Prestonburg

Petersburg

CAPE HENRY

Norfolk

Suffolk

PLATEAU

Saltville

MTS.

Danville

Bristol

umberland Gap

Greeneville

ville

APALACHIAN

GREAT SMOKIES

Greensborough

ROANOKE I.

Salisbury

Raleigh

CAPE HATTERAS

Goldsborough

Charlotte

New Bern

CAPE LOOKOUT

Greenville

Cheraw

Ft. Macon

Anderson

Florence

Wilmington

Greenwood

Columbia

Ft. Fisher

CAPE FEAR

Athens

Frying Pan Shoals

Washington

Augusta

Branchville

Charleston

Ft. Moultrie

Ft. Sumter

Scale of Miles

0   50   100

Savannah

Ft. Pulaski

Ossabaw Sound

Ft. McAllister

N.

Brunswick

W.   E.

Waycross

Troupsville

Fernandina

River

Jacksonville

Alligator

S.

Suwanee

St. Augustine

IN THE WEST

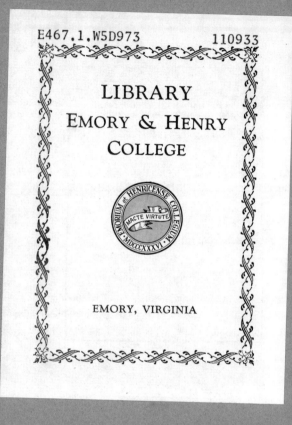

"Fightin' Joe"
WHEELER

Veterans recall with a certain grimness the iron discipline of Forrest and his magnificent, sweeping charges; they think of Stuart and Morgan for their devil-may-care insouciance and cavalier style. But their eyes twinkle when they remember Wheeler, and they marvel that one so small could accomplish so much. For the career of the diminutive Confederate cavalry general touched most of the great events in American history from Lincoln to the first Roosevelt. After serving as chief of cavalry in the Army of Tennessee in every campaign from Shiloh to Atlanta, Joseph Wheeler became successively a New Orleans businessman, an Alabama planter-lawyer, a United States congressman, then, in the Spanish-American War, a major general of cavalry again.

J. P. Dyer's exciting study of Wheeler's life reveals those striking contradictions of character that made him a unique figure in American history. Slight and wiry—he weighed but 120 pounds—Wheeler possessed a dynamic energy which contemporaries said made him "restless as a disembodied spirit." So mild was his temperament, so scholarly and meek his appearance out of uniform that strangers could hardly credit him with the indomitable fighting spirit that caused his men to call him "Fightin' Joe," or the daring exploits that made such good newspaper copy.

SOUTHERN
BIOGRAPHY
SERIES

Edited by
WENDELL HOLMES
STEPHENSON
and
FRED C. COLE

The paradoxes of Joe Wheeler's personality were reflected in his career. He was hailed in part of the South as a deliverer, and in another as a destroyer more terrible than Sherman. Although one of the South's great military leaders, he was a general without a victory, since the Army of Tennessee won no decisive campaign. Ironically, his most brilliant achievements lay in covering his army's retreats. He was the youngest American ever to be commissioned major general and the only man ever to become a corps commander in both the Confederate and United States armies.

After Johnston's surrender to Sherman in 1865, Wheeler was sent to prison along with Jefferson Davis. Upon his release he engaged in business in New Orleans for a short while, eventually moving with his bride to North Alabama. There he became a lawyer-planter. In politics he was a mild "Bourbon," but he showed enough interest in the "wool hat boys" to be returned to Congress term after term from 1883 to 1898. At the outbreak of the Spanish-American War, Wheeler volunteered and was promptly commissioned major general of volunteers in command of cavalry, in which position he commanded American troops in this nation's first engagement on foreign soil. He served in the Santiago campaign and in the Philippines, and was retired in 1901 as brigadier general in the regular army.

Chronicled here for the first time is the whole story of "Fightin' Joe" Wheeler's singular career. Mr. Dyer's happy combination of thorough scholarship with a vivid, dramatic style makes this book fascinating reading as well as a noteworthy contribution to historical writing.

SOUTHERN BIOGRAPHY SERIES
LOUISIANA STATE UNIVERSITY PRESS

From De Leon

MAJOR GENERAL JOSEPH WHEELER, C.S.A., 1864

"*Fightin' Joe*" WHEELER

By

JOHN P. DYER

LOUISIANA STATE UNIVERSITY PRESS

University, Louisiana, 1941

PRINTED IN THE UNITED STATES OF AMERICA
BY THE VAIL-BALLOU PRESS, INC., BINGHAMTON, N. Y.

TO FRANCES

PREFACE

I have found many people who think of General Wheeler as a Confederate officer, and many more who know of him because of his service in the United States Army during the war with Spain. I have found few who know him in terms of his whole career as a Confederate army officer, planter, lawyer, politician, and United States army officer. It is my hope that this volume may picture the whole man, in so far as he is reflected in available sources. A full-length portrait has not been done before; and perhaps this attempt is little more than a rough and imperfect sketch.

So many people have assisted in the preparation of this volume that any brief statement of acknowledgment is wholly inadequate. Miss Annie Wheeler kindly gave me access to her father's private papers, thereby greatly facilitating the task of interpreting what seem to me to be the significant aspects of Wheeler's career. To Professor Frank L. Owsley of Vanderbilt University I extend my profound gratitude for constructive criticism and wise counsel. Without his encouragement the task would have been much more difficult. Professors William C. Binkley and Irby Hudson of Vanderbilt and Professor Fremont P. Wirth of George Peabody College for Teachers were also generous in their assistance. My first research on Wheeler was done under the direction of the last-named.

Numerous persons have read all or parts of the manuscript and have made suggestions for its improvement. Among these are Professor Reuben W. Holland of Armstrong Junior College, Thomas Gamble of Savannah, Andrew Nelson Lytle, and Robert Penn Warren. To these I express my appreciation. The staffs of the public library of Savannah, Fort Pulaski National Monument, the public library of Atlanta, and the Division of Manuscripts, Library of Congress, have been unstinting in their assistance. I express gratitude to the editors of the "Southern Biography Series" and the director of the Louisiana State University Press for their generosity.

Finally, I would be remiss if I did not remember my paternal grandfather and the tall tales he told me of service as a private in Company E, Second Mississippi Cavalry, C.S.A.

JOHN P. DYER

Savannah, Georgia
April 19, 1940

CONTENTS

ILLUSTRATIONS

Chapter I

"FIGHTIN' JOE"

"TELL me about General Wheeler. What was he like?"

I have put that request to scores of people in all walks of life—to old soldiers at reunions, to politicians, to grizzled farmers on the porches of their dog-run houses in Alabama, to retired army officers puttering about in their gardens. And almost invariably the reply has been the same, so much the same that one might suspect collusion. They all express the same estimate as that given by a North Alabama farmer who had been the General's neighbor for years. "I'll tell you," he said, "Joe Wheeler was the gamest little banty I ever seen. He warn't afraid of nuthin' or nobody."

They all smile when they remember Wheeler. Not a smile of disparagement but one of affectionate amusement, the type of smile often brought to the face by the memory of very small men or very fat men regardless of how serious they may have been or how much they may have accomplished. They smile when they remember him because he was so small, so dignified, and so terribly in earnest about everything he undertook. And they all want to tell a story about him and his eccentricities. The Spanish War veteran likes to relate how Wheeler in the heat of battle in Cuba forgot where he was and ordered his troops to charge the Yankees; or how in the Philippines he stripped himself and wearing only his dignity, his flowing beard, and a campaign hat, he dived into a swollen stream to examine the foundations of a railroad trestle. Congressional colleagues remember with delight his little flyaway speeches on every conceivable topic. They recall with a chuckle Speaker Thomas B. Reed's comment that Wheeler would be around for a long time, for "he never stays in one place long enough for God Almighty to put his finger on him."[1] Confederate veterans tell that he could ride longer and fight harder on less food and rest than almost any other officer in the war, and then after being in the saddle for hours would ride on an additional twenty miles or more for a few moments of sleep in a feather bed in some friendly farmhouse; or how, often, he would ride along the road looking upward at the trees, searching for a "bee tree." And there are others who remember, or think they do, that a former Confederate officer of high rank encountered Wheeler dressed in a United States uniform in 1898 and said bitterly to him: "Wheeler, I hope I die and go to hell before you do because I want to see Beauregard rake you over the coals for having on that damned Yankee uniform."[2]

People never forgot Joe Wheeler once they had seen him. They usually are a bit hazy about certain of his battles and about his speeches in Congress, but they never forgot how he looked and acted. They, of course, likewise never forgot Morgan or Stuart or Forrest, but there is a distinctly different flavor in their memory of Wheeler. Veterans recall with a certain grimness the

[1] Related in T. C. DeLeon, *Joseph Wheeler: The Man, The Statesman, The Soldier* (Atlanta, 1899), 138.

[2] The story was widely circulated around 1898 but cannot be verified.

iron hand of Forrest's discipline and the magnificence
of his terrible, sweeping charges; they look back on
Stuart and Morgan and their devil-may-care insouciance and cavalier style. But when they remember
slight, mild-eyed, bearded Wheeler their eyes twinkle
and they marvel that one so small could accomplish so
much. And small he was—five feet, five inches tall,
weighing around a hundred and twenty pounds, but
withal possessing a restless energy which sent him hither
and yon "with the speed of a record breaking sprinter."
"A small, slight man, very quick and alert in his movements," one observer describes him.[3] He was "sur-
charged with electricity," another writes. "He never
walked—he loped. . . . He possessed a wonderful
memory; was restless as a disembodied spirit and as
active as a cat." [4] "His are a nervous force, a quick in-
tellectuality and a restless energy," still another adds.
"He is as frank as he is fearless; outspoken, to the verge
of bluntness." [5] From earliest youth he seems to have
possessed an inordinate dignity which, as the years
wore on, caused him to be somewhat pompous and
pedantic. Certainly he was never cast in the warrior
mold except for his indomitable spirit and terrific
energy. So mild an appearance did he make out of uniform that one might easily have mistaken him for a
scholar wizened by long hours spent poring over old
manuscripts.[6] In uniform, in action, however, he was a

[3] G. Moxley Sorrel, *Recollections of a Confederate Staff Officer*
(New York, 1905), 209.

[4] Champ Clark, *My Quarter Century of American Politics* (New
York, 1920), II, 44.

[5] DeLeon, *Joseph Wheeler*, 10, 12.

[6] "No able bodied man in America looked less like a son of Mars
. . . than Mr. Secretary [Daniel S.] Lamont unless it was General Joe
Wheeler." Clark, *My Quarter Century*, I, 241.

fighter in every sense of the word. Truly he "warn't afraid of nuthin' or nobody."

Sometimes his zeal overran itself but this only made better copy for the newsmen. One reporter wrote of Wheeler in 1898 that the most terrible thing about him was his utter lack of any sense of humor. "Nothing is funny to Wheeler," the account runs, "and he has no more conception of a joke than [Nelson] Dingley. Wheeler never laughs, but buzzes about, taking himself and everybody about him frightfully in earnest. . . . He'll fight; game as a pebble is Wheeler. But there's one trouble with Wheeler's valor. It overruns itself. He'll fight flies as ferociously as he has Spaniards. Wheeler doesn't discriminate nor match his fighting to his foes. He's the sort of man who tips over the stove putting coal on the fire and burns down the house he only meant to warm." [7] Even his fellow officers could not refrain from making an occasional joke about his size. It is related that during the Spanish-American War he popped into General James F. Wade's tent at Santiago, made some quick query, and disappeared. Shortly after, a panting aide came looking for his general.

"General, is General Wheeler here?" he asked.

"I really can't tell you," General Wade answered. "He was here, and I did not see him go. Look behind that cracker box!" [8]

And at the same time almost anyone probably would have agreed with the statement that he was "a little fellow with a soft Southern voice and so polite as to convey

[7] New York *Telegraph,* September 4, 1898, in Clipping Files, Wheeler Papers (in possession of Miss Annie Wheeler, Wheeler, Alabama).

[8] Related in DeLeon, *Joseph Wheeler,* 117.

an impression of self deprecation. He was one of the mildest and gentlest of men." [9]

All of which may indicate that Wheeler's life had more than its share of the contradictions that make up the average man's personality. He was pompous and possessed of a high degree of pride, and yet on more than one occasion he humbled himself. At one time during the Civil War he offered to place himself under the command of a none too friendly fellow officer if that officer would consent to a union of their commands at a critical moment in a campaign. Toward the close of the same war he had his entire command taken from him and placed under another officer; instead of resigning or sulking he continued as busily as ever in his job of fighting the Yankees. Assuredly he was fiery and possessed the spirit of a soldier, yet at the close of the war when he and President Davis's party were on their way to prison he walked the decks of the prison ship with the infant Winnie Davis in his arms, gently consoling the child while her mother rested below. And he showed the same gentleness in his home and community life; with marked restraint he ruled his family and conducted his civic obligations. He was dashing, yet conservative; proud, yet humble; small physically, yet possessed great stamina; mild in temperament, yet a vicious fighter.

And the same contradictions and singularities which are so obvious in his personal life are also to be found when his career is examined. He was the only officer ever to become a corps commander in the United States Army after holding the same position in the Confederacy. He was in years the youngest and in stature probably the smallest officer in America ever to be commis-

[9] Houston *Post*, August 23, 1896, in Clipping Files, Wheeler Papers.

sioned a major general. He was born in Georgia, educated in Connecticut, appointed to West Point from New York, and served his military apprenticeship in New Mexico. He graduated near the foot of his class at the Military Academy and yet was the only one of the group to attain national prominence. Making his poorest grades at the Academy in cavalry tactics, he became a renowned cavalry leader, and, it is said, was characterized by General Lee as one of the two outstanding cavalrymen in the Civil War.[10] Commissioned an officer in the forces of Georgia, he commanded Alabama troops who fought in Kentucky and Tennessee. In a part of the Confederacy he was hailed as a deliverer and in another part was denounced as a destroyer worse than William T. Sherman; and always he did his best work when the army to which he was attached was retreating. He was in command of the first engagement ever fought by American troops overseas (Guásimas), and while on active duty with the military was still a member of Congress. Trained as a soldier, he became a successful planter, lawyer, and politician. As a Democratic member of the national House of Representatives for some twenty years he was one of the best-known figures in Washington where it was laughingly said that he fought Republicans and the tariff as viciously as he once fought the Yankees; and yet when he encountered what he believed to be an unjust and unwarranted attack upon the integrity and honor of a former high officer in the ranks of the Federal

[10] Thomas J. Betts, "Joseph Wheeler," in *Dictionary of American Biography* (New York, 1928–1937), XX, 51, says: "Gen. Robert E. Lee bracketed Wheeler with J. E. B. Stuart as one of the two outstanding Confederate cavalry leaders." Andrew Nelson Lytle in his *Bedford Forrest and His Critter Company* (New York, 1931), 357, makes a similar claim for Forrest. Neither author cites sources.

army he brought to the floor of the House a spirited defense of this officer and eventually had the satisfaction of knowing that he had been instrumental in seeing that justice was done.

Wheeler's restless energy, his utter seriousness, his paradoxical personality which combined gentleness with fire, his services to the Confederacy and to the United States, all tend to give him a unique place in American history. In his life span he saw the Union dissolved and then rebuilt to fight a foreign war. He saw the transformation of the United States from an agricultural nation, and then saw that nation abandon its isolation and become an active participant in world imperialism. He saw the great West won. In short, he was either spectator or participant, usually participant, in almost every major movement in which the United States engaged from 1860 to 1906—from Lincoln to the first Roosevelt.

To understand Wheeler's background and early life one must first think of those unsatisfactory years immediately following the War of 1812 in New England. Trade had been seriously damaged by prewar restrictions and by the postwar dumping of English goods on New England shores. Depression and unemployment became widespread. Shops closed their doors; artisans wiped their tools and put them away; ships lay idle in the harbors, their masts like forests of naked trees. Men looked around them for relief, and finding it neither in their own crippled industries nor in their sterile soil, they turned to the great empire of the West. The majority who migrated found new homes and a new life in Pennsylvania, New York, and in that part of the old Northwest Territory recently made into the states of

Indiana, Illinois, and Ohio. Others came South to the almost virgin lands of cotton and slaves; and, in the course of time, both these groups oriented themselves. Sons of transplanted Yankees from Illinois and Indiana came down with Grant in 1862 to Shiloh and there met in combat many sons of other Yankees who had moved to the South, among them a certain young Colonel Joseph Wheeler.

The elder Joseph Wheeler, a merchant, was among the minority that moved southward to escape this New England economic blight.[11] A shrewd son of Connecticut, he apparently had a little capital and many schemes for making money in the cotton country of Georgia. He and his wife settled in 1819 at Augusta at the head of navigation on the Savannah River and here he became a banker, cotton factor, promoter, and farmer. He bought and traded real estate; he helped organize the Augusta Savings Bank and the Merchants and Planters Bank of Augusta; and eventually bought a farm and a few slaves.[12] His wife, Sara, died shortly after the arrival in Georgia; but soon he married again, this time to Julia Hull, daughter of General William Hull, the marriage uniting two old New England families. Both the Wheelers and Hulls traced their ancestry in America to 1640, and from there to England where the family records show a knight or two and even a trace of higher nobility. For the most part, however, both families were of the middle class—merchants, farmers, and now and then a

[11] Related by Miss Annie Wheeler to the author, August 12, 1929. Apparently Mrs. Wheeler's poor health was also an important factor in the removal of the family to Georgia.

[12] Wheeler Account Books, in Wheeler Papers. Richmond County (Georgia) Tax Returns, 1826–1835 (Tax Collector's Office, Augusta, Georgia), show that Wheeler probably never owned more than eleven slaves.

soldier.[13] It is true, the soldier tradition was somewhat overcast by General Hull's surrender of Detroit without firing a shot in the War of 1812; but occurrences like this were probably not long remembered in the semi-frontier town that was Augusta, particularly when a man was as prominent in business life as was Joseph Wheeler. There were so many other things to occupy one's mind. Augusta was growing, and business activity was everywhere apparent. Warehouses grew up along the river's edge and the coarse notes of steamboat whistles echoed through the framework of uncompleted houses.[14]

The second Mrs. Wheeler had inherited a small amount of money from her father's estate and apparently this inheritance she and her husband invested in a brick residence near the water front. With the increasing business activity in that region, however, it became unsuitable as a residential district and they moved to a recently purchased farm a short distance from town. And it was a farm rather than a plantation. It was a home-place with just enough slaves to keep it running and to raise a few bales of cotton to pay taxes. Joseph Wheeler probably never considered himself a planter; he lived on his farm but continued his business activities in town.[15]

Julia Wheeler bore her husband four children, two boys and two girls. The youngest was a boy born on September 10, 1836, and his name was entered on the

[13] MS. genealogical records of the Wheeler family, in Wheeler Papers. See also, *Proceedings of the Association of the Graduates of the United States Military Academy* (Saginaw, 1906), 63.

[14] Charles C. Jones and Salem Dutcher, *Memorial History of Augusta, Georgia* (Syracuse, 1890), 273.

[15] The Court of Ordinary Records of Richmond County, Georgia, Bks. S, T, U, V, and XX, contain the record of Wheeler's many investments.

records of St. Paul's Episcopal Church as Joseph.[16] He
bore his father's name, and as the boy grew older it was
observed that he was much like his father in many other
ways. The physical characteristics of the two were much
the same—the same slight build and mildness of counte-
nance. In temperament they showed similar traits, especially a mixture of shrewdness, impetuosity, and caution. Too, there was in both father and son an aloofness
and a reserve which few men ever really penetrated. Perhaps the Wheelers compensated for their slightness of
stature by assuming an atmosphere of dignity. And these
characteristics have continued in the family. The late
Joseph Wheeler III, also an army officer, bore in his
body the marks of the father and the grandfather, the
same diminutiveness, the same dignity.

Perhaps it was a lack of balance between impetuosity
and caution which led to Wheeler's financial disaster in
Augusta. With his small capital and native shrewdness
he built himself into a comfortable situation by the
time Joseph was born. He had several pieces of town
property, bank stock, some ready cash, part interest in a
Connecticut textile mill, and a six-hundred-acre farm.
But practically all this was swept away within a brief
period of time, the circumstances under which it all happened being very vague. There is a family legend that
he threw caution to the winds and signed notes as security
for numerous friends, trying to tide them over a bank
failure and depression. Another source not so vague has
it that the failure resulted from "unjustifiable impru-
dence" in handling the investments of the Merchants

---

[16] The other children were: William, the older son; two daughters,
Lucy Josephine and Sara Louise, by Julia Hull Wheeler; one daughter,
Sara, by Wheeler's first wife.

and Planters Bank.[17] Whatever the cause, however, the fact remains that his financial ruin was almost complete, everything going except the farm and the partnership in the mill.

In 1842, shortly after his business failure, Julia Wheeler died; and following this came a decision to move to Connecticut—to go back home. Joseph Wheeler took his children with him and put them in the public school on Gilbert Street in Derby. Years afterward men who were his schoolmates at the time remembered, or thought they remembered, that the younger Wheeler boy was a fighter and that he usually licked boys much larger than himself; [18] but it is hardly likely that the boy made much of an impression, for his stay in Derby was too short. In 1845 his father sold his interest in the mill and went back to Georgia where he tried, without success, during the rest of his life to recoup his losses. Relatives in Connecticut, however, stepped in to help the harassed father with the task of rearing and educating the children. In 1849 Mary and Augusta Hull, sisters of Julia Hull Wheeler, took the undersized, younger Wheeler boy into their home and put him in school at the Episcopal Academy at Cheshire; and here the record grows dimmer. Few stories have survived Joseph Wheeler at Cheshire except that he was aloof, stiffly polite, and

[17] *Acts of the General Assembly of the State of Georgia, 1833*, pp. 399–408, gives the report of a legislative committee appointed to investigate the failure of the bank. This committee made serious charges of illegality and corrupt practices against Wheeler, who was president of the institution, and his associates. The report also stated that Wheeler's property and that of his associates was sold at public auction to satisfy claims against the bank.

[18] Related in New York *Evening Post*, January 25, 1906, in Clipping Files, Wheeler Papers.

very serious. He is reported to have carved his name on
the beam that supported the school bell,[19] but otherwise his conduct seems to have attracted no special attention. He passed his courses at Cheshire, he did the
chores around his aunts' home, and in the course of time
finished his secondary school work.

Upon completion of this phase of his education, young
Wheeler went to New York to make his home with his
sister who had married Sterling Smith, a prominent businessman of the city. This brother-in-law could have
given the youth employment and a chance at a career
in business, but apparently Wheeler had other ideas.
He wanted a military career, a West Point appointment,
and he stuck to his decision until one was forthcoming.[20]
On July 1, 1854, at the age of seventeen he was admitted
as a cadet under the new ruling of the War Department
that required five years at the Academy instead of four.
The appointment was made by Representative John
Wheeler, himself a Connecticut Yankee and a graduate
of the Cheshire Academy.

Brevet Colonel Robert E. Lee was superintendent
of the Military Academy when Wheeler entered in 1854,
and remained in that capacity until he was transferred to
line duty in 1855, but it is not likely that young Wheeler
or any of the other plebes saw very much of him in-
formally. Considerable building was going on at the
Academy and there were a thousand details requiring
the Superintendent's attention. The cavalry horses had
glanders, the tenure of the faculty was uncertain, the
War Department had to be placated over purchases, the
curriculum was undergoing change, and there were fre-

[19] Related by the elder J. P. Morgan, himself a Cheshire alumnus, in
New York *Sun*, January 21, 1900, *ibid.*
[20] Related by Miss Annie Wheeler to the author, August 12, 1929.

CADET JOSEPH WHEELER, UNITED STATES
MILITARY ACADEMY, 1857

quent cases of discipline among the cadets. All this kept
Lee from knowing individual cadets as intimately as he
desired.[21] Frequently cadets came to his attention through
breaches of discipline, but since Wheeler had an ex-
emplary record he probably did not know his commanding officer in this capacity. In fact, it is highly
probable that, outside Lee's Sunday night suppers for
the cadets in his quarters, contacts between him and
Wheeler were limited to the parade ground and chapel.
But there were others on the faculty with whom contacts
were not so restricted. There was, for example, Brevet
Major Fitz-John Porter, Instructor of Artillery and Cavalry. Later Lee was to hurl his divisions against those
of this officer at Mechanicsville; and much later Cadet
Wheeler would defend Porter's good name on the floor
of Congress. Lieutenant Colonel William J. Hardee was
sent to the Academy to take Porter's place when the
latter was assigned to line duty. Together Hardee and
Wheeler, within a few years, would help train an army
for Shiloh, Perryville, Chickamauga, and Atlanta. Then,
too, there were among the faculty such men as Lieutenant John M. Schofield, Lieutenant Oliver O. Howard,
and Lieutenant Alexander McD. McCook—all destined
for fame in the impending Civil War.

Among the cadets, also, were many whose names later
became prominent both in American history and in the
life of Wheeler. There was young Judson Kilpatrick
who entered as a plebe in 1857. Later, as the commander
of Sherman's cavalry, he would march to the sea and
have his every move contested by a rebel General
Wheeler; and not only to fight Wheeler by day but on an
occasion to flee from him in his night clothes. And there

[21] Douglas S. Freeman, *R. E. Lee: A Biography* (New York, 1934–
1935), I, Chap. XIX, *passim*.

were others—William B. Hazen, George D. Ruggles, Wesley Merritt, Fitzhugh Lee, John T. Magruder, Richard K. Meade, Horace Porter. In Wheeler's own class, however, which started with thirty-five members, he was the only one who earned any considerable reputation for himself during the struggle of the sixties.[22]

Progress at West Point was painfully slow for young Wheeler. At the end of his first year he stood twenty-fourth, four others outranking him in deportment. During his second year he stood eighteenth in a class of twenty-nine. In his third year there was little improvement either in academic or military subjects. In 1859 at graduation he stood fourth from the bottom of his class, his poorest grades being in cavalry tactics.[23] He seems to have been the same timid youth he had been at Cheshire, apparently taking little part in athletics but spending a great deal of time in the library. It was a period in the history of the Academy when hazing was widely practiced, yet he apparently did not participate in these practices. Perhaps he was sensitive about his size, for his classmates began to call him "Point" because he had neither height, breadth, nor thickness.[24] At any rate, his activities at West Point are almost as obscure as his life at Cheshire. "Had the corps of cadets been called upon to predict who of the class would be the last to emerge from obscurity," a contemporary wrote of him, "the chances are that the choice would have fallen upon Wheeler." [25] He was "a docile, obedient and punctilious

22 *Official Register of the Officers and Cadets of the U.S. Military Academy, West Point, New York, 1855–1859* (n.p., n.d), *passim*.

23 *Ibid.*

24 John W. Dubose, *General Joseph Wheeler and the Army of Tennessee* (New York, 1912), 51.

25 Morris Schaff, *The Spirit of Old West Point* (Boston, 1907), 56.

pupil; rarely deserving a demerit, and equally patient with professors and classmates." [26]

No commission being vacant in the cavalry when Wheeler graduated, he was brevetted a second lieutenant and sent to the cavalry school at Carlisle Barracks, Pennsylvania, for further instruction. After a few months there he was raised to full rank and assigned to duty with the Regiment of Mounted Rifles at Fort Craig, New Mexico.[27] Thus, as with J.E.B. (Jeb) Stuart and so many other officers of the old army, the West became Wheeler's training ground for the Civil War, a circumstance which afforded him particularly excellent schooling for service in the cavalry arm of the service. The Regiment of Mounted Rifles with which Wheeler began active duty was really mounted infantry rather than cavalry. In contrast to the heavy Dragoons of the regular cavalry the Mounted Rifles traveled light and thus had an extensive cruising range. Their equipment included carbines and pistols, weapons equally useful on horseback or afoot; and, although these mounted infantrymen were not as effective in a mass charge as the Dragoons, they proved more valuable for scouting purposes and other duties requiring speed. It was the tactics of the Mounted Rifles which Wheeler used so well in the Confederate service that lay ahead of him.

On June 2, 1860, almost exactly a year after his graduation from West Point, Wheeler reported to Hannibal, Missouri, to join a wagon train for the long trip southwestward to Santa Fe and Fort Craig. Ever since the

[26] DeLeon, *Joseph Wheeler*, 21.

[27] *Historical Register and Dictionary of the U.S. Army* (Washington, 1903), II, 184. In 1861 the designation of the Regiment of Mounted Rifles was changed to Third United States Cavalry.

United States had acquired the Mexican territory and had established forts therein, these wagon trains had been running on a more or less regular schedule from Hannibal and Independence across the plains to the far frontier. Thus to most of the plainsmen and troopers who were to go along, the scene was no strange one. The mingled odor of bacon frying over small cooking fires with that of harness grease and mule manure was all part of a common olfactory experience. Bronzed troopers in blue tunics, their sabers slapping their thighs, only completed the familiar picture.[28] But there were two people to whom all this was undoubtedly very strange and a bit confusing. One was a woman in an advanced stage of pregnancy; the other was Lieutenant Wheeler. Obviously it was no place for a pregnant woman, even though she did have permission from the War Department to join her officer husband at Santa Fe; and certainly the frail young officer did not appear to be a type for frontier duty. Even the half-grown black beard did not hide the youthfulness of his face.

The wagon train uncoiled itself and slowly crawled over a ridge to the plain below. For two days it traveled without incident, but on the third day the surgeon ordered a halt while he delivered the woman's child. An ambulance was detached and the main train sent on a few miles to a water hole. With the ambulance was left the surgeon, a half-breed driver, and Lieutenant Wheeler. Throughout the night these three kept the birth vigil and just before morning a child was born. The journey was resumed only to be interrupted again by an attack from a small band of marauding Indians. The driver applied the lash to the mules and the ambu-

[28] Henry Inman, *The Old Santa Fe Trail* (New York, 1898), gives many interesting scenes such as this.

lance careened and bumped its way along but could not outrun Indian ponies. Soon they were circling the wagon just out of gunshot range. Riding closer they sent in a few arrows. The surgeon took the driver's place, the latter priming his rifle and getting ready for the fight. "We had gained the crest of a slight hill," Wheeler told in later years, "the Indians closing in on us, when the driver swung directly toward an Indian, sprang from his horse, dropped to one knee, and fired. A redskin tumbled, and instantly the Indians were after the driver in a bunch. The air seemed filled with arrows. That was my chance. I charged the crowd knocking down a horse with a shot from my musket. Then I threw away my gun and went at them with my Colt pistol. The driver came in with his Colt and the Indians were on the run." [29]

When the ambulance overtook the train that afternoon and the surgeon told with what spirit and relish the young officer had emptied his pistol into the Indians, the soldiers, half-jestingly and half in earnest, began to call him "Fightin' Joe," and Fightin' Joe it remained the rest of his life—a gentle, mild-mannered little man who really loved to fight. He had begun his military career standing guard while a child was born; five years later he would bring his Confederate career to a close walking the deck of a prison ship with a child in his arms.

Fort Craig, Wheeler's destination, was located on the upper Rio Grande approximately a hundred and fifty miles south of Santa Fe, a position near the center of the territory occupied by the Apaches, Kiowas, Comanches, and Navajoes. The period from 1850 to 1860, however, was one of comparative quiet among the Indians of the

[29] MS. account, in Wheeler Papers, obviously prepared for some newspaper or magazine.

Southwest. It was before the days of Manuelito the Navajo and Geronimo the Apache, and therefore border duty consisted largely of drill and maneuvers, with now and then a brush with small bands of wandering Apaches.[30] But there were many events that the officers and men could discuss in the evenings before taps, and many of the conversations doubtless centered around the state of the Union. Secession was in the air and had been for months. In April, 1860, the Democrats had split over a Presidential candidate, and in May the Republicans met in convention at Chicago and nominated as their candidate Abraham Lincoln—a sectional candidate, the Southerners said, and one with whom they could not live under the same political roof. He talked about a house divided against itself not being able to stand; and it was a divided nation in 1860. Nowhere was that division felt more keenly than in the army.

The Regiment of Mounted Rifles at Fort Craig was officered by Southerners, and the charge was openly made that Secretary of War John B. Floyd had purposely brought about this condition so that New Mexico might be brought over to the Confederacy when secession came.[31] The colonel of the regiment was William W. Loring, a native of North Carolina and resident of Florida, who had won honors at Chapultepec and had served under Albert Sidney Johnston in the "Mormon War" of 1857–1859. Quixotic George B. Crittenden, who had seen service in the Black Hawk, Texan, and

[30] A good general account of Fort Craig may be found in Hubert H. Bancroft, *A History of Arizona and New Mexico* (San Francisco, 1899). See also, Comte de Paris, *History of the Civil War in America* (Philadelphia, 1875–1888), I, Chap. V.

[31] Bancroft, *History of Arizona and New Mexico,* Chap. XXVII. The same accusations were made against Jefferson Davis when he was secretary of war. Freeman, *R. E. Lee,* I, 349.

Mexican wars, was lieutenant colonel; and convivial little Daniel H. Maury, a Virginian and former commander of the Carlisle Cavalry School, was adjutant until April, 1860. These men were secessionists, and when the war came they resigned their commissions and entered the Confederate service. Loring became a major general and fought at Vicksburg, in Jackson's Valley Campaign, and with the Army of Tennessee; Crittenden became a brigadier general in the forces of Kentucky only to resign his commission under censure; and Maury became a major general fighting at Pea Ridge, Corinth, in East Tennessee, and at Mobile.

Talk of secession and consequent resignation from the army undoubtedly occupied a great deal of the time of these officers during the closing months of 1860, but there is no evidence to indicate that Wheeler took a pronounced stand. Certainly it would not have been unnatural or strange if he had remained in the United States Army. He had selected that as a career and was doing well for a young officer. His people had been New Englanders for generations; and, although he was born in Georgia, many of his impressionable years had been spent in the North. But when the actual time of decision came, there seems to have been no hesitation on his part. A short while before Georgia seceded he wrote his brother, William, in Augusta: "Much as I love the Union, and much as I am attached to my profession, all will be given up when my state, by its action, shows that such a course is necessary and proper." [32] On January 9, 1861, the convention in session at the capitol in Milledgeville solemnly revoked Georgia's articles of union. William Wheeler began organizing a battery of artillery for the Confederacy, and at the same time took up with

[32] Quoted in Dubose, *Wheeler and the Army of Tennessee*, 52.

Governor Joseph E. Brown the matter of a commission for his younger brother. "I have a brother, Joseph Wheeler, Jr. in the Regiment of Mounted Rifles U.S.A.," he wrote. "He is now stationed at Ft. Craig, New Mexico. He is a graduate of the West Point Military Academy and was in the first class that remained under the new system of five years at that institution. He was appointed from the state of New York, but Georgia is his home and always has been, he being a native of this county. I have just received a letter from him which states that he will resign his present position and return to this State. It will probably be two or three weeks before he arrives here where he will offer his services to you. I write this letter to inform you that you may expect his services to be offered to the State." [33] On February 23, 1861, a commission as lieutenant in the forces of Georgia was issued for young Wheeler; and on March 6, William Wheeler accepted for his brother stating that "Joseph resigned as soon as he heard that Georgia had seceded." [34]

[33] William H. Wheeler to Governor Joseph E. Brown, February 2, 1861, in Catalog File, Miscellaneous Papers (Georgia State Archives, Atlanta, Georgia).

[34] *Id.* to Adjutant General Henry C. Wayne, March 6, 1861, *ibid.* Wheeler resigned from the United States Army on April 22, 1861. Whether he knew his brother had accepted a commission for him in the Confederate army over a month earlier does not appear.

Chapter II

WINNING RECOGNITION
(April, 1861—April, 1862)

WHILE Joseph Wheeler, late of the United States Army, was slowly making his way by horse from Fort Craig to Fort Smith, Arkansas, preparatory to the trip back home to Georgia, national events were in kaleidoscopic confusion. Everyone seemed to recognize that the long impending storm was about to break, yet none could find a way to stay it. A short while before Wheeler had left his frontier post, Abraham Lincoln had quit his Springfield home to go secretly into Washington where an inaugural address was to be written. In the President's chair sat the aged Buchanan filled with doubts and premonitions but determined not to force the issue and thus cause war. The lobbies of hotels and the cloak rooms of Congress buzzed with excitement; wherever men met the topic of conversation quickly turned to secession and war. From corner saloons to fashionable drawing rooms men and women were asking the same questions. What tone would President Lincoln assume in his inaugural address? Would the other southern states join South Carolina in her attempt to disrupt the Union? And above all, if war should come what would be done with Federal property, especially the forts, located within the boundaries of the seceding states?

But soon the force of circumstances answered these questions. War did come, and the forts were occupied by the Confederates. Six of them were without garrisons, and two, Pickens at Pensacola and Sumter at Charleston, were garrisoned. As a result of General P. G. T. Beauregard's action in reducing Sumter, the air was cleared as by a stroke of lightning. Lincoln and Davis issued their calls for volunteers, and the North shouted, "On to Richmond!" Bishop Leonidas Polk down in Louisiana buckled his sword over his priestly robes and joined the Confederates. Professor Thomas J. Jackson at Virginia Military Institute offered his services to Virginia. Lieutenant Colonel William J. Hardee on leave in September, 1860, resigned his place at West Point and hurried south. Near Memphis, Nathan Bedford Forrest left his plantation to raise a company of cavalry for his state. Robert Edward Lee came to the defense of Virginia. Braxton Bragg wrote from his plantation retreat in Louisiana to offer his services to President Davis. Younger officers like Wheeler who were in active service and had delayed their decision now were forced to make a choice. It was the first flush of war and everywhere the call for troops met with an enthusiastic response. Men quit their plows and fields to report at local recruiting offices. Gallant young Southerners rode away to the echo of toasts drunk on wide verandas—toasts to Davis, to the Confederacy, and to the victory which they felt could not be long in coming.

In the excitement of the bombardment of Sumter the country for a brief period almost forgot the Gulf region where the important point was Fort Pickens, the fortification which bore much the same relation to Pensacola that Sumter did to Charleston. Pickens was located at the southern tip of Santa Rosa Island, which guarded the entrance to Pensacola Bay. Directly across the channel from Pickens was Fort McRae, and a few miles northward toward Pensacola was Fort Barrancas and the United States Navy Yard. These last two forts were only slightly fortified whereas Pickens was comparatively strong. After Florida passed her secession ordinance on January 10, 1861, Lieutenant Adam J. Slemmer of the United States Army decided to transfer everything from the other forts to Pickens for safety.[1] This he did, leaving behind him a few spiked guns at Barrancas. The Confederates moved in as the Federals moved out and soon from opposite sides of the narrow entrance to the bay were the "Stars and Bars and the Stars and Stripes— flouting defiance at each other."[2]

General Bragg, who had been assigned to the defense of the Gulf area, decided to mount some of the spiked Federal guns left behind at Barrancas, guns which in turn might be used to defend Pensacola against a possible Federal naval attack. But the raw Alabama and Georgia volunteers and their political officers were completely ignorant of how to proceed with the mounting of siege guns, so ignorant that Bragg despaired of ever getting the guns into their emplacements ready for use. One evening, however, a shy young officer slipped unobtrusively into headquarters and asked to see the commanding general. He was, he explained to the choleric general, Joseph Wheeler, late of the United States Army and now a lieutenant in the forces of Georgia. He had

[1] *War of the Rebellion: A Compilation of the Official Records of the Union and Confederate Armies* (Washington, 1880–1901), Ser. I, Vol. I, 334, 362–63. Cited hereafter as *Official Records*. In instances where the author deems it expedient the exact time of day and the exact place are cited. Otherwise only the date is given.

[2] William H. Russell, *My Diary North and South* (New York, 1863), 201.

studied engineering at West Point and would be glad to assist in mounting the troublesome guns. "With alacrity" Bragg accepted his offer and the next day young Wheeler appeared on the ramparts clothed with the authority to push the work.[3] And within two weeks he had achieved unexpected success, so much so that the wife of a young Confederate officer could write her mother: "It seems now to be generally believed that hostilities will commence about the middle of this week [week of May 13, 1861]. I suppose they judge by the state of the batteries, and someone told us all of them were completed and could be started in ten minutes." [4]

It was, of course, an excellent beginning for an ambitious but unknown young officer. He had brought himself to the attention of the commanding general under the most favorable circumstances and had proved himself capable of carrying through a job. His elation, however, shortly received considerable deflation as he found himself the subject of a controversy between General Bragg and the Confederate War Department. Among the Alabama political officers in camp were some who took it upon themselves to get a promotion for him. They applied to the War Department for the promotion without consulting the commanding general and straightway received the desired commission that lifted Wheeler from lieutenant to colonel in one jump, a move which very naturally brought a protest from Bragg to the Confederate government. Wheeler was made a party to the scheme in that he consented to make formal application and this, no doubt, increased Bragg's ire.[5] For some time,

---

[3] Wheeler to John W. Dubose, September 12, 1905, in Wheeler Papers.
[4] Mollie Weakely to her mother, May 13, 1863, in author's possession.
[5] Dubose says that the men were "Pugh, Baker and others" of Alabama. Obviously he meant James Lawrence Pugh and Alpheus Baker.

he wrote Secretary Judah P. Benjamin, there had been a growing dissatisfaction among his older officers, and this discontent could be traced to the fact that their government had overlooked the point that they had served long and well in the United States Army prior to secession. They had seen themselves overlooked by their government, while their juniors in years and service were put over them in rank. "The last feather, however, has broken the camel's back," he continued. "The Department, just before your entrance on its duties, came into their midst, and selected one of the very youngest of their number for the grade of colonel. Lieutenant (Colonel) Wheeler is a very excellent officer, and none envy him his good fortune, but they cannot see the justice of the apparent reflection on themselves." [6]

Bragg, as later events were to prove, apparently did not dislike Wheeler personally, but he was submitting uneasily to the dictates of a citizen-commander. Too, it hurt his vanity and pride, for his officers could clearly see that his "personal influence, heretofore exerted, had availed them nothing." Secretary Benjamin's reply was evasive, and General Bragg complained that, "Though very grateful to my wounded feelings, yours was not entirely satisfactory to me." The matter ended there, for Secretary Benjamin apparently was too busy getting saltpeter for the New Orleans arsenal and brigadiers and pork for Richmond.

Bragg, also, was too much occupied to push the matter

Both these men were prominent in Alabama politics at the time and both were at Pensacola with the Eufaula Rifles. Why they should have been so much interested in Wheeler does not appear. See W. Brewer, *Alabama: Her History, Resources, War Record, and Public Men* (Montgomery, 1872), 128, 132.

[6] Braxton Bragg to Judah P. Benjamin, September 25, 1861, in *Official Records*, Ser. I, Vol. VI, 744.

further. The air around Pensacola was charged with electric suspense. No one seemed to know what was going to happen, yet everyone expected something; and whatever was to be, they hoped the batteries could withstand it. At Fort Gaines in Mobile Bay the soldiers were chafing under the monotony. They didn't like this kind of waiting war. What they wanted was to "touch off a few pills" which would be good for the Yankee complaint.[7] The citizens of Mobile were busy drilling, marching, and beating drums. On the streets in the evening were crowds of "negroes, mulattoes, quadroons, and mestizos of all sorts, Spanish, Italian, and French, speaking their own tongues . . . and dressed in very striking and pretty costumes." There were Alabama volunteers "in homespun coarse gray suits, with blue and yellow worsted facings and stripes." There were Zouaves and Chasseurs from New Orleans all "drilling, parading, exercising, sitting in the shade, loading tumbrils, playing cards, or sleeping on the grass." [8] Small wonder Bragg was busy; he and Colonel Hardee had to mold an army out of this medley of race and color.

Bragg, however, had no intention of attacking Fort Pickens and thus disturbing the status quo in the Gulf region. He confided to an English newspaperman that his batteries were far from being in a state, either as regarded armament or ammunition, that would justify him in meeting the fire of the fort and the ships in the harbor.[9] Then, too, Jefferson Davis had telegraphed, "Pickens is not worth a drop of blood." Instead of attacking he would delay a few months and spend the time in organizing and drilling an army, a decision doubtless forced upon him

7 Russell, *My Diary North and South,* 194.
8 *Ibid.,* 191, 194, 206.   9 *Ibid.,* 215.

by the very unmilitary conduct of his alleged troops. And to make matters worse the former Confederate Secretary of War, Leroy Pope Walker, brought down his brigade of volunteers from Huntsville, Alabama. It had been Walker who had handed down Wheeler's premature commission and had overlooked the older officers. Now he had made up a brigade and had handed out the commissions before arrival at Pensacola. To his Fourteenth regiment he assigned Colonel Thomas J. Judge, a lawyer; to the Seventeenth, Colonel Thomas H. Watts, a lawyer; to the Eighteenth, Colonel Edward C. Bullock, a lawyer; and to the Nineteenth, Colonel Joseph Wheeler. Wheeler was the only trained officer in the entire brigade, a fact not long in becoming obvious to all. Soon General Walker distributed his troops by regiments and billeted himself in a private residence on Government Street.[10]

The Alabama troops spent the fall and winter of 1861–1862 in the pine barrens near Mobile. Many of the officers took up their quarters at the Battle House and trained, it is reported, on a diet of whisky, music, and women. One of the few officers remaining in camp was Wheeler. Here he spent his time drilling, reviewing, and conditioning his regiment. The routine of duty shows how severe was his regime. From six to seven in the morning there was officers' drill; from eight until nine, regimental drill; from half-past nine until half-past ten, officers' recitation and lecture in tactics; from half-past ten to half-past eleven, sergeants' and corporals' recitation in tactics; from half-past eleven to half-past twelve, company drill. In the afternoon from one till three the camp was policed, and from four until twenty minutes past five

[10] Dubose, *Wheeler and the Army of Tennessee*, 54–55.

there was regimental drill. At sunset came dress parade and the mounting of the guard.[11]

Wheeler seems to have been one of the few officers who realized the seriousness of his job and the need for discipline and training. Although not an officer of distinctly military bearing, there was something about him that commanded attention. Perhaps it was his utter seriousness and his high concept of duty that singled him out; certainly it was not his hauteur or his force of personality. He was not a genius in the ordinary, loose sense of the word; indeed, he was in most respects not much more than an average officer. His meteoric rise seems due, not so much to brilliance, as to his ability to take an order and then stay on the job day and night until it was executed. He always lacked much of the dash and audacity of John H. Morgan and Forrest, but in the matter of subordinating himself and of playing the part assigned him in a campaign he probably excelled them both.[12] Wheeler worked well with his superiors; there seems to have been no part of him that cried out for the wild excitement of a "raid," although when one became necessary he performed his duty well.

After nearly a year of drilling and watchful waiting round Mobile and Pensacola, Bragg became restless. Ex-

---

[11] W. C. Dodson, *Campaigns of Wheeler and His Cavalry* (Atlanta, 1899), Appendix, 1.

[12] Captain Alonzo Gray, in his *Cavalry Tactics as Illustrated by the War of the Rebellion* (Fort Leavenworth, 1910), 13–14, says: "Wheeler was, without doubt, the ablest Confederate cavalry leader in the West. He was always ready to work in the team and play a subordinate part to his commanding general. . . . Forrest was a very able man, but, like Stonewall Jackson, was at his best when operating alone. He could not bear restraint and did not work well to the central idea. . . . Morgan was essentially a raider; although a hard fighter when the occasion demanded, he preferred a loose sort of warfare to working in conjunction with other troops."

cept for a skirmish between some New York Zouaves attached to Fort Pickens and a small detachment of Confederates, there had been no fighting. Pensacola was not a vital point. Why couldn't the President and the War Department see that Kentucky was the place to strike? The Confederate forces were scattered when they should be concentrated upon strategic points. On February 15, 1862, Bragg wrote Secretary Benjamin:

Our means and resources are too much scattered. The protection of persons and property, as such, should be abandoned, and all our means applied to the Government and the cause. Important strategic points only should be held. All means not necessary to secure these should be concentrated for a heavy blow upon the enemy where we can best assail him. Kentucky is now that point. On the Gulf we should only hold New Orleans, Mobile, and Pensacola; all other points, the whole of Texas and Florida, should be abandoned, and our means there made available for other service.

.   .   .   .

We have the right men, and the crisis upon us demands they should be in the right places. Our little army at Pensacola could furnish you hundreds of instructors competent to build batteries, mount guns, and teach the use of them. Our commanders are learning by bitter experience the necessity of teaching their troops.[13]

Bragg probably overemphasized the value and number of his instructors at Pensacola, but doubtless he was partially correct in the contention that Kentucky was the place to strike. On the very day on which the above letter was written, Fort Donelson had been surrendered, and with that the Confederate defenses in the West began to

[13] Quoted in Don C. Seitz, *Braxton Bragg* (Columbia, S.C., 1924), 82–84.

crumble. Fort Henry had fallen earlier and the mouth of the Tennessee had passed into Federal hands. Now with Fort Donelson lost, the control of two great rivers that went deep into the heart of the Confederacy was in the enemy's hands. This severe blow to the Confederacy made necessary many changes in the disposition of troops. In answer to Bragg's suggestions, Secretary Benjamin wrote that while he did not fully know the extent of the loss at Donelson it was evident that the plan of attacking Kentucky must be abandoned and the Tennessee line held. With this in view Bragg was instructed to abandon Mobile and Pensacola and come to the assistance of Beauregard in keeping the Mississippi open at Memphis and the Memphis and Charleston Railway clear from Memphis to Chattanooga.[14] General Albert Sidney Johnston was near Bowling Green with about fifteen thousand troops. General Earl Van Dorn was ordered to concentrate his troops at Little Rock, Arkansas, and move to Beauregard's aid. The Confederate high command had decided that the Federals probably would attack at Savannah, on the Tennessee River. Therefore, all troops would move to the defense of the Tennessee line.[15]

After the fall of Fort Donelson, Grant's troops were moved up the Tennessee River to Pittsburg Landing. From this point Grant expected to move overland to Corinth, the junction of the Memphis and Charleston and the Mobile and Ohio railroads, capture it, and thus drive a wedge deeper into the West. He established his headquarters at Savannah, eight miles down the river from Pittsburg Landing, and kept in constant touch with

[14] Benjamin to Bragg, February 18, 1862, in *Official Records*, Ser. I, Vol. VI, 828.
[15] *Ibid.*

his troops stationed at Crump's Landing and Pittsburg Landing.

In the meantime, the Confederate army was gathering at Corinth. Bragg arrived from Pensacola with three brigades during the latter part of February, 1862. In the first week of March five thousand troops sent from Louisiana to General Polk arrived and were united with Bragg's command. Polk himself arrived shortly thereafter from Jackson, Tennessee, with his four brigades. General Albert Sidney Johnston in retiring from Nashville marched by Murfreesboro, Tennessee, where he added George B. Crittenden's troops to his existing strength of five brigades, eventually reaching Corinth on March 24 and taking command of the entire army five days later. Thus the Army of the Mississippi was complete—Polk's corps of four brigades; Bragg's corps of six brigades; Hardee's corps of three brigades; and John C. Breckinridge's corps of three brigades.[16]

The task of assembling the army was an arduous one beset by many difficulties. Bragg, upon whom fell the task of receiving and co-ordinating the divisions as they arrived, gave voice to his woe in unmistakable terms. Writing to General Beauregard, who had not arrived at Corinth from Jackson, Tennessee, he described how demoralized and disorganized the troops were. The whole country seemed paralyzed, he said. The railway system was deranged, wood and water stations were abandoned, supplies were lacking—and, to make matters worse, depredations committed by the Confederates were becoming extremely serious.[17] And if this were not enough for one

[16] George J. Fiebeger, *Campaigns of the American Civil War* (West Point, N.Y., 1914), 96–97.

[17] Bragg to P. G. T. Beauregard, March 18, 1862, in *Official Records*, Ser. I, Vol. X, Pt. II, 339–40. Depredations became so serious that Gen-

general to endure, there were the additional tribulations of bad roads, inaccurate maps, and insufficient cavalry to observe the enemy's movements.[18] Indeed, it is difficult to imagine that this heterogeneous collection of straggling Confederates assembling at Corinth would within a few days display the most superb courage in hurling itself in reckless abandon at the Federals—difficult unless one stops to realize that these butternut-clad farmers were equally oblivious to fear and discipline. They were horrible examples of soldiers, but at the same time were unexcelled as fighters.

Nor did the situation improve as the day of battle approached and the army marched out from Corinth headed northwest toward Pittsburg Landing on the Tennessee River. The orders for the advance were given on the second of April to take effect on the third. Since the two armies were only twenty-five miles apart, it was assumed by General Johnston that the Confederates would be able to get in position by the fourth, ready to attack by the fifth. By the night of the fourth the army was encamped within six miles of Shiloh Church ready to move into position early the next morning. Instead of accomplishing this, however, the entire day of the fifth was spent in negotiating three additional miles and in deploying for attack. Thus the battle began on the morning of April 6, just twenty-four hours later than had been anticipated.[19]

---

eral Beauregard in "mortification and humiliation" had to order the death penalty for those found guilty. *Ibid.*, 338.

[18] *Id.* to *id.*, March 19, 1862, *ibid.*, 341–42.

[19] When deployed, the Confederate positions were as follows: The front line was formed by three brigades of William J. Hardee's corps with one brigade of Bragg's corps on their right. Six hundred yards in rear of Hardee, Bragg had five brigades, each in mass with regimental front, ready to support Hardee. Leonidas Polk's four brigades, formed

Somewhere in the midst of all the confusion was Colonel Wheeler and his Nineteenth Alabama regiment of infantry. They had come up with Bragg from Pensacola and had, we may conjecture, performed the routine of garrison duty during the month of March. Certainly there is nothing to indicate any particular activity of this regiment or its commander during the five weeks before Shiloh. When the battle lines were formed on the morning of April 6, General John K. Jackson's brigade, which included Wheeler's regiment, was assigned to duty on the right wing of the second line next to General James R. Chalmers's brigade which formed the extreme right of Bragg's corps.[20] Six hundred yards to the front of Wheeler's position lay General Adley H. Gladden's brigade forming the extreme right of General Hardee's line. Upon these three brigades—Gladden's, Chalmers's, and Jackson's—would depend to a great extent the success of the battle, for General Johnston's strategy involved turning the Federal left and pushing it back toward Snake Creek at the same time that the center was pushed back on Owl Creek. While these three brigades, with the assistance of General Breckinridge's reserves, turned the left, Generals Thomas C. Hindman and Patrick R. Cleburne supported by the troops of Bragg and Polk would push straight ahead toward Sherman's headquarters at Shiloh.[21]

---

in a single mass of brigade front, were in rear of Bragg. John C. Breckinridge was in column in rear of Polk. See Fiebeger, *Campaigns of the American Civil War*, 99.

[20] Wheeler's Report, April 12, 1862, in *Official Records*, Ser. I, Vol. X, Pt. I, 558.

[21] For the strategy and tactics of the campaign, see articles by William Preston Johnston, P. G. T. Beauregard, Thomas Jordan, S. H. Lockett, and Alexander Robert Chisholm, in Robert U. Johnson and Clarence C. Buel (eds.), *Battles and Leaders of the Civil War* (New York, 1887–1888), I, 540–606. Cited hereafter as *Battles and Leaders*.

Wheeler's part in the battle shows how the Federal left was turned and slowly driven counterclockwise toward the banks of Snake Creek and the Tennessee. When Gladden's brigade just ahead of Wheeler's regiment went into action, a few stray bullets from the enemy's answering volleys struck home in the ranks of the Nineteenth Alabama, giving the regiment its initial experience in seeing men pitch forward and lie lifeless [22]—a sight that would grow common as the day wore on. But there was no time for contemplating life and death now. Jackson's and Chalmers's brigades moved forward and joined the first line busily engaged in loading and firing in an irregular staccato rhythm. Then the entire Confederate first and second lines surged forward through the more advanced camps on General Benjamin M. Prentiss's left. Here the Federals resisted so stubbornly that assault after assault was thrown back. Early morning mists gave way before the advancing sun and still the Federals held. Leaving Gladden to hold at this point, Chalmers's and Jackson's brigades were withdrawn from Prentiss's front and sent to the Federal extreme left to strike Brigadier General Stephen A. Hurlbut's and Colonel David Stuart's positions.[23] Here on the extreme left as in the center there was bitter fighting as the Confederate charges were hurled back. General Johnston, up to this time giving almost his entire attention to the flanking operations on his right, rode upon the scene and ordered Wheeler together with the commands of Brigadier General John S. Bowen and Colonel W. S. Statham of Breckinridge's

[22] Wheeler's Report, April 12, 1862, in *Official Records,* Ser. I, Vol. X, Pt. I, 558–59. This is supported by reports of Generals Jones M. Withers, June 20, 1862, and James R. Chalmers, April 12, 1862. *Ibid.,* 535, 552.

[23] Wheeler's Report, April 12, 1862, *ibid.,* 558–59.

corps to charge the Illinois brigade in their front. Bowen
and Statham were held but Wheeler's regiment managed to gain a footing. They had swept forward across a
ravine, up a brushy slope, and into the camps of the
Fifty-seventh Illinois regiment. Re-forming his lines
quickly, Wheeler ordered his men down while Captain
Isadore P. Girardey's battery of artillery shook the position to which the enemy had retired. It was well past
noon and still the left had not been turned.

Near by the Forty-fifth Tennessee refused to act on further orders to advance and General Johnston elected to
lead them in person. Aroused by their General's example
the regiment responded and followed him up the slope to
the attack. The Illinois regiments retired firing as they
went, and one of the bullets found a costly target. General Johnston was shot in the hip and died within a short
time from loss of blood.[24] Colonel Stuart's brigade, however, was compelled to fall back to a new position, and
presently to a third. Hurlbut's left had been turned.

In the meantime, the battle raged on Prentiss's front.
After Wheeler had been detached during the morning
General Gladden was mortally wounded while leading
his command in a charge. Colonel Daniel W. Adams, who
succeeded to the command, seized the brigade's battle
flag and, calling on his troops to follow him, led a magnificent charge which threw Prentiss back. Colonel Ever-
ett Peabody commanding Prentiss's First Brigade was
killed. Major John Powell of the Twenty-fifth Missouri
also fell. The entire division was badly shattered, but it
took a new position along an old sunken road near the
main road from Corinth to Pittsburg Landing. From this
new position, "the hornets' nest," a withering fire was

24 Walter G. Shotwell, *The Civil War in America* (New York, 1923),
I, 211.

poured into the Confederates.[25] Chalmers's brigade was brought from the Confederate right and placed in support of Gladden's brigade. Soon Wheeler with the Nineteenth Alabama and other scattered miscellaneous units of Jackson's brigade were also brought from the right and placed in support of Chalmers.[26] Prentiss was still holding on in spite of the repeated Confederate thrusts. His men were well protected behind the embankments of the sunken road, and the fire from Captain A. Hickenlooper's battery tore great gaps in the Confederate lines as they surged forward, wavered, re-formed, and advanced again, the men yelling and firing not only at the visible Federals but at those unseen ones who were hiding in the bushes.

Since dawn when it received orders to join Chalmers's and Gladden's brigades, Wheeler's regiment had been marching and fighting. It had been through three separate engagements before it wheeled left and marched toward Prentiss's front, and now the regiment was to participate in the hardest fighting of the day. Marching through a burning wood on its way to join Chalmers, the regiment was almost constantly under enemy rifle fire; and when it eventually reached Chalmers, it plunged into the assaults on "the hornets' nest." [27] None of the reports of the battle, not even Wheeler's, relate the specific details of the part played by the Nineteenth Alabama as it faced Hickenlooper's canister and the deadly fire of Prentiss's infantry, but the fact that the regiment lost one third of its roster, killed and wounded, is evidence enough of what it did. Colonel Wheeler's only comment was: "The regiment here exhibited an example of cool,

[25] *Ibid.*, 207–208.

[26] Withers's Report, June 20, 1862, in *Official Records*, Ser. I, Vol. X, Pt. I, 535–36.

[27] Wheeler's Report, April 12, 1862, *ibid.*, 558.

heroic courage which would do credit to soldiers of long experience in battle. Subjected as they were to a deadly fire of artillery and a cross-fire of infantry, they stood their ground with firmness and delivered their fire rapidly, but with cool deliberation and good effect." [28]

And the same might be said for most of the other Confederate and Federal regiments engaged. It has been said that raw troops can be depended upon to " 'run like the dev–l or fight like h—l,' " [29] and, although there was some running at Shiloh, the great majority of the troops on both sides fought bravely. In this terrific conflict at "the hornets' nest," however, someone had to give way, and it was General Prentiss who was outmaneuvered so that he was forced to surrender. General Daniel Ruggles brought eleven batteries of artillery to bear on Prentiss's front while Bragg moved in from the Confederate right and Hardee from the left. With the batteries enfilading his line at the same time that a deadly cross fire from Bragg and Hardee began to be effective, General Prentiss was forced to surrender late in the afternoon.[30] With his surrender there was hardly a Federal left flank to speak of.

That night Wheeler with the remnant of his regiment bivouacked four hundred yards from the Tennessee River.[31] If General Johnston had lasted out the day he might have ridden unmolested from Wheeler's camp and carried out his boast that he would water his horse in the

---

[28] *Ibid.*

[29] Shotwell, *Civil War in America*, I, 206. Although a book of fiction, Andrew Nelson Lytle's *The Long Night* (New York, 1936), 282–301, gives one of the most dramatic yet accurate accounts of the battle the author has ever read.

[30] See General Ulysses S. Grant's account of the surrender in "The Battle of Shiloh," in *Battles and Leaders*, I, 473.

[31] Chalmers's Report, April 12, 1862, in *Official Records*, Ser. I, Vol. X, Pt. I, 552.

Tennessee by nightfall. The General was dead, but his strategy had prevailed; the enemy had been pushed into a corner and his line of retreat at Pittsburg Landing rendered precarious.

But there was another day at dawn, a day when the Confederates yielded up all they had won. The Federals had received a transfusion during the night in the reinforcements of Generals Lew Wallace, Thomas L. Crittenden, and William Nelson; and the Confederates, bled white by yesterday's charges, slowly, grudgingly, yielded up the field. Wheeler's regiment, long since detached from its brigade, was joined in a miscellaneous brigade commanded by General Jones M. Withers and deployed as skirmishers in front of Hardee's corps.[32] But the terrific Confederate charges of the day before were missing. The spirit was willing but the flesh was weak; binding up its wounds as best it could, the Army of the Mississippi limped back toward Corinth. At first it was an orderly retreat, but by noon of the eighth (the retreat began in earnest on the afternoon of the seventh) it had become almost a rout. "Our condition is horrible," Bragg notified Beauregard. "Troops utterly disorganized and demoralized. No provisions and no forage; consequently everything is feeble." [33]

General Breckinridge was assigned command of rear guard operations and his dispatches only complete the picture of confusion. "The whole road presents the scene of a rout, and no mortal power could restrain it," [34] he advised Bragg. Regiments and brigades were intermingled, wounded men hobbled along on improvised crutches, and those who escaped without wounds were gaunt, weary, and half-starved. If the enemy had pursued,

32 *Ibid.*   33 Bragg to Beauregard, April 8, 1862, *ibid.*, Pt. II, 398.
34 Breckinridge to Bragg, April 8, 1862, *ibid.*, 400.

as Beauregard feared they would, the slaughter would
have been terrible beyond words.

On the ninth at half-past nine in the morning Breckinridge notified Bragg that he himself was "unwell and
nearly unfit for duty." [35] Upon Wheeler fell the task of
completing the rear guard operations. He was given a
"demi-brigade" with which to check the Federals if they
should pursue.[36] But the enemy did not pursue; as later
reports were to reveal, they were glad to come out of the
battle as well as they did and were hardly in a position to
pursue any military unit larger than a brigade. Wheeler's
duties, therefore, were largely those of rounding up
stragglers and observing any movements on the enemy's
front. On April 12 there was a skirmish with Federal cavalry, but it amounted to little.[37]

When the army was safely back in Corinth and the
officers had an opportunity to write up their reports,
Wheeler came in for considerable praise and attention
from his superiors. General Chalmers made a special note
of Wheeler "with a small remnant of his regiment, fighting with the Mississippians, on foot himself, and bearing
the colors of his command." Again the same general noted
the promptness and vigor with which the young Colonel
took up the fight.[38] General Withers reported that "Colonel Wheeler . . . throughout the fight, had proved
himself worthy of all trust and confidence, a gallant commander and an accomplished soldier." General Bragg
himself reported that "the excellent regiment of Col.
Wheeler . . . did noble service." He especially noted

---

[35] *Id.* to *id.*, April 9, 1862, 9:30 A.M., *ibid.*, 403.

[36] Bragg to Breckinridge, April 9, 1862, *ibid.*, 404. Colonel Wheeler
had commanded John K. Jackson's brigade through a part of the battle,
General Jackson having become separated from his command.

[37] Wheeler to Jackson, April 12, 1862, *ibid.*, 414.

[38] Chalmers's Report, April 12, 1862, *ibid.*, Pt. I, 552.

that in spite of the fact that Jackson's brigade became badly scattered Wheeler was able to keep a semblance of it intact.[39]

But official compliments were not all that Wheeler received. From his home town of Augusta several young ladies sent a small silk battle flag for his sword, done in the colors of the regiment. With the flag was a note: "The heart of woman is ever proud to honor and delight in the brave, and it is this feeling, fresh and sincere, that would offer Colonel Wheeler a banner with the fervent prayers that God will especially bless him. Let Colonel Wheeler be assured that he is ever named with praise and gratitude and Augusta claims him proudly as her son." [40]

But over and above all this, Shiloh was important to Wheeler because it offered him needed experience in handling large bodies of troops. He was a young man only twenty-five years of age who had never led more than a platoon and that only in border warfare; but he seems to have displayed the same zest and coolness in the roar of Shiloh that he did that morning on the plains when he and the teamster and the surgeon fought off the marauding Indians. Too, he had a chance after Shiloh to observe at firsthand what a broken and retreating army looked like from the rear, an experience that would prove of incalculable value to him in the three years that lay ahead. As he covered the retreat to Corinth, so he covered Bragg's retreat from Kentucky. Likewise, he protected Bragg's withdrawal from Middle Tennessee to Chattanooga and then Joe Johnston's retirement to Atlanta. He became a coverer of retreats, so much so that many years

[39] Withers's Report, June 20, 1862, *ibid.*, 535; Bragg's Report, April 30, 1862, *ibid.*, 464.
[40] Augusta *Chronicle*, May 9, 1862.

after the war a political opponent [41] characterized him as "a general without a victory," thereby paying him an unintentional compliment. Wheeler performed every rearguard operation of the Army of Tennessee from Shiloh to Atlanta, and during this three-year period that army was never able to stay on the field to claim a single victory.[42]

[41] Colonel William M. Lowe of Huntsville, Alabama. See below, Chap. X.

[42] At this time these Confederate forces were known as "The Army of the Mississippi." On November 20, 1862, this designation was changed to "The Army of Tennessee." See Ben LaBree (ed.), *The Confederate Soldier in the Civil War* (Louisville, 1895), 341.

Chapter III

THE KENTUCKY CAMPAIGN
(May–October, 1862)

THE Confederate army was allowed to withdraw from Corinth to Tupelo without a struggle. Grant seemed to lay the blame for the delay on Henry W. Halleck, his superior officer. General Halleck arrived at Pittsburg Landing on April 11 and took command of the army. Preparations were slowly made for the advance upon Corinth, but it was April 30 before the preparations were complete and the advance begun.[1] Halleck would advance cautiously, avoiding any conflict with the enemy outposts. It was a progressive siege in which the country was honeycombed with roads and trenches. The Federals would advance a short distance and dig themselves in, then throw other lines forward. This process was repeated over and over until most of the territory between Pittsburg Landing and Corinth was a network of fortified positions.

In Corinth, General Beauregard had been reinforced by Van Dorn from Arkansas with about thirty thousand available troops. Halleck was creeping forward with a force which Grant estimated at a hundred and twenty thousand.[2] Beauregard sent out raiding parties with the

---

[1] *Personal Memoirs of U. S. Grant* (New York, 1885), I, 308.
[2] *Ibid.*, 394. The number probably was nearer 100,000. See James Kendall Hosmer, *The Appeal to Arms, 1861–1863* (New York, 1907), 218.

idea that he might divide the Federal force and then send an army in their rear which would block a possible retreat to the Tennessee River.[3] But the enemy refused to be divided. Instead it kept up its relentless digging of trenches and planting of guns, drawing a circle of steel around the already doomed town.

Colonel Wheeler commanded the principal raiding party sent out from Corinth. His command consisted of portions of the Nineteenth, Twenty-fifth, and Twenty-sixth Alabama regiments and about two hundred men from the Seventh, Ninth, Tenth, and Twenty-ninth Mississippi regiments, in all about six hundred men with two guns from F. H. Robertson's battery.[4] His task was to destroy bridges, obstruct fords, and otherwise delay the approach of the enemy until Beauregard could make plans for evacuating the town. Again Wheeler was covering a retreat. In addition to the work of destruction of bridges and fords, he was to engage the enemy and, if necessary, sacrifice his command in the effort. But the enemy had other plans and would not fight. Wheeler engaged their pickets, he dared the infantry to come out, but with the exception of skirmishes between pickets they kept digging. In the entire operations the Confederates lost only forty-three men killed, wounded, and missing.[5]

In Corinth privation and disease were prevalent. The salt meat furnished the Confederate troops was not fit to

[3] Beauregard to Colonel William Preston Johnston, June 22, 1862, in *Official Records,* Ser. I, Vol. X, Pt. I, 776.

[4] Wheeler's Report, June 6, 1862, *ibid.,* 853. This is an excellent example of "mixed brigades . . . formed of infantry and light cavalry." See *Regulations for the Army of the Confederate States* (New Orleans, 1861), 72.

[5] Wheeler's Report, June 6, 1862, in *Official Records,* Ser. I, Vol. X, Pt. I, 855.

eat. The water was terrible, so bad that the men had to hold their noses while drinking it. Beauregard complained that the Commissary General had assured General Johnston before the battle of Shiloh that the army would have fresh meat five times a week. Instead, the men got the meat once every ten days, if at all, and then no vegetables to go with it. Beauregard was ill, the men were ill, the town was doomed.[6] By May 25 Beauregard was convinced that he should evacuate Corinth and fall back to Tupelo. He issued secret orders on the next day, and the movement began with Wheeler's raid just described.[7]

On the morning of May 30, 1862, the Federal siege guns began the bombardment of Corinth. There was no response from the Confederate guns, which could be plainly seen protruding from the fortifications with the gunners standing by. Halleck's forces closed in and cautiously entered the town. They found two or three men and a few women and children "gathered around little heaps of furniture they had snatched from the burning buildings." Beauregard had "flown the coop taking with him his guns and baggage." [8] The guns which the advancing army had seen protruding from the fortifications were wooden guns and the gunners standing by were dummies. A newspaperman who was present wrote to his paper: "I do not know how the matter strikes abler military men, but I think we have been fooled . . . the old joke of quaker guns has been played off on us." [9] Beauregard was on his way to Tupelo, and Halleck's vise had closed on a deserted town.

At Tupelo Beauregard, ill since before the battle of

6 Beauregard to Johnston, June 22, 1862, *ibid.*, 776.

7 Beauregard's Report, June 13, 1862, *ibid.*, 766.

8 Chicago *Tribune*, May 30, 1862, quoted, *ibid.*, 771.

9 Cincinnati *Commercial*, May 30, 1862, quoted, *ibid.*, 773.

Shiloh, retired from the command on the urgent advice of his physician and General Bragg was placed in his stead, June 17, 1862.[10] Conditions among the men at Tupelo were much better than at Corinth. Wells were dug and a bountiful supply of clear, cool water was obtained. The moral tone of the men improved as the skeleton regiments began to fill up and the convalescents returned. Bragg was drilling his army five hours a day getting ready for a movement, but his exact plans, if he had any, were kept to himself. Even William Preston Johnston, who visited Bragg on a tour of inspection, did not learn the plans and was able to report to President Davis only that there were two possible moves—either attack Halleck at Corinth or cross the Tennessee and attack Don Carlos Buell, who had moved into North Alabama. Which of these Bragg intended to make, Colonel Johnston did not pretend to know.[11] Indeed, it was a problem of strategy the solution of which might determine the fate of Confederate arms in the West. Halleck, whose troops were directly commanded by Grant, was too strong at Corinth to risk an attack there; an invasion of West Tennessee would open Alabama and Georgia to the enemy; an advance toward Nashville crossing the Tennessee at or near Florence, Alabama, would place the Confederates between the upper millstone of Buell in North Alabama and the nether of Grant at Corinth. The most promising maneuver was a rapid march to Chattanooga and thence into Middle Tennessee or into Kentucky, depending upon the enemy's movements in the meantime.[12]

Bragg determined upon the last of these movements

[10] *Ibid.*, Ser. I, Vol. XVII, Pt. I, 1.

[11] Johnston's Report, July 15, 1862, *ibid.*, Vol. X, Pt. I, 780–86.

[12] Joseph Wheeler, "Bragg's Invasion of Kentucky," in *Battles and Leaders*, III, 2.

and Colonel Wheeler was called into conference to prepare the way for the advance. He was to take his new brigade and make a demonstration into West Tennessee to create the impression that Bragg's entire army was on the move in that direction. While Wheeler was thus engaging the attention of the enemy, the Confederates would move to Chattanooga. An unexpected visit from Colonel Philip H. Sheridan then in camp between Rienzi and Booneville aided Bragg's plans. On July 12, 1862, Colonel Sheridan under a flag of truce called upon the Confederates at Guntown and was received by Colonel Wheeler, Colonel E. D. Tracy of the Nineteenth Alabama, Captain T. M. Lenoir of General Bragg's staff, and Captain F. H. Robertson of the artillery. There was the customary polite small talk; but during the course of the conversation Wheeler and his companions apparently were very indiscreet in their remarks. They let fall some information which seemed of vital importance to the Federals. They said that Beauregard was out of command and in disgrace and that Bragg was reorganizing the army. They further stated that no movement was contemplated until harvest time, when sufficient corn could be obtained to feed horses and men. But most important of all was the information that when the movement did come it would be westward toward Holly Springs, Mississippi, and West Tennessee. At that very moment Bragg was planning his invasion of Kentucky. After an exchange of newspapers the meeting adjourned, and that night Captain Robert O. Selfridge, Assistant Adjutant General of the Federal Cavalry Division, transmitted to his chief the information that Bragg would move westward.[13] The

13 Robert O. Selfridge's Report, July 12, 1862, in *Official Records*, Ser. I, Vol. XVII, Pt. I, 22.

young Confederate officers had accomplished their purpose. They had told enough of the truth to insure cred-
ibility, and then by an apparent indiscretion had deliberately misled Sheridan.

In furthering the ruse, Wheeler left Tupelo late in
July with about a thousand men for a demonstration into
West Tennessee. Arriving at Holly Springs, Mississippi,
he called upon General John B. Villepigue at that place
for infantry reinforcements to aid in attacking the
Federal garrison at Grand Junction, Tennessee. These
troops being supplied him, he moved on Grand Junction
only to find that the enemy had evacuated the town, leaving about two hundred bales of cotton. These Colonel
Wheeler destroyed and then moved on toward Bolivar
in the wake of the evacuating Federals. The plan was to
menace the enemy at Bolivar and then concentrate his
troops for an attack on Jackson, Tennessee, where large
quantities of stores had been collected. The plan, however, was thwarted. General Villepigue recalled the infantry detachments which he had furnished, and Wheeler
had to content himself with the destruction of about
three thousand bales of cotton at Bolivar.

From the last place Colonel Wheeler sent a Confederate "deserter" into the Federal lines to spread the information that a large force was advancing. General John
A. McClernand, acting on this information, promptly
ordered reinforcements from Jackson on the west and
from Corinth on the east. Wheeler fell in behind the
reinforcing army from Jackson, and destroyed the railroad bridge which cut it off from a retreat. He then
swung around Bolivar to the west and tore up the track
from Corinth. A large Federal force was thus bottled up
and useless at Bolivar. Wheeler stated that with his troops

much jaded by previous privations he "penetrated some 70 miles behind the enemy's lines, destroyed the railroad bridges in the rear, and met him in eight separate engagements, in all of which . . . he was thoroughly defeated, many of his horses and men being killed, wounded, or taken prisoners by our troops." [14] But above all, the enemy had been kept occupied while Bragg was moving.

General Bragg established his headquarters in Chattanooga on July 29, 1862. His infantry, since the enemy held the Memphis and Charleston Railroad, moved from Tupelo via Mobile and Atlanta by rail and the cavalry and artillery marched overland through northern Alabama. The trans-Mississippi army under Van Dorn and Sterling Price, which had arrived too late for the Battle of Shiloh, was left at Tupelo with instructions to attack William S. Rosecrans at Corinth, and either take the position or prevent reinforcements from going into Tennessee. From Chattanooga Bragg wrote Price that he would dispose of General Buell; but "Sherman and Rosecrans we leave to you and Van Dorn, satisfied that you can dispose of them, and we shall confidently expect to meet you on the Ohio and there open a way to Missouri." [15]

On July 30 General Edmund Kirby Smith came down from Knoxville for a conference with Bragg. The result was an agreement on a double movement. Smith would move against Cumberland Gap, where General George W. Morgan had assembled about nine thousand Federals. If this movement should prove successful, then Bragg thought a corresponding success was assured in his offensive against Buell. Smith took the field on August 13, but

[14] Wheeler's Report, August 1, 1862, *ibid.*, 23–25. Wheeler was officially transferred to the cavalry division on July 18, 1862.
[15] *Ibid.*, Vol. XVI, Pt. II, 783.

it was two weeks later before Bragg was ready to move.[16] On August 28 he crossed the Tennessee from Chattanooga, his right wing under Polk, 13,537 strong; his left wing under Hardee, 13,763 strong.[17] Colonel Wheeler was given three regiments of cavalry and assigned to duty on the left wing under Hardee, his old instructor at West Point.[18] To meet this threat of an invasion of Middle Tennessee, Buell hastily concentrated his divisions at Altamont, only forty miles as the crow flies northeast of Chattanooga. Finding this position impracticable he fell back to Murfreesboro on September 5, from which point he decided to develop Bragg's intentions.

Bragg's army crawled slowly over Walden's Ridge, descended into the Sequatchie Valley, and followed it northeastward to Pikeville. Here Bragg turned northwest toward Sparta, making a wide circle and leaving the Federals at Altamont far to his left. On the morning of August 30, two days after leaving Chattanooga, Wheeler turned sharply to the left out of the Sequatchie Valley, rode twenty miles across the plateau, and struck the Federal outposts at Altamont. It was a brief engagement but of sufficient intensity to cause Buell to conclude that Hardee's corps was trying to effect a passage through the gap.[19] Turning eastward again Wheeler rejoined Hardee's corps and hovered on its left flank until the army reached Carthage, Tennessee, some fifty miles east of Nashville, on September 7.

[16] David Urquhart, "Bragg's Advance and Retreat," in *Battles and Leaders*, III, 600. Colonel Urquhart was a member of Bragg's staff.

[17] *Ibid.*

[18] Special Orders, No. 164, August 26, 1862, in *Official Records*, Ser. I, Vol. XVI, Pt. II, 781–82.

[19] Wheeler's Report, October 30, 1862, *ibid.*, Pt. I, 893. Don C. Buell in his testimony before the military commission appointed to investigate his conduct of the campaign stated that he had on this occasion repulsed Hardee's corps. See *ibid.*, 43.

In the meantime, Kirby Smith moved out of Knoxville toward Cumberland Gap. Instead of attacking the Federal force there he sent about ten thousand men under General Carter L. Stevenson to threaten it while he passed with his remaining six thousand troops into Kentucky about twenty miles below the gap.[20] Once across the mountains General Smith swept like a fury across eastern Kentucky. On August 30, the very day that Wheeler struck Buell's outposts at Altamont, Smith defeated the Federals at Mt. Zion Church near Richmond, Kentucky. Pressing the enemy back Smith fought a second battle the same day at White's farm and then a third when he took Richmond just before sundown. Giving his men one day's rest he pushed on to Lexington, reaching there on September 2. From this point he sent a small force to occupy Frankfort a few miles away and another small force to threaten Cincinnati.[21]

Bragg received the news of Smith's victory and with the news a letter urging him to turn northward immediately and join him in the invasion of Kentucky. Bragg was elated. His hopes of victory were running high, so high that he felt constrained to let his soldiers know about it. At Sparta, where he decided upon the invasion of Kentucky, Bragg issued a proclamation on September 5. "We are again called upon to rejoice," he said, "and give thanks to God for a victory as brilliant and complete achieved in our own campaign by the troops under Maj. Gen. E. Kirby Smith at Richmond, Ky." The Alabamians present were reminded that the campaign had drawn the

20 Edmund Kirby Smith to Davis, August 21, 1862, *ibid.*, Pt. II, 768; Wheeler, "Bragg's Invasion of Kentucky," in *Battles and Leaders*, III, 4.
21 Smith's Report, August 30, 1862, in *Official Records*, Ser. I, Vol. XVI, Pt. I, 931–35.

remaining Federals from their state, and that as a result "An arrogant foe no longer treads her soil." Since Buell had decided to move out of Nashville toward Louisville, Bragg called the attention of his Tennessee troops to the fact that "the restoration of your capital and State government is almost accomplished without firing a gun." [22]

But Kentucky even without Smith's victory was of great concern to Bragg. Ever since he had written Secretary Benjamin nearly twelve months previously he had planned for the time when he could win over the people of that state to the Confederate cause. "Kentuckians," he proclaimed, "the first great blow has been struck for your freedom. The manacles will soon fall from your limbs, when we know you will arise and strike for your freedom, your women, and your altars." [23] But this was wishful proclaiming, for he was soon to receive strong intimations that the Kentuckians were very well satisfied with their manacles, and considered their women and altars fairly safe under the Union flag.

General Forrest joined Bragg's army at Sparta, apparently expecting to be placed in charge of the cavalry. Certainly he had a right to expect such an appointment. He was the only brigadier general of cavalry. His raids and his spectacular capture of Murfreesboro had marked him as an officer deserving of promotion. Moreover, at this time he was forty-one years of age, a mature and experienced man. But the cavalry was not put under him. Wheeler was allowed to retain his command and Forrest was given the remainder; [24] and from this time on the two cavalry leaders operated under Bragg, but often in separate directions and with separate commands. While

[22] General Orders, No. 128, September 5, 1862, *ibid.*, 937.
[23] *Ibid.*   [24] *Ibid.*, Pt. II, 824.

Forrest made no display of his disappointment at this time, as the campaign developed he became more and more critical of Bragg.[25]

Thus the race for Kentucky began. Bragg was in the center of the movement, Kirby Smith to the right on the northeast, and Buell paralleling Bragg's left on the west.

Wheeler reached Carthage, Tennessee, some fifty miles east of Nashville, on September 7. Here he was ordered to proceed toward Nashville and strike Buell's columns moving toward Louisville. Hovering just out of range of the main Federal column Wheeler busied himself with the task of destroying telegraph lines and the railroad.[26] Arriving near Woodburn, Kentucky, on September 11 Wheeler placed his force of nearly seven hundred men in ambush hoping to entrap General Thomas L. Crittenden's division, but the ruse was discovered and the plans came to nought. There was a brief skirmish after which Wheeler drew off. The next day he proceeded to Merry Oaks, midway between Bowling Green and Glasgow, to cover the Confederate army and watch the movements of the enemy, remaining in this position until the sixteenth.[27] His orders were to "feel the enemy and harass him without endangering his command," [28] orders that called for patient watchfulness more than for daring exploits of bravery. It was routine cavalry duty, but upon the faithful performance of that duty depended the safety and success of the main army. Wheeler was displaying some of the traits which were to loom so large in his rapid rise to distinction in the days ahead of him, namely,

25 For an account of the growing estrangement between Bragg and Forrest, see Lytle, *Bedford Forrest,* 110–11.

26 Dubose, *Wheeler and the Army of Tennessee,* 89.

27 Wheeler's Report, October 30, 1862, in *Official Records,* Ser. I, Vol. XVI, Pt. I, 893.

28 Special Orders, No. 14, September 7, 1862, *ibid.,* Pt. II, 801.

persistence, patience, and a strict regard for orders.

On the Federal side of the picture Bragg's change of plans at Sparta which resulted in the decision to invade Kentucky caused confusion within the Federal lines. With Kirby Smith at Lexington threatening Cincinnati and Bragg somewhere in Middle Tennessee ready to strike, the Federal leaders during late August and early September, 1862, were in a state of mild panic. Major General Horatio G. Wright at Cincinnati wired Governor Oliver P. Morton of Indiana for reinforcements, stating that "this place is threatened." [29] In Washington President Lincoln became alarmed. "Where is General Bragg?" he wired General Jeremiah T. Boyle at Louisville, and Boyle was forced to admit: "I do not know where General Bragg is." [30] Then Lincoln turned to General Wright at Cincinnati. "Do you know to any certainty where General Bragg is? May he not be in Virginia?" he wired; and Wright answered: "Nothing reliable about Bragg." [31] Finally Lincoln turned to Buell. What degree of certainty had he that Bragg was even in Tennessee? But Buell knew. Wheeler had routed his outposts at Altamont and had destroyed his railroad and telegraph lines north of Nashville. He notified the President that "Bragg is certainly this side of the Cumberland Mountains with his whole force, except what is in Kentucky under Smith. His movements will probably depend upon mine. . . . I shall endeavor to hold Nashville, and at the same time drive Smith out of Kentucky." [32]

In the region of Cincinnati, Kirby Smith also had the Federals guessing. General Boyle at Cincinnati had wired

[29] Horatio G. Wright to Oliver P. Morton, September 7, 1862, *ibid.*, 495.

[30] Abraham Lincoln to Jeremiah T. Boyle, September 7, 1862, *ibid.*

[31] *Id.* to Wright, September 7, 1862, *ibid.*, 496.

[32] Buell to Lincoln, September 10, 1862, *ibid.*, 500.

for reinforcements from Louisville and Governor James F. Robinson protested to Halleck against any troops leaving the city. "We protest," he wired on September 10, "against the withdrawal of any of the forces from this place for Cincinnati. There is reliable information that this city is the object of the enemy. There are defenses at Cincinnati, natural and artificial, also an ample force; and there are none here and none ordered. If Louisville is taken the State is gone. Our officers here deplore any order to take away our troops. We insist that it shall not be done." [33] And Halleck could not overlook such strong words, for he wanted to retain Kentucky as badly as Bragg wanted to take it. Accordingly, he instructed General Wright, if possible, not to abandon Louisville; for if it fell, "with it we lose Kentucky." [34]

Military historians are in agreement that this would have been a most appropriate time for Bragg to turn westward a few miles and fight Buell. Van Dorn and Price were keeping the Federals occupied in the region of Corinth and in West Tennessee; Kirby Smith had them watching Cincinnati, and Buell himself was nearly *hors de combat*. He had just written: "Cut off effectually from supplies, it is impossible for me to operate in force where I am." [35] But Bragg did not seize the opportunity. "This campaign must be won by marching, not by fighting," [36] he said as Buell passed on his left going toward Louisville. Wheeler and many staff officers urged a battle but their advice was disregarded.[37]

[33] James F. Robinson to Henry W. Halleck, September 10, 1862, *ibid.*, 504.

[34] Halleck to Wright, September 11, 1862, *ibid.*, 508.

[35] Buell to Lincoln, September 10, 1862, *ibid.*, 500.

[36] Urquhart, "Bragg's Advance and Retreat," in *Battles and Leaders*, III, 601.

[37] In 1884 Wheeler wrote: "Early on the morning of the 18th, General

Bragg arrived at Glasgow on September 12. At the same time Buell arrived at Bowling Green about thirty miles to the west. At Glasgow Bragg decided to rest and feed his horses and soldiers, to rest while Buell beat him to Louisville. While he was thus taking his ease, reports came to him that General Chalmers, whom he had sent northward on outpost duty, had attacked the small town of Munfordville and had been repulsed. The event loomed large to Bragg; the very first battle of his campaign of deliverance had been unfavorable to him. Sending Forrest northward beyond Munfordville he made preparations to move on the town. On September 17, 1862, Bragg reached Munfordville which, being overpowered, surrendered its garrison of four thousand men.[38] The honor of the invading army had been vindicated, but at a dear price. While Bragg was engaged here, Buell began the occupation of Louisville.

Although military historians are in agreement that Bragg's conduct of the campaign was bad, they have failed to explain in a satisfactory manner why this is true. He waxed hot and cold. He was overcautious and then extremely bold. He seemed to lack fixity of determination and then suddenly to make up his mind, only to change it at the last moment.[39] He quarreled with his

---

Bragg sent for me and explained his plans. I never saw him more determined or more confident. The entire army was in the best of spirits. I met and talked with Generals Hardee, Polk, Cheatham, and Buckner; all were enthusiastic over our success, and our good luck in getting Buell where he would be compelled to fight us to such a disadvantage. . . . But after the arrival of General Thomas, Bragg did not deem it advisable to risk a battle with the force then under his command, believing that another opportunity would offer after being joined by Kirby Smith." Wheeler, "Bragg's Invasion of Kentucky," in *Battles and Leaders,* III, 10.

[38] Shotwell, *Civil War in America,* I, 277.

[39] The best explanation seems to be that Bragg considered his mission

officers. Matters between him and Forrest had been growing worse and worse, and now after Munfordville he rid
himself of his senior cavalry commander. He took away
most of Forrest's old command and gave it to Wheeler,
sending the former back to Murfreesboro ostensibly to
cope with the Federal raiding parties sent out from Nashville [40]—a fact, incidentally, which paved the way for
Wheeler's promotion to chief of cavalry.

While Bragg was feeding at Glasgow before the battle
at Munfordville and while Buell was at Bowling Green,
Wheeler had been assigned the task of watching the enemy and of guarding the road from Bowling Green to
Glasgow. His orders read: ". . . to picket strongly the
Bowling Green road and to keep . . . [General Hardee]
well advised of all movements of the enemy. He wishes
you to employ secret agents to penetrate the enemy's lines
at Bowling Green and obtain information of his force,
position, probable movements, &c." [41] On the night of
September 16 Wheeler observed the enemy moving a
large cavalry force over the Green River in the direction
of Glasgow. He thought Buell contemplated an attack,
and the secret agents lately returned from Bowling Green
confirmed his views. He sent word back to Hardee that
Buell was about to attack, but instead it was merely an
empty wagon train on its way to Louisville under heavy

---

political rather than military. See Thomas R. Hay, "Braxton Bragg and
the Southern Confederacy," in *Georgia Historical Quarterly* (Athens),
IX (1925), 290.

[40] See Lytle, *Bedford Forrest*, 111. Probably one of the greatest mistakes made in military operations in the West was the failure of Confederate authorities to recognize the abilities of General Forrest. Mr.
Lytle has said to the author many times in private conversation that if
Forrest had been in command of the Army of Tennessee the results
probably would have been quite different.

[41] Hardee to Wheeler, September 14, 1862, in *Official Records*, Ser.
I, Vol. XVI, Pt. II, 820.

BRAGG'S
INVASION OF KENTUCKY.

BRAGG —x—x— SMITH —•—•—
BUELL'S ARMY --------
RAILROADS ------

SCALE OF MILES
10 20 30 40 50

From Battles and Leaders of the Civil War

guard.[42] In fact, Buell's outposts and Wheeler's were playing a game of peek-a-boo. Neither of them wished to provoke a fight, for no lasting results could be obtained from an engagement at this time. Buell's outposts were to screen his movements. Wheeler was to screen Bragg's movements. The net result was that neither of them did very much screening. With two large armies so close together and moving rather leisurely toward the same objective, secrecy was next to impossible. Neither side could do more than make fruitless demonstrations.

There was, however, a sharp brush now and then. On the morning of September 20, when the Confederate army was moving from Munfordville, Buell pushed forward his outposts to learn, if possible, Bragg's movements. The next morning they encountered Wheeler's pickets posted four miles in front of his main position behind Green River. Gallantly Wheeler's First Alabama regiment charged the Federals, losing their commander, Lieutenant Colonel T. B. Brown, to a Federal bullet. That night Wheeler asked permission from Buell for Colonel Brown's brother to enter the Federal lines to claim the body. This permission was refused in a polite note which read: "He was killed outright in the handsome cavalry charge executed by your troops yesterday afternoon. His body was taken to a neighboring house and cared for. He will be interred to-day, and doubtless in the vicinity. His watch was taken charge of by an officer of rank in our service, and I will make it a point to have it forwarded to you." [43]

Wheeler's handling of the cavalry here furnishes an excellent illustration of the work which this branch of the

[42] Wheeler's Report, October 30, 1862, *ibid.*, Pt. I, 894.
[43] General Thomas J. Wood to Wheeler, September 22, 1862, *ibid.*, Pt. II, 535.

service properly handled is called upon to do. There were few magnificent sweeping charges; no highly exciting pitched battles such as popular imagination often attributes to the mounted service. It was not the duty of the cavalry to fight major battles any more than it is the function of the airplane in modern warfare to do so. In both instances the chief duty is making contact with the enemy and operating on lines of communication. This may, and often does, involve daring exploits and much fighting, but these are secondary. To use the words of an English military critic: "In the first place . . . [the cavalry] is required to cover the front and flanks of the army to which it is attached, securing it from surprises, and enabling it to carry out movements of concentration or other strategic maneuvers unobserved. In the second place, it is required to burst through the screen which covers the movements and maneuvers of the opposing army and to obtain the information which is absolutely essential to the commander in chief." [44] Therefore, in measuring the value of a cavalry commander these points must be taken into consideration. The question to be answered is how well Wheeler performed the true functions of a cavalry commander and not how glamorous he was or what a superb strategist he did or did not turn out to be. Wheeler had few opportunities to demonstrate whether he was a great strategist or not and in those the failures and successes about balanced each other. It seems perfectly clear, however, that he did not perform as well on detached missions as when operating in close conjunction with the main army.

Buell reached Louisville in full force on September 25 and found there several thousand raw troops waiting to join his army. He spent five days equipping and organiz-

[44] G. F. R. Henderson, *The Science of War* (New York, 1905), 58.

ing them into brigades and then marched forth in search of Bragg.

On September 27 Bragg issued another proclamation to the people of Kentucky in which he painted a vivid picture of the "meddlesome, grasping and fanatical disposition of the east" which had imposed a protective tariff and internal improvements upon them, raising their taxes and imposing unnecessary burdens. Their only hope of salvation was an alliance with the Southern cause. He appealed again to the men of Kentucky to flock to him and arm themselves with the rifles he had brought along for that purpose. If they would do this the secession government about to be inaugurated at Frankfort would be successful and Kentucky would be won for the Confederacy. Thus he spoke and, mounting his horse, rode away to Frankfort to see the Honorable Richard Hawes, the secession governor, inaugurated. There General Smith and his army were in attendance.[45]

In the meantime, Buell was moving his army southward from Louisville in three divisions, each taking a separate road.[46] The division under General Joshua W. Sill called by Frankfort and participated in the inaugural ceremony by throwing shells into the town and dispersing the crowd. Bragg, riding away from the town, ordered Smith with his victorious troops to Bardstown. He detached Withers's division of about eight thousand men from Polk and ordered it to attack Sill's front at Salvisa, while Smith would come up from the rear. All the plans miscarried. Sill passed Salvisa before Withers reached it.

[45] For a discussion of the political effects of Bragg's invasion, see E. Merton Coulter, *The Civil War and Readjustment in Kentucky* (Chapel Hill, 1926). See also, J. G. Randall, *The Civil War and Reconstruction* (New York, 1937), 317–22, 524–28.

[46] Don Carlos Buell, "East Tennessee and the Campaign of Perryville," in *Battles and Leaders*, III, 47.

As matters now stood the Confederate army was badly divided: part under Polk at Bardstown, part under Hardee at Perryville, part under Smith moving from Frankfort, and part under Withers at Salvisa. Buell was moving on Hardee at Perryville and the latter general's salvation lay in the speed with which Polk joined him.[47]

Colonel Wheeler was with Hardee at Perryville, his cavalry deployed in front of the army. His task was of the utmost importance, to delay Buell until Polk could arrive with the necessary reinforcements. His tactics were the same that he had previously used to such good advantage. He would engage the enemy until forced by superior numbers to retire; then he would fall back, re-form his lines, and repeat the process. Two sentences from his report are sufficient to show this: "We engaged them with artillery and small-arms, compelling them to advance very slowly, frequently deploying their infantry. We were obliged to fall back slowly when their infantry fired too heavily; but succeeded in so checking their progress that they only advanced about 4 miles from 8 a.m. until dark." [48]

This was on the sixth of October. On the morning of the seventh the process of fighting and falling back began all over again, and was kept up intermittently throughout the day. Polk was moving with all possible speed to join Hardee, and Wheeler was exerting every effort to slow up Buell. By nightfall of the seventh Wheeler could report: "By keeping our lines continually skirmishing until night we prevented the enemy from making any demonstration that day upon our in-

47 Wheeler, "Bragg's Invasion of Kentucky," *ibid.*, 14–16.
48 Wheeler's Report, October 30, 1862, in *Official Records*, Ser. I, Vol. XVI, Pt. I, 896.

fantry, which had deployed in line of battle to meet the enemy on the field of Perryville." [49]

In later years Wheeler wrote that when he rode in to General Hardee's bivouac on the night of the seventh to discuss with his commander the plans for the following day and to inform him of the disposition of Buell's troops he urged that the Confederate attack should by all means begin very early in the morning.[50] But obviously there was no general agreement among the ranking officers as to when the attack should come. General Polk had arrived at Perryville some time near midnight of the seventh with instructions from General Bragg which read: "In view of the news from Hardee you had better move with Cheatham's division to his support and give the enemy battle immediately. Rout him and then move to our support at Versailles. No time should be lost in these movements." [51] Apparently General Polk either misunderstood the orders, taking them to be merely suggestive, or he deliberately disobeyed, for about daylight on the eighth he called a conference of his officers and it was decided to take a "defensive-offensive" attitude.[52] Thus, instead of the main battle getting under way early in the morning, the only definite movement was to send

[49] *Ibid.*, 897. General Polk in writing of cavalry activity here said: "The enemy had been held in check along the whole line of march from in front of Louisville up to our present position [Perryville] by those gallant cavalry commanders Colonels Wharton and Wheeler, and we were constantly advised of his position and movements." Polk's Report, November ?, 1862, *ibid.*, 1109.

[50] Wheeler, "Bragg's Invasion of Kentucky," in *Battles and Leaders,* III, 15.

[51] Bragg to Polk, October 7, 1862, 5:40 P.M., in *Official Records,* Ser. I, Vol. XVI, Pt. I, 1098.

[52] General Polk stated afterward that he considered Bragg's communication as merely suggestive. Polk to Hardee, April 17, 1863, *ibid.*, 1101.

Wheeler reconnoitering. Pickets and scouts were thrown out by him on all the approaches to Perryville from the south and southwest as far as the Lebanon and Danville road, and all precautions were taken to prevent a possible enemy flanking movement. About ten o'clock Wheeler found himself confronted by a large body of troops deployed for battle, the line being steadily increased by troops from the rear.[53] The enemy was at least partially ready for battle.

It was about this same hour that General Bragg reached Perryville from Harrodsburg and found that General Polk had not ordered the attack. Taking charge himself, he set the Confederates in motion and for the next eight hours the two armies charged and counter-charged each other, the prize for the winner being the water holes of Chaplin and Doctor's creeks.[54] The Confederates had selected the heights above Chaplin Creek (or river) just west of Perryville for their lines; General Benjamin F. Cheatham's corps on the Confederate right, General Simon B. Buckner in the center, and General J. Patton Anderson on the left. In front of Cheatham and Buckner were the Federal divisions under Generals Alexander McD. McCook and James S. Jackson with General Sheridan confronting Buckner's left and Anderson's right. Generals Thomas J. Wood, Horatio P. Van Cleve, and William S. Smith took position on the Federal right. John A. Wharton's cavalry was in position on Cheatham's right while Wheeler covered Anderson's left.[55] Cheatham's corps was the first to go into battle; then Generals Bushrod Johnson and Cleburne moved

---

53 Wheeler's Report, October 30, 1862, *ibid.*, 897.

54 See Shotwell, *Civil War in America*, I, 281–83. A most interesting account of the battle is found in *Reminiscences of General Basil W. Duke, C.S.A.* (New York, 1911), 304–33.

55 See map of battle in *Battles and Leaders*, III, 24.

into action. By two o'clock in the afternoon fighting had become general all along the line. Slowly, as at Shiloh, the Confederates pushed the Federals back by vicious charges until the field was theirs; and as at Shiloh, night came and the Confederates yielded up what they had won. At midnight the Confederates withdrew to Perryville and at sunrise moved to Bardstown expecting a Federal pursuit, but as at Shiloh there was no immediate pursuit.[56]

Wheeler's part in the main battle was of little importance. Just before ten o'clock when he withdrew from picket duty previous to the start of the battle his troops were pressed by the enemy's cavalry and he resisted by throwing the First and Third Alabama regiments at them [57] and then retired with his command to the Confederate left flank where he remained on guard against any possible Federal flanking movement. With Bragg's decision to retire to Bardstown, however, Wheeler assumed a more important role. He was directed to prevent any advance by the Federals along the Danville road, a rear guard action such as he had performed at Shiloh.[58] But there was no pursuit the next day (the ninth) nor the next nor the next. For three days Bragg waited at Bardstown expecting the Federals to attack, three busy days for Wheeler observing enemy move-

[56] There were approximately sixteen thousand Confederates engaged. Not all the Federal troops present took part in the battle, but the number engaged was from twenty-five to thirty-six thousand. The Confederates lost approximately five hundred killed and twenty-six hundred wounded. Federal losses were approximately eight hundred killed and twenty-eight hundred wounded. See Thomas L. Livermore, *Numbers and Losses in the Civil War* (New York, 1901), 95–96.

[57] Wheeler's Report, October 30, 1862, in *Official Records*, Ser. I, Vol. XVI, Pt. I, 897. General Polk described this as "a most brilliant charge." Polk's Report, November ?, 1862, *ibid.*, 1112.

[58] Wheeler's Report, October 30, 1862, *ibid.*, 898.

ments in the rear of his own army. Becoming convinced
that the enemy was massing for a belated attack, Wheeler
sent a message to that effect to General Polk and shortly
received a message from General Bragg: "I opened your
dispatch to General Polk regarding the enemy's movements. The information you furnish is very important.
It is just what I needed and I thank you for it. This information leaves no doubt as to the proper course for
me to pursue. Hold the enemy firmly until to-morrow." [59]

This probably was Bragg's first announcement that he
intended to abandon Kentucky and retreat to Cumberland Gap. His injunction to Wheeler to "hold the enemy
firmly" was but the first of many such orders issued during the next twelve days, for a retreat is always fraught
with peril. There were the sick and wounded to be
collected. Baggage wagons and supply trains had to be
loaded for the long journey back. A junction of the units
of the army had to be effected. And above it all there
hung the dread likelihood that Buell would pursue and
attack the slow, creaking, retreating columns. Obviously,
the cavalry had to protect the rear, and sound military
judgment demanded that some one cavalry leader be
given sole responsibility. For this Wheeler was selected.
Before dawn on October 13 while on rear guard duty
Wheeler received this order:

Headquarters Department No. 2
Bryantsville, Ky., October 13, 1862—3 a.m.
Special Orders,
No. 14
I. Colonel Wheeler is hereby appointed chief of cavalry
and is authorized to give orders in the name of the command-
ing general. He is charged, under Major-General Smith, with

59 Bragg to Wheeler, October 10, 1862, *ibid.*, Pt. II, 930.

covering the rear of the army and holding the enemy in check. All cavalry will report to him and receive his orders.[60]

On the same day he received a message from Kirby Smith's Chief of Staff which read: "Maj. Gen. E. Kirby Smith directs me to say to you that you are hereby placed in command of all the cavalry of the whole army." [61]

On the thirteenth the retreat began in earnest. All the supplies which it was impossible to carry along were burned. Provisions, muskets, merchandise of all sorts, were hauled away in wagons. There were refugees with their families, slaves, and goods. Straining oxen dragged artillery along behind and between omnibuses, stages, and almost every other variety of vehicle. Mingled in the din was the shouting of Texas Rangers as they swore at frightened droves of bellowing cattle.[62] This was what Wheeler had to protect. His orders stated, in part: "The condition of that army, with its large train, &c., being now considerably in the rear, will require that you should send your largest cavalry force for covering well its rear. . . . The officer commanding the force covering the rear of the column on this road must keep his position well, and *not fall back on the infantry unless driven back by the enemy.*" [63]

"The pursuit was conducted by its commander, ac-

[60] *Ibid.*, 940.

[61] Smith to Wheeler, October 13, 1862, *ibid.*, 939. In addition to Kirby Smith's cavalry which came temporarily under his command, Wheeler's corps consisted of two brigades—John A. Wharton's consisting of the First Kentucky, Fourth Tennessee, and Eighth Texas; and Wheeler's own composed of the First Alabama, Third Alabama, Sixth Confederate, Second Georgia, Third Georgia, and First Kentucky.

[62] Urquhart, "Bragg's Advance and Retreat," in *Battles and Leaders*, III, 603.

[63] *Official Records*, Ser. I, Vol. XVI, Pt. II, 941. Author's italics.

cording to my orders, with judgment and energy," reported Buell,[64] but apparently the pursuit was accomplishing little. "We are pressing the rebel cavalry back, skirmishing with them at every turn of the road," General William Sooy Smith reported. "They have so obstructed the road by felling timber that our progress is very slow. . . . They fell trees until we come up to them, then fall back rapidly and chop away again." [65] Apparently Wheeler's tree felling was something new and unexpected in the war, for it evoked no little comment from the Federal officers. Buell mentioned it in his report of the campaign and the matter came up again in General George H. Thomas's testimony before the Buell Commission in Nashville, to say nothing of the complaints handed in by colonels and captains to their superiors in the field.[66]

The two armies of Bragg retreated as a unit as far south as Lancaster. There the roads forked and the armies divided, one under the command of General Kirby Smith and the other under Bragg. Both were moving toward a common point where the roads merged at Barboursville just north of Cumberland Gap. It was while the army was thus divided that Colonel Wheeler did his best work.

To General Smith was entrusted much of the baggage and the supply wagons. His road, as well as that of Bragg, traversed a thinly settled and extremely rough section of eastern Kentucky. The autumn of 1862 was very dry, so dry that springs and creeks were turned into burning beds of sand and polished pebbles. The Confederates were thirsty and many of them were deserting. The

64 Buell's Report, November 4, 1862, *ibid.*, Pt. I, 1029.
65 Smith to Buell, October 17, 1862, *ibid.*, 1140.
66 George H. Thomas's testimony, *ibid.*, 199.

Federal army threatened from the rear. General Smith grew discouraged and wrote Bragg: "I have little hope of saving any of the trains, and fear much of the artillery will be lost." [67] Not only was he discouraged but he believed that Bragg had deliberately chosen the easier road. To General Polk he wrote: "He gives up the Wild Cat Pass, exposes my flank, and leaves the enemy only 9 miles to march to meet my front. . . . I have marched by a circuitous route, while he has taken the direct one. . . . My train is now turned off by a circuitous route and one that is almost impassable, and on which . . . [the wagons] must be delayed a long time, if not abandoned." [68]

While General Smith was in this frame of mind there came a cheering message from Wheeler. "Tell General Smith," he wrote, "to abandon nothing; we will save all." [69] Wheeler and his lumberjack cavalrymen were bringing up the rear, fighting by day and obstructing the roads by night. It was a steady and dogged falling back in the face of the advancing enemy. At times the cavalry was dismounted and fought from behind stone fences and hastily erected rail breastworks. At other times, when opportunity presented itself, there were swift and devastating charges. Each plan was adapted to their daily needs, and always there were the tree chopping operations which so irritated General Sooy Smith.

As the retreat neared its conclusion, Polk at Cumberland Ford, Tennessee, wrote encouragingly to Bragg: "A large number of General Smith's wagons have also passed this point. General Smith himself came forward to-day and met me. . . . The rear of his army, he informs me, will be at Flat Lick on to-morrow night, *the whole of his*

[67] Smith to Bragg, October 15, 1862, *ibid.*, Pt. II, 949.
[68] *Id.* to Polk, October 17, 1862, *ibid.*, 959.
[69] Quoted in Dubose, *Wheeler and the Army of Tennessee*, 104.

trains being in advance of his column." [70] Wheeler had staved off the pursuing army and had made possible the junction of the two Confederate armies without their losing a single wagon or piece of artillery to the enemy. Congratulations were in order. Assistant Adjutant General George W. Brent of Bragg's staff was instructed to write a letter of commendation to the young Colonel to say that his conduct of operations was "particularly gratifying, and supports the reputation you have already won for high soldierly qualities." Then General Brent apparently could not restrain his own feelings. In a post-script he added: "I congratulate you, my dear fellow, upon the success with which you have conducted operations in our rear." [71] To this General Kirby Smith added his thanks and "appreciation of the thorough manner in which you have performed your important duties during this retreat." He added that he would take "especial pleasure in bringing your services to the notice of the Department at Richmond." [72]

But aside from being an outstanding personal accomplishment for Wheeler, the cavalry operations in the retreat from Kentucky furnish an excellent example of a new development in cavalry tactics. This new development was the use of mounted infantry.[73] When the Civil

[70] Polk to Bragg, October 19, 1862, in *Official Records*, Ser. I, Vol. XVI, Pt. II, 963. Author's italics.

[71] George W. Brent to Wheeler, October 19, 1862, *ibid.*, 965.

[72] John Pegram to *id.*, October 20, 1862, *ibid.*, 971.

[73] It is interesting to note how foreign writers on cavalry tactics came to take notice of the new development. The English cavalry tactician, Captain L. E. Nolan, in his *Cavalry: Its History and Tactics* (London, 1860), entirely omits any reference to mounted infantry. Three years later J. Roomer, an officer in the service of The Netherlands in his *Cavalry: Its History, Management, and Uses in War* (New York, 1863), puts emphasis only on the heavy cavalry which "by its terrible shock

War began, the American cavalry, with the exception of the experimental Regiment of Mounted Rifles, was organized along traditional European lines, that is to say, consisting of heavy cavalry or dragoons armed with sabers and pistols and trained to charge in heavy mass formations. But before the war had progressed very far the new type developed, a type exceedingly mobile. It could charge with saber, carbine, and pistol, and, in addition, was so equipped that it could fight dismounted as readily as in the saddle; and when dismounted it was but little, if any, inferior to the infantry. In fact, it was more mounted infantry than cavalry proper that Wheeler used to such excellent advantage and came to recommend later in his book on cavalry tactics. It could not be said, of course, that Wheeler originated this new style of fighting. It had been used, as has been pointed out, to a slight extent in the United States Army, but Wheeler apparently was the first Confederate officer to use it effectively in such a large scale campaign as that of Bragg's invasion of Kentucky. Undoubtedly the physical environment of the South had much to do with its development. Over wooded and broken areas large bodies of heavy cavalry were almost useless. A few men armed with rifles could successfully retard the progress of a much larger group of infantry or dragoons, a fact which Wheeler had so successfully demonstrated.

Now that General Bragg was safely out of Buell's reach he issued another proclamation and went to Richmond

is designed to complete what infantry and artillery have begun." By 1877 writers on cavalry tactics had begun to recognize the contribution made by the Southern cavalryman. For example, in 1877 Lieutenant Colonel George T. Denison, in his *History of Cavalry from the Earliest Times with Lessons for the Future* (London, 1877), devotes considerable space to the use of mounted infantry.

to explain everything to President Davis,[74] and his explanation seemed satisfactory. The President gave him a handshake of confidence and sent him back to the army. Shortly afterward Wheeler received his brigadier general's commission. It was now Brigadier General Joseph Wheeler, Chief of Cavalry—age, twenty-six years.[75]

[74] Bragg to Samuel Cooper, October 3, 1862, in *Official Records,* Ser. I, Vol. XVI, Pt. II, 976.

[75] Dubose, *Wheeler and the Army of Tennessee,* 110, states: "The general returned with the commission" after some discussion with President Davis, who was reluctant to grant it because of Wheeler's youth. The commission was dated October 30, 1862. LaBree (ed.), *Confederate Soldier in the Civil War,* 346.

Chapter IV

THE RAIDER
(November, 1862–July, 1863)

WHILE Bragg was away on his visit to the President, the Confederate army rested at Knoxville from the strain of its retreat from Kentucky. Upon Bragg's return about November 1 he ordered it to break camp and move into Middle Tennessee. Breckinridge went from Chattanooga to Murfreesboro in the last days of October. Forrest was already at this town trying to arm his brigade of newly recruited cavalry. Morgan had returned from the Kentucky campaign. Wheeler was sent over the mountains from Knoxville to escort the wagon trains of his army.[1]

At Nashville Buell was removed from command because of his failure in the Kentucky campaign and was replaced by Rosecrans.[2] However, the new commander

[1] Breckinridge had come from Earl Van Dorn's army in Mississippi to join the Kentucky expedition, but had arrived too late. Wheeler's corps consisted of four brigades, one commanded by him personally and the other three by Brigadier Generals Pegram, Wharton, and Abraham Buford. In addition, Wheeler as chief of cavalry had under his command the two brigades of Brigadier General John H. Morgan and the one brigade of Brigadier General Forrest. See *Battles and Leaders*, III, 612. The entire Confederate army composed of Polk's and Hardee's corps of infantry and Wheeler's cavalry included: twenty brigades of infantry, seven brigades of cavalry, and twenty-nine batteries of artillery—total present for duty after detachment of Carter L. Stevenson's brigade sent to Vicksburg, 38,000. See Fiebeger, *Campaigns of the American Civil War*, 137.

[2] A new department was created for William S. Rosecrans, the Department of the Cumberland, embracing all of Tennessee east of the

adhered largely to Buell's plan: to hold and repair the railroad from Louisville to Nashville and to collect enough supplies to make his army independent of service over this road. Having thus made himself secure from the threat of Confederate attacks on his line of communication he proposed to march on Chattanooga. Between him and his goal lay Bragg's army around Murfreesboro waiting to engage in battle. Apparently it did not occur to General Bragg that he had sufficient cavalry, ably led, to keep the railroad to Louisville cut and thus to delay and discourage almost indefinitely the Federal advance. Instead he permitted the enemy to get its supplies collected around Nashville and actually to take up the march toward Chattanooga before he sent his cavalry to destroy these supplies. Then he weakened his cavalry force by sending Forrest to West Tennessee in mid-December, 1862, to operate on Grant's line of communication from Columbus, Kentucky, to Vicksburg— an expedition which, in spite of the almost incredibly magnificent manner in which it was carried out, did little more than cause Grant to shift his base from Columbus to Memphis. This detachment of Forrest left Bragg six brigades of cavalry, four in Wheeler's own corps and two under John H. Morgan. Bragg then employed almost all of Wheeler's men in watching for the approach of Rosecrans, leaving only Morgan to carry on against the Federal line to Nashville. It seems that if General

Tennessee River, and portions of Alabama and Georgia. The strength of the Federal army during the campaign was: Major General Alexander McD. McCook, nine brigades and nine batteries of artillery; Major General George H. Thomas, ten brigades and nine batteries of artillery; Major General Thomas L. Crittenden, nine brigades and nine batteries of artillery; Brigadier General David S. Stanley, three brigades of cavalry and one battery of artillery—total present for duty, 45,000. *Ibid.*, 136.

Bragg had been trying deliberately to nullify the useful-
ness of his cavalry in the Tennessee campaign he could
not have done a better job.[3]

The Confederates moved leisurely into Middle Tennessee during late October and November, 1862. General Bragg was in high spirits when he joined them in
November to establish his headquarters at Tullahoma
and later at Murfreesboro. He even sat with his staff
around the campfire and told them amusing incidents
about the Mexican War.[4] But his optimism seems to have
been shared by very few. Southern newspapers were condemning him with violent editorials. Most of his officers
had quarreled with him, and even the subordinate officers and private soldiers were beginning to doubt his
ability. One of his company surgeons, H. McGaughey,
wrote to Miss Rebecca Harris in Russellville, Alabama:
"I shouldn't wonder if we fall back to the M. & C.
[Memphis and Charleston] R.R. or the Tennessee River
soon. Our army is famous for running you know." [5] This
surgeon had "run" with Bragg from Kentucky.

On November 24 the commands of John C. Pemberton at Vicksburg and Bragg in Tennessee were placed
under Joseph E. Johnston, with headquarters at Chattanooga. Immediately General Johnston set out on an
inspection tour of Bragg's army at Murfreesboro. This

---

[3] There is a very great need for a comprehensive study of Confederate
cavalry operations both in the East and the West. Numerous writers,
notably Lytle, Hay, Dubose, and the English critics B. H. Liddell Hart
and Alfred H. Byrne have commented briefly upon the relative ineffec-
tiveness of Confederate cavalry when it should have been the most effective arm of the service. However, no exhaustive study of it has been
accomplished.

[4] Urquhart, "Bragg's Advance and Retreat," in *Battles and Leaders*,
III, 604–605 n.

[5] H. McGaughey to Miss Rebecca Harris, November 13, 1862, in author's possession.

visit was followed the second week in December by one from the President himself. Could not Bragg spare a few thousand men to relieve Pemberton who was being sorely pressed at Vicksburg? Bragg thought so. The President then sent eight thousand of Bragg's army under General Stevenson to reinforce General Pemberton, thus cutting a strip from the bottom of the blanket and sewing it on the other end to make the whole fabric longer. It was done over the advice of Johnston.[6] And Rosecrans was almost ready to start for Chattanooga!

In the meantime, while the President and the generals were discussing, inspecting, and planning, the army was enjoying Middle Tennessee. It was the height of the social season and the presence of so many officers and men made many a Tennessee belle pause longer in front of her mirror. There were parties and dances and flirting and serious courtship. Lee, so the soldiers heard, had "whipped McClellan badly again on the Potomac" and "the news came down to-day that England and France had recognized our Confederacy." Rosecrans was not showing much inclination to come out of Nashville and fight. Maybe the war was about over after all. Even if it was not, Christmas was in the air. Surgeon McGaughey again addressed Miss Harris. "We are 22 miles from Nashville," he wrote. "Have been serenading several times since I got here. Made the acquaintance of some nice young ladies. First time I went I got some excellent home-made wine and heard some sweet piano music accompanied by vocal from a pair of sweet lips." "I was field officer of the day," he continued, "and we had some

6 Joseph E. Johnston, "Jefferson Davis and the Mississippi Campaign," in Battles and Leaders, III, 473. See also, id., Narrative of Military Operations, Directed, During the Late War Between the States, by Joseph E. Johnston (New York, 1874), 150.

pickets posted near her gate. Told her I would be by to visit my pickets the next day. She gave me a very cordial invitation to dine. I accepted. After dinner [evidently 12 o'clock] which was luxurious, accompanied the young lady to our drill ground to witness a brigade drill. . . . Another time we had good supper, good music and good looking young ladies." [7]

The outstanding event of the social season was the marriage of General Morgan on December 14, 1862. While on duty at Murfreesboro he, like Surgeon Mc-Gaughey, had had some affairs of the heart and one of them had proved serious. In the midst of preparations for the forthcoming battle the wedding took place. "General John H. Morgan a few evenings ago to Miss Mattie Ready of Murfreesboro. His attendants were Lieutenant General Hardee and Major-General Cheatham. Was married by Lieutenant General Polk (Bishop of the Diocese of Louisiana) and the bride was given in marriage by President Davis. Was that not grand?" [8] Shortly after the wedding Morgan and his command left on a raid toward Kentucky.

In the midst of these social activities Wheeler was fifteen miles in front of the encamped army. His task was twofold. First, he had to reorganize, or rather organize, his command. While doing so he had to be on the lookout for Rosecrans's advance.[9]

The cavalry under Wheeler, as well as most of the other cavalry units of Bragg's army, was possibly the most nondescript of all the fighting forces of the Con-

[7] McGaughey to Harris, November 13, 1862, in author's possession.

[8] Id. to id., December 27, 1862, ibid. See also, Urquhart, "Bragg's Advance and Retreat," in Battles and Leaders, III, 605; Basil W. Duke, Morgan's Cavalry (New York, 1906), passim.

[9] General Wheeler arrived at Murfreesboro on November 13, 1862. See Official Records, Ser. I, Vol. XX, Pt. II, 402.

federacy. At the outbreak of the war they had quit their farms and, mounting whatever animal they might have handy, had ridden to join the army. Part of them were formally mustered into service but some never were. Some of them had been issued horses, saddles, pistols, and sabers. Many equipped themselves at the expense of dead "Yankees" on the field. Gaunt, bearded fellows, unaccustomed to discipline, they roved and raided friend and foe alike. If there was whisky they got drunk. If there was food to be had for themselves or their horses, they took it with little regard for the source.[10]

Then there were the partisan rangers, semimilitary groups, officered by men of their own choice and responsible to no central authority. Probably they were the worst offenders in the matter of depredations. So serious did their marauding become that they were considered a nuisance, almost a terror, in Middle Tennessee. The commanding general took steps to curb the plundering by authorizing General Breckinridge to look into the matter and by providing that "parties acting without his authority will be at once arrested." [11] In addition, all distilleries were to be seized and turned over to the staff authorities.[12] These troops had to be curbed and turned into a semblance of a fighting unit. General Wheeler was assigned this task.

Wheeler received his orders to take full command of all the cavalry on November 14, 1862. Forrest, who had been in temporary command pending Wheeler's arrival, was sent on a raid into West Tennessee, leaving Wheeler

10 See photographs and descriptions in Francis T. Miller (ed.), *The Photographic History of the Civil War* (New York, 1911), IV, 145. The entire volume is devoted to the cavalry of both armies.

11 Special Orders, No. 21, November 16, 1862, in *Official Records*, Ser. I, Vol. XX, Pt. II, 405.

12 General Orders, No. 146, November 15, 1862, *ibid.*, 404.

with the services of Wharton's and John H. Morgan's brigades and two regiments of infantry doing cavalry duty. Recruits were being added to these regularly organized units of Bragg's cavalry and, in addition, the numerous "partisan ranger" groups were being mustered in as rapidly as arms could be found for them. It was an administrative problem of considerable complexity to make an efficient fighting force out of this heterogeneous array of raw material mixed with the seasoned troops.[13]

Many interesting and amusing stories are related by Wheeler's old troopers about this period of reorganization and discipline. Wheeler's forces, it is related, had been joined by a motley group of about sixty mounted men from Arkansas who styled themselves the "Dixie Rangers." They were armed with all manner of firearms from the old-time flintlock musket to shotguns and squirrel rifles. They were entirely without military training, but they "joined up" and went along with Wheeler. During the fighting between Nashville and Murfreesboro when the cavalry was constantly engaging Rosecrans's pickets, there was a skirmish reported and the Dixie Rangers were in the midst of it. A forced retreat became suddenly necessary, and the captain found his men jammed against a fence which blocked further retreat. Not knowing just what command to give and with bullets zipping uncomfortably close he is reported to have roared at his men, "Hyar, ye infernal galoots. Unbuckle a part of that fence and go through one by one or the Yankees will blow daylights through every one of ye. After ye're through, line up three by three and make like lightnin' for that piece of woods over yonder whar ye will stop fur further orders." General Wheeler had observed this very unmilitary maneuver and after the skirmish laughingly called in the captain for a conference which resulted in the Rangers being constituted an awkward squad and given some rudiments of drill tactics and field movements.[14]

Another instance is related. After a day of skirmishing with Rosecrans's outposts Wheeler had bivouacked his men, but had issued orders for no fires to be built lest they reveal their position. On a final round of inspection before retiring for the night Wheeler sighted a fire down the picket line. On closer inspection, the story goes, he found a Tennessee mountaineer minutely inspecting the dismantled parts of his rifle.

"Put that gun together at once," the General is reported to have commanded, "and tell me why you have committed this breach of military discipline."

"Well, it's this way, ginral," replied the mountaineer, "this here confounded shootin' iron of mine had been doin' some pore shootin' lately and I thought I'd take 'er apart and fix 'er. In that fight we had today I shot three Yankees an' when they fell back I went up and examined them and all three had been shot in the body. Now, Ginrul Wheeler, that wuz mighty pore shootin' fur the likes uv me. So, sez I, that ole rifle has nachuly started to shoot crooked, so I tuk her apart so I could hit 'em in the head." [15]

Wheeler was engaging the enemy's pickets daily. Even before Rosecrans's general advance had begun, the outposts of both armies had been involved in sharp conflicts. During the months of November and December

14 Related in Florence (Alabama) *Gazette*, August 26, 1880.
15 *Ibid.*

Wheeler and his ever-faithful brigadier, John A. Wharton, were in no less than twenty separate fights. In fact, during this period Bragg found it necessary to reprimand Wheeler for "reckless exposure."[16] The mild reprimand came after a shell had exploded under his horse, tearing the animal to pieces and slightly wounding the rider. Soon, however, there was more serious work than picketing to do. Learning that the Federals were collecting supplies at Hartsville, Tennessee, on the Cumberland River, General John H. Morgan asked from Wheeler permission to destroy these stores. Receiving approval, he set out on December 6 with four regiments of his cavalry, striking the Federals at Hartsville the next day, destroying large quantities of stores and capturing some eighteen hundred prisoners. To cover the raid, Wheeler with two brigades of Cheatham's infantry made a demonstration toward Nashville, encountered the enemy's outposts, and kicked up enough dust to distract attention from Morgan while he did his work.[17]

Then it was back to picket duty for Wheeler, to the weary routine of skirmishing and watching for more than two weeks for the inevitable enemy movement. As one author has expressed it, the cavalry "placed Rosecrans under a kind of distant siege by pestering him with raiding parties. When the Union general came out to brush away the flies there would be a fight."[18] On December 21 Bragg grew apprehensive and called on Wheeler to "press forward in order to ascertain the true condition of things." He pushed forward within sight of the

---

[16] Bragg to Wheeler, November 27, 1862, in *Official Records*, Ser. I, Vol. XX, Pt. I, 19.

[17] Urquhart, "Bragg's Advance and Retreat," in *Battles and Leaders*, III, 605.

[18] Fletcher Pratt, *Ordeal by Fire* (New York, 1935), 153.

capitol at Nashville and then rode back to inform his chief that the movement had begun. What Wheeler saw was the stir and commotion which always accompanies an army when it moves out and gets under way. The actual advance began the day after Christmas.

On the same day, December 26, 1862, General Bragg called a conference of his corps leaders, Polk, Hardee, and Wheeler.

"How long can you hold them on the road?" it is reported that Bragg asked Wheeler.

"About four days, general," Wheeler quickly replied.[19]

Then Bragg concentrated his army in line of battle in front of Stone's River just outside of Murfreesboro near the point where the river, the Nashville turnpike, and the Nashville and Chattanooga Railway converge. Breckinridge took position on the Confederate extreme right, Polk's corps formed the center, and Hardee took position on the extreme left. Bragg's plan was Shiloh reversed. Hardee would strike the Federal right and fold it back toward the river, Polk would drive in the Federal center, and Breckinridge would apply the pincers on the Federal left.[20]

Wheeler was, of course, well acquainted with these plans as he and Wharton rode out to make contact with the advancing Federal columns. On the twenty-seventh there was brisk skirmishing as Wheeler employed his favorite tactics of engaging the enemy cavalry until infantry reserves were brought up and then falling back to make another stand. This was repeated the next day, and on the night of the twenty-ninth he and his weary troopers joined Hardee on the Confederate left at Stone's River. It was not particularly brilliant fighting, but was

[19] Quoted in Dubose, *Wheeler and the Army of Tennessee,* 120.
[20] Shotwell, *Civil War in America,* I, 299.

determined and vigorous enough for Wheeler to keep his promise that he would delay the enemy four days. Rosecrans's "march was so delayed by the energetic resistance which the Confederate cavalry under Wheeler and Wharton offered from the moment of its commencement that he did not arrive in the vicinity of Murfreesboro until the afternoon of the 30th." [21] This was the testimony of a fellow officer who could not, by the wildest stretch of the imagination, be counted as an ardent admirer of the Chief of Cavalry.

Wheeler's cavalry badly needed sleep and rest after these three days of fighting, but such was not forthcoming. About midnight of December 29 he was ordered to destroy the enemy's supply trains running between the battlefield and Nashville. By daylight on the thirtieth he reached Jefferson, well behind the enemy lines. Here was encountered Colonel John C. Starkweather's brigade of Lovell H. Rousseau's division on guard duty. The head of his brigade train of sixty-four wagons had just arrived in camp and was driving into the campgrounds when Wheeler and his cavalry charged. The Federals resisted and Wheeler had to content himself with the destruction of twenty wagons. Leaving Jefferson and bearing to his left Wheeler struck the entire wagon train of General McCook at La Vergne and completely destroyed it. Seven hundred prisoners were taken and nearly a million dollars' damage was done, according to a member of General Crittenden's staff. Around La Vergne "the turnpike, as far as the eye could reach, was filled with burning wagons. The country was overspread with disarmed men, broken-down horses and mules. The streets were covered with empty valises and trunks, knapsacks, broken guns, and all the indescribable débris of a captured and rifled

[21] *Reminiscences of General Basil W. Duke, C.S.A.,* 334–35.

army train." [22] Leaving the scene and still bearing to his left, Wheeler rode on and struck Rock Creek, destroying a few supplies, and then on to Nolensville where the La Vergne destruction was repeated. Passing on beyond Nolensville he allowed his men to sleep a few hours, and then rousing them "at 2 o'clock on the morning of the 31st Wheeler came up bright and smiling on the left flank of the Confederate army in front of Murfreesboro', having made the entire circuit of Rosecrans's army in forty-eight hours, leaving miles of road strewn with burning wagons and army supplies, remounting a portion of his cavalry, and bringing back to camp a sufficient number of minie-rifles and accouterments to arm a brigade." [23] And, this Yankee staff officer might have added, the Confederates lost not a man killed.

The havoc wrought by this raid of Wheeler's is well described in a letter written by Captain George K. Miller of the Eighth Confederate cavalry immediately after the raid. "We were aroused from our slumbers at midnight," he wrote, "saddled up, mounted, and in a few minutes were following General Wheeler at full gallop up the Lebanon road. It was raining and so dark that one could not see the trooper by his side. When we struck the ford at Stone's River, we only knew we were riding in water by the splashing noise of our horses' feet. Proceeding out of camp about five miles and crossing to the north side of this river, we continued about two miles, then left the Lebanon Pike and took the one leading to the little village of Jefferson, directly in the rear of the Yankee army. Daylight found us near that village, when we halted and

[22] Gilbert C. Kniffin, "The Battle of Stone's River," in *Battles and Leaders,* III, 614. Colonel Kniffin was on General Crittenden's staff. [23] *Ibid.*

fed our horses. Soon in the saddle again, leaving the main road, we took by-paths, and about noon came up close to the village of La Vergne. Into this we dashed—four or five regiments of us—at full speed, firing a few shots as we rode. At once we found in our possession a large train, over 300 heavily loaded wagons with quartermaster's and commissary's stores, and some 300 prisoners captured. The officers went quickly to work paroling the prisoners while the men burned the wagons. It was a sight to make all rebeldom glad. Mules, stampeding with burning wagons hung to their traces, Yankees running, all appliances for our subjugation!" [24]

After the destruction at La Vergne they passed on. "Applying the spurs for two hours," Captain Miller continued, "we dropped like a tornado upon quiet little Nolensville. Here it was La Vergne repeated. We found squads of Yankees here and there and some 150 wagons, mostly loaded with ammunition and medicines, together with several fine ambulances. These latter we preserved; the others we set the flames upon. The Yankees we sent on their way rejoicing, as paroled prisoners of war, back to their New England households.

"We tarried but a short time at N——, then pushed down a rich little valley where we found large numbers of their wagons filled with corn, bedclothing, poultry, house-furniture, eggs, butter, etc., etc., of which they had just plundered farms. We relieved them of their plunder, put the prisoners, bareback, on mules, burned their wagons and rode on."

Summing up the results of the raid, the Captain was rather modest in his appraisals. "Four hundred and fifty to five hundred wagons, 600 prisoners, hundreds of mules

[24] Quoted in Dubose, *Wheeler and the Army of Tennessee*, 141.

and horses captured, sums up our achievements of the day." And he added rather whimsically, "We also had an immense deal of fun." [25]

When Wheeler rejoined his own left flank on the morning of December 31, he found it engaged with the enemy. While he had been away General Rosecrans had formed his line of battle and had made his plans. McCook, whose wagon trains had just been destroyed, had three divisions on the Federal right opposite Hardee; Thomas with five divisions held the center opposite Polk; Crittenden with three divisions was on the Federal left across Stone's River opposite Breckinridge. Curiously enough the Federal and Confederate plans were almost exactly the same —strike from the left, hold in the center, then push the left back on the right and crush it. As one officer expressed it: "If both could have been carried out simultaneously the spectacle would have been presented of two large armies turning upon an axis from left to right." [26]

At dawn, just as Wheeler arrived from Nolensville, General Hardee with Cleburne's and John P. McCown's divisions attacked McCook's corps on the extreme Federal right, the recently arrived cavalry covering Hardee's flank. When the Federals resisted stoutly, Polk advanced with Withers's and Cheatham's divisions; and McCook was driven back steadily so that by nightfall the attack had pivoted the Federals on their center, bending back their left for a distance of between three and four miles. It was, it appeared, a Confederate victory—so much so that General Bragg could wire the President the next day: "God has granted us a happy New Year." [27]

[25] *Ibid.,* 143.

[26] Kniffin, "The Battle of Stone's River," in *Battles and Leaders,* III, 618.

[27] Urquhart, "Bragg's Advance and Retreat," *ibid.,* 607.

New Year's Day, 1863, was bitterly cold and the lines on Stone's River were singularly quiet, so quiet that General Bragg was sure the silence meant a Federal retreat. He sent Wheeler to strike at what he thought were enemy lines in retreat, but what he saw were hospital trains carrying the wounded back to Nashville. These Wheeler left unmolested, but while he was out in the enemy's rear he decided to strike again at their supply depots. At La Vergne new stores and wagons had been collected, and these he struck, causing momentary confusion; he then retired to his own lines bearing the information that the Federals were not retreating but were digging in and bringing up fresh supplies of food and ammunition.[28] Rosecrans had decided to fortify his positions and let Bragg use up his army in futile assaults—and his strategy worked. About noon of January 2 Bragg issued orders for Breckinridge to attack on the Federal left, to capture the high bluff on the north side of the river occupied by Van Cleve of Crittenden's corps. At four o'clock in the afternoon Breckinridge assaulted the position all too well. His men rushed up the eminence and instead of halting as they had orders to do they rushed on beyond into a nest of Federal artillery where they were slaughtered like trapped animals.[29] More than two thousand Confederates were killed and wounded in this charge which deserves to rank with Pickett's at Gettysburg.

Stone's River was Shiloh all over again, and Perryville. Victory had been within the Confederate grasp only to be lost again. With the gloom of Breckinridge's losses hanging over it like a pall, the Army of Tennessee

[28] Wheeler's Report, January 26, 1863, in *Official Records*, Ser. I, Vol. XX, Pt. I, 959.

[29] Urquhart, "Bragg's Advance and Retreat," in *Battles and Leaders*, III, 607.

marched out of Murfreesboro on January 3 and the day
following General Rosecrans entered.

Wheeler's cavalry again covered a retreat, as it had
from Shiloh and from Perryville. General Polk brought
up the rear and to him Wheeler reported very briefly:

I left Murfreesborough last night [January 4], about 9 o'clock
p.m., having engaged the enemy between Murfreesborough
and the river for about an hour before sunset. I left a picket
in front of the town. We formed our first line this a.m. [January 5] 4 miles from Murfreesborough. The cavalry we kept
back with greatest ease, but finally they brought up several
regiments of infantry in line of battle, colors flying, with
cavalry on the flanks and artillery placed in a favorable position. The last attack was 5 miles from Murfreesborough.[30]

Rosecrans showed no inclination to pursue. He contented himself with additional preparations for the march
to Chattanooga and General Bragg remained unmolested
at Tullahoma almost six months. He stationed Polk at
Shelbyville with Duck River at his back and Hardee at
Wartrace on the main line of the Nashville and Chattanooga Railroad. The cavalry was strung along the front
—Forrest and Van Dorn at Columbia on Polk's left,
Wheeler in Hardee's front and right, and Morgan at
McMinnville farther on Hardee's right. In this position
the infantry and artillery rested while the cavalry from
Forrest on the left to Morgan on the right did the fighting. "Raid and counter-raid, thrust and feint" was the
daily order for the mounted branch of Bragg's army.[31]

But, while Bragg and Rosecrans were inactive so far as

30 Wheeler to Polk, January 5, 1863, in *Official Records*, Ser. I, Vol.
XX, Pt. I, 957–58.

31 Robert S. Henry, *The Story of the Confederacy* (New York, 1931),
287.

campaigning was concerned, the rear of the Federal army
and the base at Nashville presented scenes of great activity. The battle at Stone's River had left Rosecrans's army
badly crippled and the activities of the Confederate cavalry had inconvenienced him by disrupting train service between Nashville and Louisville. Crews were set to
work under heavy guard to repair the railroad, and by the
middle of March supplies were again flowing into Nashville and from there to Murfreesboro. As a secondary
line of supply Rosecrans took Forts Henry and Donelson
into his department, thus making the Tennessee and
Cumberland rivers accessible to him in case they were
needed.[32] It was this secondary line which attracted
Wheeler's attention and against which he made two
raids during January and February, 1863.

Wheeler's first raid of the new year took place on January 7, less than a week after the retirement from Murfreesboro. The point of attack was Ashland, a small landing on the Cumberland some twenty-five miles below
Nashville. Here steamboats were bringing supplies from
Paducah and Louisville to be hauled overland to Nashville. Five days were spent in burning bridges and dodg-
ing Federals until January 12 when the famous attack of
the "horse marines" took place.[33]

In preparation for the attack Wheeler divided his
forces. One part, consisting of the Eighth Confederate
and the First Alabama, he gave to Colonel William B.
Wade with orders to ride up the south bank of the Cumberland and attack any transports in sight. The other
part Wheeler personally commanded. It crossed the river
to the vicinity of Clarksville, Tennessee.

Late in the afternoon of the twelfth Wheeler and his

[32] Shotwell, *Civil War in America*, I, 313.
[33] Dubose, *Wheeler and the Army of Tennessee*, 151.

men were watching the Cumberland near the latter town. Suddenly the steamer *Charter* with a boat in tow hove into sight round a bend in the river. The raiders on the shore opened a vigorous fire. The boats came to shore and surrendered to their certain fate of burning. The raiders slept near the scene of their activities that night, and when morning came there was nothing visible to remind them of war except the blackened hulks of the boats half sunk in the shallow water near the shore. Suddenly two armed vessels swung round the same bend, their guns raking the shore. They had heard of the fate of the *Charter* and were seeking the cavalry that had no more sense than to think itself a detachment of marines. The gunboats' fire was returned, but it soon became evident that it was a hopeless task to take them. Wheeler withdrew.[34]

In the meantime, Wade and his detachment had been playing havoc farther up the river. This fighting Irishman placed his men behind breastworks of steamboat wood which he found near the Ashland landing and waited for the enemy to appear. Presently a transport without escort appeared and was captured. Next morning the transport *Trio* suffered a like fate. Hardly had she been received when the *Parthenia* and the *Hastings,* the latter a hospital boat loaded with wounded from Murfreesboro, came along. Both were captured, the hospital boat being sent across the river for safety, while the *Parthenia* and *Trio* were burned. Scarcely had this job been completed when the gunboat *Slidell* appeared, shelling the banks as she came. She too was captured, making five in a row—a gunboat and four transports.

Some idea of the consternation which Wheeler's men had wrought may be gleaned from Federal reports of the

34 *Ibid.,* 152.

WHEELER'S MIDDLE
TENNESSEE RAIDS

---o---o--- The Ride Around Rosecrans, Dec. 29 - 31, 1862
---x---x--- The Horse Marine Expedition and the
　　　　　　 Attack on Ft. Donelson, Jan. 7 - Feb. 3, 1863
---+---+--- The Sequatchie Valley Raid, Sept. 30 - Oct. 9, 1863
--↑---↑-- The Disastrous Raid of Aug. 10 - Sept. 2, 1864
--|---|-- Forrest to the Attack on Ft. Donelson

Scale of Miles
0　10　20　30　40　50

operations. General Robert B. Mitchell reporting to Rosecrans grew petulant: "The steamer Charter was burned last night about 8 o'clock with her cargo. But two regiments have arrived from Gallatin yet. . . . Damn the railroad, say I!" [35] The testy general, however, should have "damned" Bragg's cavalry instead of the railroads. The locomotives were entirely ready to pull troop trains if the tracks would stay intact for a few hours.

On the same day General Mitchell sent another report —in fact, he sent four that day. "The rebels are burning everything on the river." "One of the gunners of the gunboat Slidell has arrived, and confirms the report of the burning of the boat. He says the pilot left the wheel. . . . [Confederate Minié balls were drilling holes in the windows of the pilot house.] He furthermore says that they knocked out the side of the boat next the enemy with their own guns, endeavoring to elevate their pieces to reach the enemy on the high bank. Van Dorn is a prisoner," he added. "The balance were paroled by Wheeler." [36]

Colonel Wade and his men seem to have been ruthless in their attacks on the steamers. Chaplain Maxwell P. Gaddis of the Second Ohio infantry was on the *Hastings* and his report of the affair places the Confederates in a rather sorry light. "As soon as the boat struck the steamer that had been captured," he wrote, ". . . a gang of drunken rebels, under command of Colonel Wade, took possession of the Hastings." "Then," he continued, "followed a scene of plunder and theft never before witnessed. They robbed soldiers and passengers indiscrim-

---

[35] Robert B. Mitchell to Rosecrans, January 13, 1863, in *Official Records*, Ser. I, Vol. XX, Pt. I, 982.

[36] *Ibid.*, 983.

inately; took from . . . wounded soldiers their blankets, rations, medicines and in many instances their clothing; robbed the officers of their side-arms, overcoats, hats, &c."

The Chaplain reported further that he demanded of Colonel Wade "some explanation of this inhuman course" but that the Colonel was so drunk he made an "idiotic reply." Then an appeal was made to Captain E. S. Burford, Wheeler's assistant adjutant general, who reported the facts to his superior.[37] The *Hastings* was paroled on condition that she not engage in further transportation of supplies of war, and that her partial cargo of cotton be burned when the boat should reach Louisville.

The affair attracted quite a bit of attention in official circles. Rosecrans reported it to Washington stating that he could "multiply documentary evidence on these outrages and many others." [38] General Bragg, on the other hand, reported it as reflecting "distinguished merit" on his chief of cavalry and asked his promotion as a "just reward." [39]

In accordance with Bragg's recommendation, Wheeler was promoted to the rank of major general,[40] and the Confederate Congress passed this resolution, approved May 1, 1863, "That the thanks of Congress are due, and are hereby tendered to Brigadier-General Wheeler and the officers and men of his command, for his daring and successful attacks upon the enemy's gunboats and transports in the Cumberland River." [41]

While Wheeler was engaged in his marine expedition

---

37 Maxwell P. Gaddis to Rosecrans, February 4, 1863, *ibid.*, 980.

38 Rosecrans to Adjutant General Thomas, February 15, 1863, *ibid.*

39 Bragg to Adjutant General Cooper, January 17, 1863, *ibid.*, 983.

40 Commission dated January 22, 1863.

41 *Journal of the Congress of the Confederate States of America,* in *Senate Documents,* No. 234, 58 Cong., 2 Sess., III, 419.

General Forrest was at Columbia, Tennessee, reorganizing, re-equipping, and resting his men and horses after his West Tennessee raid, a task which consumed about three weeks.[42] While he was thus engaged, Wheeler and Bragg were laying plans for another and more ambitious raid which they believed might permanently interrupt Federal traffic on the Cumberland River. The plans called for a combined attack of the commands of both cavalrymen which would sweep all transports from the river and thus render the Federal land positions less tenable.

On January 26 Wheeler ordered Forrest to proceed from Columbia to the vicinity of Fort Donelson with about eight hundred men and there to begin the proposed raid on whatever boats might be caught out.[43] At the same time Wheeler left Bragg's headquarters at Tullahoma expecting to join Forrest. This he did, but upon arrival he found that Forrest's movements had been detected by the Federals and as a result there was no river traffic to obstruct. Both commands had ridden more than a hundred miles over winter roads only to find that their prey had taken flight. Wheeler, as the commanding officer, now had to decide the next move, and the decision was not long delayed. Wheeler proposed to Forrest that they should recapture Fort Donelson (Dover) from the Yankees. If Donelson could be recaptured, he explained, it would seriously threaten Rosecrans's line of supplies in that direction; in fact, it would render the Cumberland practically useless to the Federals. And in addition, the attack, if successful, would solve the problem of what to do with their commands if the river boats

[42] Thomas Jordan and J. P. Pryor, *The Campaigns of Lieut. Gen. N. B. Forrest and of Forrest's Cavalry* (New York, 1868), 224.
[43] *Ibid.*, 224–26.

did not show up. The cavalry could not long remain idle without serious depredations on the friendly countryside.

If not brilliant, the plan certainly was feasible, but it came to naught save confusion and tragedy. Wheeler in his report, without mentioning names, wrote that "'after maturely considering the matter, we concluded that nothing could be lost by an attack upon the garrison at Dover." On the other hand, General Forrest after the war in his personally sponsored book, *Campaigns of General Forrest*, states positively there had been a difference of opinion and that he had protested vigorously against the plan; that his protests had been based upon his observation that his command had insufficient ammunition; and that even if they should succeed in taking the position it could not be held for long.[44] Wheeler was of the opinion, however, that by a simultaneous and swift attack from two sides the garrison could be taken with little bloodshed even though it was defended by some eight hundred men well supplied with artillery. Thus Wheeler issued orders for the advance and his command arrived in sight of the fort about noon on February 3, advancing immediately to the attack.

General Wharton was sent with the Eighth Texas to the road leading from Dover toward Fort Henry on the west. He would assail the west and southwest portions of the fortification. Forrest's men were dismounted and deployed on the east side and ordered to advance on foot simultaneously with Wharton's movement. And having thus arranged his men, Wheeler sent in to the fort under a flag of truce a formal demand for surrender.[45] This being

44 *Ibid.*, 225.

45 Wheeler's Report, February ?, 1863, in *Official Records*, Ser. I, Vol. XXIII, Pt. I, 39–40.

refused, the Confederate artillery opened fire upon the advanced batteries of the enemy and these quickly retired within the fort. The initial portion of the attack had succeeded. On the west Forrest and his men calmly awaited Wharton's attack so that they might join in, but as they waited Forrest observed several companies of Federal troops moving toward the river. Mistaking this for the abandonment of the fortification and an effort to escape, Forrest ordered his men to mount and charge the apparently retreating enemy.

The Federals, however, were entertaining no idea of yielding up the fort; the men apparently trying to escape were merely being shifted to an entrenched position outside the walls. Reaching this position before Forrest's charge was well under way, the Federals received him with a vicious musketry and artillery fire. Here and there a horse went down and a man was blown to bits; then Forrest himself went down, his horse shot from under him, and both he and his men retreated to form a new line of assault, this time simultaneously with Wharton's attack. Again Forrest led his mounted men against the fortifications and again received a withering fire. Another horse was shot from under Forrest, and again a number of men were literally shot to pieces. Again there was a movement of men toward the trenches and again Forrest was fooled. Abandoning his position he rode after them, leaving Wharton to keep up the fight from the eastern side, a fight which was going favorably for the Confederates.[46] They had reached a position not more than ninety yards from the main rifle pits when Forrest's strange maneuvers forced them to retire; that is, Forrest's unforeseen charges, plus a shortage of ammunition, plus the fact that Federal reinforcements were arriving.

[46] *Ibid.*, 41.

It had been a tragedy of errors and there was nothing else to do at nightfall except to abandon the attack and retire. This they did, burning a boatload of Federal supplies on the river and collecting enough blankets to keep out the bitter cold which descended upon them.

The next action took place four miles from the scene of the battle. The stage was a cabin, crudely furnished with a bed in each corner, a table near the fire, and three rickety chairs. The actors were Forrest, Wheeler, and Wharton. Around the stage were its properties—tired, half-frozen men wrapped in their blankets, trying to keep out the cold. Wheeler sat at a table on one side of the blazing fire composing his report. Wharton sat on the opposite side of the fireplace, and in between them lying sprawled on the floor with his feet to the fire was Forrest, apparently lost in thought.[47]

Wheeler was youthful and small with mild eyes and courtly demeanor. Forrest was tall, gnarled, and fierce. Each of them was a fighter. One of them was a West Pointer trained in all the finer points of combat. To him war was a mathematical problem. It involved maneuvering of division, each movement fitting perfectly into a whole. It involved dress parade and inspection, general orders, discipline, and a religious regard for orders. In short, war was to Wheeler what it was to every professional soldier. In his scheme of things the individual was but an atom—a necessary atom, but an atom just the same. The individual must fit into the general situation and if this required sacrificing a few men for the good of the whole, it must be done, and there must be no

---

[47] A most dramatic account of the scene may be found in Lytle, *Bedford Forrest*, 142–43. Mr. Lytle has drawn heavily upon John A. Wyeth, *Life of General Nathan Bedford Forrest* (New York, 1901). Dubose in *Wheeler and the Army of Tennessee*, 156–58, gives substantially the same general facts as Lytle and Wyeth.

whimpering. If his orders required him to remain long hours in the saddle and to fight viciously and to destroy ruthlessly, he unquestioningly did so, but he did so because it was all a part of a plan. There was no fierce exultant shout of victory in his throat as his horse's hoofs beat the turnpikes. He was first a soldier, then a fighter.

On the contrary, Forrest was something of a savage. To him war was not mathematical—it was blood and sweat and dead men. He was a killer and to him war meant killing. He cared little for tactics as such, and had little patience with the academic soldier. "Git thar fust with the most men" was reputed to be his slogan. To him there were no niceties in war, the whole bloody business consisting in getting his men to a certain point, doing as much fighting as possible, and then with a fierce note of triumph in his voice, riding his men away to safety. To him orders were merely suggestive; and although he maintained unflinching discipline among his own men, he himself was probably the most undisciplined of all the ranking Confederate officers. He was a fighter first, then a soldier; and withal, perhaps the most brilliant natural strategist of the whole war.

To return to the fireside.

General Wharton began his account of the battle; and as he mentioned Forrest's men and the part they had played in the battle, the reclining general is reported to have arisen to a sitting position, his eyes flashing.

"I have no fault to find with my men. They did their duty," he is reported as having said.

"General Forrest, my report does ample justice to your men," Wheeler is said to have answered.

And then apparently all the recent past seemed to surge up before Forrest's eyes—what he considered as mistreatment by Bragg, his humiliation in being superseded in command by Wheeler, his sorry part in the day's battle.

"General Wheeler," he is quoted as having retorted, "I advised against this attack and said all a subordinate officer should have said against it, and nothing you can now do will bring back my brave men lying dead or wounded [the Confederate loss was approximately a hundred, killed and wounded] and freezing around the fort tonight. You can have my sword if you demand it, but there is one thing I want you to put in that report to General Bragg. Tell him that I will be in my coffin before I will fight again under your command."

"Forrest, I cannot take your sabre," Wheeler is said to have responded, "and I regret exceedingly your determination. As the commanding officer I take all the blame and responsibility for this failure." [48]

And he did assume the responsibility as he rightly should have done. In his report to Bragg he wrote: "The unfortunate circumstance of our having so little ammunition I cannot attribute to any want of energy or care on the part of subordinate commanders. After they received my orders to carry the full complement, every exertion was used by them to supply the deficiency, but without success." [49]

Too, Wheeler refused to let the incident embitter his attitude toward Forrest.[50] Perhaps he understood For-

48 Lytle, *Bedford Forrest*, 143.

49 Wheeler's Report, in *Official Records*, Ser. I, Vol. XXIII, Pt. I, 41.

50 The Forrest-Wheeler controversy, however, reached the newspapers. During December, 1863, the Memphis *Appeal* published a series of articles dealing with various Southern generals. The cavalry came in for its share of the praise and blame. Forrest was pictured as the dramatic and daring fighter that he was. In the issue of December 6, 1863, Wheeler was characterized as overcautious, slow, and, by implication, inefficient. Moreover, he was said to be "Bragg's favorite" and the impression was left that the commanding general had made a great mis-

rest's violent temper and that the Donelson episode was the climax of a series of incidents all apparently directed at him personally. Perhaps, also, Wheeler might have understood that the blast was directed as much against General Bragg as against himself; that it was Forrest's way of protesting against academic soldiering which resulted in indecisive battles and retreats. After Donelson, however, Wheeler and Forrest saw little of each other, and the promise not to fight under Wheeler, Forrest kept. General Bragg, taking advantage of the fact that enlistments in the cavalry were heavy, divided the cavalry commands. Forrest's brigade was joined with those of

---

take in his selection of a chief of cavalry. Immediately other papers took up the controversy. "There is no branch of the service so little understood as that of the cavalry," opined the Augusta (Georgia) *Constitutionalist,* December 19, 1863. "The mounted man in our service must not only fight, picket and scout, but is required to bring reliable intelligence to the commanding general. . . . The information communicated may lead to a great victory—and yet the cavalry officer meets with nothing but blame and abuse from the press and people. . . . Why is it that the Memphis *Appeal* takes every occasion to cast a slur upon the able commander of cavalry in the Army of Tennessee? Is it because he ranks General Forrest? . . . Let no rash hand seek to tear from the brow of this gallant Georgian the wreath which he wears with so much justice and such modesty." Far away from the scene of the controversy the *Southern Literary Messenger* (Richmond), XXXVIII (1864), 232, defended Wheeler. "His entire career as an officer in our army clearly shows that he did not buckle on his sword and go forth to seek merely the bubble reputation at the cannon's mouth, but from an honest desire to give his life and energies to the cause of human liberty, the rights and principles of this country, bought and bequeathed to us by the patriots of '76." This magazine thought Wheeler was no aspirant for political or military honors and that "the laurels which now cluster about his brow" were not placed there because "he had the popular favor" but because the President saw in him a capable and faithful officer who always did his duty.

And the controversy did not die with the men. The author has seen old troopers of both men at Confederate reunions reach the fist-shaking and foot-stamping stage of argument over the relative merits of the two cavalry leaders.

Generals George B. Cosby, Frank C. Armstrong, and J. W. Whitfield and given to Major General Van Dorn, lately come from Mississippi where he had been replaced by Pemberton. The brigades of Generals John A. Wharton, John H. Morgan, and James Hagan constituted a separate division under Wheeler.[51] Forrest joined Van Dorn at Columbia and within two weeks these two officers were quarreling violently.[52]

Bragg was feeling much better about things in general. "I am very happy to say," he wrote, "that all seems to be subsiding into quiet satisfaction, and the only dissatisfaction that ever existed was fomented by a few disappointed generals, who supposed they could cover their own tracks and rise on my downfall." [53] His chronic headache must have been considerably better, for he even took occasion to praise Forrest in a congratulatory order.[54]

In Nashville, Rosecrans, also ill, was trying to find some way of dealing with the rebel cavalry which had been harassing him so much of late. In January he had wired Halleck, "I must have cavalry or mounted infantry. . . . With mounted infantry I can drive the rebel cavalry to the wall. . . . Not so now." In addition, he "must also have some bullet-proof, light-draught transports for the

51 Dubose, *Wheeler and the Army of Tennessee*, 160. On March 14, 1863, Brigadier General William T. Martin who had been in command of a brigade of Stuart's cavalry was transferred to the West and assigned to Wheeler. See *Official Records*, Ser. I, Vol. XXIII, Pt. II, 695. Wheeler sent Martin to Van Dorn.

52 Lytle, *Bedford Forrest*, 146.

53 Bragg to Colonel B. S. Ewell, February 27, 1863, in *Official Records*, Ser. I, Vol. XXIII, Pt. II, 652.

54 General Orders, No. 68, March 31, 1863, *ibid.*, 732. Bragg stated that Van Dorn's fighting and that of Forrest were "worthy of imitation by all commands, and deserve the applause and gratitude of their comrades in arms and their country." Shortly after this General Van Dorn was murdered by a jealous husband at Spring Hill, Tennessee.

Cumberland." [55] Wheeler had played havoc with his wooden ones.

He kept the telegraph wires hot. On February 1 he again wired his superior. "We must bring down all the cavalry available. . . . If you will back me up, I am determined to command the country instead of giving it to the enemy." [56] His requests were almost pathetic in their appeal. The rebel cavalry was making his position extremely precarious. He could do nothing to prevent this because he had not the necessary cavalry and "one rebel cavalryman takes on an average of 3 of our infantry to watch our communications." [57] Failing in his appeals to Halleck he went over his superior's head and took up the matter with Secretary Stanton at Washington. General Halleck had misunderstood his appeals, he said, and instead of sending the necessary equipment had reprimanded him for complaining. "We command the forage of the country only by sending large train guards," he continued. "It is of prime necessity in every point of view to master their cavalry." [58]

Tardy assistance finally arrived, and a cavalry expedition under Colonel Abel D. Streight was sent through Alabama and Georgia to threaten the Confederate lines of communication in that direction. Bragg sent Forrest to follow Streight. Now both generals could breathe a little easier. Rosecrans had his cavalry in action and Bragg was rid of Forrest for a time.

After the division of the cavalry Wheeler set about reorganizing his new command. Bragg, always ready to praise his favorite officer, wrote that he was gratified at

[55] Rosecrans to Halleck, January 14, 1863, *ibid.*, Vol. XX, Pt. II, 326.

[56] *Id.* to *id.*, February 1, 1863, *ibid.*, Vol. XXIII, Pt. II, 31.

[57] *Id.* to Secretary of War Edwin M. Stanton, February 2, 1863, *ibid.*, 33.

[58] *Ibid.*

the efforts his young chief was making in regulating and disciplining his command.[59] In addition to this reorganization Wheeler was making daily raids on the enemy communications between Nashville and Tullahoma, and was writing a book on cavalry tactics during his spare time.

Wheeler's line of pickets extended over a front of seventy miles before the main army encamped at Tullahoma. Wharton was in front of Shelbyville, and Forrest was at Spring Hill after his return from the pursuit and capture of Streight. Van Dorn was dead, and Forrest was serving under the direct orders of the commanding general.

Several minor engagements took place during March and April between Wheeler and the enemy, but they were of small consequence. On one occasion Rosecrans lost two trains to Wheeler, together with several prisoners and $30,000 in greenbacks. The rebel cavalry was a constant threat, however. There is abundant evidence to support the idea that Rosecrans was almost ready to abandon Nashville because he could not cope with this branch of Bragg's army.[60]

Wheeler grew restive during this period of inactivity and proposed an attack on Louisville. He knew that this post had been considerably reduced in numbers and believed that he might transport his men by boat, take the city, and be back in fifteen days.[61] The plan was vetoed by Bragg, however, on the ground that Rosecrans might move any day and that the services of the cavalry could

[59] Bragg to Wheeler, March 11, 1863, *ibid.*, 684.

[60] Wheeler's Report, April 11, 1863, *ibid.*, Pt. I, 218. See also, Rosecrans to Halleck, January 13, 1863; *id.* to Stanton, January 14, 1863; *id.* to Montgomery C. Meigs, January 16, 1863, *ibid.*, Vol. XX, Pt. II, 323, 328, 331.

[61] Wheeler to Bragg, March 7, 1863, *ibid.*, Vol. XXIII, Pt. II, 668.

not be spared from picket duty.[62] Rosecrans, it seems, had planted a vegetable garden and he wished very much to remain long enough to gather his lettuce and radishes—at least that is what the soldiers jokingly said about his inactivity.

Wheeler had seen from the very beginning that there was a vital need for some system of cavalry tactics which would insure uniformity among heterogeneous elements of mounted divisions calling themselves cavalry. Forrest and many other officers had not even known how to conduct an inspection. So the Chief of Cavalry set himself to the task of preparing a manual which, if adopted, might bring this much desired uniformity of tactics. The title was simply *Cavalry Tactics;* and, although parts of it were entirely superfluous, it proved valuable in systematizing Bragg's cavalry.

The Augusta *Constitutionalist* commented on the publication of the manual, and pointed out that "it is almost incredible that, in the midst of the exciting scenes of so active a branch of the service as the cavalry, an officer having the largest command in the Confederate service could find the leisure and have the additional energy necessary to prepare so extensive and elaborate a work." [63] This paper went further and pointed out that the main features included the "Single Rank Formation"; a system of platoon, squadron, battalion, and brigade drill; and "music prepared with the greatest care . . . as that adopted by the best cavalry of Europe." Although the cavalry had little use for music, the manual as a whole was so valuable that General Johnston adopted it for use in the cavalry of the Army of Tennessee. As one reads the manual today, he is inclined to marvel at its

[62] Bragg to Wheeler, March 8, 1863, *ibid.,* 669.
[63] Quoted in Dodson, *Campaigns of Wheeler,* 80.

detail, its scholarly preparation, and its manifest utility. Profiting by his experience in the Kentucky campaign, Wheeler unhesitatingly advocated the use of mounted infantry of the type he had used so successfully. Heavy cavalry, he thought, was too expensive to maintain and well-nigh useless as skirmishers and in reconnoitering. Likewise dragoons, originally intended to act both as horse and foot soldiers, had failed, after a loss of much time and exertion, to perform their true functions. The mounted infantry, however, became "of great value in covering the retreat of an army, or in obstructing the advance of the enemy; and in broken and wooded countries . . . the mounted rifleman becomes indispensable to an army." [64] As far as the records show, this work of Wheeler's was the first one openly to advocate practically the abandonment of heavy cavalry and the substitution of mounted riflemen.

At McMinnville, thirty miles on Bragg's right, there was little action, and General Morgan was not a soldier built to endure such a situation long. If fighting did not come his way he was likely to ride out in search of it; and by the middle of June he was ready to abandon his job of picketing and to go looking for the Yankees. On June 13, 1863, he applied to Wheeler for permission to take his entire force and make a raid on Louisville. Wheeler, after consulting with Bragg, authorized him to take fifteen hundred men and whatever artillery he needed and proceed with the raid.[65] Apparently he failed to receive Wheeler's message, for on the fifteenth came an almost

---

[64] Joseph Wheeler, *A Revised System of Cavalry Tactics for the Use of the Cavalry and Mounted Infantry, C.S.A.* (Mobile, 1863), Appendix, 23.

[65] Wheeler to Morgan, June 14, 1863, in *Official Records*, Ser. I, Vol. XXIII, Pt. I, 817.

boyishly insistent letter from Morgan. With two thousand men he promised he could "accomplish everything."
"Can I go? The result is certain." [66]

Again Wheeler sent his consent. Morgan would take
two thousand men, make the raid, "after which he will
return to his present position." [67]

But Morgan never returned. Sweeping through Kentucky he crossed the Ohio early in July. Through southeastern Indiana he kept up a running fight into Ohio,
passing through Cincinnati to the region of Blenner-
hasset's Island by midmonth. Here he was surrounded
and more than half his men were killed or captured.[68]
Instead of operating on Rosecrans's line of communication he had followed his own plan and as a result ended
up in the penitentiary at Columbus, Ohio. And Bragg's
cavalry force was reduced almost 20 per cent at a most
crucial time.

Meanwhile, on May 18 Halleck had wired Rosecrans:
"Dispatches just received say that General Joe Johnston,
with a considerable force, has left Tennessee to re-enforce
Vicksburg. . . . The best way to counteract this is to
concentrate your forces and advance against the enemy in
Tennessee, moving, if possible, in such a manner as to
threaten East Tennessee." [69]

"We have scouts in every direction," Rosecrans replied, "and, according to our best information no considerable force of any arm, and none of the infantry,
have left our front." [70]

Halleck was literally pushing Rosecrans toward East

---

[66] Morgan to Wheeler, June 15, 1863, *ibid.*, 818.

[67] Wheeler's Orders, June 18, 1863, *ibid.*, 817.

[68] For an account of this raid, see Howard Swiggett, *The Rebel Raider:
A Life of John Hunt Morgan* (Indianapolis, 1934), 129–152.

[69] *Official Records,* Ser. I, Vol. XXIII, Pt. II, 337.   [70] *Ibid.*

Tennessee and the latter wasn't quite sure he wanted to go. His urgent need was cavalry. "If I had 6,000 cavalry, in addition to the mounting of the 2,000 now waiting horses, I would attack Bragg within three days. As it is, all my corps commanders and chief of cavalry are opposed to an advance, which they think, hazards more than the probable gains." [71]

"There is no more cavalry to send you," wired Halleck in reply. "We have none, and can get none until a draft is made." [72]

But, as events were about to demonstrate, Rosecrans's cavalry was better than he thought.

Finally, the long-delayed advance got under way on June 24, 1863. The two armies as they faced each other were substantially as follows: Bragg, 31,000 infantry, 13,500 cavalry, 2,250 artillery; Rosecrans, 41,000 infantry, 6,800 cavalry, 3,000 artillery.[73]

Rosecrans's plans for the advance involved a feint at Bragg's left at Shelbyville while the main portion of the Federal army was sent through Liberty and Hoover's gaps, somewhat to the right of Bragg at Tullahoma. By sending a heavy detachment of cavalry and infantry down the Shelbyville pike Rosecrans created the impression that his whole army was moving in this direction. Bragg was fooled to the extent of sending reinforcements to Polk at Shelbyville and of concentrating his cavalry on the Shelbyville pike.[74] General William T. Martin was already there with some fifteen hundred men. Forrest was ordered from his base at Columbia with his three

71 *Ibid.*, 351.   72 *Ibid.*

73 Gilbert C. Kniffin, "Maneuvering Bragg Out of Tennessee," in *Battles and Leaders*, III, 635–36.

74 Shotwell, *Civil War in America*, II, 4. See also, Seitz, *Braxton Bragg*, 321.

thousand mounted men. Wheeler, who had been giving his attention to the entire right side of the Confederate line from McMinnville to Tullahoma, moved a brigade of his own men from Dug's Gap.[75] If the concentration had been completed, the Confederates would have had some sixty-five hundred cavalry; but Forrest was late, Martin was defeated, and Wheeler was almost captured as he attempted to rally enough men to stop the Federals.

This hopeless confusion and defeat of the Confederate cavalry was on June 27, and happened as follows: General Bragg learned of Rosecrans's trick and ordered Polk to abandon Shelbyville and join Hardee at Tullahoma. The cavalry was to cover Polk's withdrawal and then guard his rear as far as Tullahoma where the junction with Hardee would take place. The Federal cavalry under the leadership of Major General David S. Stanley performed remarkably well, driving Martin to the banks of Duck River. When General Wheeler arrived on the twenty-seventh, he found that Forrest had not arrived, that Martin's men were in a state of confusion and retreat, and that the rear of Polk's columns were exposed and unprotected.[76] Hastily collecting some six hundred men Wheeler determined to make a stand in front of the bridge over Duck River. He led his forces in a charge but was repulsed and driven across the bridge into the town. Re-forming his men on the courthouse yard he made a stand and the fighting became hand to hand.

Where was Forrest? Why didn't he hurry? Earlier in the day Wheeler had grown apprehensive lest Forrest

[75] See Wheeler's instructions, in *Official Records,* Ser. I, Vol. XXIII, Pt. II, 794.

[76] On June 27 at 11 P.M. Bragg notified Polk: "Push on your trains at once with the greatest dispatch. Martin's cavalry has been utterly defeated before Shelbyville." *Ibid.,* Pt. I, 620.

should be delayed and had sent two staff officers to meet and advise him of the desperate situation at Shelbyville. These officers, it is said, received assurance that all possible speed would be made. Then Forrest is said to have added: "Tell General Wheeler to, at all hazards, hold the town until I arrive, or I will be cut off, as the Shelbyville bridge is my only means of crossing Duck River." [77]

Wheeler, it appears, was doing his best to hold on. For two hours he charged and countercharged; and then, concluding that Forrest was not coming, he decided to abandon the task of trying to hold the bridge. As he was ready to withdraw, several of Forrest's staff officers arrived with the information that they had left their general only a few minutes before and that he was but a short distance up the road.[78] Wheeler, calling for volunteers, charged the head of the Federal column and drove it across the bridge, but the lone piece of artillery he dragged along stuck fast on the bridge, cutting off a possible retreat.[79] Wheeler and some fifty of his men were trapped. Calling to his men to follow, Wheeler broke through the encircling enemy line and plunged his horse over an embankment fifteen feet into the swollen river below. His men followed, but only thirteen reached the other side.

Forrest never got there. He had approached to within three miles of the town, found a place where the river could be forded, and had ridden on to the rear of Polk.[80] He had made good his oath never to fight under Wheeler again.

[77] Dodson, *Campaigns of Wheeler*, 88. See also, Dubose, *Wheeler and the Army of Tennessee*, 176.

[78] Lytle, *Bedford Forrest*, 184.

[79] Shotwell, *Civil War in America*, II, 5.

[80] Lytle dismisses this act of Forrest with the statement: "Forrest, in the meantime, sensed the danger before him. He veered to the right and crossed over another bridge, eight miles away." *Bedford Forrest*, 184.

Wheeler's dramatic leap soon became the talk of the army. In later years John A. Wyeth, famous New York surgeon and Forrest's biographer, wrote about the incident. "Without a moment's hesitation, and without considering the distance from the top of the river-bank, which was here precipitous, to the water level, these gallant soldiers followed their invincible leader, and plunged at full speed sheer fifteen feet down into the sweeping current. They struck the water with such velocity that horses and riders disappeared, some of them to rise no more. The Union troopers rushed to the water's edge and fired at the men and animals struggling in the river, killing, or wounding and drowning a number. Holding to his horse's mane, General Wheeler took the precaution to shield himself as much as possible behind the body of the animal, and although fired at repeatedly, he escaped injury and safely reached the opposite shore. Some forty or fifty were said to have perished in this desperate attempt. 'Fighting Joe Wheeler' never did a more heroic and generous deed than when he risked all to save Forrest from disaster." [81]

The junction of the two wings of Bragg's army was effected and the Confederates retired behind the Tennessee to the region of Chattanooga, yielding up Middle Tennessee to the enemy. It had taken the Federals from June 24 to July 4, only ten days, to force the Confederates back.

[81] John A. Wyeth, "General Wheeler's Leap," in *Harper's Weekly* (New York), XLII (1898), 601.

Chapter V

CHICKAMAUGA AND THE RAID ON
ROSECRANS
(July–December, 1863)

THE Appalachian system, one hundred and fifty miles wide, divides the South into two unequal parts. Eastward are Virginia, North and South Carolina, and to the west are Kentucky, Tennessee, Alabama, Mississippi, Louisiana, and the trans-Mississippi states of Texas and Arkansas. Each of these geographic divisions had from the very first become a natural theater of war. In the East the major Federal objective was the Confederate capitol at Richmond. In the West it was the military control of rivers, mountain passes, and railway junction points— steps through which the economic life of the South in the West might be paralyzed. By July of 1863 this paralysis of the West was becoming evident, and with it the hopes of the Confederacy ebbed fast. Within the first ten days of this month Bragg entered Chattanooga, thereby yielding up Tennessee to the enemy, and Pemberton surrendered Vicksburg. Lost to the Confederacy were Nashville, Memphis, Corinth, Holly Springs, New Orleans— all strategic points. Lost also were the Tennessee, Cumberland, and Mississippi rivers, and the greater portion of the railroad systems from Louisville to New Orleans and from Memphis to Chattanooga.

In the East, General Lee had during early July left an inconclusive battlefield at Gettysburg. The end was not far off for the Confederacy; but before it expired, the Army of Tennessee was to bare its teeth like a wounded animal and slash viciously at the enemy on Chickamauga Creek in September, 1863, at Atlanta in the summer of 1864, and finally, to see the last of its lifeblood trickle down the icy slopes at Nashville in December, 1864.

General Rosecrans had, during late June and all of July, 1863, occupied Bragg's old fortifications around Tullahoma, and it was only after considerable prodding that he took up the march toward the mountains which concealed the Confederates at Chattanooga.[1] It was well into August before he reached the mountains east of Chattanooga and not until the last of the month before he was ready to scale the wall.

In the meantime, Bragg had been making what preparations he could to resist the advance.[2] Since the Confederate line of communication was now the railroad from Chattanooga to Atlanta, the commanding general called upon Wheeler for plans by which this line could be protected. For the first time in a major campaign the Army of Tennessee had to make preparations against the danger of Federal cavalry raids. Streight's raid had not been successful but it had demonstrated the possibility of two armies playing the game of interrupting communications.[3] Too, the affair at Shelbyville had shown beyond question that the Federal cavalry had developed into an important threat.

[1] General Halleck's impatience is plainly shown in the almost constant stream of letters fired at Rosecrans during July, 1863. See *Official Records,* Ser. I, Vol. XXIII, Pt. II, 550–56.

[2] Seitz, *Braxton Bragg,* 326, denies that Bragg was confused.

[3] Federal cavalry had grown in strength from 5,816 effectives in January, 1863, to 12,636 effectives in July of the same year. During the same period the Confederate cavalry had increased from 8,062 to 13,954 effectives. *Official Records,* Ser. I, Vol. XXIII, Pt. II, 573, 957.

Obviously with this in mind Wheeler submitted a plan for protecting the line of communication. Stockades were to be built along the railway at bridges from Chattanooga to Atlanta and from Atlanta to Columbus, each stockade to be supplied with artillery and garrisoned by state troops and men unfit for field service. Timber for temporary trestles was to be cut, squared, and scattered in the woods near the bridges. At Rome and Atlanta rifle pits were to be thrown up and a few stockades scattered about. In addition a division of cavalry was to be stationed near Gadsden, Alabama, at Rome, Georgia, and at Calhoun, Georgia. With these precautions Wheeler felt that "Georgia would be quite secure from the cavalry of General Rosecrans's army." [4]

While these plans were being executed, pickets were established along the Tennessee River to watch for the Federal advance. General Philip D. Roddey with his independent command was to watch the river from Corinth, Mississippi, to Decatur, Alabama; Wheeler's pickets were responsible for the river from Decatur to Chattanooga; and Forrest patrolled the area from Chattanooga to Kingston, Tennessee, toward Knoxville. [5] In order to supervise the remounting and re-equipping of his brigades, General Wheeler established his headquarters at

[4] Wheeler to Bragg, July 19, 1863, *ibid.,* 916.

[5] Lytle, *Bedford Forrest,* 188. The detailed position of Wheeler's cavalry was as follows: "[W. N.] Estes' regiment, of Wharton's division, picketing the Tennessee River from Bridgeport to Guntersville, [Alabama]; [William B.] Wade's regiment, Martin's division, from Guntersville to Decatur; and detachments from [Philip D.] Roddey's brigade from Decatur to the mouth of Bear Creek. The main body of Wharton's division was stationed near Rome, Ga.; of Martin's division near Alexandria, Ala.; and of Roddey's brigade near Tuscumbia, Ala." See Wheeler's Report, October 30, 1863, in *Official Records,* Ser. I, Vol. XXX, Pt. II, 520.

Gadsden, Alabama, and remained in that vicinity until the first of September.[6]

There were two directions from which Rosecrans might approach Chattanooga: from the north across Walden's Ridge or from the south by way of the Tennessee River and the Nashville and Chattanooga railroad. If he came in from the north he would encounter Forrest's pickets; if from the south, Wheeler's. As it developed he chose to feint toward the north and then to come in through the south gate. On August 29, 1863, he commenced crossing his troops over the Tennessee at Shell Mound, Bridgeport, and Caperton's Ferry, by means of improvised ferries and bridges.[7] In all, some fifty-eight thousand Federal troops were sent across, divided into corps as follows: the Fourteenth commanded by Major General George H. Thomas; the Twentieth commanded by Major General Alexander McD. McCook; the Twenty-first under Major General Thomas L. Crittenden; the Reserve Corps under Major General Gordon Granger; the Cavalry Corps under Brigadier General Robert B. Mitchell.[8]

Once across the river, the Federal army faced Raccoon Mountain which runs roughly north and south parallel to the river. Beyond this mountain lies Wills Valley, the northern end of which opens at Chattanooga. Across this valley lies Lookout Mountain, and beyond it another valley through which runs Chickamauga Creek, shut off

[6] A great deal of the information concerning Wheeler's activities during this period comes from Federal reports. See especially, McCook to Thomas, September 4, 1863, *ibid.*, Pt. III, 345.

[7] Shotwell, *Civil War in America*, II, 6.

[8] Fiebeger, *Campaigns of the American Civil War*, 224. Figures are approximate.

from Dalton, Georgia, by Taylor's and White Oak Ridges. It all makes up three bowling alleys. The first alley is between Raccoon and Lookout mountains; a ball rolled down it would pass to the west or left of Chattanooga. The second is between Lookout and Missionary Ridge at the open end of which are the pins, the houses in Chattanooga. The third alley is between Missionary Ridge and Pigeon Mountain. Here the bowler would find his ball passing to the east or right of Chattanooga. This is the Chickamauga battlefield. Into this maze of mountains and coves both commanders took their armies. Rosecrans held Crittenden's corps in Wills Valley sending Thomas into McLemore's Cove just beyond Lookout. McCook's corps was sent beyond Thomas's position across Pigeon Mountain to Alpine.[9] From these positions Rosecrans expected to move against Bragg's line of communication.

On September 8, however, while Rosecrans's army was thus divided into three parts, Bragg moved out of Chattanooga southward to La Fayette, there to await the reinforcements which were being hurried to him. General Buckner was on his way from Knoxville with a corps; General Breckinridge was bringing troops from Mississippi; and James Longstreet was hurrying from the Army of Northern Virginia with the divisions of John B. Hood and Lafayette McLaws.[10] It was an excellent strategic movement on Bragg's part, for it saved him from a siege within Chattanooga and also afforded him an opportunity to make contact with his reinforcements. But beyond

---

9 Daniel H. Hill, "Chickamauga—The Great Battle of the West," in *Battles and Leaders*, III, 641.

10 The Confederate strength at Chickamauga was approximately 66,000 effectives. The odds on strength alone were about 6 to 5 in favor of Bragg. See Fiebeger, *Campaigns of the American Civil War*, 225.

this, fortune did not smile so broadly upon him. As a matter of fact, both armies were almost totally ignorant of the disposition and intentions of the other. Rosecrans thought Bragg was in precipitous retreat on the day that Chattanooga was evacuated. In turn Bragg apparently was for a time almost as ignorant of the Federal positions. In this maze of coves and passes almost anything could happen.

General W. W. Mackall, Bragg's chief of staff, wrote General Daniel H. Hill on August 29: "The night has brought us no news." [11] At one o'clock in the afternoon, however, Colonel W. N. Estes of Wharton's division notified General Wheeler: "Enemy crossed the Tennessee River 10 miles below Bridgeport . . . by fording." [12] This gave Bragg information that the enemy was actually crossing the river, but Mackall was still apprehensive. On September 2 he wrote Wheeler:

I am uneasy about the state of affairs. It is so vitally important that the general should have full and correct information. One misstep in the movement of this army would possibly be fatal.

Your line of pickets now occupy on Lookout Mountain about the same advantages they possessed on the river or Sand Mountain. The passage at Caperton's Ferry [on August 29] broke the line, and a week has passed and we don't know whether or not an army has passed. If this happens on Lookout, say to-night, and the enemy obtain that as a screen to their movements, I must confess I do not see myself what move we can make to answer it.[13]

Wheeler's response to this message was a redoubling of his efforts. His pickets on the river were notified: "Ordi-

11 W. W. Mackall to Daniel H. Hill, August 29, 1863, in *Official Records,* Ser. I, Vol. XXX, Pt. IV, 564.

12 *Ibid.*   13 Mackall to Wheeler, September 2, 1863, *ibid.,* 584.

narily you will report to these headquarters three times a day, but in case of any demonstration of the enemy you will report every hour at least, and oftener if you have anything important to communicate." [14] By the fourth General Bragg was well informed of the enemy's movement across the river. He wrote General Hill: "There is no doubt of the enemy's position now; one corps opposite you, and two this side of river from Shellmound by Bridgeport to Caperton's, the point of first crossing. A part of the latter are reported moving down Will's Valley towards Gadsden or perhaps Rome; Wheeler is gone to develop them." [15]

When the Federals had completed their crossing and had established themselves in the valleys below Chattanooga the difficulties of the Confederate cavalry in obtaining information only increased. These difficulties, were, it appears, due largely to two factors—the nature of the terrain, and the fact that the Federals themselves were well supplied with cavalry. The result was that when General Bragg evacuated Chattanooga on September 8 and moved southward toward his new base at La Fayette he lacked the complete information which a commander needs at such a time. General Hill in a most positive observation said that Bragg was "encircled by foes, without knowing who they were, what was their strength, and what were their plans." [16]

Illustrations of the cavalry's problems in attempting to determine the enemy's position and strength are afforded by some of Wheeler's experiences. When Bragg was preparing to evacuate the city on September 5, he ordered Wheeler without delay to move with his command "into

14 Wheeler to T. H. Mauldin, September 2, 1863, *ibid.*, 585.
15 Bragg to Hill, September 4, 1863, *ibid.*, 594.
16 Hill, "Chickamauga," in *Battles and Leaders,* III, 664.

the valley, drive in the enemy's pickets, and assail him so as to develop his designs, strength, and position." "This must be done," the order concluded, "even at the sacrifice of troops." [17] Before the battle at Stone's River this would have been an order easy to obey, but at Chickamauga the situation was much different: the difference between cavalry operations in open country and in densely wooded mountainous areas; between assailing an enemy with a negligible cavalry force and one with an effective mounted branch.

When Wheeler received this order he was at Alpine in Chickamauga Valley. If he carried it out it meant that he was to select a mountain pass, ride through it over Lookout Mountain into Wills Valley, and encounter the Federals there. Then, having engaged them sufficiently to determine their strength, he and his men were to retreat through this or some other closely guarded pass and rejoin the army. It obviously was an order issued without consideration of the fact that every pass was strongly picketed by enemy cavalry; and even if Wheeler had succeeded in forcing an entrance his retreat could have been shut off by the simple process of closing the gap behind him. As a result, Wheeler, who made a fetish of obeying orders, disobeyed one. Instead of going over the mountain in force, he sent observers to the top and contented himself with the information they furnished.[18] In explanation of his disobedience of orders Wheeler wrote: "Had I attempted to go over into the valley I am very certain I could not have obtained any information beyond what I now have, as when I got into the valley I could only see that portion of the enemy's force immedi-

[17] Bragg to Wheeler, September 5, 1863, in *Official Records,* Ser. I, Vol. XXX, Pt. IV, 602.

[18] Wheeler's Report, September 6, 1863, *ibid.,* 614.

ately opposed to me, while my scouts from various cliffs on the mountain had the whole of Will's Valley almost continually under observation." [19] Not only this, he reported, but his march over to the valley and back would have rendered numbers of his horses unserviceable. If General Rosecrans were commencing a campaign, he thought it was of prime necessity that the cavalry should be in as good condition as possible. "Though I consider it to be the duty of officers generally to obey orders to the letter, I feel it is also their duty to carry out the intentions of their commander, even though a departure from the strict letter of the instruction be involved." [20]

But it should not be understood that all the difficulties were encountered by the Confederate cavalry, for the Federals were operating under the same difficulties. On the eighth, for example, when Rosecrans thought Bragg to be in hasty retreat he sent General David S. Stanley to break through the railroad line toward La Fayette and to gain what information he could. Rosecrans had been incorrectly informed that Forrest and Wharton of Wheeler's corps were near Chattanooga. They were not in this position but confronted him in Chickamauga Valley. Stanley did not wait for a fight but hastily retreated back into Wills Valley without the information which would have been so vital to his chief—the information that Bragg's retreat was strategic.[21] As a matter of fact, General Rosecrans's army was in more danger from the ninth to the fourteenth of September than was the Army of Tennessee. By September 11 the three corps of the Federal army were separated and out of touch with each other; and not only the corps but different

19 *Ibid.*   20 *Ibid.*, 615.
21 General Stanley's Report does not mention the incident, but Lytle in his *Bedford Forrest*, 199, gives an account of the movement.

divisions of the same corps had no communication with each other.[22] General McCook was at Alpine, forty miles from Chattanooga; Thomas was twenty miles nearer Chattanooga; James S. Negley was in McLemore's Cove; and Wood of Crittenden's division was at Lee and Gordon's Mill, ten miles from Ringgold. The positions made the situation highly favorable to Bragg. He could crush the divisions one by one.

This attempt to fall upon the separated divisions and crush them Bragg attempted, but all his plans miscarried. On the ninth he ordered General Hindman's division of Polk's corps to join with Cleburne's division of Hill's corps and Walker's reserve corps to attack Thomas on the tenth in McLemore's Cove. Hill did not get Cleburne's division up and Hindman delayed the attack until the afternoon when there was no one to attack. Thomas had quietly withdrawn his troops and joined McCook at Alpine.[23] Failing in this attempt, Bragg then determined to turn upon Crittenden's corps at Ringgold. Polk's and Walker's corps were moved toward that point and directed to attack at dawn on September 13; but no attack was made and Crittenden withdrew and joined Thomas.[24]

Disappointed in his attempts to destroy the Federals when they were divided, there was nothing left for Bragg now except to fight them as they stood united. Accord-

[22] Hay, "Braxton Bragg and the Southern Confederacy," in *loc. cit.*, 300, gives a brief but comprehensive survey of the situation. See also, Hill, "Chickamauga," in *Battles and Leaders*, III, 643–45.

[23] General Hill attributes the failure to "Bragg's ignorance of the condition of the roads, the obstructions at Dug Gap, and the position of the enemy." "Chickamauga," in *Battles and Leaders*, III, 642.

[24] See Polk's Report, September 12, 1863, in *Official Records*, Ser. I, Vol. XXX, Pt. II, 44. On September 29, 1863, both Polk and Thomas C. Hindman were suspended from their commands and sent to Atlanta. See *ibid.*, 56, 298.

ingly, he sent his trains and supplies to safe positions behind Taylor's Ridge and concentrated his army on the seventeenth in line of battle along the Chickamauga.

While Hindman and Polk had been engaged in their unsuccessful attempts to crush Thomas and Crittenden, Wheeler had been almost constantly engaged in the type of cavalry skirmishing which presages a great battle. The left flank of Bragg's army pointed toward McLemore's Cove, the right toward the Tennessee River; Wheeler on the left, Forrest on the right, each observing, picketing, fighting sharply upon occasion. Neither cavalryman could accomplish much, however, except to prevent surprises and strike the enemy's advance cavalry. With Bragg's line of battle drawn, both cavalry leaders concentrated their forces on the wings and prepared to go into battle.[25]

On September 18 there was almost constant skirmishing between the two armies but the main battle did not open until the nineteenth, a Saturday. Bragg's plan was his old favorite one of striking the enemy's left and pushing it back with the center as a pivot.[26] If he could successfully accomplish this he could cut Rosecrans's contacts with Chattanooga. Early in the morning of September 19 the Confederates struck the Union left, but instead of finding an exposed flank as they had anticipated they encountered "lines of soldiers commanded by Thomas, good soldiers, well placed and well led." [27] Throughout the day the battle lines wavered back and forth, and when night came Thomas was content to intrench himself and let his troops sleep on their arms.

25 See Wheeler's and Forrest's reports, October 30, 1863, and October 22, 1863, *ibid.*, 520, 525.

26 Shotwell, *Civil War in America*, II, 12. See also, Hill, "Chickamauga," in *Battles and Leaders*, III, 649–51.

27 Henry, *Story of the Confederacy*, 310.

During the night Longstreet arrived at Ringgold from Lee's army, and near midnight General Bragg reorganized his army into two wings: a right wing under Polk which was made up of Hill's corps, Cheatham's division, and Walker's corps recently come from Mississippi; a left wing under Longstreet composed of Buckner's, Alexander P. Stewart's, William Preston's, and Bushrod Johnson's corps, and Hood's and McLaw's divisions which had come with Longstreet from Virginia. Under the new organization Wheeler operated on the left under Longstreet and Forrest on the right under Polk.[28]

Orders were for the Confederates to attack at dawn the next morning (September 20) with the Confederate right again assailing the Federal left as it had on the previous morning. The attack was delayed, however, until near ten o'clock. During the night everything had become confused. Officers could not be located, orders could not be delivered, troop movements lacked synchronization.[29] When the Confederate attack did come it was almost a repetition of the previous day's fighting. The Confederate right under Polk assailed the Federal left under Thomas and kept up a fierce fight until near noon when the left under Longstreet went into action. On the right Thomas asked for reinforcements and Rosecrans, acting, it is said, upon an erroneous statement by a courier, withdrew Wood's division from the center and sent it to the left.[30] This created a gap in the Federal front, and Longstreet was quick to take advantage of it

[28] Fiebeger, *Campaigns of the American Civil War*, 222.

[29] See reports of Generals Polk, Hill, and James Longstreet, in *Official Records*, Ser. I, Vol. XXX, Pt. II, 43–48, 136, 287.

[30] Federal divisions from left to right were: James S. Negley's, Absalom Baird's, Richard W. Johnson's, John M. Palmer's, and Joseph J. Reynolds's under George H. Thomas; John M. Brannan's, Thomas J. Wood's and H. P. Van Cleve's under Thomas L. Crittenden; Jefferson

by hurling Hood's division into the space and following with all his remaining divisions.[31]

The Federals broke, and soon retreat became rout. Officers lost control of their men, and in the face of a plunging fire of musketry and artillery Rosecrans's center broke and fled toward Chattanooga. It approached a panic. A mob of fugitives swept General Rosecrans himself away from the battle, "fugitives, wounded, caissons, escort, ambulances, thronged the narrow pathways." [32] When the Federal commander reached Chattanooga about dark he sent his staff officer, General James A. Garfield, with a message to Thomas reported as: "Ride to the front. Find General Thomas, if he is still alive. Tell him to cover the retreat with Granger's men. I will wire to have Cincinnati and Louisville put in order for a siege." [33]

The battle seemed an overwhelming Confederate victory, and it doubtless would have been except for two factors—Thomas held behind his breastworks and Longstreet was unable to get the necessary troops to pursue and annihilate the fleeing Federals. Near three o'clock in the afternoon Wheeler was ordered to cross the Chickamauga at Lee and Gordon's Mill and strike the enemy cavalry to prevent its covering the retreat.[34] General George Crook commanding the right wing of the Federal

---

C. Davis's and Philip H. Sheridan's under Alexander McD. McCook. To comply with the order Wood had to move his men back out of the front lines and march them to the rear of Brannan and thence to the left. See map of battle, in *Battles and Leaders,* III, 648.

[31] Longstreet's Report, October ?, 1863, in *Official Records,* Ser. I, Vol. XXX, Pt. II, 288.

[32] Gates P. Thruston, "The Crisis at Chickamauga," in *Battles and Leaders,* III, 664.

[33] Quoted in Pratt, *Ordeal by Fire,* 281.

[34] Wheeler's Report, October 30, 1863, in *Official Records,* Ser. I, Vol. XXX, Pt. II, 521.

cavalry had been picketing the fords of Chickamauga
Creek to the south of Crawfish Springs and had throughout the day been skirmishing with Wheeler's patrols.
When Crook received word that the Federal right was in
retreat he collected his men and moved toward the rear
to hold the pursuing Confederates.[35] But there were no
pursuing Confederates. Wheeler rode herd on the stragglers, rounding up, he reported, a thousand of them,
twenty wagons, and a large supply of stores,[36] but he did
not strike the fleeing columns in full force. General
Longstreet requested reinforcements from Bragg which
could be used to clinch the victory, but the request was
refused.[37] Over on the right near Chattanooga, Forrest
climbed a tree and through a pair of captured field glasses
saw the rout. Hastily he dispatched a note to Polk with
the request that it be sent on to Bragg: "Can see Chattanooga and everything around. The enemy's trains are
leaving, going around the point of Lookout Mountain.
. . . I think they are evacuating as hard as they can
go. . . . I think we ought to press forward as rapidly as
possible." [38] That night he rode in to headquarters and
repeated his advice, but it fell on deaf ears. "What,"
Forrest angrily demanded of anyone within hearing,
"does he fight battles for?" [39]

On the twenty-first, the day after the battle, Wheeler
was busy clearing up the wreckage left in the wake of
the retreat. Two regiments were detached with orders
to pick up stragglers and collect abandoned arms. An-

---

[35] George Crook's Report, September 29, 1863, *ibid.*, Pt. I, 918.

[36] Wheeler's Report, October 30, 1863, *ibid.*, Pt. II, 521.

[37] H. J. Eckenrode and Bryan Conrad, *James Longstreet: Lee's War
Horse* (Chapel Hill, 1936), 237.

[38] September 21, 1863, in *Official Records*, Ser. I, Vol. XXX, Pt. IV,
681.

[39] Lytle, *Bedford Forrest*, 233.

other was sent under orders from Longstreet to determine the Federal position; and a third, some seventeen hundred strong, moved directly under Wheeler to protect the captured property.[40] During the afternoon a force of enemy cavalry bent upon saving what it could from the wreckage was encountered by Wheeler. There was a brief but brisk fight in which the Confederates, so Wheeler reported, captured eighteen stands of colors and ninety loaded baggage wagons.[41] This was routine cavalry work.

On this same day, however, momentous decisions were being made and unmade at Longstreet's and Bragg's headquarters. At sunrise Bragg came to Longstreet's bivouac and asked for advice. What should be the next move? And the reply was: cross the Tennessee above Chattanooga and move against the Federal communications. If Rosecrans evacuated Chattanooga the Confederates could either pursue him or move against the Federal force at Knoxville.[42]

Bragg seemed to acquiesce, but then changed his mind,[43] and the plan which Longstreet advocated was undertaken piecemeal fashion. Wheeler alone was sent against the Federal communications, and after his return was sent with Longstreet against Knoxville.

On the twenty-second, the day after this conference between Bragg and Longstreet, Wheeler pushed within a mile and a quarter of Chattanooga to watch the movements of the enemy within the city. While on this mission he received orders to "cross the Tennessee River and

---

40 Wheeler's Report, October 30, 1863, in *Official Records,* Ser. I, Vol. XXX, Pt. II, 521.

41 *Ibid.*   42 Eckenrode and Conrad, *James Longstreet,* 240.

43 *Ibid.,* 241. See also, Longstreet to Secretary of War James A. Seddon, September 26, 1863, in *Official Records,* Ser. I, Vol. XXX, Pt. IV, 705.

press the enemy, intercept and break up all his lines of communication and retreat." [44] But before this could be carried out it was countermanded and new orders issued: "The commanding general directs that before crossing the Tennessee you ascend Lookout Mountain and sweep up toward Chattanooga, clearing the top of the mountain of the enemy." [45] And later that same day he was notified: "After executing the order clearing the top of Lookout Mountain you will suspend the execution of the order to cross the Tennessee River." [46]

Obviously, during the two days while Wheeler was away, General Bragg had made two decisions: to lay siege to Chattanooga with his main army and to strengthen Wheeler's command before he sent it against the Federal communications. Both of these moves he made. After Wheeler had driven the Union pickets off the point of Lookout, General Bragg placed pickets there and then spread his army fanwise south of Chattanooga. Then, having placed his army, he turned to the matter of operating on the enemy's communications.

On September 28 General Forrest, who was on outpost duty near Athens, Tennessee, received an order which from all reports provoked somewhat the same response as that received from applying a match to a keg of blasting powder. The order read: "The general commanding desires that you will without delay turn over the troops of your command previously ordered to Major-General Wheeler." [47] The order, of course, meant that Bragg was sending Wheeler against Rosecrans's communications with the combined cavalry force of the Army of Tennessee, a move which from this distance seems a reflection of

44 Bragg to Wheeler, September 22, 1863, *ibid.*, 695.
45 *Id.* to *id.*, September 23, 1863, *ibid.*, 698.
46 *Id.* to *id.*, September 23, 1863, *ibid.*, 699.
47 *Id.* to Forrest, September 28, 1863, *ibid.*, 710.

distressingly bad judgment on Bragg's part. Forrest had demonstrated a remarkable ability to command large bodies of cavalry on independent expeditions. Wheeler could not claim this special talent,[48] but did his best work when operating in close conjunction with the main army. It therefore seems that Bragg, who apparently had a positive genius for making mistakes, rid himself of the one leader who might have had a chance to impair permanently Rosecrans's communications. A union of the two commands at this time seems to have been a necessary move, but it also appears that, temporarily at least, Forrest should have been the commander; not only because he was better fitted for this type of work, but for the additional reason that Wheeler's troops apparently showed no resentment in being commanded by Forrest while the same could not be said in the reverse order.

But these considerations Bragg seems to have ignored, indeed, if he ever had them in mind; and Wheeler was sent on an expedition which began with tremendous success and ended in near disaster. He was to take his own and Forrest's command, cut the Union line of communications through Sequatchie Valley north of Chattanooga, and then sweep westward toward Nashville, tearing up the railroad and destroying supply depots.[49]

General Forrest protested to Wheeler that his men

[48] In reporting on Wheeler's corps Colonel Alfred Roman wrote Beauregard: "The proposition that all able officers are not fit to be efficient cavalry commanders is assuming, more and more, the proportions of a self-evident proposition: the Van Dorns, the Forrests, the Hamptons, are not easily found, in this or any other country." MS. report of Assistant Inspector General Roman to General Beauregard, December 28, 1864, in Beauregard Papers (Division of Manuscripts, Library of Congress).

[49] Wheeler stated he received his orders on September 29, 1863. See Wheeler's Report, October 30, 1863, in *Official Records*, Ser. I, Vol. XXX, Pt. II, 722.

and horses were in no condition for such an expedition.[50] General Frank C. Armstrong, Forrest's senior brigadier, also protested that his brigade was "totally unfit to start on any expedition" and that he himself was too sick to accompany his troops.[51] There also is evidence that considerable dissatisfaction was expressed by the troops themselves.[52] But to make his position clear beyond a doubt, Forrest mounted his horse and rode to Bragg's headquarters where he gave the commanding general a sound "cussing," ending, it is said, with these words: "You have threatened to arrest me for not obeying your orders promptly. I dare you to do it, and I say to you that if you ever again try to interfere with me or cross my path, it will be at the peril of your life." [53] So saying, Forrest rode away to a conference with President Davis at Montgomery, which resulted in his being given an independent command in Mississippi and West Tennessee.

In the meantime, Wheeler proceeded with his raid. Leaving John H. Kelly's brigade on duty with the army before Chattanooga, Wheeler with Wharton's and Martin's divisions moved up the left bank of the Tennessee toward the rendezvous with Forrest's men near Cottonport, Tennessee, some thirty-five miles northeast of Chattanooga. As Wheeler moved, enemy cavalry paralleled him on the right bank as closely as shadows thrown across the stream. Not a shot was fired by either side for several miles until Wheeler, apparently irritated by the comic opera state of affairs, determined to fight his way across. Under cover of his artillery he forded the river, drove back the enemy cavalry, and continued the march.[54]

[50] Forrest to Wheeler, September 28, 1863, *ibid.*, Pt. IV, 711.
[51] Armstrong to *id.*, September 30, 1863, *ibid.*, 719.
[52] Lytle, *Bedford Forrest*, 237.   [53] *Ibid.*, 238.
[54] Wheeler's Report, October 30, 1863, in *Official Records*, Ser. I, Vol. XXX, Pt. II, 723.

On the afternoon of September 30 Wheeler joined
Forrest's men near Cottonport,[55] and here he found that
General Forrest's report of the condition of his command
was no exaggeration. "The three brigades from General
Forrest were mere skeletons, scarcely averaging 500 effective men each. These were badly armed, had but a small
supply of ammunition, and their horses were in horrible
condition. . . . The men were worn out, and without
rations," [56] reported Wheeler later. Calling an inspection Wheeler weeded out the worst of the unfit and took
with him three skeleton brigades commanded respectively by Brigadier General H. B. Davidson and Colonels
John S. Scott and George B. Hodge.[57] With his own command Wheeler's total force probably numbered near
four thousand men with six pieces of artillery.[58]

At Cottonport with the river to his back Wheeler could
look westward across the valley of the Tennessee some
twenty miles to Walden's Ridge rising fifteen hundred
feet and extending north and south like a huge spine
with Chattanooga to the south as its head. Across this
ridge was the Sequatchie Valley and across this valley
were more mountains which gradually faded into the
rolling country of Middle Tennessee. All day of October 1 was spent by Wheeler in organizing his new command and in making preparations for the march toward
Walden's Ridge. Toward evening the command moved,
but because of the heavy rain it was able to move only

---

[55] George B. Hodge's (of Forrest's corps) Report, October 11, 1863,
ibid., 726.

[56] Wheeler's Report, October 30, 1863, *ibid.*, 723.

[57] Hodge's brigade was attached to Simon B. Buckner's corps until
August 24, 1863, when it was put under Forrest. John S. Scott's and
H. B. Davidson's brigades were of Pegram's division.

[58] Dubose, *Wheeler and the Army of Tennessee*, 207, puts the number at 3,937.

nine miles during the night.[59] The day of October 2 was spent in reaching the top of the ridge; but, before it moved into the valley below, Wheeler called a conference of his division commanders.[60] It was his purpose, he explained, to divide the force, detaching some fifteen hundred men whom he proposed to lead personally in a raid on the valley below while the balance moved on to McMinnville, Tennessee, where large Federal stores were reported to be collected. Wharton, it is said, objected to the move on the grounds that it was unsafe to divide the command in the face of the enemy,[61] but in spite of this Wheeler went through with his plans. Wharton and Forrest's men under Davidson were sent on to McMinnville while Wheeler tarried to harass the valley.

In the meantime, word of Wheeler's movements had reached the Federals who were on the point of starvation in Chattanooga. On the night that Wheeler moved his men from Cottonport, General Garfield acting for Rosecrans sent a warning to the cavalry patrolling the Tennessee River. "The enemy's cavalry has crossed the river in heavy force a short distance below Washington, and designs making a raid on our communication.

"The general commanding directs you to leave one or two small regiments that are down the river to watch the crossings and move with all dispatch with the balance of your force to Anderson's Cross-Roads, in the Sequatchie Valley, to protect our wagon trains. Three regiments of infantry and a section of artillery have been ordered there to support you." [62] As an additional measure to insure the safety of the train General Crook was ordered to fol-

[59] Hodge's Report, October 11, 1863, in *Official Records*, Ser. I, Vol. XXX, Pt. II, 726.

[60] Dubose, *Wheeler and the Army of Tennessee*, 208. [61] *Ibid.*

[62] James A. Garfield to McCook, October 1, 1863, 12:15 A.M., in *Official Records*, Ser. I, Vol. XXX, Pt. IV, 21.

low and attack Wheeler, and at about the same time that
Wheeler was having the conference with his officers
Crook pulled up at the foot of Walden's Ridge. "The
enemy's rear passed this place at 12 m. to-day," he reported. "I shall pursue them at daylight in the morning,
and expect to overtake their rear to-morrow. . . . I'll
follow them until I come up with them, if I have to go
to Nashville." [63]

But daylight was too late for Crook to carry out Rosecrans's injunction that "they must not be allowed to
enter Sequatchie." [64] At almost the hour when General
Crook planned to overtake the Confederates, Wheeler
struck the wagon trains in the valley. On the morning of
October 3 at three o'clock he roused his men and put
them in motion southward down the valley toward Chattanooga. After traveling some ten miles he overtook and
captured thirty-two six-mule wagons loaded with provisions for the Federals,[65] but this was a mere preliminary
incident to the main business of the day. An hour or so
later the main wagon train was overtaken, infantry and
cavalry guarding it front and rear. "Parts of two regiments under Colonel John T. Morgan," a participant
wrote, "were ordered to charge the escort of the train,
which they did, but were repulsed and came back in dis-
order. I was standing near Colonel A. A. Russell who
commanded the Fourth Alabama Cavalry, when General
Wheeler rode up and ordered him to lead his regiment
in. As soon as our lines could be formed, we rode forward at full speed, and receiving a volley at close quarters, were successful in riding over and capturing the entire escort within a few minutes. We found ourselves in

[63] Crook to Rosecrans, October 1, 1863, 8 P.M. *ibid.*, 24.
[64] Rosecrans to Mitchell, October 1, 1863, *ibid.*, 20.
[65] Wheeler's Report, October 30, 1863, *ibid.*, Pt. II, 723.

possession of an enormous wagon train, and such a scene of panic and confusion I had never witnessed." [66]

It was the first time in many days that the Confederates had had an opportunity to fill their haversacks. The young trooper who was standing near Colonel Russell when the charge began now tied his horse to a wagon and dived under the canvas top after cheese. General Wheeler riding by ordered the youth to be about his business of destruction, and, in the young man's own words: "I obeyed, and had the honor of riding side by side with my commander for some distance further among the captured wagons." [67]

Wheeler and his young companion saw the Federal teamsters take to their heels for safety, leaving their teams to run wild. "Some of the wagons were overturned, blocking the road in places with anywhere from ten to fifty teams, some of the mules still standing, some fallen and tangled in the harness, and all in inextricable confusion." For miles this scene was repeated over and over again until the valley was a smoking corridor of destruction and death. Men were detailed to burn the wagons while others shot or sabered the mules. Soon the explosion of ammunition in the burning wagons assumed the proportions of artillery in action. For eight hours the destruction went on within twenty miles of Chattanooga and with McCook closing in from the direction of Chattanooga and Crook across Walden's Ridge in pursuit.[68]

Estimates of the total damage vary. General Wheeler stated that "the number of wagons was variously estimated at from 800 to 1,500." [69] General Rosecrans placed

[66] John A. Wyeth, "The Destruction of Rosecrans' Great Wagon Train," in Miller (ed.), *Photographic History of the Civil War*, IV, 160.
[67] *Ibid.*, 162.   [68] *Ibid.*, 164.
[69] Wheeler's Report, October 30, 1863, in *Official Records*, Ser. I, Vol. XXX, Pt. I, 723.

the loss at five hundred wagons.[70] But it is not difficult to see what the effect was in Chattanooga. Rosecrans's only line of supply was the railroad from Nashville to Chattanooga, this road reaching the Tennessee River at Bridgeport, Alabama, and following the river from there into Chattanooga. This part of the river and railroad being in possession of Bragg's army, all Federal supplies had to be hauled by a sixty-mile circuitous route through Sequatchie Valley. Now that Wheeler had destroyed the line, at least temporarily, conditions already bad within the city became worse. Many were daily dying of starvation. Clothing and shoes were so scanty that the frosty autumn nights were becoming intolerable. "The condition of the army, indeed, was fast becoming pitiable." [71] Rosecrans was forced to have built at Bridgeport a crude steamboat which in a measure served to alleviate conditions in Chattanooga,[72] but in the end the predicament in which he had placed his army cost him his job as commander.

While Wheeler was engaged in his work of destruction in Sequatchie Valley, Wharton and Davidson with Forrest's men had made their appearance before the Federal garrison at McMinnville commanded by Major Michael L. Patterson, Andrew Johnson's son-in-law. After a preliminary skirmish with the Federal outposts Colonel Hodge, acting under orders from Wharton, went in under a flag of truce and demanded surrender of the town. Major Patterson requested that he be allowed to count the attacking force, and this being refused he sur-

[70] Rosecrans to Ambrose Burnside, October 5, 1863, in *Official Records,* Ser. I, Vol. XXX, Pt. IV, 114.

[71] Shotwell, *Civil War in America,* II, 26.

[72] For an account of the "cracker line" which the steamboat opened, see William G. LeDuc, "The Little Steamboat That Opened the 'Cracker Line,' " in *Battles and Leaders,* III, 676.

rendered "himself and command, some 600 in number, prisoners of war unconditionally, with several million dollars' worth of stores, provisions, and munitions." [73]

Following the surrender, according to Major Patterson, there occurred "the most brutal outrages on the part of the rebels ever known to any civilized war in America or elsewhere." The Confederate cavalrymen, he said, proceeded to outfit themselves in new clothes from head to foot, to take "boots, watch, pocket-book, money, and even finger-rings, or, in fact, anything that happened to please their fancy." With a pistol cocked in one hand the rebel held out his other for whatever attracted him, "even compelling captains to sit down in the middle of the road and pull off their boots." Appeals were made, the outraged Major stated, to General Wheeler who had arrived on the scene, but from him he received no aid in checking the pillaging. He "would reply that he (Wheeler) could not control his men; that they would do as they pleased, &c.," a statement which probably was true considering the half-starved, ill-clad condition of Forrest's men and their known reluctance to obeying Wheeler's orders. [74]

Wheeler, his command united and a portion of it reclothed, rode from McMinnville toward Murfreesboro. Close in pursuit, Crook reported: "On arriving at McMinnville I found that the garrison had surrendered without making any resistance. The enemy sacked the place, destroying a great deal of public and private property, and left in the direction of Murfreesborough." [75] He was gaining on the raiding Confederates, but still was unable to check them. Closely behind Crook came Gen-

[73] Hodge's Report, October 11, 1863, in *Official Records,* Ser. I, Vol. XXX, Pt. II, 727.
[74] Michael L. Patterson's Report, October 20, 1863, *ibid.,* 711.
[75] Crook's Report, November 5, 1863, *ibid.,* 685.

eral Mitchell with a division of cavalry. He had arrived
at Anderson's Cross Roads too late to prevent Wheeler's
destruction, so now he was joining the chase. On October 6 he arrived at Murfreesboro where he drew rations.
Here he found that Crook had drawn his rations the
night before and was ready to depart. Forming a junction with Crook's command he moved to Shelbyville on
the seventh to cut off Wheeler. Colonel Edward M.
McCook was sent with a division toward Unionville and
Crook with his division of cavalry and Colonel John T.
Wilder's mounted infantry was dispatched to the Farmington road.[76]

In the meantime, Wheeler had made a demonstration
upon Murfreesboro, destroyed a stockade, and burned
the bridge over Stone's River. On the day following he
destroyed the railroad bridges and trestles between Murfreesboro and Wartrace and on October 6 sacked Shelbyville,[77] crossing over the same bridge he had so gallantly
held for Forrest five months before. He was nearing the
end of a successful raid, having encountered no stiff opposition and having lost very few men killed and wounded.
He had destroyed millions of dollars' worth of enemy
stores and had further imperiled the position of the Federals at Chattanooga; but now that full success was so
near, disaster almost overtook him.

The night of the sixth, Wheeler reported, he ordered
Davidson's division to encamp on Duck River near War-
ner's Bridge, Martin's division two miles farther down,
and Wharton's two miles below Martin's.[78] Learning that
Crook and Mitchell were not far away, Wheeler notified
Davidson that in case the enemy attacked he was to fall
back and join Martin. A short while later he amended

[76] Mitchell's Report, October 20, 1863, *ibid.*, 669–70.
[77] Wheeler's Report, October 30, 1863, *ibid.*, 724.   [78] *Ibid.*

the order and requested Davidson to fall back on Martin immediately whether the enemy attacked or not.[79] For some unknown reason Davidson failed to comply with these instructions, and on the morning of October 7 the enemy moved against him. Davidson fell back, but instead of falling back directly on Martin he moved in the direction of Farmington.[80] About ten o'clock in the morning Scott's brigade received the impact of the enemy and as Colonel Hodge rode to reinforce it he found it in wild retreat. To quote his own account:

Being ordered by General Davidson to lead them and to take command of the rear in person, I countermarched with my brigade and was proceeding at a gallop with my command back, when, ahead of me, I encountered the whole of Scott's brigade crowded in frightful and horrible confusion, wild and frantic with panic, choking the entire road and bearing down upon me at racing speed. It was too late to clear the way; they rode over my command like madmen, some of them stopping only, as I am informed, when they reached the Tennessee. I was ridden over and my horse knocked down, but succeeded in extricating myself and Captain Larmer's company, Twenty-Seventh Virginia Battalion, which I threw into position behind a fence running at right angles with the road, and opened fire upon the enemy, who were fiercely charging the rear of the panic-stricken crowd.[81]

Galloping ahead, Colonel Hodge succeeded in extricating his own brigade from among the fleeing mass and formed it in line. Farther along General Davidson attempted to halt and re-form a few of Scott's men to reinforce Hodge, but the enemy now in the flush of victory pushed ahead, often sabering Confederate riders in the

[79] Wheeler to Davidson, October 6, 1863, *ibid.,* Pt. IV, 731, 732.
[80] Wheeler's Report, October 30, 1863, *ibid.,* 724.
[81] Hodge's Report, October 11, 1863, *ibid.,* Pt. II, 727.

saddle. "For five hours and a half, over 7 miles of country, the unequal contest continued," Hodge wrote. "My gallant brigade was cut to pieces and slaughtered." [82]

Upon receiving word that Davidson was moving toward Farmington and was being pressed by the enemy, Wheeler started immediately at a trot with Martin's division to assist him.[83] At three o'clock in the afternoon, Hodge reported, he received the welcome news that Wheeler was in his rear with reinforcements. "I passed at 4 o'clock through his lines into Farmington, but only to resume the retreat; when, at 5, the division he had placed in position was charged and broken by the enemy." [84]

It was a race from this point on to the Tennessee River where Wheeler put his men across to safety. It was the second almost successful, almost disastrous expedition undertaken by Wheeler in command of Forrest's troops. The first had been at Donelson, and now it was at Farmington. One wonders what Forrest would have done in the presence of such a rout or what his commanding personality on the field might have been worth. It seems likely from his precautions in other instances that he would have taken steps to prevent a third of his command from straying and being trapped. But Wheeler seems to have lacked Forrest's dominating way with men and also to have lacked that sense of movement and coordination which is so essential to an independent commander in the field. It seems probable that General Bragg never realized that in Wheeler and Forrest he had perhaps the most valuable combination of cavalry leaders

82 *Ibid.*, 727–28.
83 Wheeler's Report, October 30, 1863, *ibid.*, 724.
84 Hodge's Report, October 11, 1863, *ibid.*, 728.

possessed by any commander during the war—that is, if these men were employed in the tasks to which they were best adapted.

It was almost sundown on the afternoon of October 9 when Wheeler began to put his men across the river near the head of Muscle Shoals, some twenty miles above the site of the present Wilson Dam. Behind him was Crook's cavalry, but across in front of him was friendly soil and food for his men and horses. The condition of the Tennessee at this time of the year made the crossing difficult. Although the river was at a low stage, the way across was strewn with boulders beyond which lay deep pools.[85] Horses and riders would scramble onto a boulder and then drop with a splash into the pool beyond, then repeat the performance a few yards ahead. "Every one of us got about six duckings" was the testimony of one old trooper who crossed that evening.[86]

Wheeler sat on his horse until the last rider had filed by and then he himself plunged into the river. As he sat there looking at the river and at the opposite shore he had no way of knowing that someday he would put through Congress legislation providing for a canal around these shoals, and that he also was destined to be master of those broad acres just across the river. Yet within a few years this would come to pass.[87]

It was midnight when he crossed. Already his men were busying themselves around the campfires, cooking, drying their clothes, and polishing pistols and sabers. Near by was a rambling, two-story house facing the river.

[85] Dubose, *Wheeler and the Army of Tennessee,* 213.

[86] Related by J. M. Smith of Augusta, Georgia, to the author, June 17, 1930.

[87] The Tennessee Valley Authority's "Wheeler Dam" is located almost precisely at the point of the river where Wheeler crossed.

Wheeler dispatched a member of his staff to ask permission of the owner for his men to camp in the vicinity. The staff officer was admitted by the master of the house, Colonel Richard Jones, reputed to be the third largest land owner in North Alabama.[88]

"General Wheeler presents his compliments," the officer is reported to have said, "and asks your permission for his men to camp here for the night."

"General Wheeler, did you say?" queried a young woman who had now joined her father. "I'd like to see him."

"Well, madam," responded the officer, "you won't see much when you do." [89]

Laughing, the officer returned to inform his commander that it was perfectly agreeable with the master for his men to camp there, and that a beautiful young woman had asked to see him.

On the morning after, the cavalry general was presented to Mrs. Daniella Sherrod, lately widowed daughter of Colonel Jones. Before Wheeler broke camp and moved on, a love affair between the two began. This was the first time he had ever seen his future wife, but she had seen him before; and now they recalled the incident. In 1858 Wheeler and three fellow cadets from the Military Academy had attended a theater in New York. During the performance the stage scenery caught fire and the four cadets sprang onto the stage to extinguish the flames. In the audience at the time were Mr. and Mrs. Benjamin Sherrod from Alabama, who were in New York on their wedding trip. They had witnessed the incident,

---

[88] James E. Saunders, *Early Settlers of Alabama* (New Orleans, 1899), 217.

[89] Related by Miss Annie Wheeler to the author, August 26, 1928. This is, Miss Wheeler states, her father's version of the incident.

and somehow the young bride had remembered the sprightly little cadet and his furious fire fighting.[90]

[90] *Ibid.* Benjamin Sherrod was the grandson of Colonel Benjamin Sherrod, one of the wealthiest men in the early history of Alabama. See Saunders, *Early Settlers of Alabama*, 234.

Chapter VI

KNOXVILLE AND NORTH GEORGIA
(November, 1863–May, 1864)

WHEELER remained at his headquarters at the Jones home near Courtland for nearly two weeks; from October 9 to 20. During this time he appears to have been waiting for orders from General Bragg, trying to get his command in marching condition, and, one suspects, enjoying during his spare hours the comforts of the home and the company of Mrs. Sherrod. His correspondence during the period is filled with references to shoeing horses, collecting stragglers, accumulating supplies and ammunition, and securing reinforcements from the portion of his command left with the army in Chattanooga. But mostly it is concerned with the problem of what his next move should be.[1]

General Stephen D. Lee had come up with his cavalry command numbering some thirty-five hundred men from Joseph E. Johnston's department in Mississippi. Lee expected to join Wheeler's and Roddey's commands in the task of further harassing Rosecrans's communications in Middle Tennessee; and the general was rather insistent that they should get going. Wheeler, however, does not appear to have been so anxious. He should, he thought, wait for specific orders from Bragg, and, pending the

[1] For the correspondence between Lee, Wheeler, and Roddey, see *Official Records*, Ser. I, Vol. XXX, Pt. IV, 746–48.

arrival of such, keep the respective commands in camp.
To this Lee objected. Roddey was across the Tennessee,
he pointed out, and the rising waters were likely to cut
him off. Also, Sherman was moving slowly from Memphis
toward their positions near Muscle Shoals, and as Sherman moved, the chances for a surprise attack in Middle
Tennessee grew less likely of success.[2] But Wheeler remained firm in his stand, and finally on October 20 General Lee reported to Johnston that "up to the 19th in-
stant General Wheeler declined to cross the Tennessee
River with me, not deeming his command in condition
to do so and feeling it incumbent on him to await instructions from General Bragg." Wheeler's command,
he added, was "much demoralized by plunder" after the
retreat from Farmington. Officers and men had "behaved
unbecomingly" on the retreat, "thinking more of their
plunder than of fighting the enemy."[3]

As a matter of fact Wheeler had, on October 19, received instructions from Bragg which authorized him to
take his command to the region of Guntersville, Alabama, where further orders would be delivered.[4] When
he reached Guntersville he received orders to leave Roddey in North Alabama and to proceed with his own command to the region of Cleveland, Tennessee, on Bragg's
right wing, some twenty-five miles east of Chattanooga.
Wheeler himself was to report personally to headquarters "for conference and instructions";[5] a conference, as
later events were to show, concerning a proposed movement toward Knoxville.

[3] Lee to Joseph E. Johnston, October 20, 1863, *ibid.*, Vol. XXXI, Pt.
I, 25.

[4] Bragg to Wheeler, October 17, 1863, *ibid.*, Vol. XXX, Pt. IV, 763.
Delivered by messenger to Wheeler on October 19.

[5] *Id.* to *id.*, October 24, 1863, *ibid.*, Vol. XXXI, Pt. III, 586–87.

The commanders of both armies at Chattanooga were in a state of doubt and confusion at the time Wheeler returned late in October, and had been since the battle. On the Confederate side General Bragg was greatly perplexed as to what his next move should be, but most of his general officers were not at all hazy about one move he should make. He should resign the command of the army, they thought, and they so informed Richmond. Longstreet and Bragg had quarreled almost from the very first moment Longstreet arrived on the scene, and now several of Bragg's officers came to "Lee's war horse" and asked him to take up Bragg's deficiencies with President Davis. Longstreet felt that he was not in the President's confidence but agreed to take up the matter with the War Department.[6] Not content with this, the officers themselves signed a "round-robin" letter and sent it to President Davis,[7] a message which was soon followed by a personal protest from General Polk.[8] At these Bragg struck back. Polk was put under charges for failing to open battle on schedule on the twentieth, and Hindman was relieved under charges. On October 9, the same day on which Wheeler crossed the Tennessee during his retreat from Farmington, President Davis visited the army at Chickamauga to straighten out the troubles. Polk was sent to Mississippi to take Hardee's place there, the latter rejoining Bragg's army.[9] Daniel H. Hill was relieved

[6] A minor point of controversy between Longstreet and Bragg was Longstreet's criticism of the cavalry for "not riding in response to my calls" on September 20. Bragg, it is said, came to Wheeler's defense. See James Longstreet, *From Manassas to Appomattox* (Philadelphia, 1896), 453. See also, Eckenrode and Conrad, *James Longstreet*, 247. For Longstreet's letter to Secretary of War Seddon, see *Official Records*, Ser. I, Vol. XXX, Pt. IV, 705–706.

[7] October 4, 1863, *ibid.*, Pt. II, 65–66.

[8] October 6, 1863, *ibid.*, 67–68.

[9] It seems that Hardee and Wheeler were the only important officers

of his command and sent back to North Carolina. Buckner took a leave of absence. It was a house cleaning for nearly all except Bragg. He was left in command of the army and Wheeler continued as chief of cavalry.

Within Chattanooga among the Federals conditions in many respects were no better than among the Confederates on the mountain. Starving soldiers followed army wagons around hoping to pick up a few grains of corn. Feed troughs had to be guarded to keep men from snatching the grain allotted to the horses. General Crittenden was relieved from duty along with General McCook, both men being directed to appear before a court of inquiry. Charges were brought against General Rosecrans which sound strangely like those directed against Bragg. The Federal commander, Charles A. Dana thought, "seems to be insensible to the impending danger, and dawdles with trifles in a manner which can scarcely be imagined . . . all this precious time is lost because our dazed and mazy commander cannot perceive the catastrophe that is close upon us, nor fix his mind upon the means of preventing it. I never saw anything which seemed so lamentable and hopeless." [10] On October 18 General Grant was put in command of the newly created Military Division of the Mississippi, and one of his first official acts was to relieve Rosecrans by telegraph and give the command to Thomas.[11]

The personal disaffection which existed among Con-

---

in the Army of Tennessee who were not severe in their criticism of Bragg. Hardee, however, had expressed an earlier conviction that Bragg did not possess the confidence of the army. See Hay, "Braxton Bragg and the Southern Confederacy," in *loc. cit.*, 294–308. Wheeler, it appears, was very much in Bragg's favor.

[10] Quoted in J. T. C. Fuller, *The Generalship of Ulysses S. Grant* (New York, 1929), 166.

[11] *Ibid.*, 162–63.

federate officers was perhaps not the most important problem facing the army, however. It appears that General Bragg was in the throes of indecision as to what steps he should take to follow up the victory of Chickamauga. About all he had done since the battle was to plant his army on the heights south of the city, send Wheeler on his raid, throw a few random shells into the city from Lookout, and post a detachment of sharpshooters; all of which proved ineffectual. Wheeler's raid, although it increased the discomfort of the besieged Federals, did little more than demonstrate what might have been accomplished if Bragg had taken Longstreet's advice and moved in force against the Federal communications. The random shells bothered the Federals not at all, and the sharpshooters were less than a mild irritant.[12]

On the Federal side, however, steps were being taken to remedy their bad plight. On September 24 General Joseph Hooker with some twenty thousand men was sent from the Army of the Potomac, arriving at Bridgeport, about thirty miles southwest of Chattanooga, on October 1. Immediately Grant set about the task of opening a line for Hooker. At 3 A.M. on the morning of October 27, General William F. Smith with about fifteen hundred men loaded in small boats floated past the Confederate pickets on Point Lookout, effected a lodgment on the left bank of the river a few miles below the city, drove in the Confederate pickets, and established himself in the hills.[13] That night Hooker made contact with Smith and the next day was well on his way to Chattanooga. On the night of the twenty-eighth Longstreet attacked Hooker but was repulsed.[14] Having thus quickly

---

12 Seitz, *Braxton Bragg*, 395.

13 Fuller, *Generalship of Ulysses S. Grant*, 166–67.

14 Longstreet in *Manassas to Appomattox*, 476, attributes his defeat to a confusion of orders among his subordinates.

secured a workable line of supply, Grant next turned his
attention to bringing up Sherman from Memphis. Sending a messenger in a small boat down the Tennessee
to Sherman at Iuka, Mississippi, Grant ordered him to
abandon his railroad building activities and hurry to
Chattanooga. Sherman complied, meeting no opposition
except from General Lee's cavalry near Muscle Shoals.
On November 13 he reached Bridgeport and was in contact with Grant.[15]

With the Federals thus reinforcing, Bragg with Longstreet's advice, consent, and assistance, arrived at the
novel decision of dividing his force and sending Longstreet's corps to attack and capture Knoxville.[16] The plan
as conceived involved a hasty campaign against General
Ambrose Burnside at Knoxville and a return before
Sherman reached Chattanooga—a plan which military
experts have characterized as nothing less than pure
folly. But "the decision was made, the madness was completed." [17] By November 4 Longstreet was ready to go.
With him he took McLaws's and Hood's divisions (the
latter commanded by Brigadier General Micah Jenkins),
Colonel E. Porter Alexander's and Major A. Leydon's
artillery, and four brigades of Wheeler's cavalry—two
under William T. Martin and two under General Frank
C. Armstrong, formerly with Forrest.[18]

The infantry and artillery were to move by rail to
Sweetwater, Tennessee, and from this point, after being
joined by the cavalry under Wheeler, the expedition was
to move against Burnside at Knoxville. The Confederate

[15] B. H. Liddell Hart, *Sherman: Soldier, Realist, Statesman* (New
York, 1929), 212.

[16] Eckenrode and Conrad, in *James Longstreet,* 249, take the position
that Longstreet knew the movement was unwise, but encouraged it
because he "longed to get away—anywhere, if only away."

[17] *Ibid.,* 251.   [18] Longstreet, *Manassas to Appomattox,* 482.

force, including the cavalry, numbered near twenty thousand, while the Federals numbered possibly twelve thousand with an additional two thousand raw recruits from East Tennessee.[19] As Longstreet's army gathered, however, it must have been evident to the most uncritical that any hopes for a lightning stroke at Knoxville and an early return to the main army had slight chances for realization. Transportation difficulties delayed the arrival of the last of the Confederate troops at Sweetwater until November 12, the day before Sherman established contact with Grant at Bridgeport. There were supplies and military stores at Sweetwater, but General Stevenson, in command of the post, declined to turn these over to Longstreet on the grounds that he was under orders to send everything directly to Bragg. As Longstreet expressed it: "Thus we found ourselves in a strange country, not as much as a day's rations on hand, with hardly enough land transportation for ordinary camp equipage, the enemy in front to be captured, and our friends in rear putting in their paper bullets."[20] The "paper bullets," of course, had reference to Bragg's messages urging a vigorous and rapid movement, messages which Longstreet considered a deliberate attempt on Bragg's part to build up a "paper case" against him. The two officers, now that they were separated, renewed their feud and vigorously bombarded each other from afar.[21]

Wheeler reached Sweetwater on the night of November 11, and on the following morning Longstreet issued his marching orders. Wheeler was to leave sufficient cavalry to picket the river from Kingston to Loudon, and

---

[19] Eckenrode and Conrad, *James Longstreet*, 252, gives the numbers as "something more than 15,000" for Longstreet and 25,000 for Burnside.
[20] Longstreet, *Manassas to Appomattox*, 486.
[21] See *Official Records*, Ser. I, Vol. XXXI, Pt. III, 679–81, 686–87.

with the balance of his command was to swing south of Knoxville some twenty miles and disperse the Federal garrison at Maryville. Generals McLaws and Jenkins were to move directly across the Tennessee and proceed toward Knoxville.[22]

At dark on November 13 Wheeler with Martin and Armstrong moved out on a night march on Maryville. On finding that the garrison was composed of only one brigade he pushed rapidly to the attack. Riding ahead with his escort and a squadron of George Dibrell's men Wheeler unexpectedly rode into the midst of the enemy's outposts. Immediately Dibrell's brigade closed up from the rear, and the outpost scattered. Soon Colonel John T. Morgan's brigade was engaged with the main force of the Federals, quickly forcing them to retreat.[23]

With the coming of dawn Wheeler recrossed Little River and moved to carry out the balance of his orders which were to seize and hold the heights overlooking Knoxville on the southeast; or, if that were not possible, to take actual possession of the approaches to the city, to create a diversion in that region so that the infantry and artillery might approach more easily to an attack on the north and west. As it developed, Wheeler was not able to get possession of the southeastern approaches. As he marched from the direction of Maryville he had encountered three brigades of Federals who fell back behind Stock Creek, destroyed the bridge, and took a strong position on an elevation overlooking the city. Wheeler dismounted half of his command, crossed the swollen creek under cover of fire from his artillery, and struck

[22] General Orders, No. ?, November 12, 1863, *ibid.*, 687. See also, Longstreet, *Manassas to Appomattox*, 487.

[23] Wheeler's Report, December 31, 1863, in *Official Records*, Ser. I, Vol. XXXI, Pt. I, 540.

the left wing of the Federal line. While he was thus engaged, a detail of his men repaired the bridge allowing
Armstrong and the artillery to cross and attack the enemy positions. The Federals retreated, crossed the Holston at the city limits, and withdrew their pontoon
bridge.[24]

After Wheeler had retired from the attack he received
a message from Longstreet which read: "Unless you are
doing better service by moving along the enemy's flank
than you could do here, I would rather you should join
us and co-operate. I presume that you could unite with
us by crossing the Holston." [25] This left the move up to
Wheeler's judgment, and he later reported: "As there
was little prospect of accomplishing any further good in
that vicinity, I determined to march without delay to
join the main body of the command." [26] Finding it necessary to move fifteen miles down the Holston before he
could find a ford, it was November 17 before he joined
Longstreet.[27]

Longstreet had crossed the Tennessee River at Huff's
Ferry on November 13 and 14, at the same time that
Wheeler was striking at Maryville. With Longstreet's
approach the Federals fell back within their fortifications, leaving heavy skirmish lines in their front,[28] and
at this point Longstreet's "blitzkrieg" degenerated into
a siege. The Confederates, including the cavalry, began
to dig themselves in as though the campaign were

---

24 *Ibid.*, 541–42.

25 Longstreet to Wheeler, November 14, 1863, *ibid.*, Pt. III, 696.

26 Wheeler's Report, *ibid.*, Pt. I, 542.   27 *Ibid.*

28 The city was protected by a series of earthwork forts surrounded
by ditches and wire entanglements. Beyond the entanglements were rifle
pits. Each part was connected with the other by a series of protected
roads and trenches. See Orlando M. Poe, "The Defense of Knoxville," in
Battles and Leaders, III, 735–51.

planned to last all winter. On November 22 McLaws
thought he was ready for an attack and was ordered to
make it that night. In preparation for it Wheeler was
instructed to advance his skirmishers and prepare his
artillery; but the attack did not occur. McLaws said his
officers preferred a daylight attack.[29]

On the twenty-first Longstreet had written Wheeler
that Colonel H. B. Lyon, commanding a detachment of
Confederate cavalry near Kingston, had sent in the information that two regiments of Federal cavalry were
near by. Could not Wheeler, Longstreet asked, run over
to Kingston and capture them?[30] Wheeler, busy in-
trenching his command and preparing to assist McLaws
in his attack, let the matter rest until the next afternoon when Longstreet again called it to his attention as
a matter of great importance. Bragg had telegraphed, he
said, that reinforcements were being sent to supplement
the Confederate forces at Knoxville, and since Kingston
would be an important base for the troops, it must be
captured and held. Therefore Wheeler should "try and
reach Kingston before day on the 24th, drive in the pickets there, and you will then ascertain whether the enemy
has been re-enforced there. If he has not, capture or disperse the force that is there."[31]

Acting on Longstreet's instructions, Wheeler ordered
Martin and Armstrong to get their commands in marching order with two days' supply of cooked rations.[32] Leaving the command to follow, Wheeler rode with his escort
on the night of November 22 to the region of Kingston

[29] General Lafayette McLaws was later relieved under charges by
Longstreet and was convicted by a court-martial on one charge. The
verdict was disapproved at Richmond and McLaws was restored to his
command. See *Official Records*, Ser. I, Vol. XXXI, Pt. I, 471–506.

[30] Longstreet to Wheeler, November 21, 1863, *ibid.*, Pt. III, 733.

[31] *Id.* to *id.*, November 22, 1863, 6 P.M., *ibid.*, 736–37.   [32] *Ibid.*, 736.

and learned that the enemy had been reinforced by infantry. Near three o'clock in the morning his command
arrived, sleepy, tired, and hungry. Many of the men,
Wheeler reported, had been left at various points along
the road, being unable because of their exhaustion to
keep up.[33] After an hour's rest the command was put
in motion with the hope that the enemy might be surprised before daybreak. They were not caught unprepared, however, and Wheeler reported that he encountered a strong line of infantry, artillery, and cavalry, all
in position. After preliminary skirmishing had revealed
the strength of the enemy Wheeler retired from the
field.[34] He had failed to take and hold the base for the
expected reinforcements from Bragg, but the troops were
never sent,[35] and for very good reasons.

The affair at Kingston concluded Wheeler's services
with Longstreet. On the twenty-fourth he received orders
to rejoin Bragg,[36] and leaving Martin in command of the
cavalry,[37] he and his escort rode over the mountains to
North Georgia. Arriving early in the afternoon of No-

[33] Wheeler's Report, December 31, 1863, *ibid.*, Pt. I, 543.

[34] *Ibid.*, 544. Longstreet reported later that Wheeler was mistaken;
that the garrison had not been reinforced. *Ibid.*

[35] On November 25 Bushrod Johnson's division arrived, and Cleburne's division was ready to take the cars from North Georgia, when
Sherman's movement from Chattanooga caused Bragg to recall this division. See Seitz, *Braxton Bragg*, 395.

[36] Bragg to Wheeler, November 24, 1863, in *Official Records*, Ser. I,
Vol. XXXI, Pt. I, 544.

[37] Martin remained with Longstreet until February 25, 1864, when he
rejoined the Army of Tennessee in North Georgia. Eckenrode and Conrad, *James Longstreet*, 269, states that "on December 9, . . . he parted
company with Wheeler's cavalry, which made its way to Bragg in
Georgia." Longstreet says, however, in *Manassas to Appomattox*, 512,
that he recalled Martin on December 10. See Longstreet to Martin,
February 25, 1864, in *Official Records*, Ser. I, Vol. XXXII, Pt. II, 803,
for Longstreet's order for Martin's return to Georgia.

vember 25, he found the Army of Tennessee broken and almost overcome by disaster. On November 23, Wheeler discovered, Grant had thrust Thomas at the Confederates on Missionary Ridge and had occupied the picket lines on Orchard Knob.[38] That night Sherman had ferried the Tennessee at Brown's Ferry and had made contact with Thomas. On the next day Hooker had pushed two divisions through the mists up Lookout Mountain and had driven back the Confederates from that vantage point.[39] On the morning of the twenty-fifth while Wheeler was still riding toward his own lines, Hooker advanced his corps and engaged Stewart, who occupied the Confederate left wing, driving him back. Early in the afternoon, with Hooker fully engaged on the left, Sherman struck Cleburne on the right and Cleburne held. With the right and left engaged, Grant threw eleven brigades of Thomas's army at the Confederate center. In a magnificent charge these troops swept up Missionary Ridge and broke the Confederate lines, forcing them back in precipitous retreat.[40]

It was shortly before the Confederate center gave way that Wheeler arrived.[41] By the time he found his scattered cavalry regiments the day had ended; but not the retreat. On November 26 the Federals pursued, forcing Bragg's army back to Ringgold and then beyond. At Ringgold, however, Cleburne's division was faced about and ordered to halt the pursuit. Wheeler's small cavalry

[38] Fuller, *Generalship of Ulysses S. Grant*, 172.

[39] Liddell Hart, *Sherman*, 215.

[40] For a summary of the campaign, see Ulysses S. Grant, "Chattanooga," in *Battles and Leaders*, III, 679–711. See also, Thomas R. Hay, "The Battle of Chattanooga," in *Georgia Historical Quarterly*, VIII (1924), 121–41.

[41] Wheeler reported the time of his arrival at about 1 P.M. on November 25. Wheeler to Longstreet, November 26, 1863, in *Official Records*, Ser. I, Vol. XXXI, Pt. III, 760.

force, hastily collected, hugged the flanks.[42] On the morning of the twenty-seventh Hooker with two divisions attempted to dislodge Cleburne. Failing in this, he sent two brigades to drive Wheeler's forces from the flanks. There was a sharp engagement in which Wheeler was wounded in the foot; but this movement also failed, and with the failure Grant temporarily abandoned the pursuit.[43]

With his army in a safe position, temporarily at least, Bragg turned his attention to the matter of Longstreet's siege of Knoxville. One third of the Army of Tennessee was engaged there with no apparent results, and those troops were sorely needed in Georgia. On November 26 Wheeler wired Longstreet: "General Bragg desires me to say he wishes you to fall back with your command upon Dalton if possible. If you find that impracticable, he thinks you will have to fall back toward Virginia. At all events he desires that you order all the cavalry to Dalton." [44] Three days later Wheeler again wired his former commander, this time to say that he would move to the Hiwassee to assist in the movement of the troops.[45]

Longstreet, however, on the day this last dispatch was sent, wrote General Robert Ransom that he did not think it practicable to attempt to rejoin Bragg.[46] On December 2 he confirmed this decision in a letter to Bragg. He was grieved, he said, to know that the army had been forced to fall back to Dalton, but he hoped everything would work out all right and that Bragg would be able to prevent Grant from succoring Burn-

[42] Present at the time were three brigades of Wharton's and John H. Kelly's divisions. See *ibid.*, 887.
[43] Dodson, *Campaigns of Wheeler,* 155.
[44] See *Official Records,* Ser. I, Vol. XXXI, Pt. III, 760.
[45] November 29, 1863, *ibid.*, 762.
[46] Longstreet to Robert Ransom, November 29, 1863, *ibid.*, 758.

side. He could not spare the cavalry, he continued, until he had changed his base from Loudon to some point nearer Virginia toward which he would retire.[47]

This letter arrived shortly after two important events had transpired, each of them having direct bearing on Longstreet's campaign. On November 30 Sherman left with his corps to move to Burnside's relief; [48] and on December 2 General Bragg relinquished command of the Army of Tennessee, General Hardee being named temporary commander.[49] Sherman's move meant, of course, that Longstreet, having failed already to dislodge a smaller force, would likely be compelled to abandon the siege in the face of a greatly augmented one. It also meant that the door to Georgia definitely was closed to him even had he desired to rejoin the Army of Tennessee. The fact that Bragg was out and Hardee (shortly to be succeeded by Joseph E. Johnston) in meant a probable reorganization of the army and the formulation of a new plan of campaign. At any event Knoxville remained in Federal hands.[50]

There was no campaigning for the Army of Tennessee during December, 1863, and January, 1864, but this in no wise indicates that activity had ceased. The army changed commanders and began to prepare for the inevitable fighting which would come in the spring. Just what the nature of this fighting would be and what proportions the spring campaign would assume was a matter of conjecture and debate among the higher-ups at Richmond and the officers in the field.

[47] *Id.* to Bragg, December 2, 1863, *ibid.,* 777.

[48] Liddell Hart, *Sherman,* 217.

[49] See General Orders, No. 214, in *Official Records,* Ser. I, Vol. XXXI, Pt. III, 775–76.

[50] Eckenrode and Conrad, *James Longstreet,* 269. Longstreet withdrew to winter quarters, eventually joining General Lee in April, 1864.

General Hardee's tenure of office was, at his own request, brief. He did little more than assume command, write an encouraging address to the soldiers, and await Johnston's appointment.[51] He did warn Richmond that the army was in no condition for any sort of offensive, nor would it be, in his opinion, until adequate reinforcements had been secured.[52] Richmond, however, overlooked this bit of advice, for within a short time the administration was urging upon Johnston the desirability of his taking the offensive.

On December 27, 1863, General Johnston quietly assumed command. On his arrival at Dalton he found a letter from Secretary James A. Seddon which sought to impress upon the new commander the necessity of restoring discipline in the ranks and of improving the morale of the discouraged officers. He was also reminded that Richmond expected him to take the offensive.[53] This offensive, Richmond thought, should be a movement into East Tennessee to join Longstreet and thus separate the two Federal armies, one at Chattanooga and one at Knoxville. Then the Confederates could move into Middle Tennessee. Johnston objected to this, insisting that reinforcements should be sent to him so that they could be organized before any campaign should begin.[54]

While plans were being thus debated with Richmond, Johnston began the task of rebuilding the army. There

---

[51] See *Official Records*, Ser. I, Vol. XXXI, Pt. III, 776.

[52] Hardee to Adjutant General Cooper, December 17, 1863, *ibid.*, 839–40. Hardee's returns show the strength of the Army of Tennessee on December 26 to be 36,017, exclusive of cavalry. Wheeler's cavalry at the time numbered about 5,000—3,500 with Longstreet and 1,500 at Dalton.

[53] Robert M. Hughes, *General Johnston* (New York, 1893), 214.

[54] *Ibid.*, 215.

was an alarming deficiency in every phase of his command, in infantry, small arms, artillery, supplies, cavalry. The infantry was described as "dispirited and destitute . . . barefoot and half naked"; the cavalry poorly mounted and equally destitute; and the artillery "incapable of movement for the same causes." [55] One of the first steps in this rebuilding program was a furlough order on December 22, permitting large numbers of men and officers to go to their homes for a visit.[56] Johnston reorganized his army into two corps under Hardee and Hood with Wheeler retained as commander of the cavalry.[57] Strict orders were issued concerning breaches of discipline and depredations. Warm clothing and shoes were secured and deficiencies in munitions gradually eliminated. "The good effects of these efforts toward increasing the comfort and discipline of the troops were soon apparent; their spirits returned, [and] laggards rejoined their commands." [58]

The cavalry under Wheeler came in for its share in the reorganization and refitting, a procedure most sorely needed. The cavalry was in a deplorable state. Shortly before he returned from East Tennessee, Martin reported on the condition of his troops, a description which speaks for itself. "A very large proportion of my men, and even officers," he wrote, "are ragged and barefooted, without blankets or overcoats. Owing to the want of attention to the duties of his office, the quartermaster of General Wheeler's corps left my command in great need of clothing. We have drawn none for fall or winter.

---

[55] *Ibid.,* 217.

[56] General Orders, No. 227, December 22, 1863, in *Official Records,* Ser. I, Vol. XXXI, Pt. III, 855.

[57] Later when Polk joined Johnston's army the third corps which Johnston desired was added.

[58] Hughes, *General Johnston,* 218.

A very large number of my horses are unshod. The men have received no pay for six months." [59] Not only this, but the straggling and marauding propensities of the men apparently had lowered the morale of the entire command, a situation which seems to have grown worse after such defeats as those at Dover, Shelbyville, Farmington, and Kingston.[60]

These two factors of poor equipment and the tendency toward depredations upon enemy and friend alike were, of course, not confined wholly to Wheeler's command, but were common to all the Confederate cavalry units to a greater or lesser degree. In Wheeler's case, however, there appears another factor which is difficult to account for except in terms of his own personality and the way in which he apparently was regarded by his officers and men. There is no evidence that anyone ever doubted his personal bravery, his activity, his faithfulness, or his devotion to the cause; but there seems to have been lacking in him the ability to inspire his men, and that trait was particularly important to a man commanding these "ragged and reckless" farmer-cavalrymen. It should be remembered that these men were not trained soldiers with a military point of view; they were citizen soldiers with a frontier outlook. They were excellent fighters, but poor soldiers. Tactics and orders meant little to them; they fought well if they were inspired by superb leadership, otherwise they were apt to straggle. Wheeler, it appears, talked the language of West Point to men whose vocabularies were limited to simpler terms. As a result there seems to have been more than a little mutual misunderstanding between Wheeler and his officers and

[59] Martin's Report, January 8, 1864, in *Official Records*, Ser. I, Vol. XXXI, Pt. I, 549.

[60] See Stephen D. Lee to Johnston, October 20, 1863, *ibid.*, 25.

men. There was little overt hostility, but under the surface there probably was a feeling that perhaps Wheeler could not manage men if orders and military etiquette failed him.[6] Too, the fact that Wheeler had always stood high in the regard of General Bragg did not help him any in the estimation of the army.

The lull in fighting during January and February, 1864, gave Wheeler an opportunity to correct some of these deficiencies, and apparently he did a very thorough job of it. There were roll calls, drills, officers' schools, reviews, and field tactics. No one escaped the scrutiny of the commander. One young officer writing home about his experiences in the cavalry described Wheeler's activities. "Last Thursday the officers of our regiment went before the examining board, composed of Generals Kelly and Humes. Some were subjected to a very slight examination, while others passed through a severe ordeal. Captain —— and myself were examined orally and had only some two dozen questions put to us each. Others stood written examinations of several hours length. . . . This [Sunday] morning, the great day for inspection and review, we had a grand review of our brigade. Generals Wheeler, Kelly, Humes and Allen, with their gay, dashing staff, rode before us.[62] Unfortunately, about half the

---

[61] Reporting to Beauregard in January, 1865, Colonel Roman said of Wheeler: "No one admires General Wheeler more than I do. He is a modest, conscientious, industrious officer. He takes a fatherly interest in his command. His activity is proverbial, and is equalled only by his gallantry. But he is wanting in firmness. His mind and his will are not in proper relation to one another. He is too gentle, too lenient; and we know how easily leniency can be made to degenerate into weakness. General Wheeler's men like him, but do not appear to be proud of him. They know he will always fight well, but seem to feel that he cannot make them fight as well." Beauregard Papers.

[62] Brigadier Generals Kelly, William C. Y. Humes, and William W. Allen. At this time Wheeler's command consisted of four divisions of

different regiments were off on duty, rendering the display less imposing. . . . We were all aroused about three o'clock this morning by an alarm on the picket line. Judging by the time of the alarm, I concluded we were about to have a bloody day, but it turned out a fake and we returned to camp fully satisfied." [63]

A few days later this same officer made the observation that "General Wheeler is either becoming vain or likes his cavalry so well that he keeps it all the time under his eye. Our discipline is the most rigid that I have ever known volunteers to be subjected to. Some of it has good effect, some bad. The routine of camp and field duty is so great that we can scarcely find time to eat half rations." [64] Small incidents and diversions were welcomed by the troops if they interrupted the tedium. And nothing probably provoked more amusement than the appearance one morning of Dr. Mary E. Walker who claimed to be an assistant surgeon in the Union army. She "rode with sang-froid in her bloomer costume, with marks of military rank" to Wheeler's picket line. Under a flag of truce she came to headquarters where she explained that she had ridden over to bring a letter from a Confederate prisoner. But the letter was never delivered, and the nattily attired lady was sent to Richmond.[65]

Fighting in North Georgia was desultory. The active cavalry fighting was in North Mississippi where Forrest in a series of magnificent maneuvers and battles seriously interrupted Grant's scheme for capturing Atlanta.

two brigades each. Division commanders were Major General Wharton and Brigadier Generals Martin, Armstrong, and Kelly. General Humes was, during the Atlanta campaign, promoted to the command of a division. See *Official Records,* Ser. I, Vol. XXXI, Pt. III, 806–807.

[63] Quoted in Dubose, *Wheeler and the Army of Tennessee,* 273–74.
[64] *Ibid.,* 274.   [65] *Ibid.,* 276.

Grant's plans involved a double movement. Sherman with a force of twenty thousand was to march out from Vicksburg, to which he had been sent after the battle of Chattanooga, and move across Mississippi to Meridian where he would be joined by General William Sooy Smith from Memphis with seven thousand picked cavalry. Then from Meridian the united force would move across central Alabama, destroy the Confederate arsenal at Selma, and strike Atlanta from the south. While this movement was in progress, Thomas was to move out of Chattanooga and crush Johnston at Dalton.[66]

Both movements failed, however. Sherman moved from Vicksburg on February 3 and proceeded without opposition toward Meridian. Smith moved on the eleventh from Memphis through Holly Springs, New Albany, and Tupelo. On February 22 he encountered Forrest at Okolona, Mississippi, and was disastrously defeated.[67] Thus Sherman was unable to carry out the intended strategy. The same day on which Forrest defeated Smith, Thomas carried out a reconnaissance in force on Dalton. Moving down the Western and Atlantic railroad, Major General John M. Palmer with the first division of the Fourteenth Army Corps and Brigadier General Charles Cruft with the first division of the Fourth Army Corps advanced on Dalton. At Tunnel Hill they encountered Wheeler's outposts, which offered spirited resistance and then fell back on the infantry. The Federal thrust was turned back and the Atlanta campaign was delayed until May.[68]

But this was not the only result of Thomas's reconnais-

---

[66] Fuller, *Generalship of Ulysses S. Grant,* 179–81.

[67] See Lytle, *Bedford Forrest,* Chap. XVI.

[68] See Charles Cruft's Report, March 2, 1864, in *Official Records,* Ser. I, Vol. XXXII, Pt. I, 422.

sance in force, for Wheeler's regiment of Texas Rangers profited greatly. Soon after the fight they appeared in resplendent new uniforms. No one knew where they got them or how, but the whole army soon learned of them and laughed. The new uniform consisted of frock-tailed morning coats and high stiff collars. Evidently the Rangers had appropriated a shipment of these articles destined for some haberdasher's shop in Georgia, but the Southern gentlemen for whom they were intended never saw them—that is, unless these gentlemen were fighting with Joe Johnston at Dalton.[69]

[69] Dodson, *Campaigns of Wheeler*, 171–72.

Chapter VII

THE ATLANTA CAMPAIGN
(April–August, 1864)

THE failure of Thomas's February reconnaissance in force and the defeat of Smith by Forrest halted temporarily the Federal plans for taking Atlanta. Other events also intervened to slow up the process, chief of which was the change in Federal commanders. Early in March, 1864, Lincoln called Grant to the White House and made him lieutenant general in command of all Federal armies. Grant immediately divided the South into three departments and put a commander over each. He gave to General Nathaniel P. Banks the Southwest, including Texas. The middle section comprising Georgia, Alabama, Tennessee, and Mississippi he gave to Sherman. The third part, in Virginia, he reserved for himself. As soon as the season opened, it was planned, all the Union armies would assume the offensive by "concentric lines" on the common enemy, and then finish the job in a single campaign. The main objectives were Lee's army behind the Rapidan and Joseph E. Johnston's army at Dalton.[1]

Sherman took up his headquarters at Chattanooga on April 28 preparatory to the drive against Atlanta. On May 5 the campaign began with the movement of Sher-

[1] William T. Sherman, "The Grand Strategy of the Last Year of the War," in *Battles and Leaders*, IV, 247.

man's forces in three armies, one under Thomas, one under James B. McPherson, and the third under John M. Schofield with a total strength of 98,797.[2]

The army against which Sherman moved was a better one than that which had evacuated Missionary Ridge in the fall. The drilling and maneuvering through which Wheeler put his men was an example of what was going on throughout Johnston's army.[3] Desertion had been reduced through a sensible policy of granting furloughs. Major breaches of discipline were dealt with harshly, even to the point of shooting men at the foot of their graves, while minor offenses were dealt with in a less serious manner.[4] Nor were sports neglected. There were "gander pullings" and snowball fights and, what was almost capable of being classified a sport, revival meetings.[5] It was all a continuation of his systematic scheme to improve the discipline and morale of the army. Johnston's forces were divided also into three corps, Hood's, Hardee's, and Polk's Army of the Mississippi—total strength, including Wheeler's cavalry, approximately 63,408 men and 189 pieces of artillery.[6]

[2] William T. Sherman, *Memoirs of General W. T. Sherman Written By Himself* (New York, 1891), II, 23–24.

[3] Johnston, *Narrative, passim.*

[4] Henry, *Story of the Confederacy*, 378.   [5] *Ibid.*, 379.

[6] On April 30, 1864, General Johnston reported his strength as present for duty as 49,911. Wheeler's cavalry strength is given as 7,327, but at least half this number were absent for one reason or another. On June 10, after Polk's Army of the Mississippi had joined Johnston's army, the strength is reported as 63,408, which includes 12,328 cavalry. Polk's cavalry numbering 4,628 under Brigadier General William H. Jackson swelled Johnston's cavalry strength to the above figure. The organization of Wheeler's corps during the Atlanta campaign was as follows: William T. Martin's division composed of William W. Allen's and Alfred Iverson's brigades; John H. Kelly's division composed of Robert H. Anderson's, George G. Dibrell's, and Moses W. Hannon's brigades; William Y. C. Humes's division composed of Henry M. Ashby's,

On May 3 Grant crossed the Rapidan, putting his army between Fredericksburg and Lee's army of northern Virginia. Two days later he attacked Lee and fought the opening battle of the last campaign against Richmond. On the same day, as though he had heard Grant's guns bark in the Wilderness, Sherman deployed his men in front of Tunnel Hill, Georgia. The united movement calculated to crush the Confederacy had begun.[7]

Wheeler received the initial impact of Sherman's onslaught at Tunnel Hill. For several days before the Federal advance had begun, Wheeler with the brigades of J. Warren Grigsby, Moses W. Hannon, William Y. C. Humes, and William W. Allen had been picketing the territory in the front of his own army from Ship's Gap on the left (east) to the Connesauga River on the right.[8] In addition to desultory skirmishing with the enemy, Wheeler's troops had busied themselves felling trees and otherwise obstructing the roads over which the Union army would move. On May 6 the Federals came up in force near Tunnel Hill and at daylight on the morning of the seventh advanced on Wheeler's breastworks. Wheeler brought up his artillery and for four hours he held against vastly superior forces until forced to fall back on the infantry.[9]

Sherman, now in possession of Tunnel Hill, rode upon a slight elevation and surveyed the situation, and what

Thomas Harrison's, and John S. Williams's brigades; William H. Jackson's division composed of Frank C. Armstrong's, Lawrence S. Ross's, and Samuel W. Ferguson's brigades reporting directly to Polk. See *Official Records,* Ser. I, Vol. XXXVIII, Pt. III, 665, 676–77.

[7] Fuller, *Generalship of Ulysses S. Grant,* 229–33; Liddell Hart, *Sherman,* 243.

[8] The other regiments were at Dalton, Calhoun, Resaca, and Tilton, and in the various mountain gaps around Dalton.

[9] Wheeler's Report, June 1, 1864, in *Official Records,* Ser. I, Vol. XXXVIII, Pt. III, 944.

he saw was not very encouraging for a frontal assault. Before him was Dalton, and around the town every hill was bristling with artillery. The connecting lines of infantry lay behind well-constructed breastworks and rifle pits. Joe Johnston was ready, but Sherman did not choose to fight. Instead he decided upon a flanking movement with Thomas and Schofield holding before Tunnel Hill while McPherson with some thirty thousand men was sent southward to the east of Rocky Face.[10] At Dug's Gap, four miles southeast of Dalton, or at Snake Creek Gap, ten miles farther south, McPherson might be able to force a passage and move toward the Confederate rear at Resaca, thus catching Johnston in a trap.[11]

The strategy worked. Although, as will be seen shortly, Dug's Gap was defended by a portion of Wheeler's cavalry, Snake Creek Gap was not fortified, and through this opening McPherson was able to threaten Resaca. With a little more boldness he might have put an end to the Atlanta campaign.[12]

Nothing reveals the unfolding of Sherman's scheme better than a study of Wheeler's movements from May 7 to 15. It was May 7 when Wheeler's dismounted men received Sherman at Tunnel Hill. On the next day Wheeler, apparently seeing the possibility of a flanking movement, divided his command, sending Grigsby's brigade of Kentuckians to strengthen Dug's Gap on the Confederate left, while he and the balance moved to the right on the Cleveland road. Near Varnell's Station

---

[10] Sherman, *Memoirs*, II, 32. [11] *Ibid.*, 33.

[12] See Hughes, *General Johnston*, 230. A recent excellent, critical account of the Atlanta campaign is Alfred H. Burne, *Lee, Grant and Sherman* (New York, 1939). Regarding the Snake Creek Gap incident Colonel Burne says (p. 81): "Johnston's conduct of the operations had been flawless—if we except the failure to hold Snake Creek Gap, about which there is some dispute."

he was joined by Kelly who had moved with his division from Resaca, and there on May 9 he encountered a portion of Sherman's cavalry under McCook. Sherman had sent this force to create a diversion on his left. It moved boldly to the attack and was as gallantly received. Dibrell's brigade and a part of Allen's brigade were dismounted to receive the Federals, but instead of awaiting their attack the dismounted Confederates charged. Near by the Eighth Confederate and the Eighth Texas regiments, still mounted, likewise charged. The enemy broke in confusion leaving behind about a hundred prisoners, including Colonel Oscar H. LaGrange, who commanded McCook's second brigade.[13] To Wheeler the captured colonel vented his disappointment. " 'If my men had fought as well as yours,' " he is reported to have said, " 'I would have got the brigadier's commission promised to me this morning by General Sherman if I succeeded.' " [14]

This fight at Varnell's Station was of brief duration and, of course, in no way interfered with Sherman's plans; but it was important to Wheeler in that it was a demonstration of the renascent morale of his command. Such a fight as this would hardly have been possible during his Middle Tennessee raid shortly after Chickamauga, or at Knoxville. Wheeler's cavalry had almost disintegrated at the time Johnston took command of the Army of Tennessee. Now it appears to have been revivified; and the satisfaction in the army, it is not difficult to imagine, was very great. "General Wheeler fought the Yankee cavalry for three hours this morning," General Cleburne's adjutant wrote, "drove them two miles;

[13] Wheeler's Report, June 1, 1864, in *Official Records*, Ser. I, Vol. XXXVIII, Pt. III, 944.

[14] Dubose, *Wheeler and the Army of Tennessee*, 286.

captured 200 prisoners, horse equipment, &c." [15] General
Mackall added his appreciation. "Let me congratulate
you on your splendid success till the general can speak
his thanks," he wrote.[16] In fact Wheeler was so pleased
and so confident in the renewed morale of his men that
he asked for permission to ride around the enemy's rear
as he had done at Stone's River, but this was refused him
on the grounds that "to make the entire circuit of the
army would take too much time." [17]

In the meantime, the detachment of Grigsby's men
sent to Dug's Gap had gallantly met the enemy. On the
morning of May 8 scouts of the Ninth Kentucky regiment of Grigsby's brigade discovered the southward
march of McPherson screened by Hooker's corps.
Hooker would seize Dug's Gap, Sherman planned, and
then push forward sufficiently to protect McPherson's
flank. While Hooker's possession of Dug's Gap would
threaten Dalton, McPherson would move through Snake
Creek Gap and gain the railroad in Johnston's rear at
Resaca. These were the plans, but they were not carried
to completion. On the afternoon of the eighth General
John W. Geary's division of Hooker's corps attempted to
force a passage through Dug's Gap but was held by Grigsby's men. So important was the fight that Generals Hardee and Cleburne with their staffs rode to the scene to
add encouragement if needed.[18] But the Kentuckians
needed no encouragement. They had "posted skirmishers thickly across the steep face of the ridge, behind rocks,
logs, and trees, and their fire was galling and destruc-

[15] D. G. White to Cleburne, May 9, 1864, in *Official Records,* Ser. I,
Vol. XXXVIII, Pt. IV, 682.

[16] Mackall to Wheeler, May 9, 1864, *ibid.*

[17] *Id.* to *id.,* May 9, 1864, *ibid.,* 681.

[18] W. C. P. Breckinridge, "The Opening of the Atlanta Campaign,"
in *Battles and Leaders,* IV, 279.

tive." [19] As the main Federal lines surged forward the fighting came to be hand to hand, and "stones as well as bullets became elements in the combat," the Confederates rolling them over the precipice upon the Federals below.[20] "The enemy made several assaults upon the brigade," General Wheeler reported, "which repulsed them with great slaughter, killing and wounding nearly as many of the enemy as the effective total of Grigsby's brigade." [21]

While this attack had been going on, McPherson had steadily marched toward Snake Creek Gap which Johnston had left unfortified. At night, May 9, General James Cantey of Edward C. Walthall's division reported that he had been engaged with the enemy, and immediately General Johnston dispatched Hood to Resaca with three divisions. The next morning Hood reported that the Federals were retiring and as a result he was recalled, leaving two divisions midway between Resaca and Dalton where they could be rushed either to the northern front if the attack should come from that direction, or back to Resaca in case the movement there was genuine and not a feint.[22] The move of the Federals, of course, was not a feint, but McPherson chose to intrench himself in Snake Creek Gap rather than to strike boldly, and the delay gave time for Loring's division of Polk's army moving in from Mississippi to move into position to protect Resaca.

As a matter of fact, the Confederate leaders up to May 12 did not know fully the Federal intentions. On May 10 Hardee had written Wheeler: "I am unable to

[19] General John W. Geary's Report, September 9, 1864, in *Official Records*, Ser. I, Vol. XXXVIII, Pt. II, 115.

[20] *Ibid.*   [21] Wheeler's Report, June 1, 1864, *ibid.*, Pt. III, 944.

[22] Joseph E. Johnston, "Opposing Sherman's Advance to Atlanta," in *Battles and Leaders*, IV, 263.

decide what the Yankees are endeavoring to accomplish.
. . . I am only uneasy about our right. . . . Report
promptly any movement of troops on Varnell's Station
road. It is from that point I apprehend danger." [23] On
the morning of May 11 Wheeler was ordered by Johnston to find out what was really happening behind Rocky
Face.[24] Taking all his available cavalry, he moved upon
Varnell's Station, drove back Stoneman's cavalry, causing the Federals to burn a large number of wagons, and,
most important of all, discovered that all but two divisions of the enemy were moving behind Rocky Face
toward Resaca.[25] Hardee had guessed wrong; the enemy
was not moving on the Confederate right, but behind
the protecting slopes of Rocky Face had turned the Confederate left.

Under the circumstances Johnston decided to abandon Dalton and fall back upon Polk at Resaca. The
movement began on the morning of May 13, and when
the army reached Resaca a few hours later it found Loring's division already engaged with the enemy. General
Johnston, however, had ample time to form his battle
lines—Polk's corps on the left, Hardee in the center, and
Hood on the right.[26] On May 14 spirited fighting began
with Hood's corps the object of a vigorous attack. In the
meantime, Wheeler was ordered by Johnston to ascertain the position of the Federal left which faced Hood.[27]
His report indicated that the Union left was in a position

[23] Hardee to Wheeler, May 10, 1864, in *Official Records*, Ser. I, Vol.
XXXVIII, Pt. IV, 687.

[24] Mackall to *id.*, May 11, 1864, 7:50 A.M., *ibid.*, 692.

[25] Wheeler's Report, June 1, 1864, *ibid.*, Pt. III, 945.

[26] Johnston, "Opposing Sherman's Advance to Atlanta," in *Battles
and Leaders*, IV, 265.

[27] John B. Hood to Wheeler, May 14, 1864, in *Official Records*, Ser.
I, Vol. XXXVIII, Pt. IV, 710.

favorable to a Confederate attack, and so Hood was instructed to drive it from the railroad.[28] Hood's efforts were successful after a sharp attack on the fourteenth, and on the next day fighting was renewed; but by this time Johnston had decided that his position at Resaca was untenable, and at nightfall fell back behind the Oostenaula River expecting to find a favorable position at Calhoun ten miles to the south on the Western and Atlantic railroad.

As usual, the cavalry covered the retirement as it had from Dalton to Resaca. On the thirteenth when the retirement from Dalton began, all of Wheeler's troops not engaged in picket duty occupied the Confederate fortifications until the last wagon was on its way and then slowly fell back as a rear guard. At Resaca the cavalry was placed in the trenches, a part on the right under Hood, a part on the left under Polk, and a part in the center under Hardee. At times the fighting was at close range with soldiers concealing themselves as best they could behind trees and rocks. One of Wheeler's swearing troopers partially concealed himself behind a tree, his hinder part protruding. Suddenly a bullet plowed through the exposed portion of his anatomy. The trooper yelled with rage and pain, but kept firing away. Someone suggested that he go to the rear and have the wound dressed.

"Go back to the rear, hell!" he is reported to have stormed; "I would be only too glad to go back if wounded anywhere else, but I will be d—ned if I go back, shot where I have been." [29]

Didn't the infantry always say the cavalry couldn't

[28] Johnston, "Opposing Sherman's Advance to Atlanta," in *Battles and Leaders*, IV, 265.

[29] Dodson, *Campaigns of Wheeler*, 184.

fight and that one never found a dead Confederate with spurs on? How could he explain to the infantry how he happened to be shot in the buttock?

Johnston's retreat continued southward from Calhoun toward Atlanta. The territory over which he was marching was a comparatively level valley between the Etowah and Oostenaula rivers. At Adairsville, halfway across, Sherman caught up and there was a fight on May 17. It was sharp but so indecisive that it did not interfere seriously with the Confederate plans. At Adairsville Johnston planned to administer a crushing blow. Two roads about five miles apart led southward from Adairsville to Cassville. Sherman, Johnston hoped, would divide his forces and use both roads. If he did this, then Johnston would attack while the enemy was divided. Sherman acted as Johnston hoped. He started his divided army over the two roads. It was evident from the map that the distance between the Federal columns would be greatest when they should arrive at a point opposite Kingston. Therefore, Johnston prepared to deliver the blow at that place. Polk was to strike the Federal front while Hood simultaneously struck the rear. Hood misunderstood his orders and the plan miscarried.[30] The Confederate retreat continued to Cassville.

Johnston had planned to make a stand here. Fortifications were thrown up and every preparation made to receive Sherman. A council of the generals was called. Polk and Hood thought the position should be abandoned. Hardee favored making the stand. Johnston yielded to the opinion of the majority and again ordered a retreat. On May 20 the Confederates crossed the Eto-

[30] See Thomas R. Hay, "The Atlanta Campaign," in *Georgia Historical Quarterly*, VII (1923), 19–43, 99–118.

THE ATLANTA CAMPAIGN

⌐⌐⌐⌐⌐ Principal Confederate Positions
- - - - - - Principal Union Positions

Scale of Miles
0   5   10   20

wah drawing themselves a little closer to Atlanta.[31] Confederate losses since the campaign began were 3,388
killed and wounded—more than the South could afford
to lose.[32]

Since the intervention of the Etowah prevented close
observation of the movements of the enemy, Wheeler
was directed to cross the stream on May 23 in the direction of the recently evacuated town of Cassville to ascertain the location and movements of the Federals and to
interrupt their communications as much as possible.
Resting his command for one day he set out near midnight on May 24. The First Georgia and the Eleventh
Texas commanded by Colonel Samuel W. Davitte and
Major O. M. Wessick, respectively, he sent to create a
demonstration at Cass Station while he with portions of
Kelly's, Humes's, and Allen's commands moved directly
upon Cassville some six miles east of Kingston and a mile
north of Cass Station.[33]

At daylight on the twenty-fourth the Georgia and
Texas regiments encountered a detachment of Stoneman's cavalry at Cass Station and were forced to retire
and join Wheeler's main force about to attack Cassville.
When they rejoined Wheeler they brought the news
that there was a large supply train at Cass Station. This
Wheeler determined to capture. Taking Kelly's brigade
with him to the attack he left Humes's division to protect his rear in case the force protecting the trains was too
strong to be driven off. With comparative ease he drove
off the guard and captured, he reported, about eighty
wagons in addition to those burned, and then proceeded

[31] Johnston, *Narrative*, 324.   [32] *Ibid.*, 325.
[33] Wheeler's Report, June 1, 1864, in *Official Records*, Ser. I, Vol.
XXXVIII, Pt. III, 947.

with the plan to move on Cassville. Allen's brigade, which had not participated in the fight, was given the task of bringing off the captured wagons and mules. As it moved toward Cassville a force of enemy cavalry closed in to rescue the supply train. Observing this movement, Wheeler ordered the Eighth Texas and the Second Tennessee to stop it. They were to wait, he directed, until the enemy wavered to charge and then they themselves were to charge. This order, Wheeler stated, was "magnificently obeyed; the enemy came up in fine style and charged with great ferocity. They were met, however, as directed and driven back in utter confusion. We continued our charge, killing and wounding large numbers of the enemy, and capturing over 100 prisoners." [34] But he did not attack Cassville, explaining in his report that "having, from prisoners, citizens, and personal observation, learned all regarding the enemy, I withdrew quietly toward the river, crossing with my prisoners, wagons, mules, horses, &c." [35]

For this raid Wheeler received a congratulatory message from Johnston,[36] the second within two weeks; but the important aspect of the raid was the fact that Wheeler obtained information which confirmed the opinion that Sherman had abandoned his southeastward course directly along the Western and Atlantic railroad and had swung almost due south across the country toward Marietta.[37] The movement had begun on May 23, the day before Wheeler's thrust at Cassville, and by May 25 Sherman had reached a position at New Hope Church nearly thirty miles northwest of Atlanta and twenty miles

[34] *Ibid.*   [35] *Ibid.*

[36] May 25, 1864, *ibid.*, 949. The message read: "General Johnston congratulates you on your success in the enemy's rear. He wishes the captured wagons sent to the chief quartermaster."

[37] Burne, *Lee, Grant and Sherman*, 91.

due west of Marietta.[38] When he reached this position, however, he found Johnston there in full force. On the twenty-seventh Sherman attempted to turn Johnston's right, but to no avail. On the next day he tried the left, but Hardee's attack on McPherson was so fierce that any future plans in this direction were abandoned. "Sherman had, for the time being, been foiled." [39]

In this situation Sherman changed plans and decided to resume operations along the railroad. In the words of one of his biographers he began "side-stepping eastwards towards the railroad." [40] To meet this move, Johnston retired to a new line of intrenchments covering Marietta, his right on Brush Mountain, his center on Pine Mountain, his left on Lost Mountain. "Johnston was resting on his base while Sherman was cut off from his and with his transport always in potential danger from Johnston's daring cavalry." [41]

This "daring cavalry" had, after its raid on Cassville, fallen back to regain the main army in position near New Hope Church. Portions of Hannon's and Allen's brigades were placed upon Cleburne's right. These men were dismounted and intrenchments were thrown up which extended Cleburne's line nearly eight hundred yards. General Martin's command was placed on the Confederate left and the space of some two miles in between Martin and Kelly was filled by a line of skirmishers from Humes's command, the remainder of this

[38] Liddell Hart, *Sherman,* 258, states: "The Confederate cavalry, far more efficiently led and manned than the Federal, was quick to detect signs of the circling move of Sherman's left wing, so that early on the 23rd Johnston had sufficiently penetrated Sherman's intention to lead him to begin moving Hardee's and Polk's corps south-westwards to block Sherman's path, and Hood's followed on the 24th."

[39] Burne, *Lee, Grant and Sherman,* 91.

[40] Liddell Hart, *Sherman,* 260.   [41] *Ibid.,* 261.

command being "held in reserve to move to any point which might be attacked." [42] In these positions the cavalry served as infantry during Sherman's attack on May 27, and the following day assisted in covering Johnston's retirement to his new position.[43]

The increasing length of Sherman's communications rendered his position particularly vulnerable. If these communications could be seized by a strong force in his rear and permanent injury inflicted on the railroad, then Sherman might be forced to abandon the campaign. Johnston, apparently aware of this, had from the beginning urged such a move. In the words of Johnston's biographer: "As early as May 7th, before Polk had joined him, he had asked him by telegraph whether he could not throw a cavalry force into Middle Tennessee; and on May 10th he repeated the suggestion to Polk and to S. D. Lee, his successor in Mississippi. On June 3rd in telegrams to Bragg and S. D. Lee he renewed the request, claiming that such a step, if successful in breaking Sherman's communications, might produce great results. He renewed the recommendations on the 11th, 12th, 13th, 16th, and 26th. On the latter date Bragg replied for the first time, saying briefly that there was no force available for that purpose. It was not until July 11th that President Davis communicated to Johnston his ideas on the subject. They were that a strong cavalry detachment should be sent from his own army and charged with that duty. As Johnston needed all his cavalry, not only to protect his own communications but also to hold portions of his lines against the superior numbers of his foe, this did not meet the approval of his judgment." [44]

---

[42] Wheeler's Report, June 1, 1864, in *Official Records*, Ser. I, Vol. XXXVIII, Pt. III, 948.

[43] *Ibid.*, 949.   [44] Hughes, *General Johnston*, 237.

Johnston had suggested that Forrest be assigned "such parts as he may select of the commands of Gideon J. Pillow, Chalmers, and Roddey" to conduct the operations.[45] He planned to keep Wheeler close to him doing the job for which he was best equipped—covering the flanks, covering retirements, obtaining information, and protecting communications. General Stephen D. Lee in command of the Department of Mississippi was not occupied and could spare the services of Forrest very easily. Wheeler, knowing that the latter would not serve under him, removed the last practical obstacle to the success of the plan by offering to place himself under the orders of Forrest.[46]

But nothing was attempted. Bragg showed no more comprehension of what cavalry might accomplish than he had in Middle Tennessee; and both he and Davis revealed their well-known aversion to yielding up territory even though it might result in the enemy's defeat. Both men were afraid that Mississippi might have to be abandoned if Forrest should be detached. "General Lee in Mississippi, where Forrest is serving, is in proportion to the enemy confronting him much weaker than General Johnston," Bragg wrote Davis, "and needs his troops now with Johnston more than the latter can need Forrest." [47] The matter was dropped temporarily to be revived later by General Hood under almost disastrous circumstances.

On June 1 Sherman began his "side-stepping eastwards towards the railroad" from New Hope Church. On June 4 he moved his whole army across to the rail-

[45] Johnston to Bragg, June 3, 12, 27, 1864, in *Official Records*, Ser. I, Vol. XXXVIII, Pt. IV, 756, 770, 772.

[46] Dubose, *Wheeler and the Army of Tennessee*, 312.

[47] Bragg to Davis, June 29, 1864, in *Official Records*, Ser. I, Vol. XXXVIII, Pt. IV, 805.

road and Johnston paralleled him placing his center at Pine and Kennesaw mountains.[48] Now rain began to fall and the roads became soft and slippery, making operations extremely difficult. On June 14 the rain slackened and Sherman pushed part of Thomas's army "east of Pine Mountain, while concentrating the fire of his batteries on it. Johnston, Hardee, and Polk were there at the time" looking over the situation and discussing plans. At the first enemy volley Johnston and Hardee took to cover but the ponderous Bishop Polk refused to run and as a result was killed by a shell from the second volley.[49]

On the morning of June 27 Sherman ordered a direct frontal assault on Kennesaw which was repulsed with a loss of twenty-five hundred men. Being foiled here he again decided to threaten Johnston's left flank toward the Chattahoochee west of Atlanta. Again he "sidestepped," this time from the railroad to the open country, directly the reverse of the movement he had made on June 4. Schofield's and McPherson's corps were transferred from the Federal left to the right and on July 3 were pushed toward the Confederate left. General Johnston met this by falling back to a new and strong position at Smyrna eight miles nearer Atlanta; and again Sherman was confronted by the fact that he must maneuver his opponent from his position rather than risk a fight.[50]

In this maneuver Sherman sent his cavalry out on each flank. On the right Stoneman was to demonstrate while on the left Kenner Garrard was to secure Roswell Ford and hold it. Then Schofield was to be shifted from the Federal right to the left and with Thomas was to cross

---

48 Pine Mountain lies contiguous to Kennesaw on the north.
49 Liddell Hart, *Sherman*, 263.
50 Shotwell, *Civil War in America*, II, 288.

the Chattahoochee at or near Roswell. And the plan
worked. For the first and last time during the Atlanta
campaign General Sherman was able to utilize his cavalry in a really effective manner.[51] General Stoneman
demonstrated against the Confederate left, the Confederate cavalry moved to intercept him, and Garrard secured his foothold at Roswell on the Confederate left.[52]
On July 8 Schofield and Thomas crossed the river. The
next day McPherson's corps was transferred from the
Federal right to the left and took position at Roswell.
Again Sherman had "side-stepped"—the third time in a
little more than a month. He had moved from the railroad to the open country on May 23 to fight at New Hope
Church. Thence he had gone back to the railroad to
fight Johnston at Kennesaw on June 27; and now he
was moving away from the railroad again.

Johnston's answer to this latest maneuver was to fall
back again, directly in front of Atlanta on the north and
west, his right resting on the Georgia Railroad near Decatur, his left on the Western and Atlantic Railroad near

[51] Military critics are pretty well in agreement that Sherman's cavalry
was not well handled during the campaign. The English critic Burne
in his *Lee, Grant and Sherman*, 88, says: "Sherman's handling of the
cavalry was not impressive. Though he possessed four divisions he never
employed them as a whole. Instead he used them individually, usually
one on each flank, and one, or two, in reserve. Consequently when he
ordered some big effort, such as the breaking of the line behind the
Confederates, the cavalry failed him—as they did between Resaca and
Allatoona."

[52] George Stoneman's Report, July 13, 1864, in *Official Records,* Ser.
I, Vol. XXXVIII, Pt. II, 912; also Sherman to Kenner Garrard, July 4,
1864, *ibid.,* Pt. V, 48–49. General Kelly on picket duty on the Confederate right apparently did not extend his picket lines as far east
as Roswell and thus did not know of Garrard's gaining a foothold.
On the morning of July 5 he reported to Wheeler: "everything quiet
in front. No enemy reported on this, the Powers' Ferry, or Papermill
road." *Ibid.,* 865.

where it crossed the Chattahoochee in the direction of
Marietta. While in this position General Johnston was
relieved of the command and General John B. Hood
placed in his stead, an event which, in spite of its re-
percussions in the Confederate ranks, changed Sherman's
plans none at all at the time. He pushed ahead to turn
the Confederate right, cut the railroad to Decatur, and
approach Atlanta from the east.[53]

McPherson's Army of Tennessee was selected to do the
turning. McPherson was to move out from his position
at Roswell, cut the railway east of Decatur, and then
move toward Atlanta along the railway. While he was
thus engaged Thomas was to move in on the city from
the north across Peach Tree Creek; Schofield was to form
a connecting link between McPherson and Thomas.[54]
The movement began on the afternoon of July 18 and
by the following day the whole army was under way.
McPherson and Schofield moved southeast toward Decatur, and Thomas advanced to Peach Tree Creek. The
whole movement, however, encountered unexpected
and stubborn resistance from Wheeler's cavalry now
fighting as infantry-cavalry-artillery. To meet the advance of the Federals Wheeler had detached all but
about sixteen hundred of his men to guard the flanks.
With portions of Kelly's, Alfred Iverson's, Williams's,
and Samuel W. Ferguson's brigades under his personal
command he met Thomas's advance on July 17 and 18.
Fighting behind successive lines of breastworks Wheeler's men contested the ground in front of Peach Tree

[53] Oliver O. Howard, "The Struggle for Atlanta," in *Battles and Leaders*, IV, 313.

[54] Schofield's Report, September 10, 1864, in *Official Records*, Ser. I,
Vol. XXXVIII, Pt. II, 516; Sherman's Orders, July 17, 1864, *ibid.*, Pt.
V, 166.

Creek, and then on the nineteenth moved to the Confederate right to resist McPherson's advance.[55]

On this same day, July 19, General Hood, two days in command of the Army of Tennessee, issued orders which indicated his reversal of Johnston's Fabian strategy. Hood proposed to fight, and the first battle would be against Thomas as he approached Peach Tree Creek. While his own corps under Cheatham, reinforced by Wheeler's cavalry, held on the Confederate right against McPherson, Hood sent Hardee and Stewart against Thomas. The plan, excellent as it was, did not succeed, however. Hood's orders were issued on the afternoon of the nineteenth, but the attack could not begin until the next day. On the twentieth when the attack came, it was thought necessary to detach Cleburne's division and send it to the right where Cheatham and Wheeler were threatened by McPherson. Therefore, in spite of the heavy blow which Hardee struck at Thomas the Confederate plan failed in this sector.[56] In the afternoon as a sort of concluding event to the day's fighting McPherson sent General Walter Q. Gresham's division against Wheeler's position on the Decatur railroad. Wheeler's skirmish line was located in front of the railroad, and to the rear of the line the rest of his troops were intrenched on Bald Hill, an important eminence some two and a half miles east of Atlanta. General Gresham's attack drove back Wheeler's skirmish line and swept across the railroad tracks toward the hill. General Ferguson on Wheeler's right gave way and it seemed for a time that the hill would be captured.[57] Wheeler was able to re-

---

[55] Wheeler's Report, October 9, 1864, *ibid.*, Pt. III, 951.

[56] Hay, "The Atlanta Campaign," in *loc. cit.*, 106.

[57] Wheeler's Report, October 9, 1864, in *Official Records*, Ser. I, Vol. XXXVIII, Pt. III, 952.

establish this line, however, and made a "desperate and successful stand" [58] to hold the hill until reinforced by troops from Cleburne's division. The day ended with Bald Hill in Wheeler's possession. The Confederate right had not been turned.

On the morning of July 21, however, the attack on Wheeler and Cleburne at Bald Hill was renewed, and this time with success. Brigadier General Manning F. Force of Frank P. Blair's division (McPherson's corps) supported by the wounded Gresham's brigade now commanded by Brigadier General Giles A. Smith attacked the position at dawn. Again, as on the day before, it was Ferguson's brigade that received the assault. Ferguson gave way in confusion, exposing the right of Allen's brigade; and with the second assault of the Federals the hill fell into their hands. [59] McPherson, it appeared, was now in an excellent position to turn the Confederate right when he chose.

Events, however, prevented McPherson from following up the victory at Bald Hill. On the night of the twenty-first Hood withdrew two corps from Peach Tree Creek into the outer fortifications of Atlanta. Hardee concentrated four divisions within Atlanta and moved during the night with Wheeler's cavalry to the Federal left rear. [60] It was a maneuver similar to Jackson's flank march and attack at Chancellorsville, and was almost as successful. Sherman, following his consistent policy of misusing his cavalry, had sent Garrard on a railroad destroying expedition east of Decatur, and thus McPherson

---

[58] Howard, "The Struggle for Atlanta," in *Battles and Leaders*, IV, 314. General Walter Q. Gresham was seriously wounded during the assault.

[59] Wheeler's Report, October 9, 1864, in *Official Records*, Ser. I, Vol. XXXVIII, Pt. III, 952.

[60] Hay, "The Atlanta Campaign," in *loc. cit.*, 108.

was almost completely surprised by Hardee's appearance on the twenty-second.[61] Wheeler, leading Hardee's night march, rode four miles beyond the Confederate right flank and at noon struck McPherson's supply train at Decatur. The train was guarded by a large detachment of infantry. After a personal reconnaissance Wheeler dismounted his men and moved upon the Federals who threw out two regiments of infantry to meet him. These two regiments were driven back into their works. Here, supported by artillery, they poured a galling fire into the lines of dismounted cavalrymen. Seeing the strength of the enemy's position in front Wheeler threw a force upon his right flank and rear, and this synchronized frontal and flank attack was successful. Decatur fell to Wheeler and, he reported, "some 225 prisoners, a large number of small-arms, 1 12-pounder gun, 1 forge, 1 battery wagon, 1 caisson, and 6 wagons and teams, together with the captain of the battery and most of his men, were captured and brought off. We also captured his camp equipage, stores, and hospitals." [62]

In the meantime, Hardee had arrived on McPherson's left four miles east of Decatur, had faced his men to the left and launched his attack through the concealing woods. He overran a Federal battery and several hospital camps before his presence was known; but by sheer good fortune the Federals had a corps in position to repel the attack. On the morning of July 22 McPherson had ordered the corps of Major General Grenville M. Dodge to move to the left in support of Major General Blair.[63] It was while Dodge was executing this movement that

[61] Liddell Hart, *Sherman*, 282.

[62] Wheeler's Report, October 9, 1864, in *Official Records*, Ser. I, Vol. XXXVIII, Pt. III, 953.

[63] Grenville M. Dodge's Report, November 25, 1864, *ibid.*, 384.

Hardee struck. Dodge's troops were turned to meet the Confederate attack.

When Hardee realized that he was encountering stiffer resistance than he had anticipated, he hastened a courier to Wheeler at Decatur requesting him to join with all speed the main attack. Dropping his work at Decatur, Wheeler hastened to join Hardee,[64] but the slight assistance the cavalry was able to give was not enough to bring victory to the Confederates. The battle was a draw, and a draw here was equivalent to a defeat for Hood's army. The Union army, however, had sustained one serious loss. General McPherson galloped into a line of Confederate skirmishers and was shot from his horse, dying within a few moments.[65] Perhaps there was some slight comfort to the Confederacy in the fact that Atlanta had not fallen, but the Battle of Atlanta on the twenty-second had resulted in little that was decisive; it merely marked the beginning of a siege.

After the battle both sides changed their positions. Hardee dropped back on his right to a position almost due south of Atlanta with the idea of protecting the Central Railway which ran southeast to Macon and Savannah. General Stephen D. Lee, who had replaced Cheatham, occupied a position on Hardee's left just east of the city. General Alexander P. Stewart held the lines north of Atlanta facing Schofield and Thomas. The area to the west of the city was defended by one division of Stewart's corps, but until July 27 no enemy was on this front.[66] This area to the west of Atlanta opposite Stewart's one division in the neighborhood of Ezra Church,

64 Wheeler's Report, October 9, 1864, *ibid.*, 953.

65 Liddell Hart, *Sherman*, 283.

66 Sherman's Report, September 15, 1864, in *Official Records*, Ser. I, Vol. XXXVIII, Pt. I, 77; Hood's Report, February 15, 1865, *ibid.*, Pt. III, 631–32.

however, soon became the scene of fierce combat, for on the twenty-seventh McPherson's corps, now commanded by General Oliver O. Howard, was switched from the extreme left flank on the east of Atlanta to the extreme right flank on the west. Sherman proposed to loosen Hood's hold on the city by cutting his communications on the Macon railway.[67]

To further his plans Sherman turned to his cavalry. To General George Stoneman he assigned his own and the cavalry of General Garrard, making an effective force of full five thousand men. To General Edward M. McCook he gave his own and the Eighth Indiana cavalry, in the aggregate some four thousand men. Calling the two generals to headquarters Sherman carefully explained their task. The two were to move in concert, Stoneman by the left around Atlanta to McDonough nearly thirty miles southeast of Atlanta and McCook by the right to Fayetteville some thirty miles south of Atlanta. On the night of July 28 these two were to bring their commands together at Lovejoy's Station and destroy the railroad. The officers understood their orders, Sherman wrote, and "entertained not a doubt of perfect success." [68] In fact, General Stoneman was so certain of success that he asked and received permission to ride on to Macon and Andersonville and release Federal prisoners there. "There was something most captivating in the idea, and the execution was within the bounds of probability of success," Sherman wrote. "I consented that after the defeat of Wheeler's cavalry, which was embraced in his orders, and breaking the road he might attempt it with his cavalry proper, sending that of General Garrard back to its proper flank of the army." [69]

[67] Sherman's Report, September 15, 1864, *ibid.*, Pt. I, 79.
[68] *Ibid.*, 75.   [69] *Ibid.*, 76.

But Sherman's high hopes were soon dashed. Wheeler was not whipped, the road was not cut, and the whole expedition came to disaster.

General Stoneman moved by the left around Atlanta sending Garrard to Flat Rock for the purpose of covering the major movement. The movement was not unobserved, however, for Wheeler discovered it on the morning of the twenty-seventh—that is, he observed Garrard moving to Flat Rock, but as yet had no knowledge of the larger force under Stoneman.[70] By daylight on the twenty-eighth Wheeler had got ahead of Garrard and was skirmishing with him. Hearing nothing from Stoneman, Garrard slowly fell back and rejoined the left of his own army.[71] Stoneman apparently had decided to release the prisoners before he joined McCook, whipped Wheeler, and tore up the railroad. Instead of swinging in a wide arc southwestward he moved by the most direct route toward Macon, leaving Garrard and McCook to care for themselves. Learning of Stoneman's move, Wheeler sent Iverson's, Allen's, and Breckinridge's brigades to intercept him and, if possible, destroy him.[72]

While he was thus preparing to pursue Stoneman, Wheeler was informed that McCook was working destruction on the Confederate left. He had gone down the west branch of the Chattahoochee to Rivertown, had thrown a pontoon bridge across the river, moved on Fayetteville, and destroyed a large quantity of Confederate stores there. Pushing on he tore up the track of the railroad for several hundred feet and burned the station at Lovejoy's; and having accomplished this he anxiously

70 Wheeler's Report, October 9, 1864, *ibid.*, Pt. III, 953.
71 Sherman's Report, September 15, 1864, *ibid.*, Pt. I, 76.
72 Wheeler's Report, October 9, 1864, *ibid.*, Pt. III, 953.

awaited Stoneman. Stoneman was on his way to Macon and glory, however, and McCook found himself confronted by Wheeler's cavalry. With a portion of William H. Jackson's division and Henry M. Ashby's and Anderson's brigades Wheeler moved to intercept McCook. When he reached Fayetteville on the afternoon of July 29 he found that McCook had moved on the Fayetteville road toward Newman. That night at ten o'clock General Jackson wrote Wheeler suggesting that if Wheeler would strike McCook's rear on the Fayetteville road, he (Jackson) would gain their front or flank at Newman. This Wheeler agreed to, and immediately went into action. Within two hours after receipt of Jackson's message Wheeler had caught up with McCook's rear and was skirmishing with it in the darkness. At three o'clock in the morning Jackson informed Wheeler that the Federals had encamped at Shakerag and that he was moving to keep in their front. Wheeler and Jackson still had McCook between them and were slowly applying the pincers. By five o'clock Wheeler had struck McCook's camp at Shakerag and had routed him, killing forty men and capturing two hundred more. McCook moved toward Newman and Wheeler again took up the pursuit. Two miles from Newman he caught up with the rear and captured twenty prisoners. Jackson had not yet been engaged, nor indeed was he to become seriously engaged during the running battle. He simply made a noise on the front and flank while Wheeler's stalkers closed in from the rear.[73]

On approaching Newman McCook observed that the town was occupied by Confederate cavalry, which by every calculation had no right to be there. It was General

[73] *Ibid.*, 954-55.

Roddey moving from North Alabama to join Hood at Atlanta. By sheerest chance he happened to be at Newman just at a time when McCook needed refuge there. Instead of finding sanctuary in the town McCook was forced to swing to the right. Roddey joined forces with Wheeler and the chase continued down the LaGrange road. McCook found cavalry on his front, rear, and flanks striking viciously, circling, and then striking again. "The pursuing cavalry hemmed him in and forced him to fight," Sherman reported. "He was compelled to drop his prisoners and captures, and cut his way out, losing some 500 officers and men." [74] McCook's command was not entirely wiped out, but it was so badly cut to pieces that its effectiveness was destroyed. "I was finally completely surrounded," McCook reported, "and compelled to abandon everything that would impede me in order to cut my way through. I ordered Colonels [John T.] Croxton and [William H.] Torrey to cut through with their brigades. I took Colonel [Fielder A.] Jones and got through 1,200 men by a charge in column, and crossed the river below Franklin. I have not heard from Croxton's or Torrey's commands, but suppose that they got out, as they made the attempt while I was fighting. Colonel [Joseph B.] Dorr, Colonel Torrey, Major [John] Austin wounded; Major [Nathan] Paine killed; [Colonel Thomas J.] Harrison missing, supposed a prisoner. My loss very heavy. No co-operation from Stoneman." [75]

Stoneman had a very good reason for not co-operating. He, too, had been whipped, and not only whipped but captured along with a large part of his command. When news of his approach had reached Macon, Howell Cobb

[74] Sherman's Report, September 15, 1864, *ibid.*, Pt. I, 77.
[75] McCook to Sherman, August 3, 1864, *ibid.*, Pt. II, 762.

hastily collected an army of clerks, old men, boys, and nondescripts, armed them with whatever weapons were at hand, and marched them out to meet the enemy.[76] Just as Stoneman ran into this unforeseen obstacle, Iverson appeared in his rear. Stoneman and five hundred of his men attempted to escape, but Iverson cut them off and captured them. Several hundred more, largely Kentucky volunteers, ran from the battle and were captured as they attempted to cross a bridgeless gully. It was a rout—perhaps the most disastrous cavalry defeat of the whole war. "Without entering now into particulars," Stoneman wrote from prison in Macon, "we were whipped. . . . Our loss in killed and wounded was quite large. . . . I have not heard from the Kentucky brigade since it left. [Colonel Horace] Capron's brigade I learn was considerably cut up, and several hundred of it captured. I feel better satisfied with myself to be a prisoner of war, much as I hate it, than to be amongst those who owe their escape to considerations of self-preservation." [77]

Garrard had retired; McCook had been cut to pieces; and Stoneman was in prison. General Sherman's laconic comment on it all is humorous. "On the whole the cavalry raid is not deemed a success," he wrote.[78] And he proceeded to reorganize his cavalry with the hope that he might have at least one effective mounted unit. He had been impressed with the work of tall, angular, awkward young Judson Kilpatrick, commander of the Third Division of Thomas's cavalry. But for Thomas's objec-

[76] Dubose, *Wheeler and the Army of Tennessee*, 380.
[77] Stoneman to Sherman, August 6, 1864, in *Official Records*, Ser. I, Vol. XXXVIII, Pt. II, 914.
[78] Sherman's Report, *ibid.*, Pt. I, 77.

tion Sherman would have made Kilpatrick chief of cavalry. Since Thomas objected, Sherman regrouped all his cavalry in three divisions—one under McCook, one under Garrard, and one under Kilpatrick.[79]

[79] Liddell Hart, *Sherman*, 289.

Chapter VIII

APPROACHING THE END
(August, 1864–April, 1865)

WHILE the Federal cavalry raid designed to harass
the Confederate lines of communication was meeting
with failure, Sherman completed the task of switching
Howard's army from the left to the right flank. It was
just taking up its new position near Ezra Church on July
28 when Hood, taking advantage of his interior lines,
attacked with Lee's and Stewart's divisions united under
the command of Hardee.[1] The Confederate attack was
repulsed, but Sherman was no closer to Atlanta than he
had been for two weeks. His cavalry raid had failed to
break the Confederate communications and his flanking
movement with Howard had not achieved its objective.
Now Sherman figuratively scratched his head and began
thinking of a new plan to take the city. Pending his next
move he brought up some Parrott guns and sent shells
screaming into the city for several days; but, with the
exception of the excitement created among the populace
of Atlanta, the bombardment had little effect.[2]

Hood himself gave Sherman an unexpected opportunity. On August 10 he sent Wheeler with four thousand
men northward to operate upon the Federal communications in the direction of Chattanooga. Above Chatta-

1 Shotwell, *Civil War in America*, II, 293.
2 Burne, *Lee, Grant and Sherman*, 115.

nooga Wheeler was to cross the Tennessee River and swing westward toward Nashville, destroying the railroad as he went. Having accomplished this he was to leave twelve hundred men to keep the road cut, and with the remainder of his command was to return to Georgia, again destroying the Western and Atlantic Railroad from Chattanooga to Atlanta.[3] It was the same move Johnston had before his removal from command urged upon Davis and Bragg—with this important exception: Johnston had urged that Forrest be sent from Mississippi to do the work while Wheeler was retained to guard the army defending Atlanta. In brief, Johnston believed it unwise to weaken his cavalry force in the presence of the enemy. Now General Hood did just that, going Sherman one better in the unwise use of cavalry. "I could not have asked for anything better," wrote Sherman, "for I had provided well against such a contingency, and this detachment left me superior to the enemy in cavalry." [4]

Since his return from the McCook pursuit, Wheeler had rested his men and horses at Covington, well in Sherman's rear. The matter of food, however, was most serious. The country had been laid bare for miles around by frequent cavalry raids. There was no dry grain for the horses and every cavalryman knew that horses could not last long when eating only green stuff. But hardships were not strange to the cavalry, and so they made the best of it. They lived on green corn which they called "roas'n ears." "I went into a cornfield," wrote a trooper from Covington, "gathered twelve ears from the growing stalk, in the milk; gave

[3] Wheeler's Report, October 9, 1864, in *Official Records*, Ser. I, Vol. XXXVIII, Pt. III, 957.

[4] Sherman's Report, September 15, 1864, *ibid.*, Pt. I, 79.

my horse eight and kept four to roast for my dinner. I took two from him to help my dinner, but gave him the shucks from all, so I claimed to have been generous." [5] Wheeler's men scoured the country in search of meat for themselves and dry corn for their horses. If they failed to find cured meat they took chickens and eggs. After all, they argued, were they not fighting for these Georgians? If the Yankees left anything should not the Southern soldiers be allowed to appropriate it? Thus they reasoned, and thus they acquired for themselves the reputation of being first-class chicken thieves. [6]

On August 10 Wheeler led four thousand troopers out from camp at Covington to carry out his orders. In preparation for the raid he issued an order calculated to stop the thieving. This order read:

I. In the march about to commence, no soldier or officer of any grade whatever will be permitted to carry any article of private property, except one single blanket and oil-cloth.

II. The troops will be inspected daily while en route, and any additional article upon the person or horse of any trooper or officer will be immediately destroyed.

III. The ordnance wagons, ambulances, limber-boxes, and caissons will be inspected twice each day, and the officer controlling them will be arrested, and, if practicable, immediately punished if the smallest article of private property is found being thus transported. [7]

Wheeler's course lay northward along the Western and Atlantic railroad, his first objective being Dalton. At Marietta, on the way, he tore up several miles of

[5] Quoted in Dubose, *Wheeler and the Army of Tennessee*, 382–83.

[6] Virginia Clay-Clopton, *A Belle of the Fifties* (New York, 1905), 233.

[7] Circular, August 9, 1864, in *Official Records*, Ser. I, Vol. XXXVIII, Pt. V, 953.

track and captured nearly a thousand beef cattle which were sent back to the army in Atlanta. Here, General Martin was detached and ordered to strike Tilton, somewhat off the main road, and then to ride on and join his commander in the proposed attack on Dalton.

With Humes's and Kelly's divisions Wheeler proceeded to the attack at Dalton fully confident that Martin would join him in time for the fight. On approaching the garrison Wheeler sent in one of his formal and polite demands for surrender. "To prevent the unnecessary effusion of blood, I have the honor to demand the immediate and unconditional surrender of the forces under your command at this garrison," the note read. To this he received the following reply from Colonel Bernard Laiboldt in command: "I have been placed here to defend this post, but not to surrender." [8] A bold and polite refusal, but it was a bluff. Quickly Laiboldt got in touch with General James B. Steedman at Chattanooga. "Wheeler has demanded surrender of this post," he wired. "Send re-enforcements." [9]

Before these reinforcements could arrive Wheeler attacked. The defenders were quickly driven out of the town and back into their earthen fortifications on a small hill. Wheeler's men sacked the town, but it was not a very rich haul. A few wagons, some canned milk which Wheeler's men now tasted for the first time, miscellaneous small items—that was all. There was no wagon train, no large depot of supplies, no dry corn for the horses.

The attack took place late in the afternoon of August 14. Shortly after eight o'clock Steedman arrived with reinforcements. Wheeler withdrew in the face of

[8] Bernard Laiboldt's Report, August 18, 1864, *ibid.*, Pt. I, 324.
[9] *Ibid.*, 504.

these new troops and waited for Martin. There was desultory firing until past midnight, but still the tardy general did not appear. At dawn it was discovered that Martin had come within several miles of Dalton and there had put his men into camp for the night, leaving his commander to whatever fate might befall him. He was promptly relieved from duty and was eventually transferred to Mississippi.[10]

Dalton being now reinforced by cavalry and infantry, Wheeler wasted no time in a siege of the place. Instead he instituted a game of "fox and goose" with Steedman. Riding away from Dalton, Wheeler made a demonstration toward Chattanooga, Steedman in close pursuit. Having thus drawn the Federals out of Dalton to protect Chattanooga, he faced his men about and rode toward Dalton. Again Steedman took up the pursuit. For three days this game was kept going, while the railroad was left unrepaired. Steedman finally divined Wheeler's purpose, gave up the chase, and set his men to repairing the railroad.[11]

Wheeler left some two hundred men with orders to strike the railroad every night at several different points while he continued his ride toward Tennessee. He had intended crossing the Tennessee River at Cottonport, but the continuous rains had so swelled the river as to make it unfordable. Therefore he concluded it would be better to move northeastward up the river to its headwaters, the Little Tennessee and Clinch rivers, cross them, and then ride southward again. While preparing to cross the Little Tennessee he learned that the Fed-

[10] Charles S. Sydnor, "William Thompson Martin," in *Dictionary of American Biography*, XII, 349. General Martin seems to have adopted Forrest's attitude of distrust of Wheeler.

[11] James B. Steedman's Report, September 11, 1864, in *Official Records*, Ser. I, Vol. XXXVIII, Pt. II, 496–97.

erals had made extensive arrangements to procure forage for their army from the country along the line of railroad from Cleveland to Loudon. Feeling that it was important to stop this source of supply, he made a demonstration upon Cleveland and then destroyed the railroad from the latter town to Charleston. Crossing the Hiwassee River from Charleston he struck the town of Athens, captured it, and then tore up the track to Loudon.

In the meantime, Steedman set out from Chattanooga in pursuit with thirty-six hundred men. He moved in the direction taken by Wheeler as far as Madisonville, whence, learning that Wheeler had crossed the river, he returned to Chattanooga. "The enemy had destroyed a large amount of railroad track between Calhoun and Loudon; he had attacked and captured a portion of a gang of workmen employed by the quartermaster's department in getting out logs for the Government near Sale Creek, together with some 50 teams in use there, and had robbed the country generally; friends and foes seemed to suffer alike, but not an engine or car had yet been destroyed," was Steedman's report of the damages.[12]

Wheeler crossed the Little Tennessee with slight difficulty, but to his disappointment he found the Holston had risen too high to be crossed, and he was compelled to move farther up and cross above Knoxville. Just before the crossing General John S. Williams requested permission to take his own brigade and one other with half the artillery and strike the Federal garrison and bridge at Strawberry Plains. Wheeler, realizing that speed was essential to the success of the raid, at first refused permission, but finally gave in only on the con-

12 *Ibid.*

dition that Williams should march by moonlight and
overtake the main command. The garrison at Strawberry Plains was too strong to be taken, and Williams
did not attack. Wheeler, after crossing the river, waited
through the night and then set out at dawn without the
missing brigadier. Thus was lost another general and
the use of over one third the entire command.[13] Williams tried but never caught up.

The raid, however, had been continued without Williams. Riding through Sparta, Wheeler's men left the
mountains behind and entered the gently rolling foot-
hills of Middle Tennessee. At McMinnville on August
29 they struck Major Shelah Waters's command of three
companies. The officer and men barely escaped with
their lives, leaving behind their camp equipage, ten
wagons, one ambulance, and three teams. On the same
night another group of Wheeler's men cut the railroad
and telegraph line between McMinnville and Murfreesboro about four miles from Bell Buckle.[14] Other raiding
parties had struck Lebanon, Smyrna, intervening block-
houses, bridges, and railway supplies, coming within
eight miles of Nashville. Here Wheeler was urged by
some of his officers to attempt to capture the city. One
officer was particularly urgent.

"To be candid with you, General," said this officer,
"the press of the South has so vituperated and abused
you that everybody has lost confidence in you except
your own command and those of the army who have had
an opportunity of knowing what you have done. Your

[13] Wheeler's Report, October 9, 1864, *ibid.,* Pt. III, 959. Williams
never rejoined Wheeler but spent the rest of the war fighting in East
Tennessee and Southwest Virginia. See Dubose, *Wheeler and the Army
of Tennessee,* 387–89.

[14] Robert H. Milroy's Report, September 17, 1864, in *Official Records,*
Ser. I, Vol. XXXVIII, Pt. II, 490.

own reputation and that of your command demand that you take Nashville." [15]

But the odds against such an undertaking were insurmountable. Nashville was too well fortified to be taken by a mere cavalry attack; so Wheeler made this officer a little speech about caring more for the good of the cause than for his own reputation, and then put his men in motion toward Alabama and safety.[16]

Before starting south, however, he issued a proclamation to the people of Tennessee urging them to join his command and help redeem their state from Federal hands. "Georgia has called her last available citizen between the ages of seventeen and fifty," he proclaimed. "They are now fighting beside your chivalrous sons at Atlanta. Other states are now throwing their entire male population into the field. Citizens of Tennessee! You also have been always ready to respond to your country's call; every one of you must rise to duty. If all who should come will now join us, we pledge the honor of those states whose sons compose the western army of the Confederacy that Tennessee shall be redeemed." [17]

As a result of Wheeler's efforts he was able to report that some eight hundred "absentees" were reinstated and about two thousand new recruits gained for the Confederate service; [18] but they apparently were paper recruits.

The Federals now took up the pursuit of Wheeler. Steedman was ordered from Chattanooga and Rousseau was sent out from Nashville with cavalry and infantry. It was a running fight from Nashville by way of Colum-

---

[15] Quoted in Dodson, *Campaigns of Wheeler*, 260.
[16] *Ibid.*
[17] Quoted in Dubose, *Wheeler and the Army of Tennessee*, 386.
[18] Wheeler's Report, October 9, 1864, in *Official Records*, Ser. I, Vol. XXXVIII, Pt. III, 960.

bia to the Tennessee River near Florence, Alabama. In a minor affair near Franklin Wheeler suffered what probably was his most severe loss of the campaign—the death of the brilliant and dashing Brigadier General John H. Kelly. A native of Alabama, this West Pointer was the ideal cavalry fighter. He had been with Wheeler from the beginning of the Kentucky campaign and had shared with his commander the vicissitudes of every campaign. That unknown Yankee who sent a bullet through the general's brain deprived Wheeler of one of his most colorful and versatile fighters.

The enemy pursued Wheeler almost to the Tennessee River without success, trying each day to force a pitched battle. On September 2 Wheeler again forded the Tennessee as he had after his raid on Rosecrans's rear in 1863 and placed his men in safety at Tuscumbia, Alabama. It had been a barren raid. He had captured some beef cattle, had torn up a few miles of track around Dalton, had caused some consternation in East Tennessee and momentarily confused things around Nashville; but it had been at a terrible price. It had cost him two generals, Martin and Kelly. It had cost him the services of nearly half his command, counting those absent with Williams. So far as permanently endangering Sherman's line of communication, he had accomplished nothing.

General Forrest during late August and early September was near Tuscumbia preparing for his invasion of Tennessee. Wheeler called upon him and the two patched up their differences long enough to agree that they should join their forces. A few months earlier a junction of the two commands might have accomplished something. Now it was too late.

Wheeler sat down and wrote Hood of the result of

his conference with Forrest: "General Forrest thinks that the aid of my force for ten or twelve days would be of great service to him and materially affect the success of his expedition. Some of my troops are still in Tennessee, and by remaining a short time I could increase my command. . . . However, unless I hear from you, will start as directed as soon as possible. General Williams being absent with half [*sic*] my command, I will only be able to bring back 2,000 men." [19]

The truth of the matter is that Wheeler apparently was discouraged and was about to resign. On the same day that Wheeler wrote Hood, Forrest in a letter to General Richard Taylor, brother-in-law of Davis, commented on the conference:

I met Major-General Wheeler to-day at Tuscumbia. His command is in a demoralized condition. He claims to have about 2,000 men with him; his adjutant-general says, however, that he will not be able to raise and carry back with him exceeding 1,000, and in all probability not over 500. One of his brigades left him and he does not know whether they are captured or have returned, or are still in Middle Tennessee. He sent General Martin back in arrest, and his whole command is demoralized to such an extent that he expresses himself as disheartened, and that, having lost influence with the troops, and being unable to secure the aid and co-operation of his officers, he believes it to the interest of the service that he should be relieved from command. [20]

Again it was demonstrated that Wheeler could not successfully conduct large scale independent cavalry operations. After his disastrous Middle Tennessee raid in September, 1863, and his Knoxville campaign in the

[19] Wheeler to Hood, September 20, 1864, *ibid.*, Vol. XXXIX, Pt. II, 849.

[20] Forrest to Richard Taylor, September 20, 1864, *ibid.*, 859.

fall and winter of 1863 he had rejoined the main army at Dalton. From Dalton to Atlanta his conduct of cavalry operations had been almost flawless. He had protected the flanks of his army, supplied Johnston and Hood with proper information, fought bravely in the trenches, engaged in short, successful raids, and, finally, had almost destroyed Sherman's cavalry in disposing of McCook and Stoneman. In spite of this most recent failure, however, Hood declined to join the two commands. On September 16 he wired the disheartened Wheeler: "Join the left of this army without delay." [21]

While Wheeler was away on his raid Sherman sent another cavalry expedition against the Confederate communications, this one directed by his favorite cavalry leader, General Kilpatrick. Kilpatrick gained the Confederate rear, did some damage, but failed to impair for any length of time Hood's railway lines.[22] Sherman now became convinced that only the infantry could accomplish effective destruction, and accordingly developed his plans. On August 25 he moved against Hood's communications. Marching slowly he reached the railroad to Montgomery below East Point on August 28 with Howard's and Thomas's corps, Henry W. Slocum's corps being held in reserve.[23]

Within Atlanta, Hood, deprived of his cavalry, was without adequate information; and when he discovered that Sherman had disappeared from his intrenchments before Atlanta, he jumped to the false conclusion that the siege had been raised. Four valuable days he remained within the city while Sherman destroyed the railroad.[24] On the evening of the thirtieth Hood realized

[21] Hood to Wheeler, September 21, 1864, *ibid.*, 861.
[22] Liddell Hart, *Sherman,* 296.
[23] Burne, *Lee, Grant and Sherman,* 115.   [24] *Ibid.*

that Sherman was in his rear in full force and quickly sent Hardee and Lee to Jonesboro on the Macon railroad.[25]

These two arrived at Jonesboro on the morning of the thirty-first. The night before Sherman, having torn up the Montgomery road, moved toward the Confederates at Jonesboro, and in the afternoon there was a sharp engagement between Howard's and Hardee's corps. On that same afternoon Hood in Atlanta, apparently believing that Sherman was about to attack from the south, ordered Lee's corps to return to the city. It was a strange maneuver, one based on inadequate information. As one recent writer has explained the matter: "Hood was certainly in an unenviable position. He had divested himself of his 'eyes,' like so many other leaders in the Civil War, and like them he lived to regret it." [26] Hood sent encouraging messages to Hardee on September 1, "but no number of messages could compensate for the absence of Wheeler. Hood's surprise is as directly attributable to this as McPherson's surprise on July 2nd [sic] was attributable to the absence of Garrard's cavalry." [27]

On the first day of September Sherman sent his forces against Hardee and failed to crush him; but Atlanta was doomed, and Hood's problem was to get the balance of his army safely out of the city. Early on the morning of September 2 Hood, destroying what stores he could

[25] The railroad divided at East Point, one branch going southwestward to Montgomery and the other southeastward to Macon.

[26] *Ibid.*, 123. Colonel Burne uses the date September 31, but obviously this is an error. It should read August 31. Sherman occupied Atlanta on September 2.

[27] *Ibid.* Obviously Burne is here referring to McPherson's surprise by Hardee and Wheeler on July 22 instead of July 2.

not carry along, evacuated Atlanta and moved south to Lovejoy's Station where he joined Hardee. Four days later, September 6, the Federals were withdrawn from the Confederate front and moved toward Atlanta. The Atlanta campaign was at an end.[28]

Sherman, now that he had taken Atlanta, was faced with the problem of holding the city. The Confederate army had not been destroyed and was now concentrated twenty miles away in his rear. If this army should be thrown upon the long line of Federal communications from Nashville by way of Chattanooga to Atlanta, Sherman possibly could be cut off. This strategy Hood now employed: If he threw the whole Confederate army upon Sherman's communications the Federal commander would, he reasoned, follow to protect these communications. Then, Hood thought, after Sherman had been drawn out of his shelter at Atlanta he could be forced to do battle somewhere in the mountains of North Georgia.[29]

As the first step in the development of this plan, Hood shifted his army from Lovejoy's to Palmetto, still farther west on the Montgomery railroad. From here he could march northward leaving Atlanta to his right, pass on by Kennesaw Mountain, and strike the railroad anywhere near Ackworth or Allatoona. This route Hood took, starting his movement on October 1, 1864. On the second day his army had reached the railroad some forty miles north of Atlanta. By the fifth General Sam G. French's division had attacked Allatoona and had been repulsed. Sherman, as Hood had thought, was in

[28] John B. Hood, "The Defense of Atlanta," in *Battles and Leaders,* IV, 344.

[29] John B. Hood, *Advance and Retreat* (New Orleans, 1880), 245–46.

pursuit. He had left Slocum's corps to guard Atlanta while he took the balance to follow Hood's army to Tennessee.[30]

Hood swung westward from Allatoona, crossed the Coosa River below Rome, and there on October 8 met Wheeler from Tuscumbia.[31] The Chief of Cavalry had rested his men at Tuscumbia and armed the few new recruits brought out of Tennessee. After his request to join forces with Forrest had been rejected he had made his way across North Alabama working what destruction he could as he marched. At Courtland he stopped for a brief visit in the Jones home with the young widow Sherrod. Riding on he overtook his command at Huntsville. There he swung eastward and northward to enter Georgia. On October 2 he appeared before Dalton, the second time within thirty days. "Send forces immediately. Wheeler has sent a demand for the unconditional surrender of this post," Colonel Lewis Johnson in command wired his superior.[32] But Wheeler did nothing more than make a demonstration against Dalton. That night he camped near by at Snake Creek Gap and at dawn was on the move. Before departing, however, he tore up several miles of track which had just been repaired.

On October 4 Wheeler used a new device. After moving southward from Dalton he arrived at the swollen Conasauga River. Here he dismounted his men and began felling trees to build rafts. These rafts were launched in the swirling waters of the river to be carried by the current to Resaca. Here was a bridge, a very

---

[30] Liddell Hart, *Sherman,* 318.

[31] Francis A. Shoup's Journal, in *Official Records,* Ser. I, Vol. XXXIX, Pt. I, 806.

[32] Johnson to Sherman, October 2, 1864, *ibid.,* Pt. III, 31.

important one, through whose foundations these rafts
would not pass. The rafts piled up against the bridge,
the water piled up against them, and the bridge was
swept away. That night Thomas relayed the information to Grant. "Railroad torn up and burned for ten
miles. Chattahoochee bridge destroyed by high water
and 1 hundred feet of bridge at Resaca also carried
away by high water." [33]

From this point near Resaca, Wheeler and his men
turned westward again and marched toward Rome. On
the sixth General Sherman wrote that the commanding
officer at Rome reported "Wheeler all about." He was
so much "all about" that part of his command actually
entered the city on the day that he joined Hood. The
Texas Rangers rode up about noon in front of a small
hotel. Part of them dismounted and the rest relaxed
in the saddles, throwing their legs over the pommels,
sitting sideways, smoking, bantering. Suddenly a Negro
cook appeared from the hotel and began to beat a gong
for dinner. The horses reared and plunged. Riders
found themselves dumped precipitately to the ground,
and that was a disgrace to Texas Rangers. The stampede
left more riderless horsemen than the fire from a Federal battery might have done.[34]

"It will be a physical impossibility to protect the
roads, now that Hood, Forrest, and Wheeler, and the
whole batch of devils, are turned loose without home
or habitation. . . . I propose we break up the railroad
from Chattanooga, and strike out with wagons for Milledgeville, Millen, and Savannah. . . . By attempting
to hold the roads we will lose 1,000 men monthly, and
will gain no result. I can make the march, and make

[33] Thomas to Grant, October 4, 1864, *ibid.,* 79.
[34] Dodson, *Campaigns of Wheeler,* 282–83.

Georgia howl. . . . We can forage in the interior of
the State." [35] Thus did Sherman announce his intention
of turning his back on Hood and Atlanta, marching
to the sea, and establishing a new base at Savannah. This
was October 9, soon after Wheeler joined his forces
with Hood.

"At this time [October 16] I received intelligence
that Sherman had on the 13th, reached Snake Creek
Gap, where the right of his line had rested in the early
Spring of this year; also that he was marching in our
pursuit, whilst General Wheeler was endeavoring to
retard his advance as much as possible. I here determined to advance no further toward the Tennessee
river, but to select a position and deliver battle." [36]
Thus did Hood express a determination to fight.

But he did not fight. His officers were against making
a stand. "In this dilemma I conceived the plan of marching into Tennessee with the hope to establish our line
eventually in Kentucky." [37]

And so two great armies turned their backs on each
other after months of intimate contact and proposed
to fight it out in widely separated spheres. Both
leaders made preparations for their respective campaigns. Sherman had detached Thomas and sent him
to Nashville to arrest Hood's northward movement.
Hood left Wheeler to watch Sherman and called upon
Forrest to blaze the way for the advance into Tennessee.
It was the first time the Army of Tennessee had made
a forward movement that Wheeler had not had a part
in blazing the trail.

[35] Sherman to Grant, October 9, 1864, in *Official Records,* Ser. I, Vol.
XXXIX, Pt. III, 162.

[36] Hood, *Advance and Retreat,* 262–63.

[37] John B. Hood, "The Invasion of Tennessee," in *Battles and Leaders,* IV, 426.

On the eve of Hood's departure for Tennessee, Wheeler was instructed: "You must endeavor to keep the Atlanta and Dalton railroad constantly cut, and should the enemy evacuate Atlanta you must destroy all the road north of the Chattahoochee, and constantly concentrating toward your left be prepared to join at any time the main body of the army. Should the enemy advance anywhere you will drive off all the stock in their front and destroy all the mills within ten miles of their line of march, retarding them as much as possible." [38] Perhaps no soldier ever received a harder assignment. He must with forty-five hundred men destroy the railroad from Atlanta northward and at the same time be prepared to follow Sherman and fight him. He must destroy everything from which the enemy might derive sustenance and at the same time be prepared to join his main army. The attempt to carry out this order meant that he must bring his career to a close in an inglorious and fruitless dogging of Sherman's footsteps.

On the morning of November 16, 1864, General Sherman with his staff and escort rode out of Atlanta toward Milledgeville. His army had left Atlanta the day before and now as he rode along he found the roads choked with marching men and creaking wagons. Soon the flame-scarred remains of what had been Atlanta were left in the distance. He was away on his mission, but his final destination was not exactly clear in his mind. He was going first to Milledgeville, from there it might be Savannah, or Port Royal, South Carolina, or even Pensacola. The first night out was spent in camp near Stone Mountain destined in later years to be dedicated as a great monument to those leaders of the South

[38] Hood to Wheeler, October 22, 1864, in *Official Records,* Ser. I, Vol. XXXIX, Pt. III, 842.

who were engaged in fighting everything for which the invader stood. The next day the invading army marched through Covington with bands playing and colors flying. All along the way Negroes were besieging Sherman with their shouting and singing. The whites beholding the scene before them wisely kept to themselves and in spite of their hatred uttered no sound.

From Covington the army proceeded toward Milledgeville, foraging as it went. Molasses, corn, bacon, chickens, all were swallowed up to fill the gaping maw of a great army on the march. The country had not been visited before by a hostile army and thus had escaped the fate which had befallen the northern part of the state. There were vast stores of food in this goodly land, and there is abundant testimony that Sherman was not timid about taking these supplies. By the twenty-third Sherman was in Milledgeville quartered in the Governor's Mansion.[39]

Before leaving Atlanta Sherman had selected as his chief of cavalry young Judson Kilpatrick, a contemporary of Wheeler's at West Point. Both had been rivals for honors in conduct, with Kilpatrick having the edge here as in scholarship. He had no demerits at all for the year 1859 and Wheeler had only six.[40] Now they were rivals in a greater game—a game of killing and destroying, in which they could put into practice all they had learned at the old academy about those useful arts.

Sherman's march to the sea was practically uncontested except for Wheeler's continuous and dogging attacks on Kilpatrick and his cavalry. The day Sherman

---

[39] Sherman, *Memoirs,* II, 180 ff.
[40] *Official Register of the Officers and Cadets of the U.S. Military Academy, West Point, June, 1859.*

marched out of Atlanta, Wheeler made preparations to
follow him. The first of these preparations was an order
revoking that part of Hood's instructions which bade
him destroy everything in front of the enemy. Therefore he cautioned his men:

   I All orders heretofore issued regarding destroying sup-
      plies and removing stock before the enemy are modified
      as follows:
  II All mills near the enemy's line of march will be rendered
      useless to the enemy by breaking the machinery, and,
      when practicable, by drawing off the water.
 III No mill building, corn-crib, or any other private property
      will be burned or destroyed by this command.
  IV All horses, mules, and other stock which citizens have
      left on the enemy's line of march will be driven off and
      proper receipts left for the same. When no owner can be
      found, accurate accounts will be kept, so that the stock
      can be reclaimed by the owner.
   V Commanders of troops in falling back before the enemy
      will send reliable officers and men at least one day in
      advance to instruct citizens in which direction to drive
      their stock.[41]

   Wheeler seems to have realized the temptations to
which his men would be subjected in the matter of
depredations. The command was so loosely organized
that at times it apparently was not even one unit. When
Wheeler had joined Hood's army at Rome a few weeks
earlier, his original command had been reduced by
more than half during the Middle Tennessee raid. His
two leading generals, Kelly and Martin, were gone.
Captains now commanded regiments and colonels commanded brigades; and Bragg's orders read: "You are

   [41] Circular, November 15, 1864, in *Official Records,* Ser. I, Vol. XLIV,
859.

authorized to impress, for temporary use, all the labor-
ers and tools necessary, and to use the means of the people in the country, as far as they may be of advantage.
*Supplies of all kinds useful to the enemy and not re-
quired for your use must be destroyed."* Thus Wheeler
was ordered to take an undisciplined, disorganized
group of hungry cavalrymen and go into a portion of
the country to destroy anything which might be of use
to the enemy.[42]

In addition to this, every cavalryman must furnish
his own mount. The Confederacy did not furnish its
cavalrymen with horses. When they rode in to join
the cavalry they rode their own horses. If horses strayed
or were killed, then the riders must find others in any
way they might devise. Thus the Confederate government unwittingly encouraged horse-stealing. As early
as September 1 Major E. H. Ewing, Inspector of Field
Transportation, had protested against this practice.
"The policy adopted at the beginning of the war by the
Government of making cavalrymen mount themselves
is, in my opinion, the most extravagant to the Government, and has done more to demoralize the troops of
this branch of the service than any other cause," he
wrote. "When a soldier is dismounted . . . he is entitled to a furlough of thirty days to go home and re-
mount himself. This makes every cavalry soldier, or at
least all that desire to be, mere horse traders, selling
their animals whenever they desire to go home. Many
even go further than this; they steal every animal,
whether public or private, when it can be done with

---

[42] Bragg to Wheeler, December 1, 1864, *ibid.*, 916. Author's italics.
Wheeler had with him the divisions of Iverson, Humes, and Allen, and
one brigade of William H. Jackson's cavalry—a total of ten brigades
of unequal size.

any show of success in retaining him for a few days, until they can sell or swap him. . . . I respectfully suggest that all private animals now ridden by cavalrymen be taken possession of by the Government and paid for . . . and when a soldier is dismounted, if it can be shown that it was through no carelessness of his, let him be remounted by the Government. If through his negligence let him at once be sent to an infantry command." [43]

General Sherman continued his march, his right wing under Howard, the left under Slocum, Kilpatrick commanding the cavalry—total strength approximately sixty-eight thousand.[44] Each corps was independent for supplies and moved on a separate road. The right wing moved south apparently aiming at Macon, but swerved southeast before they reached the city. The left wing advanced eastward toward Augusta, but changed its course through Madison to Milledgeville. The left wing occupied Milledgeville on November 22. Simultaneously the right wing reached Gordon, ten miles away.[45] Sherman had thoroughly deceived the Confederate forces in Georgia, Wheeler and Hardee, in particular. Hardee, now in command of the Department of South Carolina, Georgia, and Florida, believed that Macon was the objective of the right wing and Augusta the objective of the left. Wheeler with his cavalry and some three thousand Georgia militia had rushed to the defense of Macon where they were joined by about twelve thousand troops from scattered points within the department. When Macon was not attacked Hardee sent

[43] Inspector E. H. Ewing to Chief of Field Transportation, September 1, 1864, *ibid.*, Vol. XXXVIII, Pt. V, 1014.
[44] Fiebeger, *Campaigns of the American Civil War*, 386.
[45] Liddell Hart, *Sherman*, 336–37.

all except Wheeler's cavalry to Savannah. Wheeler with
his three divisions swam the Oconee near Milledgeville
and gained Sherman's front. In the meantime, General
Bragg on November 30 reached Augusta from North
Carolina with ten thousand troops to protect that
point.[46]

On leaving Milledgeville November 24 Sherman
changed Kilpatrick from his right to his left (toward
Augusta) to convey the impression that this move was
preliminary to a general attack on the city. By the
twenty-sixth Wheeler had reached Waynesboro, thirty
miles up the Savannah from Augusta; and that afternoon his pickets brought in the information that Kilpatrick was moving toward Augusta.[47] Acting immediately Wheeler concentrated his troopers at Briar Creek,
whereupon Kilpatrick rode around Wheeler and struck
out toward Waynesboro with the intention of destroying the Savannah and Augusta railroad there. When
Wheeler discovered that Kilpatrick had given him the
"run around" he set out in pursuit. When he arrived
at Waynesboro it was after dark and the Federal cavalry
was busy burning the town and destroying the railroad.
"I immediately moved on and attacked the enemy, who
were engaged in tearing up the railroad," Wheeler reported. "The attack had the effect to stop their work
upon the railroad and keep them in line of battle all
night." [48]

At three o'clock in the morning Wheeler sent Humes's
division to the enemy's rear by a flanking movement to
the left. Simultaneously a regiment was sent by the right

46 *Ibid.*

47 Wheeler's Report, December 24, 1864, in *Official Records,* Ser. I,
Vol. XLIV, 408.

48 *Ibid.*

flank for the same purpose. At daylight Wheeler charged
the enemy's front and flanks, driving him from his position, capturing a number of prisoners, and killing many
who refused to surrender. General Kilpatrick himself
was almost captured.[49] It was "one of the most desperate
cavalry charges I have ever witnessed," wrote Kilpatrick; [50] but he failed to mention the fact that he had
barely escaped. As a matter of fact he reported a smash-
ing victory despite the fact that he fell back to join the
infantry at Sandersville.[51]

This was the last pitched battle between the two classmates; but soon they were engaged in a war of words.
It all started over a request of Kilpatrick that a certain
Captain Norton who had been wounded in an attack
on Wheeler's fortifications be returned to the Federal
lines. "For the memory of old associations, please let
Corpl. M. D. Lacey, Tenth Ohio Cavalry, remain to at-
tend a wounded soldier. . . . Please show him such attention as is in your power, and at some future day you
shall have the thanks of your old friend," the letter
ran.[52]

"I assure you Captain Norton has and will receive
every attention which can be bestowed upon a wounded
soldier," Wheeler replied. "I am pleased to inform you
that he was doing well and out of pain at last accounts."
It was too good an opportunity to let pass without
administering a reprimand for Federal depredations.
"Since the commencement of this sad war I have used
untiring efforts to maintain in my soldiers principles
of chivalry and true soldierly honor," Wheeler informed
his opponent. "They have been taught to despise and

49 *Ibid.*
50 Judson Kilpatrick's Report, December 27, 1864, *ibid.,* 364.
51 *Ibid.*   52 Kilpatrick to Wheeler, December 4, 1864, *ibid.,* 627.

spurn the cowardly instincts which induce low men to frighten, abuse, and rob defenseless women and children. You allude to old associations, and promise to return any kindness to Captain Norton. I have only to ask, for the sake of these old associations, for your own sake, and for the sake of the institution where military honor was taught, that you will offer some protection to the families necessarily left defenseless, and not leave them at the mercy of a brutal soldiery. . . . It is useless for me to recount the atrocities committed; suffice it to say, that the history of no war, however barbarous, can tell of atrocities equal to those daily and hourly committed by your command." [53]

"I will simply say that the same complaints have been made by the citizens of Georgia against officers and men of your own command," Kilpatrick shot back. "If you cannot control your men while they are among their friends, you cannot expect me to prevent my men from committing depredations upon their known enemies. . . . War is terrible, and the people of Georgia are now being made to feel this in all its force. Had the people of the Confederate States, and especially those of South Carolina, ever known and felt what the people of Georgia know and feel now, no hostile shot would ever have struck the sacred walls of Sumter." [54]

Kilpatrick's charge that complaints had been made by Georgia citizens against Wheeler's men for alleged depredations was assuredly true. From various parts of the state serious charges were being brought against the Confederate leader. As early as August, 1864, Robert Toombs wrote Vice-President Alexander Stephens: "The enemy care nothing for Wheeler and his seven

[53] Wheeler to Kilpatrick, December 5, 1864, *ibid.*, 635.
[54] Kilpatrick to Wheeler, December 13, 1864, *ibid.*, 706–707.

thousand cavalry in the rear. They did not obstruct his trains more than four days, if that; and Wheeler avoided all depots where there were as much as armed sutlers. He has been gone [to Tennessee] for three weeks. I cannot say he has done no good for he has relieved the poor people of this part of the country temporarily from his plundering marauding bands of cowardly robbers. . . . I hope to God he will never get back to Georgia." [55] In December, 1864, P. A. Lawson wrote President Davis characterizing the cavalry as "Wheeler's robbers" and stating that the people of Georgia had about come to the point where they did not care which army won, as Sherman was not making war any harder on them than the cavalry of their own army.[56] In January, 1865, General Daniel H. Hill from Augusta wrote that "the whole of Georgia is full of bitter complaints of Wheeler's cavalry." [57]

General Beauregard at Charleston wrote the Confederate War Department December 23, 1864, that "unless Wheeler's command of twelve so-called brigades can be properly organized into divisions, under good commanders, a large portion of it had better be dismounted forthwith; its conduct in front of the enemy, and its depredations on private property, render it worse than useless." [58] This, of course, was too important a communication to be overlooked, and so on December 28 Wheeler wrote Bragg a letter in his own defense. The

[55] Robert Toombs to Alexander H. Stephens, August 30, 1864, in Ulrich B. Phillips (ed.), *The Correspondence of Robert Toombs, Alexander H. Stephens, and Howell Cobb,* in American Historical Association, *Annual Report,* 1911, II (Washington, 1913), 651.

[56] See *Official Records,* Ser. IV, Vol. III, 967–68.

[57] Hill to Iverson, January 27, 1865, *ibid.,* Ser. I, Vol. XLVII, Pt. II, 1047.

[58] Beauregard to Seddon, December 23, 1864, *ibid.,* Vol. XLIV, 979.

charge of straggling, he admitted, was partially true, but
the great cause was the issuing of an illegal order by
General Taylor directing General James H. Clanton to
organize all absentees into ninety-day regiments. Clanton's officers, Wheeler stated, "enlisted men directly
from my ranks, and this nearly ruined one brigade and
had a bad effect upon my entire command." [59] Charges
of horse-stealing, Wheeler continued, were untrue as
were the charges of mill-burning. As a matter of fact,
Wheeler asserted, he had "positive proof that the country swarmed with organized parties who do not and
never did belong to my command." Most of these, he
claimed, were acting under orders from Governor
Joseph E. Brown, "but in all their stealing they claimed
to belong to Wheeler's cavalry." [60]

A few days after this, on January 8, General Hardee
came to Wheeler's defense. Writing directly to President Davis he said: "Wheeler's cavalry has been reorganized under my direct supervision, and now consists
of three divisions and eight brigades. It is a well organized and efficient body. The reports of its disorganiza-
tion and demoralization are without foundation, and
the depredations ascribed to his command can generally be traced to bands of marauders claiming to belong
to it. I know of nothing at present to add to its effectiveness except the promotion of Brigadier-General Allen
to major-general, and of Colonel Dibrell to brigadier-
general, for which recommendations have been sent
on." [61]

---

[59] Wheeler to Bragg, December 28, 1864, *ibid.*, 998.   [60] *Ibid.*

[61] Hardee to Davis, January 8, 1865, *ibid.*, Vol. XLVII, Pt. II, 1000.
General Hardee commanded the Department of South Carolina and
Georgia; General Bragg commanded the Department of North Carolina;
General Beauregard was in command of the entire Department of the
West.

There were other matters of greater importance during December, 1864, and January, 1865, however, which occupied the minds of Confederate leaders. On December 13 Fort McAllister at the mouth of the Ogeechee River, twelve miles south of Savannah, fell to Sherman. On the twentieth Hardee evacuated Savannah, sending his troops across to the South Carolina shore, and Sherman entered the city on the twenty-first. At Franklin, Tennessee, on November 30 the old guard of the Army of Tennessee under Hood threw itself at the Federals and left more than six thousand dead on the breastworks.[62] The remaining ones went on to meet defeat at Nashville on December 16. Now at the time that Hardee was moving his troops across the Savannah, the remnant of Hood's army was moving back toward the Tennessee.[63]

Once Hardee's troops were across the river to temporary safety in South Carolina, General Beauregard again turned to the matter of Wheeler's command. On December 28 he sent Inspector Alfred Roman to make a special inspection of Wheeler's corps, and on January 24, 1865, Roman sent his voluminous report to Beauregard.[64] According to Roman the organization, armament, equipment, discipline, and military appearance were bad. Divisions were not larger than brigades and brigades were not larger than regiments, he reported. One company had one officer and one man. Another had one man and no officer at all. The armament, he found, was deficient. There were but 3,896 rifles for near five thousand men, and only 1,978 pistols. Cloth-

---

[62] Shotwell, *Civil War in America,* II, 320.

[63] See Henry Stone, "Repelling Hood's Invasion of Tennessee," in *Battles and Leaders,* IV, 440–64.

[64] Roman's Report, January 22, 1865, in Beauregard Papers.

ing, he reported, was "very deficient." Men were "in a suffering condition, many of them in a ragged condition." Discipline, he thought, was poor, having become "loose, uncertain, wavering." Roll calls, he said, were neglected and "the careless way about most of the officers and men plainly indicates how little they value the details of army regulations and of tactics in general." As for depredations Roman reported:

Much has been said—and is still being said—of the gross misconduct of Gen. Wheeler's men. Their alleged depredations and straggling propensities and their reported brutal interference with private property, have become common by-words in every county where it has been their misfortune to pass. Public rumor condemns them everywhere; and not a few do we find in Georgia as well as in South Carolina who look upon them more as a band of highway robbers than as an organized military band.

But the inspector defended Wheeler's command against all these charges. "While I am ready to admit that much truth is hidden under some of the rumors thus brought into circulation," he wrote, "yet justice makes it a duty upon me to add that not a little is said about the command which is utterly false." The cry of "mad dog," he thought, was being brought into play. "Men, depredators, horse-thieves, purporting to be of Wheeler's command, have been arrested of late, who, when confronted have been proven to have never belonged to the corps under whose name they had striven to conceal their misdeeds, in order to avoid the punishment they justly deserved." He would not, he reported, screen the bad men which formed "only a small portion of the corps," but suggested that the corps should not be judged by their conduct. Most of the men who rode with Wheeler were, he said, of the same type, "the very same type," as found in every branch of the Confederate service.

The chief trouble, he thought, was fivefold. "After having carefully weighed the different reasons which could have brought forth the undisciplined, loose, and relative inefficiency of Wheeler's command" he came to the conclusion that five things accounted for the condition, namely:

1. The negligence and incompetency of many of the company and regiment commanders.
2. The want of system and good administration in the commissary department.
3. The great irregularity in the payment of troops.
4. The error of allowing cavalrymen to procure their own horses, instead of having them furnished by the government.
5. Excessive leniency of the corps commander.[65]

As the last item indicates, Roman held Wheeler personally responsible for part of the confusion. While, he said, he was aware that the reasons given for the loose discipline in Wheeler's corps "exist also, more or less, in Forrest's and Hampton's commands," he was strongly of the opinion that conditions could not be improved so long as Wheeler was in command. "Had I the power to act in the matter," he concluded, "I would relieve General Wheeler from his command; not as a rebuke, not as a punishment, for he surely deserves neither; but on higher grounds—that is to say for the good of the cause, and for his own reputation." [66]

No immediate changes were made by Beauregard, and in spite of charges of inefficiency Wheeler went ahead

[65] *Ibid.*   [66] *Ibid.*

fighting Sherman as best he could. Sherman had remained in Savannah almost one month. During that time he was preparing for his march through the Carolinas and eventually to make contact with Grant somewhere near Richmond. The "concentric movement" which he and his chief had planned was about to be fulfilled. During this period of rest he went over the matter thoroughly with Grant and the authorities at Washington. "The truth is the whole army is burning with an insatiable desire to wreak vengeance upon South Carolina," he wrote to Halleck. "I almost tremble at her fate, but feel that she deserves all that seems in store for her. . . . I look upon Columbia as quite as bad as Charleston, and I doubt if we shall spare the public buildings there, as we did at Milledgeville." [67] If Georgia had been scourged with whips, now South Carolina would be scourged with scorpions!

Sherman's first movement to cross the Savannah was to lay a pontoon bridge and send Kilpatrick and his cavalry across to blaze the way and feel out the country. Wheeler observed Kilpatrick's movement and made preparations to receive him. The river being at flood stage, he moved a few miles up the river, constructed rafts as he had done in Georgia, and floated these rafts down upon the pontoons. A few Federals were drowned, but engineers quickly repaired the breach and the movement went on. All the ferries across the Savannah were intact and every one was utilized by Sherman in sending his troops across. Wheeler divided his forces and sent small detachments to contest the crossing, but to little avail. Other groups were put to work felling trees across the roads over which the invader must march north-

[67] Sherman to Halleck, December 24, 1864, in *Official Records,* Ser. I, Vol. XLIV, 799.

ward. "We encountered Wheeler's cavalry," wrote Sherman in later years, "which had obstructed the road by felling trees, but our men picked these up and threw them aside, so that his obstruction hardly delayed us an hour." [68]

Wheeler had in November prevented Kilpatrick from reaching Augusta from the Georgia side. Now the Federal Chief of Cavalry attempted to reach the town from the South Carolina side. He had, in addition to his cavalry, a corps of infantry. As news of his approach reached Augusta, preparations were made to burn the cotton and stores to prevent their falling into the enemy's hands. Wheeler gathered two thousand of his scattered troops and interposed himself at Aiken between Kilpatrick and Augusta. Then he sent a message to General D. H. Hill in command at Augusta suggesting that the burning of the cotton there be delayed. "We would feel very badly to burn so much cotton if the enemy should not reach the city," he wrote.[69]

The battle of Aiken took place on February 11. Kilpatrick began his advance upon the place early in the morning. Wheeler withdrew his men to a hidden position in the rear of the town, planning to strike when the Federals broke rank to enter the town. One column was to strike the enemy's flank while the other, broken into squadrons, was to advance down different streets striking at irregular intervals. The plan worked. Every way Kilpatrick turned he encountered a squadron of rebel cavalry. His classmate had outguessed him this time. He tried to rally his troops, but the confusion of breaking rank to enter the town rendered this next to

[68] Sherman, *Memoirs*, II, 272.
[69] Wheeler to Hill, February 11, 1865, in *Official Records*, Ser. I, Vol. XLVII, Pt. II, 1163.

impossible, and he was forced to fall back on his infantry about five miles from town.

General Hill reported that the battle was a "handsome affair" with Kilpatrick being driven back some four miles.[70] Kilpatrick, however, was not willing to admit his defeat. "I lost but 25 men killed and wounded and less than 20 taken prisoners," he reported. "It was not a general fight, but simply a reconnaissance. This party fell back slowly from Aiken. . . . Wheeler has, as usual, reported a victory over my people, whose backs he has never yet seen, and from all that I can learn a portion of our army seems only too willing to believe such reports." [71]

But there were others besides his own men who were "ready to believe such reports." From Augusta General Hill wired Wheeler: "I congratulate you on your success." [72] From the Statehouse came a message from Governor Andrew G. Magrath. "I avail myself of the earliest opportunity to offer you, in behalf of the State, my thanks for the defense of the town of Aiken, and the protection given in that defense to the population of that town. To be saved, as was that town and its population, from the ruthless foes by which it was attacked calls not only for the thanks of those immediately exposed, but to the grateful remembrance of all classes of our citizens. To you, and through you to that portion of your command which participated in the conflict for the possession of Aiken, I tender you the thanks of the State." [73]

But Wheeler's victory at Aiken did not redeem his

[70] Hill to Beauregard, February 12, 1865, *ibid.*, 1170.
[71] Kilpatrick's Report, February 16, 1865, *ibid.*, 450.
[72] Hill to Wheeler, February 11, 1865, *ibid.*, 1164.
[73] Andrew G. Magrath to *id.*, February 28, 1865, *ibid.*, 1295.

waning reputation. Beauregard, long dissatisfied with the conduct of his troops, and doubtless acting on Roman's report, now recommended that Wheeler be replaced as chief of cavalry by Major General Wade Hampton, who had lately come from Lee's army. Wheeler had been ranking officer of the cavalry branch since J. E. B. Stuart's death in May, 1864. Now he was to be removed. "I earnestly recommend, for the good of the service and cause, that General Hampton be promoted temporarily to command all the cavalry of this department, which can not be rendered otherwise as effective as present emergencies demand," Beauregard wrote General Lee. "Major-General Wheeler, who ranks only a few days, is a modest, zealous, gallant, and indefatigable officer, but he cannot properly control and direct successfully so large a corps of cavalry." [74]

The transfer of command to Hampton was made quietly and without fanfare. Hampton had come from the Army of Northern Virginia in the latter part of January to Charleston. On February 7 he was assigned to the command of two small divisions of cavalry, one commanded by Major General P. M. B. Young (formerly Iverson's division), and one under Major General Matthew C. Butler, lately of the Army of Northern Virginia.[75] On February 17 Hampton's authority was extended over all the cavalry in the department. There was no bitterness on Wheeler's part. When Hampton personally informed Wheeler of the change it is said that Wheeler replied with alacrity: "Certainly, gen-

[74] Beauregard to Lee, February 12, 1865, *ibid.*, 1165.
[75] Special Orders, No. 32, February 7, 1865, *ibid.*, 1112. Wade Hampton was made a lieutenant general on February 16, 1865, the day before he was made chief of cavalry. Wheeler apparently finished the war with the rank of major general, although in after years he referred to himself as lieutenant general.

eral, I will receive your orders with pleasure." [76] Perhaps he was glad to be relieved of the responsibility.

At any rate, both men turned to the defense of Columbia, Wheeler being assigned the job of guarding the approaches to the city. These approaches were across three streams, the Saluda, the Congaree, and the Broad. All were comparatively small streams, but large enough to afford some protection to the city. Wheeler was to patrol these and keep out Sherman's army. Just how Beauregard expected the Confederate cavalry to work miracles is not recorded, but he informed Wheeler rather testily: "I regret to hear the enemy has crossed the Saluda. Endeavor by all means to prevent him from crossing the Broad. Burn the bridge should it become necessary." [77]

And it did become necessary to burn the bridge. Wheeler took his escort and crossed to the enemy's side of the stream to hold them in check while his men fired the bridge. Then when it was thoroughly ignited he and his men recrossed—that is, all of them except one. Captain John R. Mathews of the Eighth Confederate had been killed. Several of his company dashed back across the burning bridge. One of them scooped up the body of his dead captain, swung it across the pommel of his saddle, and bore it back to be buried.[78]

The Fifteenth and Seventeenth corps under Generals John A. Logan and Francis P. Blair entered Columbia on February 17. Wheeler and his men were powerless to prevent it. The entrance of the Federals was the

---

[76] Quoted in Dubose, *Wheeler and the Army of Tennessee*, 430.

[77] Beauregard to Wheeler, February 16, 1865, in *Official Records*, Ser. I, Vol. XLVII, Pt. II, 1207.

[78] Dubose, *Wheeler and the Army of Tennessee*, 431.

signal for a fresh outburst of marauding and destroying. Private homes were pillaged, jewelry was taken, cotton was burned, and at last the town was fired. Wheeler and his men hovered about but were powerless to relieve the situation. The only blow struck in the defense of the city was by him, but it was ineffectual. On the same day that Sherman entered Columbia, Charleston was evacuated, and the grip of the besieger was tightened about Petersburg.

Following the disastrous encounter with Thomas at Nashville, Hood had taken his battered and torn Army of Tennessee to Tupelo, Mississippi, for winter quarters. Now with Sherman on his rampage through the Carolinas this army was again put on the march to help fight him. The crippled Hood retired and his soldiers got their "Uncle Joe" again, for General Lee now replaced Beauregard with Johnston. It was given to the veteran Joseph Eggleston Johnston to surrender the army. To assist him came Hardee from Charleston with his garrison and Bragg from Wilmington with a few troops. In all, the Confederates mustered some twenty-five thousand troops to arrest the relentless and triumphant march of Sherman.

Soon after the burning of Columbia the Federals took up the march toward North Carolina, Kilpatrick and his cavalry leading the way and keeping back the straggling lines of Confederates. Here some of the bitterest fighting of the whole war was carried on. It was not in pitched battles, but rather it had degenerated to guerrilla warfare. The contest between Wheeler and Kilpatrick seems to have become a personal matter between their troops. Both young leaders resorted again to lectures. Kilpatrick wrote:

Yesterday a lieutenant and seven men and a sergeant of a battery were taken prisoners by one of your regiments— if I am correctly informed, a Texas regiment—armed with Spencer carbines and commanded by a lieutenant-colonel. This officer and his men after surrendering and being disarmed, were inhumanely and cowardly murdered. Nine of my cavalrymen were also found murdered yesterday, five in a barn-yard, three in an open field, and one in the road. Two had their throats cut from ear to ear. This makes in all eighteen Federal soldiers murdered yesterday by your people. Unless some satisfactory explanation be made to me before sundown, February 23, I will cause eighteen of your soldiers, now my prisoners, to be shot at that hour.[79]

Not only was Kilpatrick going to punish Wheeler's outfit, but he proposed to take it out on the neighboring country. "If this cowardly act be repeated, if my people when taken are not treated in all cases as prisoners of war should be, I will not only retaliate as I have already mentioned, but there shall not be a house left standing within reach of my scouting parties along my line of march, nor will I be responsible for the conduct of my soldiers, who will not only be allowed but encouraged to take a fearful revenge. I know of no other way to intimidate cowards." [80]

"If any of my regiments were engaged with the enemy yesterday that fact has not yet been reported to me," Wheeler answered. "I will have the matter promptly investigated and see that full justice is done. Should the report, however, by any means prove correct I prefer that the retaliation may be inflicted upon the parties guilty of the misdeeds, and not upon innocent persons.

[79] Kilpatrick to Wheeler, February 22, 1865, in *Official Records,* Ser. I, Vol. XLVII, Pt. I, 860.
[80] *Ibid.*

I have no desire whatever to make counter-threats in response to those which you have thought proper to address to me, but should you cause eighteen of my men to be shot because you chanced to find that number of your men dead, I shall regard them as so many murders committed by you, and act accordingly. I trust, however, such a painful necessity may not be forced upon me. Your threat to 'burn every house as far as your [sic] scouts can extend' is of too brutal a character for me, and I think for my Government, to reply to." [81]

The executions were not ordered by Kilpatrick and he moved along toward North Carolina with Sherman.

As Sherman continued his northward march Wheeler held himself between the Federal columns and Hardee, who had crossed the Peedee River to effect a junction with Bragg. When Wheeler reached the river he found it at flood stage. It was imperative, he said, that he should cross, but the ferryman refused. The oldest riverman declared it impossible, and so he decided to swim it. Twenty Texans volunteered to follow him. Thus twenty-one men plunged into the flood. Eighteen of them were soon swept downstream. Wheeler and two privates made the crossing. On the other side of the river he ascertained that Kilpatrick was between Hampton and Hardee at Fayetteville. Wheeler reported this fact to Hampton, and for the first time the two cavalry commands were united—united to fight Kilpatrick.

By March 9 the river had subsided enough for Wheeler's command to cross. Immediately they were put into action. That night Wheeler and Hampton came upon Kilpatrick's camp and at daylight of March 10 Wheeler's troops charged into the enemy camp. "In less

[81] Wheeler to Kilpatrick, February 22, 1865, *ibid.*

than a minute [they] had driven back my people, and taken possession of my headquarters, captured the artillery, and the whole command was flying before the most formidable cavalry charge I ever have witnessed," Kilpatrick reported. "Colonel [George E.] Spencer and a large portion of my staff were virtually taken prisoners." [82]

But the charge had been made against stubborn resistance. Among Wheeler's wounded were Generals Humes, Hannon, and Hagan, besides every field officer in Hagan's brigade. Generals Allen and Ashby had horses shot from under them.[83]

It was a signal triumph for Wheeler, however, in one respect. The attack had been so sudden and so swift that Kilpatrick was forced to flee in his night clothes. The Confederates had dashed headlong into the camp and General Kilpatrick had fled through a window minus his uniform. In after years Kilpatrick might relate a number of instances in which he had defeated Wheeler but he could never relate an instance in which he had chased the diminutive rebel general in his night clothes.[84]

[82] Kilpatrick's Report, April 5, 1865, *ibid.*, 861. Kilpatrick reported that it was Hampton rather than Wheeler who led the charge, but he obviously was mistaken. General Hampton apparently was not present at the fight and his reports make no mention of the incident. See Dubose, *Wheeler and the Army of Tennessee*, 447–48. Edward L. Wells in "A Morning Call on General Kilpatrick," in *Southern Historical Society Papers* (Richmond), XII (1884), 123–30, states that it was General Butler who actually led the charge and that Wheeler came up immediately afterwards. See also, Edward L. Wells, *Hampton and His Cavalry in '64* (Richmond, 1899), 397 ff.

[83] Wheeler's Report, March 23, 1865, in *Official Records*, Ser. I, Vol. XLVII, Pt. I, 1130.

[84] Dubose, *Wheeler and the Army of Tennessee*, 448. According to Dubose, Wheeler's men presented him with Kilpatrick's horse and pistols captured at the time.

The fighting now came rapidly to a close. The Confederates drew themselves up at Bentonville for a last desperate stand but Sherman was irresistible. He moved on toward Raleigh, Confederate cavalry still hovering on his flanks. There was random fighting, but the contest was over. General Johnston had hastily collected the battered remnants of the Army of Tennessee to say its burial rites. Following Lee's surrender at Appomattox the Army of Tennessee capitulated on April 26 near Durham Station in the state of North Carolina. The two classmates Wheeler and Kilpatrick issued farewell messages to their commands. "You have fought your battles; your task is done," said Wheeler to his troopers. "During a four years' struggle for liberty you have exhibited courage, fortitude and devotion: you are the sole victors of more than two hundred severely contested fields; you have participated in more than a thousand successful conflicts of arms. You are heroes, veterans, patriots. The bones of your comrades mark battlefields upon the soil of Kentucky, Tennessee, Virginia, North Carolina, South Carolina, Georgia, Alabama and Mississippi; you have done all that human exertion could accomplish.

"In bidding you adieu, I desire to tender my thanks for your gallantry in battle, your fortitude under suffering, and your devotion at all times to the holy cause you have done so much to maintain. I desire also to express my gratitude for the kind feeling you have seen fit to extend toward myself and to invoke upon you the blessings of our heavenly Father, to whom we must always look in the hour of distress.

"Pilgrims in the cause of freedom, comrades in arms, I bid you farewell." [85]

[85] Quoted in *ibid.*, 469.

"This day I met our great chief on the field of battle, amid the dead and dying of our enemy, who has again fled before our proud, advancing banners, and my ears were made to tingle with the grateful words of praise spoken in admiration of the cavalry," Kilpatrick's message said. "Soldiers, be proud! Of all the brave men of this army you have a right to be. You have won the admiration of our infantry, fighting on foot and mounted, and you will receive the outspoken words of praise from the great Sherman himself.

"He appreciates and will reward your patient endurance of hardships, gallant deeds, and valuable services.

"With the old laurels of Georgia entwine those won in the Carolinas, and proudly wear them.

"General Sherman is satisfied with his cavalry." [86]

[86] *Official Records,* Ser. I, Vol. XLVII, Pt. I, 864.

Chapter IX

TO PRISON WITH THE PRESIDENT

THERE is something pitifully dramatic in the efforts of Jefferson Davis to stave off defeat during the twilight hours of the Confederacy. For some months prior to April, 1865, he had practically been discredited in the eyes of many Southern people.[1] The South was perishing, the cause had visibly failed, and yet at Richmond a broken and suffering President refused to acknowledge the collapse. It seems impossible to know just what transpired in his mind during those dread days. In his *The Rise and Fall of the Confederate Government* he tells us everything but that which we most want to know.

Whatever may have been his reasons for entertaining certain ideas that the fight might be carried on in the trans-Mississippi country, it seems evident that many of his soldiers were not so inclined. There were doubtless some who would follow him to the bitter end, but there is abundant evidence that most of them were ready to go home. For four years the men of the South had fought with a courage seldom equaled in history, but now it was all over. Now they could go home, raise a crop, and settle themselves to the task of reconstruction.

President Davis was in church on Sunday morning, April 2, when General Lee's telegram came announc-

[1] H. J. Eckenrode, *Jefferson Davis, President of the South* (New York, 1923), 311.

ing the evacuation of Richmond. Late that afternoon he made his way southward toward the Carolinas by train. Next morning he was in Greensboro, North Carolina.[2] From Greensboro the party journeyed toward Charlotte. Here he received a telegram announcing the assassination of President Lincoln. Here, also, he was handed the articles of surrender agreed upon by Sherman and Johnston. The end had come. His counselors began to take their leave. One by one they departed, leaving the fallen President almost alone—a shell of a man racked with pain, yet blindly hopeful.[3]

Already the search for Davis was getting under way. The North was in a frenzy over the death of Lincoln. They had reviled and abused him through most of the four years of the war, but now that he was dead they rose up with one voice and demanded a life for a life. In his extremity President Davis called upon Hampton's and Wheeler's cavalry to protect him. Both these generals had been absent when Johnston surrendered and thus felt that they might go as guard for Davis without violating paroles.[4]

General Wheeler himself has given a picture of this last gesture of Davis. "While he saw the necessity of further retreat," he says, "he did not realize the completeness of our undoing. He still hoped that the tide of calamity might be turned. Around him was preserved

[2] Elizabeth Cutting, *Jefferson Davis, Political Soldier* (New York, 1930), 289. See also, A. J. Hanna, *Flight into Oblivion* (New York, 1938), Chap. I.

[3] Joseph Wheeler, "An Effort to Rescue Jefferson Davis," in *Century Magazine* (New York), LVI (1898), 85–91.

[4] For the plans of Hampton and Wheeler, see Hampton to Joseph E. Johnston, April 26, 1865, in *Official Records,* Ser. I, Vol. XLVII, Pt. III, 841; Wheeler to Hampton, April 26, 1865, *ibid.;* Hampton to Johnston, April 27, 1865, *ibid.,* 846; Johnston to Wheeler, April 27, 1865, *ibid.*

the semblance of power and routine of government, and on the day of my arrival I remember that a young cadet underwent a regular form of examination for promotion to the office of lieutenant." [5]

Davis was keenly interested in knowing how many men could be counted upon to support this new venture. "He was surprised and disappointed," Wheeler continued, "when, speaking with the authority of one just come from the army, I told him it was very evident that our soldiers regarded the war as over, and their allegiance to the Confederate government as no longer binding."

" 'I can do this, Mr. President,' " Wheeler suggested, " 'that is, gather from my command a body of new men who will stand by you in a new enterprise.' " [6]

At this suggestion the President visibly brightened and informed Wheeler he wanted to try it out. The two cavalry leaders, Wheeler and Hampton, were instructed to go back to their commands and see what they could do about getting volunteers.[7] Riding all night in a box car these two officers reached Greensboro in the morning. There the ways parted for them, Hampton going on to his command and Wheeler stopping with his.

Wheeler's troops were camped at Company's Shops, a village a few miles east of Greensboro. Immediately upon his arrival Wheeler gathered his men about him. Jefferson Davis, he explained in a short speech, needed men who were willing to engage in a desperate adventure. Just what this adventure was would be disclosed to them at the proper time, but above all they must be willing unquestioningly to follow Davis even to death.[8]

As Wheeler completed his speech he looked up and

[5] Wheeler, "An Effort to Rescue Jefferson Davis," in *loc. cit.,* 85.
[6] *Ibid.,* 85–86.   [7] *Ibid.,* 86.   [8] *Ibid.*

down the lines of solemn faces. There was no cheering, no great display of emotion. Six hundred men stepped forward and said they would go. Without further ado they mounted their horses and with Wheeler in the lead headed south for Cokesboro, South Carolina, where Davis expected to meet them. While on the march, however, Davis ordered a change of plans. Wheeler was notified that Washington, Georgia, would be the rendezvous instead of Cokesboro.

On Sunday evening, May 1, exactly one month after Davis had left Richmond, Wheeler and his troops reached Yorkville, South Carolina, the home of General Hampton. Wheeler called on Mrs. Hampton that afternoon to pay his respects and have tea. Soon after rejoining his troops he received a note from Mrs. Hampton which said that her husband had come home and wished to talk with General Wheeler. On Monday morning Wheeler paid a second call at the Hampton home. He found Hampton discouraged, "and I was shocked at the broken appearance of my fellow-officer," wrote Wheeler. "He was harassed in mind and worn in body; and the story of his march from Greensboro' made it plain to us all how sadly our fortunes had fallen." [9]

Few of General Hampton's troops had responded to the call for volunteers. As a result he started south with only his escort of thirty men. One by one, even they deserted him; "some begging off on account of their families, others alleging their horses could go no farther." "Their spirit was gone; they felt that the expedition was without a purpose or hope." So General Hampton had let them go, officers and men, until the day he reached home there remained only one man with him, his Chief of Staff, General Henry B. McClellan. But

[9] *Ibid.*

even McClellan had not remained with his superior to the end. When the two had reached the Peedee River near Yorkville, McClellan spoke of his wife and child and expressed the fear that his horse could not swim the river. He turned back and rode away leaving his General to plunge into the river alone. So it was that Hampton came home.[10] So did many an officer of the Confederacy come home, spirits broken, hopes blasted, their slaves free.

Now that General Hampton was at home, Mrs. Hampton insisted that his physical condition was such that he could not go on to overtake the fleeing President. In this Wheeler concurred. The two of them, Wheeler and Mrs. Hampton, prevailed upon him to remain at home, repair his health, and look after his business interests long neglected. "He finally yielded," Wheeler wrote, "and giving me a letter for Mr. Davis, asked me to tell the President that if, in the future, there should appear any way in which he could serve him, he would do so to the last." [11]

Thus Wheeler was left alone with his few ragged troops to continue the march. As they neared the Georgia line Wheeler realized that he could not keep even a small body of troops together without exciting the suspicion of Federal officers whom they might encounter. Soon after crossing the Savannah River he, according to a previous agreement with the President, divided his force into small groups and directed them to move by different routes to Washington. For his own protection he retained three staff officers and seven or eight privates armed with pistols and repeating rifles.

In the meantime, the Presidential party slowly made its way southward. Mrs. Davis had gone on to Abbe-

[10] *Ibid.*   [11] *Ibid.,* 86–87.

ville, South Carolina, and expected her husband to join her there, but Davis sent word that she should go on and not wait for him. He was discouraged and apparently had come to find out what Wheeler and Hampton already knew—that the Confederacy had collapsed and the soldiers were ready to quit fighting. On May 3 Davis wrote his secretary, Burton N. Harrison: "I have the bitterest disappointment in regard to the feeling of our troops, and would not have any one I love dependent upon their resistance against an equal force." [12]

On May 4 Davis crossed the Savannah River into Georgia, hastening on to the rendezvous with Wheeler at Washington and possible escape to the West. Here he disbanded the troops who had accompanied him. There was need for speed now, he found. The Federals were all around and the body of troops with him could only attract unfavorable attention, as he hurried on toward the Florida border.[13] On May 10, a few miles east of Irwinsville, Georgia, the Presidential party was surprised and captured by a troop of Federal cavalry under the command of Colonel Benjamin D. Pritchard.[14] The entire party was taken to Macon and turned over to General James H. Wilson, regional commander.

Wheeler and his escort reached Washington about twelve hours after the Presidential party had gone on toward Florida. On learning that Davis had disbanded his soldiers, Wheeler and his small escort headed through

[12] Davis to Burton N. Harrison, May 3, 1865, in *Official Records*, Ser. I, Vol. XLIX, Pt. II, 1277.

[13] Hanna, *Flight into Oblivion*, 93.

[14] See Robert McElroy, *Jefferson Davis: The Unreal and the Real* (New York, 1937), II, 510–17. The old story of how Davis was captured in his wife's clothes is, of course, discredited. See also, William E. Dodd, *Jefferson Davis* (Philadelphia, 1907), 363.

the woods bent on escape.[15] Federal soldiers seemed
everywhere. Davis was the man! Whoever captured Davis would be a hero!

A few evenings later, toward dark, Wheeler and his
men were overtaken by a force of about forty Federal
soldiers who came firing as they galloped. Wheeler and
one private returned the firing and then plunged into
the pine thickets. The Federal drag net was closing on
the fleeing cavalryman. As though still commanding an
army corps, Wheeler sent out scouts to secure any possible information. These scouts, pretending to be stragglers, sauntered into the enemy camp. They were on
their way home, they said, and just dropped in for a
friendly call. But they overestimated the enemy's credu-
lity. The two scouts were arrested and sent under guard
to a near-by cabin. When the guards were brought their
supper they relaxed, set their guns in the corner and fell
to the meal. The Confederates, taking advantage of the
situation, seized the guns and fled the place.[16]

"I saw at once the danger that menaced us," Wheeler
wrote afterwards, "and, calling my men to the saddle,
told them we could not remain a moment where we
were. . . . We rode all that night, taking by-paths when
possible, and frequently riding through the woods in
the hope that the enemy would lose our trail and cease
their pursuit. About sunrise we drew rein in an open
space, and, seeing a negro, gave him money to bring us
food. He went away, and presently returned with dishes
and cups containing a steaming breakfast. Having eaten,
we wrapped ourselves in blankets and lay down on the
ground for a few hours of the sleep we so much needed.

[15] Wheeler, "An Effort to Rescue Jefferson Davis," in *loc. cit.*, 87.
[16] *Ibid.*, 87–88.

The negro, meantime, . . . had been intercepted by Federal soldiers, who had been pursuing us more closely than we knew. They had followed our tracks along the road, and found the point where we had entered the woods. After that they had a plain trail before them." [17]

Thus Wheeler and his men were captured while they slept. It was useless for them to resist. They were surrounded before they were fully aware of what all the commotion was about. Although Wheeler pleaded immunity because of the parole granted the Confederates in Sherman's and Johnston's agreement, he was taken prisoner to Conyers, Georgia. From there he was taken to Athens.

At the latter town Wheeler and the three members of his staff joined a distinguished group of Confederate prisoners. There were the President, Mrs. Davis, and the children; the former executive, ill and ashen, his wife, nervous and excitable. There were also Vice-President Alexander H. Stephens, Clement C. Clay of Alabama with his wife, former Governor Francis Richard Lubbock of Texas, Postmaster General John H. Reagan, Burton Harrison, the President's faithful secretary, and Colonel William Preston Johnston, his aide. It was a most trying and uncomfortable trip. Three of the party, Davis, Stephens, and Clay, were practically invalids. The air in the crowded day coach was foul and no one was allowed to relieve the situation by strolling through the train. Telegraphic orders were sent ahead for food to be served aboard the train to anyone who might have the heart to eat.

When the party reached Augusta the town was in an uproar. Almost everyone had turned out to view the

[17] *Ibid.,* 88.

distinguished party which included the now famous townsman, Joe Wheeler.[18] Included in the milling crowd were, doubtless, the young ladies who had so proudly presented the young Colonel a small silk battle flag four years before. There, also, were two sisters and an aged father to bid the son hail and farewell.

The party did not tarry long in Augusta, but was soon put aboard a tug and started down the river toward Savannah and the open sea. Close alongside the prison boat was her man-of-war escort, the *Tuscarora,* with guns primed and sailors standing by.

Below deck the Presidential party was confined to a cabin in which there was not a couch or even a chair. Davis sat on two suitcases, suffering agony from his chronic headache. Above, on the deck, Wheeler lounged against a guardrail watching the receding shore line. Suddenly a young Federal officer appeared and struck the cavalry leader with the flat side of a sword.

" 'It is against the rule to lean on the guard-rail,' " the officer snapped.

Wheeler turned and politely touched his hat. " 'I did not know the rule, sir, or I would not have infringed it.' "

Mrs. Clay, who had come on deck in time to witness the scene, was "thrilled with admiration" at the general's self-control.

" 'General,' " she exclaimed, " 'you have taught me a lesson in self-control and courtesy I can never forget! Had I been a man, that Yankee would have been exploring the bottom of the Savannah River, or I, one.' " [19]

At Savannah the entire party was transferred to a

[18] Clay-Clopton, *A Belle of the Fifties,* 258. At this time the author was Mrs. Clement C. Clay of Alabama and was accompanying her husband to prison.

[19] *Ibid.,* 259.

larger steamer and the trip north began.[20] At Hilton Head Mrs. Davis sent her Negro servant ashore with a message to General Rufus Saxton asking kind treatment and any advantage which her present situation might warrant. Before the servant could return the ship moved on, leaving Mrs. Davis below, servantless, and with a small babe in her arms. This, in addition to the constant care which Davis had become, almost overtaxed her strength. General Wheeler sympathizing with the mother's predicament offered his services. They were accepted, and thus occurs an incident unique in military annals. For hours at a time the young general walked the decks with the infant Winnie Davis, "The daughter of the Confederacy," in his arms.[21] Five years earlier, when he had begun his active career in the United States Army, his first taste of war had been fighting Indians when they attacked an army ambulance containing a lone mother and a tiny baby girl. Now, after four years of fighting, he was bringing his Confederate military career to a close walking the decks of a prison ship with a tiny baby girl pulling at his beard. He was a soldier who could fight viciously and then soothe an infant.

Apparently, while strolling the decks, Wheeler evolved a plan for rescuing the President. The steamboat was a large three-decker not unlike modern excursion boats. The guard, composed of some sixty men from Pritchard's command, was stationed on the upper deck. Wheeler, according to his own account of the affair, realized that when these men went below for meals there might be a chance for some members of the prison party to es-

---

[20] See Myrta Lockwood Avery (ed.), *Recollections of Alexander H. Stephens: His Diary* (New York, 1910), 113–20.

[21] Wheeler, "An Effort to Rescue Jefferson Davis," in *loc. cit.,* 89.

cape. Naturally the President would be first. "I supposed that they [the guards] would go down in sections, relieving one another," wrote Wheeler; "but it
turned out differently. . . . For some reason, we prisoners were sent down to breakfast first, before the soldiers, who were grumbling and hungry.

"Finally we came up, in great good humor, for the
meal had been an excellent one, and the soldiers went
tumbling down below to take their turn, leaving their
guns stacked on the upper deck, and only two sentinels
to guard them." [22]

"Then I saw our chance," Wheeler continued, "and,
calling Preston Johnston, pointed to the stairway, narrow and steep, that led up to where the guns were. In
quick words I showed him how easy it would be for us
to rush upon the two sentinels, overpower them, take
possession of the guns, and then of the boat."

" 'What will we do with the boat when we have got
her?' " Johnston inquired.

" 'Sail to the Florida coast, the Bahamas, and finally to
Cuba, if necessary,' " was the reply.

" 'We have not got fuel enough,' " Johnston demurred.

" 'We can burn the decks,' " he was answered.

Quickly, Davis was notified of the plans, but he did
not give his approval; and while they were arguing and
discussing, the time of opportunity passed and soldiers
came back on the deck. [23]

The rest of the trip seems to have passed unevent-
fully. Wheeler and Alexander H. Stephens occupied a
stateroom together and were much concerned over their
probable fate, but there was no more contemplated dramatic action looking to Davis's rescue.

On May 19 Colonel Pritchard wired the Adjutant

22 *Ibid.*   23 *Ibid.*

General in Washington: "I have the honor to report that I have just arrived at this point [Fort Monroe] on board the steamer Clyde, in charge of a party of prisoners from Macon, Ga., consisting of Jeff. Davis and family, Alexander H. Stephens, C. C. Clay and wife, Major-General Wheeler and staff, Postmaster-General Reagan, Colonel Johnston and Colonel Lubbock, aides-de-camp to Davis, and Harrison, his private secretary, besides several other unimportant names." [24]

"You will retain your prisoners in safe custody until the arrival of Major-General Halleck, who will reach Fortress Monroe to-morrow at 12 o'clock with further instructions," wired Secretary Edwin M. Stanton in reply.[25]

When General Halleck reached Fort Monroe, he placed General Nelson A. Miles in charge of the prisoners and the following commitments were made: Davis and Stephens to be confined at Monroe; Harrison, the Secretary, was to be taken to Washington and confined in Old Capitol Prison; Wheeler and the others were to be sent to Fort Delaware, in the mouth of the Delaware River.[26]

[24] Benjamin D. Pritchard to the Adjutant General, May 19, 1865, in *Official Records,* Ser. II, Vol. VIII, 558.

[25] Stanton to Pritchard, May 19, 1865, *ibid.,* 559.

[26] *Ibid.,* 562–69. Stephens was carried on to Fort Warren in Boston harbor.

Chapter X

TRANSITION

DURING the turbulent period of Reconstruction many former Confederate officers of high rank were approaching their declining years. Within fifteen years after the war Lee, Forrest, and Hood were dead. Jefferson Davis lingered until 1889, Joseph E. Johnston until 1891, and Beauregard until 1893. For Wheeler, however, the postwar period was one of transition to a new and even more active life, one which was to see him changed from soldier to businessman to politician and then back to soldier again. He was just under thirty when the war was over.

The period in his new life from May to December, 1865, however, was one of doubt, humiliation, and uncertainty. There was the outright suffering of his prison life and, what was even worse, there was the demoralizing uncertainty of what civil life would hold for him after his release. Ever since his entrance to West Point at the age of eighteen he had worn a uniform, and almost all his activities had centered around military affairs. Now that was all over—the Confederacy had fallen and its armies were disbanded. Since he had lately been a rebel there was no chance for him to regain his standing in the United States Army. In short, he was facing civil life with the most meager preparation for it, a situation he had ample opportunity to ponder as he paced his cell and looked out through the bars on the scenes of misery around him.

It is small wonder the Confederate prisoner fortunate enough to escape or be paroled from Fort Delaware came away with horror written on his face. It was one of the most dreaded of Northern prisons. The high, gray-black walls enclosed T-shaped barracks erected on ground several feet below the level of high water, thus adding dampness to the other miseries of the unfortunate occupant.[1] In few cases did the prisoners have proper facilities for bathing and in most instances they had no change of clothing, with the result that various kinds of vermin multiplied with marvelous rapidity.[2] Disease and death were prevalent. During the months of May and June of 1865 while Wheeler was there, more than a hundred prisoners died, and more than five hundred were too ill to rise from their filthy beds. Witnesses relate how they saw Confederate prisoners picking up the scraps and refuse thrown out from the kitchens in an attempt to satisfy the gnawing pangs of hunger.[3] Unwholesome bread and water produced diarrhea in numberless cases, and suffering from this was greatly aggravated by the regulations which forbade more than twenty men at a time from going to the sinks at night. "I have seen," testified an army surgeon, "as many as 500 men in a row waiting their time. The consequence was that they were obliged to use the places where they

[1] Holland Thompson, "The Prisons of the War," in *Photographic History of the Civil War*, VII, 56.

[2] *Ibid.*, 136. See also, William B. Hesseltine, *Civil War Prisons* (Columbus, 1930); "Treatment of Prisoners During the War," in *Southern Historical Society Papers*, I (1876), 292.

[3] Report of joint committee appointed to investigate the condition and treatment of prisoners of war, in *Official Records*, Ser. II, Vol. VIII, 347.

were." [4] It was a place of horrors where gaunt, hollow-eyed men stood and gazed away into nothingness and waited for release—whether it should come by death or parole.

A study of mortality statistics shows that there were fewer deaths among officers than privates. Their treatment, however, was not essentially different, and the food was usually the same for all. Yet it seems the officers more successfully endured the hardships. Perhaps there was something left in Wheeler and his fellow officers which was heroic—a certain stoutness of heart which made them hold on. "They were determined not to lose heart and become apathetic, and for this reason they lived." [5] Prisoners' letters were few, but those that came through described conditions. Wheeler wrote his father that the food was worse than bad, "a slice of bread and a small piece of miserable meat for breakfast. The same is repeated, with the addition of a cup of soup for dinner, and for supper we have a slice of bread and a cup of water." Added to this was the punishment of solitary confinement. "I rise in the morning and remain in my prison without being permitted to communicate with anyone," he wrote. "We are permitted to purchase food from the sutler, but as my means were quite limited when I arrived here I have denied myself these privileges." [6]

Thus Wheeler, impoverished and hungry, remained in solitary confinement until late in July, 1865, when the War Department decided he should be paroled on

[4] Testimony of Dr. C. C. Herrington, quoted in *ibid*. See also, Thompson, "The Prisons of the War," in *Photographic History of the Civil War*, VII, 56.

[5] Thompson, "The Prisons of the War," in *Photographic History of the Civil War*, VII, 57.

[6] Wheeler to his father, May 30, 1865, in Wheeler Papers.

the terms granted other officers who had been included in Johnston's surrender. He returned to Augusta, but there was little in his home town for him. His aged father and a spinster sister were there to welcome him, but the family fortune was gone, the older brother had died in the Army of Northern Virginia, and the river warehouses were empty and silent. The war had deprived Augusta of her wealth as though some monster had reached a giant flipper into the town and with a stroke wiped the boats from the river and toppled the factories.[7] Wheeler found it necessary to seek a career elsewhere.

Late in August he was called to Nashville to testify for the defense in the trial of an independent Confederate cavalry leader accused of murdering Federal prisoners who fell into his hands, and while in the city for the trial Wheeler became involved in a humiliating personal altercation. Two former Federal officers forced their way into his hotel room and one of them administered a severe beating while his companion stood by with drawn pistols to ward off any intruders who might wish to interfere with the proceedings. Wheeler, it seems, was lying across his bed at the City Hotel when there came a knock at the door, and without waiting for an invitation the two entered.

"Is this General Wheeler?" one inquired.

"Yes," was the reply. "What can I do for you?"

"I am Colonel Blackburn of the 4th Tennessee Mounted Infantry," returned the man. Then as if to punctuate his remarks he struck Wheeler across the face with a stick.

[7] Jones and Dutcher, *History of Augusta, Georgia,* Chap. VII, *passim.*

Instantly the other, Captain Morton E. Quinn of Blackburn's command, went into action. Drawing his pistols he interposed himself to block any interference from the outside. Wheeler dashed by the captain however, and gained the hallway outside, Blackburn in close pursuit. Spectators attracted by the commotion soon put an end to it, but not until after Wheeler had suffered severe lacerations about the face and head.[8]

Colonel Blackburn gave as his reason for the attack that Wheeler had, about a year previously, issued an order threatening to hang every member of the Fourth Tennessee Mounted Infantry who should fall into his hands. Although a search of the records fails to reveal this order, it is entirely possible that one might have been reported to Blackburn. The Fourth Tennessee Mounted Infantry was composed largely of East Tennesseans loyal to the Union, and it is a recognized fact that antagonism among Southern troops toward men of their own section who joined the Union army was often much greater than that displayed toward Union soldiers who came down from the North.[9] For that reason Blackburn and his men might have been threatened by Wheeler or some of his men. General Thomas, however, after investigation found the attack "wholly unjustifiable and unprovoked" and said "the only reason

[8] Nashville *Dispatch*, August 22, 1865; Nashville *Daily Press and Times*, August 22, 1865; Wheeler's Report to General Thomas, in *Official Records*, Ser. II, Vol. XIII, 726–29.

[9] Records show that the Fourth Tennessee Regiment of Mounted Infantry was composed largely of East Tennesseans, most of whom were mustered into the Federal service late in 1864. Lieutenant Colonel Joseph H. Blackburn took charge of the regiment on November 26, 1864. He was then twenty-two years of age. See *Report of the Adjutant General of the State of Tennessee of the Military Forces of the State from 1861 to 1866* (Nashville, 1866), 221.

for their not being arrested and tried by court martial was the fact that the two officers in question had already been mustered out of the service." [10]

Wheeler, ill from his recent imprisonment and bandaged from his encounter with Blackburn, returned to Augusta by way of Courtland, Alabama, and the Jones home where he and his troopers had camped that night during the war when he had been presented to young Mrs. Daniella Jones Sherrod. His reason for making this call was obviously to propose marriage. Wheeler's New York brother-in-law, Sterling Smith, and his business associate, Charles Bouton, had purchased the hardware and carriage business of J. M. Denman in New Orleans and had decided to make Wheeler the manager. With a job he might care for a wife; but the young woman delayed her decision and Wheeler journeyed to New Orleans alone.[11] He returned later, however, and on February 8, 1866, the two were quietly married in the parlor of the old Jones home.[12] Immediately they packed and moved to the Crescent City.

The New Orleans firm continued under the name of "Bouton and Smith" until 1868 when it was changed to "Bouton, Smith and Company." The addition to the firm was Joseph Wheeler.[13] Evidently Mrs. Wheeler had decided to invest some of her money in her husband's business, for in 1869 Wheeler and J. D. Wandell of New Orleans bought out the interests of the two New Yorkers.[14] The soldier apparently was about to settle him-

[10] Thomas to Mason, August 26, 1865, in *Official Records*, Ser. II, Vol. VIII, 728.

[11] Related by Miss Annie Wheeler to the author, May 8, 1926.

[12] MS. Genealogical Records of Wheeler Family, in Wheeler Papers.

[13] *Gardner's New Orleans Directory for 1868* (New Orleans, 1868).

[14] *Edwards' New Orleans Directory for 1870* (New Orleans, 1870).

self to the ways of peace and to make a merchant of himself as his New England forebears had done.

He was not destined to remain long in New Orleans, however, for Richard Jones was not entirely satisfied to have his daughter and son-in-law there, particularly during the summer months. Within a few months after they were settled the father had begun to let his views be known. "I think you should frankly say to Bouton, Smith and Denman that in the future you would not spend the summer in New Orleans for any consideration," he wrote Wheeler. "If they are not satisfied with that, I would retire, withdrawing from the partnership. . . . If you think proper to quit the city, I will furnish the farm outfit and give you half of the net proceeds." [15] Doubtless he was influenced by personal desires. In his declining years it would be only natural for him to want his vivacious only daughter near him; but whatever the considerations were, in 1870 Wheeler sold his share of the business and moved to Lawrence County, Alabama, to assume the new role of lawyer-planter.

Wheeler and his wife began the construction of a house for themselves a few miles east of the old Jones home. It was not a beautiful nor a pretentious home but it was set in a grove and it was substantial and livable. To the budding young planter weary of uncertainty and insecurity it must have seemed a pleasant haven. A flower garden was laid out and a hitching post set in the clay near the frontyard gate.[16] Numbers of Negroes, finding that their new freedom did not carry a living with it, were quite willing to rent small tracts of land on the same plantation where they had been

15 Richard Jones to Wheeler, September 30, 1866, in Wheeler Papers.
16 The Wheeler home at Wheeler, Alabama, occupied at the present by Miss Annie Wheeler, is virtually unchanged from its original form.

slaves. Wheeler became their supervisor and soon his vigilance produced results. It was not long before the plantation was making a profit in spite of Reconstruction and adverse business conditions.[17] These profits were put back on the soil in the form of improvements, and the surplus above this was invested in railroad securities. The old Memphis and Charleston Railroad ran for several miles across the Jones and Sherrod property. At the close of the war the railroad was badly in need of repairs and equipment, and to raise funds for the restoration work a second mortgage to secure a million dollars' worth of 7 per cent bonds was negotiated in January, 1867. In 1877 the property of the Memphis and Charleston, now Southern, was leased to the East Tennessee, Virginia and Georgia Railroad Company, by which the credit of the former was greatly strengthened and its securities made sounder.[18] Mr. and Mrs. Wheeler had bought a block of bonds in 1875 and when this merger took place the value of their securities was greatly increased.[19] By 1880 Wheeler had become attorney for and a director of the road.

In addition to his other activities during this period, Wheeler took up the study of law, a course attended by most unusual circumstances. His wife's brother, Tom Jones, became involved in a fight with a blacksmith at Courtland which resulted in the latter's death. Jones was arrested and brought to trial at Moulton, the county seat, a few miles away. As his trial neared he quarreled with his legal counsel and summarily dismissed them. Wheeler and friends of the family succeeded in getting

[17] Wheeler Account Books, in Wheeler Papers.

[18] Guy E. Mauldin, Assistant Secretary of the Southern Railway, to the author, June 18, 1930.

[19] Wheeler Account Books, in Wheeler Papers.

a continuance of the case until the following term of court.[20] Before the next term convened, six months later, Wheeler had read enough law to pass the bar examination, and when the trial was held he appeared as attorney for the defense and secured a verdict of acquittal.[21] Thereafter Wheeler and his brother-in-law were warm friends as well as kinsmen. Together they set up a law practice in Courtland running their card in the county paper as "Jones and Wheeler, Attorneys at Law."

Carrying out the tradition of the lawyer-planter group in the South, Wheeler also began to participate in politics. His fame as a former Southern general and his position of importance in the community made this course almost inevitable. Not only was his participation inevitable but his political alignment was as surely foreordained. His connection with the Jones family, his railroad interests, and his economic status fixed his political affiliation; he, by the very nature of things, lined up with the "Bourbons," for to do otherwise meant allying himself with a political group tainted with Carpetbagism. It should quickly be said, however, that, although classed as a Bourbon, Wheeler really could not be rated as orthodox. But perhaps the terms used here should have some explanation.

It is a well-known fact that the South was never solid economically before 1865 and that after that date it was made so politically only after a prolonged struggle. During the Reconstruction period all political factions united in an effort to preserve white supremacy, but when the threat of black domination was removed there emerged a new form of the old alignment of yeoman

20 Circuit Court Criminal Docket, Lawrence County, Alabama, 1872–1875.

21 Related by Miss Annie Wheeler to the author, August 26, 1928.

farmer versus planter-industrialist—a movement which ultimately was to culminate in the Populist struggle of the 1890's. In this struggle the Bourbon as the political heir of the old not-so-aristocratic "planter aristocracy" sought to enforce a conformity which would best promote his interests; and those interests had now become industrial and commercial rather than agrarian.[22] Neglecting the "community of interest" which might have existed between small farmer and planter, many of the Bourbons who emerged from the Reconstruction period became involved in railroad building and promotion, in factories and industries—in those things that Wheeler came to say would make the South "more prosperous and more united, more Christian and more enlightened." "Southern liberals" these men came to be called —men like Henry W. Grady, Joseph E. Brown, and, to a much lesser degree, Joseph Wheeler. They believed the South should forget the war and be regenerated; that the new social pattern should be one of modernity, more nearly conforming to that of the "progressive" North. And the small farmer-agrarian group sensing their abandonment sought a political alignment all their own—a group which became articulate through men like Bob Taylor in Tennessee, Reuben Kolb in Alabama, and Tom Watson in Georgia.[23]

[22] A most interesting discussion of the Bourbon is given in Donald Davidson, *The Attack on Leviathan* (Chapel Hill, 1938), Chap. XIII. See also, Benjamin B. Kendrick, "Agrarian Discontent in the South," in American Historical Association, *Annual Report*, 1920 (Washington, 1923), 267.

[23] See Daniel M. Robison, *Bob Taylor and the Agrarian Revolt in Tennessee* (Chapel Hill, 1935); and *id.*, "From Tillman to Long," in *Journal of Southern History* (Baton Rouge), III (1937), 289. See also, Alex M. Arnett, *The Populist Movement in Georgia* (New York, 1922), and C. Vann Woodward, *Tom Watson, Agrarian Rebel* (New York, 1938).

As Wheeler emerged from the seclusion of his plantation as a district Democratic Committeeman and as delegate to local Congressional conventions he came in contact with this agrarian group variously termed "Independents," "Wool Hat Boys," or "Independent Democrats." They resided, by and large, on the plateaus and slopes bordering the Tennessee Valley and possessed little wealth, power, or organization. During the early years of Alabama's statehood their forebears had been Jacksonian Democrats wholly supporting the President in his fight for nationalism. In the period from 1830 to 1860 when the great plantations were developing in the Tennessee Valley and in the Black Belt of Alabama these small farmers came to have a distinctly antagonistic attitude toward slavery and slave politics.[24] As the controversy became more and more acute in the years immediately following the passage of the Kansas-Nebraska Act, these plateau people gave striking proof that they were not in accord with the so-called "Fire-eaters" of the South. In 1860 four of the seven counties that later were to comprise Wheeler's own Congressional district showed a distinct majority in favor of Stephen A. Douglas for President. When secession was squarely put up to them in the convention in Montgomery in January, 1861, they proved to be "co-operationists." They were willing to co-operate if secession came, but they were not willing to bring it on.[25]

There was yet a third group in Wheeler's district to be reckoned with, the Republicans. There seems to be no way of determining accurately their numerical strength,

[24] Albert B. Moore, *History of Alabama and Her People* (New York, 1927), I, 448, 478–515.
[25] Walter L. Fleming, *The Civil War and Reconstruction in Alabama* (New York, 1905), 27–34.

for elections and campaigns were conducted on a basis of Bourbon versus anti-Bourbon, that is, of anti-Bourbon against old-line Democrats whether the latter were industrially minded or not. "Bourbon" came to be a term applied to all who held to the political party of the old prewar privileged groups, the "courthouse rings." Too, in the minds of the regular Democrats or Bourbons the Independent Democrats and Republicans were put into one class as Negro lovers, traitors, or worse. "Independentism is the back door to radicalism" was a generally accepted idea among the old-line Democrats.[26] In fact, the Independent was more severely characterized than the Republican. He was described as being "the protegé of radicalism, the spawn of corruption or poverty or ignorance, come forth as the leader of ignorant and deluded blacks to attack and plunder for avarice." "There may be no God to avenge the South," the account continues, "but there is a devil to punish Independents. Satan has been in the Democratic camp and taking these Independents from guard duty, led them up into the mountains and shown them the kingdom of radicalism, his silver and his gold, storehouses and bacon, and all these things promised to give him if he would fall down and worship him, throwing down the altars of their fathers and trampling them under their feet." [27] Another newspaper resorted to less rhetorical flourish in describing the Independent's alleged radical leanings. "He is," this paper thought, "like a bob-tailed, one-eyed bull on our place. He is quiet enough in his pasture until he sees the other cattle getting the most of the grass, then he jumps into the cornfield and depredates upon his

26 Florence (Alabama) *Gazette*, October 6, 1880.
27 Opelika (Alabama) *Times*, October 14, 1874, quoted in Fleming, *Civil War and Reconstruction in Alabama*, 782.

neighbors until his dogs chew off his ears. Then he
comes limping back home and wants to be turned on
his home grass again." [28]

But denounce as they might, the Bourbons found it
difficult to force conformity on the Independents. The
rift was of too long standing and there was little inclination on their part to be turned on the "home grass"
again. Wheeler, before he had been long in politics,
discovered this and resorted to pacific means rather than
bludgeoning to win them over; and so successful were
his methods that he was able as congressman to take a
badly divided district and leave it so united that elections came to be confined almost wholly to the matter
of selecting a Democratic nominee. Before this state
of affairs could obtain, however, two things were necessary: William M. Lowe, the Independent-Agrarian
leader, had to be removed and then the discontented
groups had to be won over after their leader was out of
the way.

Just as the Democrat-Bourbons were primed for the
contest with Lowe and his Independents in 1880 a fourth
political element, the Greenbackers, made its entrance
on the stage of Alabama politics to add to the woe of
the already troubled Democratic leaders. This party entered on a wave of depression with promises of better
times through more and cheaper money. Although it
had only a minority following, it was a threat to the
Bourbons because it bid fair to win over many who
gave only lip service to the planter party. There was
also the dangerous probability of a coalition between
these minority elements; and, as it developed, that is precisely what happened. The Independents, Greenback-

28 Demopolis (Alabama) *News,* quoted in Huntsville (Alabama)
Democrat, July 20, 1880.

ers, and Republicans united in 1878 to elect William M. Lowe to Congress from the Eighth Alabama District. Lowe was one of the most picturesque figures ever to participate in Alabama politics. He was a man of commanding personality, a powerful orator, a shrewd politician who might have been another Tom Watson or Bob Taylor.[29] Indeed, he raised the banner of agrarianism and the wool hat boys before either of these leaders came into national prominence. While a soldier in the Confederate army he was wounded at Bull Run, receiving as a result an honorable discharge. Returning to his native Huntsville, he resumed his law practice and, while the Bourbons were temporarily out of control during Reconstruction, served in the state legislature and in the constitutional convention of 1875.[30] With the return of the Bourbons to power, however, Lowe's career as an Independent was temporarily checkmated. In 1876 he had aspired to an unexpired term as probate judge of Madison County, but instead the appointment went to William Richardson, a Bourbon. In the same year he tried for the Democratic nomination for Congress but the planter delegates held a sufficient number of votes to block him there. His plans being thus thwarted by the Bourbons twice in the same year, he was greatly embittered and as a result began organizing the Independents and Greenbackers into a cohesive political machine.[31] "His dream was," a contemporary said of him, "to be the leader of a powerful political organization in the state that would hold the balance of power and

[29] Huntsville *Democrat*, August 11, 1880.
[30] *Biographical Directory of the American Congress, 1774–1927* (Washington, 1928), 1241.
[31] "Political Memoirs of Judge Thomas J. Taylor of Huntsville, Alabama," MS. in possession of Judge Taylor's son, a Huntsville attorney.

open to him the road to political preferment and leading finally to a seat in the United States Senate." "And,"
added this observer, "to a man of his ambitious talent
for successful party manipulation and wonderful sagac-
ity, nothing was impossible." [32] Since this observation
was made by a staunch Bourbon it takes on the qualities of a tremendously high compliment.

Lowe's initial move in furthering his designs was entirely successful. In 1878, as has been stated, with the
support of these despised Independents, Greenbackers,
and Republicans he was elected to Congress on a platform that called for aid for "the little man whose votes
the Bourbons solicit, but whose interests they ignore."
This 1878 campaign was a savage one with both sides
bringing up the heavy artillery. The Bourbons warned
that a vote for Lowe was a vote for the return of Radicalism and Carpetbagism; but in spite of all their warning and pleading they could not stem the tide. Lowe was
a popular figure who knew the people's language.[33]
Moreover, the Bourbons lacked colorful leadership; they
very much needed a name to match that of Lowe when
he should offer for re-election in 1880.

For this leadership the Bourbons naturally turned to
Wheeler, for he possessed many of the characteristics so
sorely needed in a candidate. He was an earnest if not
a fluent speaker, he "possessed the confidence and kind
regards of the people," and, above all, his was a name to
conjure with; he was "Fightin' Joe" who had fought the
Yankees from hell to yonder all over Dixie. In the par-
lance of politics, he was a natural, and little time was

[32] *Ibid.* See also, John B. Clark, *Populism in Alabama* (Auburn,
1927), 25.

[33] Huntsville *Democrat*, August 25, 1880. Lowe was called "the life
and soul" of the Independent-Greenback party. See Clark, *Populism
in Alabama*, 27.

wasted in getting him into the race. On August 23, 1880, the District Congressional Convention met under the shed of a sawmill on the banks of the Tennessee River at Decatur and there nominated Wheeler to run against Lowe and his "Radical-Greenback-Independent-Everythingarian-Nothingania-hybrid opponents of the Democratic party." [34] The sawmill as a meeting place was a deliberate selection, a newspaper explained, "as the object is to saw asunder the Radical party and their Greenback-Independent allies." [35]

Thus they were arrayed—the wool hat boys against the silk hat boys, Lowe against Wheeler, Independent against Bourbon, and, as many believed, Carpetbagism against decency. And the latter view was greatly strengthened when on the eve of the campaign the State Chairman of the Republican Executive Committee announced that the Republican party would support Lowe, and then sharp on the heels of this came an announcement from "the leading colored journal of the South and the only Republican newspaper in Alabama" to the effect that the Negroes would support the Independent-Greenback-Lowe ticket.[36] But this was no surprise, the Bourbons insisted; it was merely a situation which they had long predicted would eventually present itself. "We have insisted time and time again," one paper wrote, "that the Radicals, Greenbackers and Independents were one and the same. Now as things stand what can any good man and true who does not desire to return to negro and scalawag rule do except renounce this Greenback-Independent-Republican party." [37]

[34] Clark, *Populism in Alabama*, 27.

[35] Huntsville *Democrat*, August 25, 1880.

[36] Announcement in Huntsville *Independent*, July 18, 1880. See also, Huntsville *Gazette*, August 6, 1880.

[37] Huntsville *Democrat*, September 9, 1880.

The Lowe-Wheeler campaign of 1880 is one the old-timers still like to talk about as one of the most viciously fought political feuds in the annals of the state. Not only were two outstanding personalities involved but also the question of the restoration of Democratic control, better known by its pseudonym of "white supremacy." In 1874 Alabama had elected a Democratic governor and legislature which meant that the state had rid itself of the carpetbag element that had dominated politics since the war. So complete was the change that by 1876 the Republicans carried only eight counties and in six of these there was a heavy Democratic vote.[38] This riddance of radical control was one of profound significance, but it did not entirely redeem the state.[39] In the Eighth Congressional District the Republicans had united with other elements and had elected Lowe to Congress in 1878, and, in the minds of the Bourbons at least, he was a renegade and a scalawag. Not until he was safely out of the way could "white supremacy" be made a certainty for the entire state, they reasoned. The hope of the Bourbons lay in associating in the minds of the people Lowe's group with Carpetbagism, and this they more or less successfully did.

Although both parties formally adopted a platform, neither of them seems to have referred to it after the campaign got under way. It was a campaign of personalities in which both sides hurled anathemas with reckless abandon. Colonel Lowe characterized the Democrats as "bitter, reactionary and intolerant," and General Wheeler preached that "It is an historical fact that when a man deserts his own people and goes over to the enemy he becomes the most vindictive of enemies." [40] Colonel

---

[38] Fleming, *Civil War and Reconstruction in Alabama*, 796.
[39] Moore, *History of Alabama and Her People*, I, 647.
[40] Huntsville *Gazette*, October 30, 1880.

Lowe threatened to "take down the little General's political breeches and lay him across my lap for correc-
tion" and Wheeler's reply was to lay on with more
charges of radicalism against Lowe.[41] Lowe challenged
Wheeler to a joint debate and Wheeler found it inconvenient to meet him; then later he challenged Lowe
and got no reply. Charges and countercharges flew back
and forth all during September, October, and early November.

But the Bourbons had other plans which were not
so much of the rough-and-tumble variety. A group of
them met in Huntsville and organized a "Hancock
Club" with Barnwell Rhett as president, the avowed
purpose being the election of all Democratic nominees.
Soon after its organization "secret" circular letters out-
lining plans for winning the election were sent to each
club throughout the district.[42] These letters reveal much
about how seriously the election was taken.

The clubs were to meet "not less than twice a month;
oftener if necessary, and in executive session behind
closed doors." Members were to make a list of the white
voters in each precinct who were not on the roll of the
club. Then, having ascertained those who were non-
members, a committee from the club was to wait on
each of these and "respectfully and cordially" invite
them to join. The Negroes were likewise to be enrolled
as members and then a committee was to be appointed
to see that all plans went according to schedule on election day.[43]

It is interesting to note the methods employed in

[41] Tuscumbia (Alabama) *North Alabamian,* September 29, 1880.

[42] This "secret" circular, as may well be imagined, did not long
remain secret. The Huntsville *Gazette* published a copy of it as early
as September 25, 1880.

[43] *Ibid.*

swinging the doubtful white vote into the Democratic column. Here was a problem which did not greatly confront the Black Belt politicians. In this region of the state the great problem was the Negro and the ballot, but this was soon solved by intimidation. A few careless shots on election day or a clever manipulation of the ballot box was sufficient to nullify the Negro vote. But in North Alabama the situation was quite different; here was a large dissenting white vote and ordinary methods of intimidation could not be used. As a matter of fact, the Bourbons seemed quite at a loss as to the best method of handling the mountain white. They could urge that he "should not by lethargy or inaction desert his kindred in this hour of deliverance," but beyond this there was little else to do except perhaps to manipulate the ballots so that his vote would be nullified. When everything else failed this is precisely what was done.

The circular went into greater detail as to the methods of handling the Negro vote. A census was to be taken in which should be set down the name and address of each Negro voter, with whom he worked and whether as hired man or tenant, and what merchant advanced goods for him. As soon as this list was completed it was to be turned over to the county chairman for distribution and the Negroes thus enrolled were to be canvassed as to their political beliefs. Those who were unwilling to support the Democrats were asked to remain away from the polls on election day; and in order that this might be carried out certain young men of the precinct under voting age were to be enrolled and each one "assigned his negro." They were instructed to "use all lawful means to watch and keep to their promises those negroes who have agreed not to vote" but "above all

things in this, be careful to avoid intimidation. . . .
Rioting before or at the polls, race collision brought
about by the whites are deemed insane folly." [44]

In addition to this method of personal evangelism the
Bourbons also attempted to influence the Negroes en
masse. In many places over the district attempts were
made to bring over to Democracy the colored brother
who was so disillusioned as to believe that the Republican party held out any advantages for him. At Courtland,
General Wheeler's home box, one of these Negro mass
meetings was held and the Negro educator, W. H. Coun-
cill of Huntsville, speaking from a platform upon which
sat General Wheeler himself and other Democratic leaders, "labored to encourage the colored people to forsake
the Republican party." The best thing for the Negro,
he urged, was "to make the best possible contact with
the Democratic party and vote the Democratic ticket." [45]

In the other end of the district Colonel Lowe was doing some evangelizing himself. At Florence a mass meeting was held early in October in which the speakers
were "vociferously and enthusiastically applauded" when
they urged the colored citizenry to vote for Garfield and
Lowe. In fact, the meeting, according to the newspapers, took on the fervor of a revival meeting with the
Negroes chanting "Amen" to Colonel Lowe's impas-
sioned plea.[46] In Huntsville the Negro newspaper coun-
seled its readers: "Colored men, you are Republicans
and want Republican success next Tuesday. Then go
to the polls like men and cast your votes for Garfield

[44] *Ibid.* See J. P. Dyer, "The Final Struggle for Democratic Control
in North Alabama," in *Alabama Historical Quarterly* VI (1930), 370 ff.
[45] Huntsville *Gazette,* October 2, 1880.
[46] Florence *Gazette,* October 16, 1880.

and Arthur. We have no nominee for Congress in this District, but your votes helped elect Col. Lowe two years ago and he has done nothing to cause you to vote against him. Let well enough alone and when you go to the polls next Tuesday, see that William M. Lowe is on your ticket." [47]

Both sides worked feverishly until election day, for all seemed to realize that the contest would be a close one. The election itself seems to have passed off quietly, however, and when the votes were counted General Wheeler had a majority of 43 out of a total of 24,773 votes cast. But in order to get this majority the election judges had rejected 601 Greenback-Independent-Republican ballots alleged to be illegal.[48]

After the election was over the Democratic-Bourbon papers dropped the Congressional issue almost entirely. Occasionally there could be found a passing reference to Colonel Lowe's attempts to contest the results, but it appears that he was not taken seriously. The Democrats had won and apparently were quite willing to let the matter drop.

But if the Democrats were complacent, the opposition was far from it. Colonel Lowe was raging and the Negro newspaper was waxing sarcastic. Lowe wrote a letter to the newspapers in which he declared in no uncertain terms that he was elected "but the Bourbon inspectors are seeking to change the result by throwing out my Greenback votes." These votes were thrown out, he said, because "the electoral districts are designated by numbers or figures." "No court," he continued, "would sustain such construction. It is a fraudulent technicality.

[47] Huntsville *Gazette*, October 30, 1880.
[48] *Congressional Record*, 47 Cong., 1 Sess., 4456.

In behalf of fair elections and an honest count I invoke the moral sentiment of the country." [49] And, backing him up, the Huntsville *Gazette* paraphrased Hamlet's soliloquy to fit the occasion:

> To count or not to count, that is the question.
> Whether 'tis better in the end to suffer
> The pangs of sorrow and inglorious defeat
> Or to take arms against a sea of ballots,
> And by rejecting end them.[50]

But Lowe did more than protest to the newspapers. Immediately after the election he asked the United States District Court at Huntsville to sustain his election, and the case came up for a hearing on November 29, 1880.[51] At this time both Lowe and Wheeler were summoned to appear and upon their appearance an agreement was reached to the effect that the court would sit at various places over the district and take testimony rather than go to the trouble and expense of having the vast swarm of witnesses report to Huntsville. And so throughout the fall of 1880 and the winter of 1881 the taking of testimony proceeded slowly from place to place.

In the meantime, General Wheeler presented himself for the oath of office at the opening session of the Forty-seventh Congress which convened on the first Monday in December, 1880. When his name was called by the Clerk of the House, Representative James H. Jones, Greenbacker of Texas, offered a resolution to the effect that neither Lowe nor Wheeler should be seated until the Committee on Elections should report and the House decide the question. The resolution was tabled and the

[49] Huntsville *Gazette,* December 6, 1880.
[50] *Ibid.*   [51] Florence *Gazette,* January 3, 1881.

entire matter referred to the Committee on Elections.
General Wheeler was sworn in and the Democrats won
the first and only skirmish of a protracted and rather
unexciting battle.[52]

The committee made its report to the House the following May 17 to the effect that "Joseph Wheeler is not
entitled to a seat in this House as a Representative in
the 47th Congress" and that "William M. Lowe is entitled to a seat in the House." The majority report gave
Lowe a majority of 848 votes and the Democratic minority of the committee said that Wheeler's majority
really should be 4,712 votes instead of the 43 as previously reported.[53]

The committee report was placed on the calendar and
in the regular order of business came up for consideration on June 2, 1881. Representative William Thompson, Republican of Iowa, made the presentation speech
on behalf of the majority, and Representative Roger Q.
Mills, Democrat of Texas, represented the minority.

Here it is that the evidence taken a year previously
in Alabama is brought to light, and in this evidence is
found mirrored the struggle that was going on for the
mastery of politics in many Southern states. Between
1874 and 1880 there were numerous contested election
cases from the South before Congress and in almost every instance the issue hinged on alleged illegal ballots.
Thus the question involved in the Lowe-Wheeler case
was more important than a matter of personal differences. The real question, as in most of the other dis-
puted election cases, was whether the old-line Democrats could whip the malcontents into line or not. If
successful, the South could be made "solid."

The contention of Wheeler and his friends through-

[52] *Cong. Record,* 47 Cong., 1 Sess., 4456.   [53] *Ibid.,* 4465.

out the fight was that the tickets cast for Lowe were illegal because they violated the Alabama election law that provided, "the ballot shall be a plain piece of white paper without any figures, marks, rulings, characters, or embellishments thereon, not less than two nor more than two and one-half inches wide, and not less than five nor more than five and one-half inches long, on which must be written or printed, or partly written or partly printed, only the names of the persons for whom the elector intends to vote, and must designate the office for which each person so named is intended by him to be chosen; and any ballot otherwise described is illegal and must be rejected." The Lowe ticket, the Democrats reasoned, was illegal because it contained figures designating Presidential electors by districts.[54]

The majority of the Committee on Elections contended that the Lowe tickets were valid, even though they might have violated a state law, for the simple reason that when a state law is made in opposition to, or in contravention of, a Federal statute it is "an unqualified nullity." Thompson was prepared to back his view that "if the ballots had been printed on red paper or on white paper, six inches long or a foot long, one inch wide or three inches wide, the only duty of the officers was to take them out and count them after ascertaining whose name was on the ballot for Congressman, irrespective of every law the State of Alabama could pass. . . . You have robbed these ballot boxes; you have denied the manhood of electors who the law says are your equals and as much entitled to cast a vote and have it counted for the man of their choice as General Wheeler or any other honorable man in Alabama or elsewhere. The evidence shows that Mr. Lowe has joined the party

[54] *Ibid.*, 4459.

that is opposed to bull-dozing, the party that is opposed
to robbing the ballot box, opposed to ballot box stuff-
ing; he has come to the front and opposed the practices
that have so long prevailed there. There has not been
a fair election from one end of the state to the other in
the last fifteen years." [55]

Apparently this last statement was a little more than
General Wheeler could stomach. He jumped to his feet
and challenged the assertion as being aimed at him personally, but the speaker hastened to smooth it over by
assuring him that "in all the fraudulent transactions
. . . I believe none of them were done at your instance
or request, or by your aid, advice or counsel." "Let us,"
he intoned, "rise above party feelings and prejudices,
and like men demand and insist upon what the constitution provides, that there shall be a fair vote and an
honest count." [56]

This display of political piety brought forth loud
hisses from the Democratic side of the House and in
reply Thompson shot at them: "You may sneer at the
Republican party if you please, my Democratic friends,
but remember that all the rights that you enjoy today,
the very flag under whose shelter you sit today, are the
gifts of the Republican party to you." And this deeply
impressed Representative Mills. In fact, he was "lost
and overwhelmed" when he contemplated the "length,
breadth, height and depth of the love of that great party
for a fair ballot and a free count." Especially was he
impressed with Republican fairness "in Louisiana, Florida and South Carolina in 1876." "I am persuaded," he
concluded, "that neither tribulation nor distress, nor
persecution, nor famine, nor nakedness, nor peril, nor
sword, nor things present, nor things to come, nor

[55] *Ibid.*, 4458.   [56] *Ibid.*, 4457.

height, nor depth, nor any creature can separate from them the love of a free ballot and a fair count." [57]

The whole affair had long since degenerated into a brawl with the original question being lost in the slugging. Representative Roswell G. Horr of Michigan helped matters along by injecting the secession issue. He charged the Democratic party: "You said that if the minority could not rule the country, then we will destroy it." He was about to proceed when a South Carolinian interrupted to proclaim that "South Carolina is not ashamed of anything she ever did."

Horr was quick to retort: "I do not think she is. The trouble I have to find with you gentlemen is that you are never ashamed of anything."

"How was it with Hayes?" a heckler inquired from the Democratic side of the House.

"I never doubted that he was elected by a majority of votes honestly cast," he shot back. "If there is anything that has soured the Democratic stomach and which they will never get over it is this Hayes business. No matter what you feed them they will even throw up their toddy at the thought of Hayes." [58]

General Wheeler must have realized, of course, that anything he might say in his own defense would be useless, but he consumed two hours getting his defense into the *Record,* and then the resolution to unseat was adopted 148 to 3, with 140 Democrats not voting. Colonel Lowe was escorted to the Speaker's desk where the oath was administered and immediately thereafter jubilantly sent his friends in Huntsville this telegram: "The fraud has been eliminated. I am seated at last. Let the honest Bourbons to whom my books, documents, seeds,

[57] *Ibid.,* 4484.   [58] *Ibid.,* 4459.

etc., have been sent now turn them over to the nearest
Independent, Republican or Greenbacker and all will
be forgiven." [59]

[59] *Ibid.*, 4505. The telegram dated June 3, 1882, was published in
the Huntsville *Independent,* June 7, 1882.

Chapter XI

THE GENTLEMAN FROM ALABAMA

WHILE the result of the Lowe-Wheeler contested election case was personally embarrassing to Wheeler, it did not seriously interrupt his Congressional career. In all, he served ten of the eleven months the Forty-seventh Congress was in session, Lowe serving the remaining one month. All the time that the case was pending Wheeler was legally a member of the House, eligible to serve on committees, participate in debate, vote, or exercise any of the other prerogatives of members. That he did not participate more freely in discussions before the House is doubtless due, aside from the fact that he was a new member, to the fact that he was consuming a great deal of time assembling evidence in his own behalf. He did find time to introduce a few private bills, but his own personal problems were too acute to permit of much participation in House discussions and committee work.

When the House finally decided Lowe was the eligible one to represent the Eighth District of Alabama, Wheeler left Washington immediately for his plantation home, there to begin a campaign of vindication. Throughout the summer of 1882 he was busy writing letters, holding conferences, and, it was rumored, preparing for a duel with Lowe. He ordered a quantity of revolver ammunition and, his friends said, went to the mountains near by for target practice.[1] The duel never occurred, however, for Lowe came home to Huntsville in the last stages of tuberculosis and was not able to leave his house before his death in October, 1882.

His death left the agrarian Independents leaderless. The Bourbons saw this and opened their arms to the erring brethren only to have the overtures rejected. "Unite, Republicans, Independents, Greenbackers," was the battle cry again as it had been two years earlier.[2] But no leader like Lowe arose to rally them. They finally selected D. D. Shelby of Huntsville as their candidate, but he was a poor substitute for their dead champion, and was not able to carry the election, or rather it might be said elections, for there were two separate matters to be voted on in November, 1882. One concerned the selection of a representative to fill the now vacated seat over which Lowe and Wheeler had fought, and the other the choice of one whose regular term would begin March 4, 1883, and run the full two years.

General Wheeler was not a candidate for the full term. His fight with Lowe apparently had engendered too much bitterness to make him the best possible choice. When the Democratic Congressional Convention met in September he, after conferring with various party leaders, declined to enter the contest and in a "well timed and appropriate speech" nominated solid, respectable, dignified, fox-hunting, former state Senator Luke Pryor of Athens.[3] At the same convention Wheeler was

[1] A bill from A. J. Vienna, Memphis gunsmith, August 10, 1882, in Wheeler Papers, indicates that the ammunition was purchased immediately after Wheeler returned home. Although accounts of the proposed duel differ widely, it seems probable that such a thing was contemplated by Wheeler.

[2] All the newspapers of the district carried the announcement.

[3] Florence *News*, September 6, 1882.

chosen to run for the unexpired term which he had begun and which Lowe had partially completed. In their choice the Bourbons showed a considerable change of opinion from previous campaigns. In 1880 they had used Wheeler the Confederate general as their chief argument. Now they turned to Pryor who during secession days had been not a mere co-operationist but a downright oppositionist, and who during the war had steadfastly refused to participate in it. The party leaders, however, were willing to overlook this if he could only lead them to victory. "He was wise and prudent and saw the folly of secession," one Democratic paper wrote. "He is not running on his war record, and the opposition is weak indeed when it can find nothing against him except that he was not identified with the late rebellion." [4] That from a Bourbon paper and, of all things, referring to the war as "the late rebellion"!

So it was Shelby the Independent-Greenbacker-Republican against Democratic Pryor for the full term, and Wheeler running without opposition for the unexpired one, the general understanding being that Wheeler would be given his chance for vindication in 1884.

The campaign was almost devoid of interest, for Pryor and Shelby were not colorful men. Neither of them could arouse the electorate as Lowe had done nor add the dignity and atmosphere of the Confederacy as had Wheeler. Nevertheless, it was a close race, Pryor winning his seat by a majority of only 137 votes, while Wheeler went in unopposed.[5] Wheeler, the electorate had decided, would go back for the short session of the Forty-seventh Congress, and Pryor would take his

[4] *Ibid.,* October 18, 1882.
[5] Copy of Secretary of State's Report, published in newspapers.

seat on March 4, 1883, for a full term of two years.

Thus when Wheeler returned to Washington in January, 1883, he was temporarily free from the threat of Lowe's Independents. It is true another man had been elected for a full term, but it was merely a temporary expediency resorted to while the district "cooled off" from the bitter struggle of 1880.[6] Matters being thus arranged in his constituency, he was freer to take part in the deliberations of the House and to consider more carefully the welfare of his district. In the latter activity he displayed a zeal and astuteness in placating all groups which returned him term after term to the nation's capitol.

The second session of the Forty-seventh Congress that convened on the first Monday in December, 1882, was a lameduck session. The off-year elections of 1882 had swept out a Republican majority in the House and filled the seats with Democrats. Thus the defeated members held on during the session although they had been repudiated at home—held on and cried to Heaven to protect the country against the "rebel Democrats." Perhaps they saw a reason to become alarmed at the large number of former Confederates being sent to Washington. Such men as Alexander H. Stephens of Georgia, John H. Reagan of Texas, Joe Wheeler of Alabama, George Dibrell of Tennessee in the House, and Wade Hampton of South Carolina, Isham G. Harris of Tennessee, Joseph E. Brown of Georgia, Zebulon B. Vance of North Carolina, and L. Q. C. Lamar of Mississippi in the Senate, were enough to frighten any good Republican who believed that the party which had "saved the Union" should govern it. In the debates, both in the House and the Senate, taunts, veiled insinuations, and outright de-

[6] Numerous letters to Wheeler, in Wheeler Papers, show this.

nunciations were hurled at the "rebels" who now proposed to help run the country.

The House was in the midst of one such debate when Wheeler returned on January 13, 1883, to take his seat. The bill under discussion was House Resolution 7135, providing a pension for Mexican War veterans. Representative Charles H. Joyce of Vermont objected to the bill because, he said, Section 4716 of the *Revised Statutes of the United States* provided that "no person, or the widow, children, or heirs of any person who had in any manner voluntarily engaged in rebellion against the United States" could ever receive a pension from the Federal government. There were, Joyce thought, many Confederates who were Mexican War veterans and thus would be able to share in the distribution of pension money—and he couldn't stomach that.

Wheeler's reply to Joyce was calculated to pour oil on the troubled waters. The South, he said, had always borne an honorable part in the nation's wars. When the settlers beyond the Alleghenies were attacked by Indians it was a Southerner, George Washington, who was the first to "fly to the rescue." When "the sound of battle was heard at Lexington and Concord" Captain Daniel Morgan "with a hardy Southern band" was first to march to the defense of the people of Massachusetts. When the second war with England came "the entire South rushed to the flag" and the last battle of that conflict was fought "by Southern soldiers, upon Southern soil, and led by a Southern general." Even during the Civil War, he reminded his opponent, many Southern soldiers joined the Union army. Thus, the South had always been ready to do its part of the fighting.

Joyce's object, Wheeler thought, was "to remind the House that this bill would give $8 a month to a few men who, after fighting bravely a score of battles on the plains of Mexico, drew their swords to fight for their own homes and fire-sides." Rather than give these few men a small allowance "the gentleman from Vermont appears to be willing to deprive of their just rights . . . brave soldiers of every northern state who fought in the various regiments of regulars under Generals Scott and Taylor." The only way in which Wheeler could account for this view of his opponent was through prejudice. Joyce was prejudiced, and prejudice "invades and poisons the reason as the malaria from the deadly swamp invades and destroys the physical system."

"This prejudice for and against locality," Wheeler continued, "clings to and controls your actions like an irresistible temptation with which it requires all the strength of your manhood to contend." And then, as if a bit weary of the whole subject of "rebel baiting" and seeing that the bill was defeated he concluded:

Now, Mr. Speaker, were our people of the North and South to use the same effort in promoting harmony as is often used in kindling strife, would not the sweet influences thus aroused . . . close our ears to the clamors of sectional strife and direct us safely in our search for the golden fleece, a prize to be realized only in a newly regenerated Union, happier and grander than before, more prosperous and more united, more Christian and more enlightened? [7]

On February 15, approximately a month after his debate with Joyce, Wheeler again took the floor for another "peace between the sections" speech. On this occasion

[7] *Selections from the Speeches of Hon. Joseph Wheeler, January 15 to March 3, 1883* (Washington, 1883), 1–41. Largely reprints from the *Cong. Record* prepared by General Wheeler covering each term he spent in Congress from 1883 until 1896. Cited hereafter as *Selections*, with date.

was presented the unusual spectacle of a former Confederate general standing before Congress and pleading the cause of a former Federal general. General Fitz-John Porter, the Northerner, had been cashiered and deprived of his commission in the United States Army on charge of disobedience of orders during the Second Battle of Bull Run. General John Pope, then in command of the Army of the Potomac, had preferred the charges and the sentence of the court-martial had been approved by President Lincoln. For ten years following imposition of the sentence Porter almost continually applied for a rehearing in the light of newly discovered evidence. In April, 1878, President Rutherford B. Hayes appointed a board of officers to investigate the new evidence in the light of the old. The report of this board was that General Porter was not guilty of the charges placed against him, but rather that his conduct was "obedient, subordinate, faithful and judicious" and that it "saved the Union army from disaster." [8] In May, 1882, President Chester A. Arthur remitted that part of the sentence that had not been carried into execution, but did not restore rank in the army. The bill upon which General Wheeler was about to speak would restore this rank and in a measure alleviate what he termed "the pangs of a living death." [9]

Doubtless, Wheeler's reasons for wishing to defend Porter were composed of a mixture of emotions. General Porter had been his teacher at West Point; the honor of an officer was at stake and an officer's honor is his honor whether he be Federal or Confederate. The House Military Affairs Committee of which Wheeler was a member had considered the case and thus a splendid opportunity

[8] Richard B. Irwin, "The Case of Fitz John Porter," in *Battles and Leaders*, II, 696.

[9] Wheeler, *Selections*, 1883, p. 137.

was afforded a "rebel" general to show the world that he was ready to forgive; all these things probably constituted parts of Wheeler's desire to defend his former enemy. Then, too, it was popular among Southern Liberals to show a forgiving spirit even as Henry W. Grady did.

The defense presented by Wheeler covers more than a hundred pages of the *Congressional Record*. Most of it is detailed military information unintelligible to those who have not studied such things. Without going into these details it may be said that Wheeler's thesis was that General Pope had "deliberately selected Porter for immolation." According to Wheeler, Pope needed a victim upon whom could be shifted the responsibility for defeat and "when a man in the high place of military power needs a victim, one can be found." [10] To support this statement page after page of statistical and reference material was cited. Although, he stated, many Republicans had thrown taunts at him for defending a Northern general his reply was: "The honor of an American soldier is as dear to us [the South] as it is to the people of any portion of our land."

As he proceeded with his remarks another reason for them becomes evident. He saw in the persecution of Porter a "marked similarity" to that which had been brought upon General Hull after his surrender of Detroit. Wheeler thought that his grandfather had been the victim of "vindictive and ambitious" men just as had Porter. Both men, he pointed out, were tried by a court "some of the members of which were directly interested in their conviction" and both cases show "shameful illegalities." [11] Perhaps he also remembered the charges of depredation which had been brought against himself during the Georgia campaign.

[10] *Ibid.*, 139.   [11] *Ibid.*, 247.

But the Porter case was passed over, not even being brought to a vote. It remained for a Democratic Congress and President finally to afford the desired relief.

Aside from his efforts to promote better feelings between the sections, Wheeler showed during his first active period in Congress a rather wide variety of interests, a variety which corresponded with his reading. As a young soldier, businessman, lawyer, and planter he had read widely. This love of books he carried with him to Congress. Perhaps it accounts for the active interest he took in the plans for an adequate national library. The question was being debated during the short term of the Forty-seventh Congress and he gave the projected library his wholehearted support. He was careful, however, to warn the other members that if the nation proposed to spend money on a library, it should be one "commensurate with the growing demands of this great people" and not a mere makeshift. He reasoned that if such a library should double every decade it would reach 4,800,000 volumes by 1923, and that a building should be erected that would accommodate the increase.[12] Just how near his prophecy came to being correct is shown by the fact that in 1933, ten years later than he predicted, the number of printed books and pamphlets in the Library of Congress was placed at 4,477,431.[13] While no action was taken at the time, appropriations totaling $6,500,000 were made by subsequent enactments in 1886, 1888, and 1889 to provide an adequate building, and in 1897 Wheeler had an opportunity to see the main collection transferred from the Capitol to what has been termed the most magnificent library in the world.

[12] *Ibid.*, 225.   [13] *World Almanac* (New York, 1933).

Closely allied to Wheeler's interest in books was his active support of legislation designed to aid the common school. Perhaps the most discussed of all the school bills before Congress between 1882 and 1890 was the so-called "Blair Bill" which provided for national aid to education out of the surplus revenues of the Federal government, the distribution to be made in proportion to each state's illiteracy. Partly because of constitutional objections and partly because of the fear of Federal supervision, many Southern representatives opposed the measure. Although the South would have received a large share of the money, her previous experience with Federal supervision had not been very pleasant and many feared the result might be another Freedmen's Bureau.[14] General Wheeler, however, was one exception to those who objected. He favored the bill because he said it would help the ignorant people of his district, people whom he described as of "moderate means, who selected abodes on the lofty plateaus and mountains of north Alabama, and who were never slaveholders." These people, he said, were "as deserving of the same opportunities" as those accorded to other sections of the country.[15] Those "who selected abodes on the lofty plateaus" were the Independents of his district, voters whom he must face in the next campaign, the Agrarians who must be kept contented.

The tariff also occupied part of Wheeler's attention

[14] Holland Thompson, *The New South* (New Haven, 1919), 27.

[15] Wheeler, *Selections*, 1883, p. 290. Associated with Wheeler in promoting the Blair bill was J. L. M. Curry, General Agent of the Peabody Fund in the South. Curry was a member of Wheeler's staff during the Civil War and today his statue stands near that of Wheeler in Statuary Hall in Washington. See Edwin A. Alderman and Armistead C. Gordon, *J. L. M. Curry* (New York, 1911), 329–32.

during his brief tenure from January to March, 1883. To the surprise of many of his friends who still looked upon him as purely a man of military affairs rather than the planter-lawyer he had come to be, he showed a profound knowledge of fiscal affairs. Perhaps no other member pointed out more clearly the faults of the "mongrel" tariff of 1883 than did he.

His objections were twofold. Not only did he protest against certain rates that he considered to be highly objectionable, but he also disapproved of the methods used in getting the bill passed. His objections seem well founded. The tariff of 1883 did not originate in the House as the Constitution provided. Congress in 1882 had passed an act for the appointment of a tariff commission that was to report at the next session what changes it thought desirable. This commission, protective in sentiment, was headed by John L. Hayes, Secretary of the Wool Manufacturers' Association. Its report was laid before the House at the beginning of the 1882–1883 session but the members were not able to agree on a schedule of duties. They did, however, pass an internal revenue bill and send it to the Senate. To this internal revenue bill the Senate tacked an amendment, a tariff bill, based on the committee's report. When this bill was referred to the House the protectionist majority succeeded in having it referred to a conference committee where details were settled and the matter reported back to the House without ever having been considered by the Ways and Means Committee, the Committee of the Whole House, or by many of the members privately. It was this procedure which Wheeler considered high-handed and which he characterized as "an effort by the Republican party to disfranchise every member of the representatives of the people in the Forty Seventh Congress." [16] The bill, he protested, consisted of "one hundred and sixteen pages of printed matter, not one line of which was ever officially within the Hall where we now stand, until a few hours ago." With this situation existing the members were to vote intelligently on a measure "before it is possible . . . with the utmost rapidity, to glance over the pages." [17]

From this he passed into a criticism of what he considered to be the glaring faults of the bill, and many he found. He saw in the bill "a reduction of the tax on silk" and a "largely increased tariff put on low priced cotton goods which are used to clothe people in moderate circumstances." He also regretted that the bill removed the tax on diamonds altogether and showed an increase on the tax on earthenware "which is used by the people who have no influence with the Republican party." Although the duty on woolen goods was slightly reduced, the reduction applied only to the better grade cloth. On cheaper textiles, which means a mixture of cotton and wool, the duty had been prohibitive and it remained so.[18] Thus, in addition to raising the duty on pure cotton goods, the bill maintained a high duty on woolen goods that contained a mixture of cotton. Wheeler saw that this would force the people of his district to pay a higher price for their cotton cloth and for their cheap wool-and-cotton suits and dresses. This he characterized as "most unwarranted, unnecessary, and oppressive." In fact, he thought that the Republican party was building up through its entire tariff policy "a tremendous autocracy and plutocracy—a great body

---

[16] Frank W. Taussig, *The Tariff History of the United States* (New York, 1914), 231.

[17] Wheeler, *Selections*, 1883, p. 364.

[18] Taussig, *Tariff History of the United States*, 242.

of people whom it is sought to have supported by a percentage levied upon the hard earnings of the people." [19] Just how large and powerful that "plutocracy" was to become Wheeler would have an opportunity to observe as the years came and went.

It is, of course, not difficult to understand Wheeler's tariff views. He came from a section where planter and small farmer alike believed that a protective tariff injured them. This was one thing upon which the Independents and many Bourbons could agree—a tariff made them pay more for the articles they had to buy. There were many tenant farmers among the Independents who depended almost wholly upon their cotton crops for cash. Practically everything the share cropper wore or used on the farm was either purchased at the village store or from a mail-order house. In many instances the proceeds from the sale of his cotton were barely enough to pay the merchant for goods advanced during the growing season. If a tariff made the cropper have to pay the merchant more for goods, then he was against it. In turn, the merchant opposed the tariff because it made him pay more for his goods in eastern markets. The district was antiprotectionist in 1883 and Wheeler well represented its views in Congress. And, it might be added, he never changed his views.

When Wheeler returned home after the adjournment of the Forty-seventh Congress he found himself much stronger politically than when he left in January. His speeches in Congress, particularly on the tariff and education, were hardly delivered before they were reprinted and scattered through the district. Reflecting as they did his interest in "people of moderate means who had

[19] Wheeler, *Selections*, 1883, p. 364.

selected abodes on the lofty plateaus and mountains of North Alabama" these speeches did much to make the Independents feel that their Congressman was not caring for the interests of the Bourbons alone. The good impressions thus created were further strengthened by many personal contacts during the time Pryor was in Congress for his one term. Wheeler became a familiar figure on court days in Moulton and at picnics and rallies. People who had only heard of the great General now met him and shook his hand. Yet there was nothing hail-fellow-well-met about him; a certain innate dignity prevented anyone from slapping him on the back and calling him "Joe." There are many people who remember him as he unobtrusively went about the business of cultivating the good will of his district. They recall that he was a sprightly little man whose clothes usually were loose and baggy, whose pockets bulged with official looking papers, who wore a black slouch hat and a beard—always the hat and the beard. Always he moved gingerly and spoke rapidly. There are those who remember chiefly his eccentricities, but few speak of him except in terms of respect and even veneration.

There was, of course, a reason for this activity. He was looking forward to the campaign of 1884 which he hoped would prove his vindication. As it developed, he was elected in 1884 but it would be difficult to determine whether it was his own popularity that was responsible for his victory or whether it was the collapse of the leaderless Independents. Probably it was due to a combination of things: the death of Lowe, the victory of the Bourbons in 1882, and Wheeler's growing popularity. One thing, however, is certain: the Independents offered but little resistance in the fall election of 1884. As a sort of prelude to the contest the Democrats of the Eighth District assembled in June for the double purpose of selecting a representative to the forthcoming Democratic National Convention and of nominating their Congressional candidate. With very little real opposition Wheeler was selected as both.[20] He would go to the convention first and then come home to run for Congress.

When the Alabama delegation headed by Wheeler as chairman reached Chicago on July 7 for the convention which would assemble on the next day, they found their choice for the Presidential nomination, Grover Cleveland, in the lead with preconvention votes but lacking enough for a nomination on the first ballot. As a matter of fact, he was lacking enough to insure his nomination on any ballot; and, what was worse, Tammany Hall was fighting him—fighting him openly and with secret intrigues and conspiracies. After the first ballot, which took place on the third day, Tammany tried to stage a rally for Thomas A. Hendricks, but to no avail. Joe Wheeler of Alabama and Wade Hampton of South Carolina were again fighting together, fighting to hold the Southern delegates firm against a possible stampede away from Cleveland.[21] On the second ballot with the South standing firm the Governor of New York was given more than the necessary two-thirds majority. Nor did these two fighters cease their activities with the end of the convention. Both went home and there helped carry their states for the Democratic nominee. In Wheeler's home district the ticket "Cleveland and Wheeler" received the largest Democratic vote of any ticket since

20 Although Judge William Richardson of Huntsville showed some strength in the convention, the majority of the delegates were for Wheeler.

21 Allan Nevins, *Grover Cleveland, A Study in Courage* (New York, 1932), 151.

the Civil War. Alabama went overwhelmingly for Cleveland and the Eighth Congressional District sent Wheeler to Congress.[22] Independentism had been defeated again. As a matter of fact, it had not put up much of a fight.

March 4, 1885, was of course a gala day for the Democrats. The inauguration of Grover Cleveland marked their return to power in national politics. Since the day in 1860 when Yancey and his fellow seceders in high dudgeon forsook the convention hall at Charleston the Democratic party had fought the taint of rebellion. Back in their local districts the leaders of the now renascent party had fought a good fight to rid themselves of the stigma of the war and to restore the party to the high position it had once occupied in the affairs of the nation. The years had been long and the famine sore, but the leaders had been faithful. Now they crowded around their newly elected chief and pressed upon him their congratulations.

This happy occasion marked the beginning of an uninterrupted fourteen-year tenure—a period in which Wheeler would be an active participant in the affairs of a rapidly changing economic and social order. He had lived through the Civil War, through the period of Reconstruction, and now he and his fellow Congressmen in 1885 stood upon the threshold of a new era. It could not be said, however, that Wheeler was a leader in these changing years. He never became a great and powerful figure in Congress directing legislation, conferring with the President, or mapping party strategy. Rather he mirrored the forces that were shaping the new order of things, particularly in the South. He came to be the incarnation of the average Southern Congress-

[22] Huntsville *Democrat*, November 11, 1884. The Greenback-Independent ticket polled about 30 per cent of the total vote.

man of the late eighties and nineties who found himself confronted by confusing new economic and political issues. His work in Congress was not to prove spectacular; in fact, the most interesting thing about his career is the man himself. This sprightly and serious little man with the black slouch hat and the flowing gray whiskers came to be one of the best known figures in Washington; what he accomplished was really secondary.

But the jubilation of a Democratic victory soon gave way to more prosaic things. Many people turned expectant faces toward the new administration and many others thought it a major catastrophe. The Democrats were hungry for office, the Grand Army of the Republic was hungry for pensions—almost everyone seemed to want something of the new President. The members of his own party soon began to complain that he made too few removals of Republican officeholders and the National Civil Service Reform League thought he made too many. The G.A.R. snarled when the President vetoed fraudulent pension bills and grew vituperative when he proposed to give back to the South its captured battle flags. The Republican Senate joined in the mêlée by reviving the Tenure of Office Act to embarrass the Executive. Friend and foe alike made Cleveland's term a Via Dolorosa.

The Forty-ninth Congress which convened on the first Monday in December, 1885, was a distinct disappointment to many who had been hopeful of its success. Bills providing for a Presidential succession act, creating an interstate commerce commission, and regulating the manufacture and sale of oleomargarine were pushed through; but this was practically the sum total of the accomplishments excepting, of course, private bills. Many other matters were under consideration. There was

Wheeler's troublesome Fitz-John Porter case and the Blair Bill, holdovers from previous congresses. There were free-silver bills, rivers and harbors bills, tariff measures, and a host of other things unconsidered. That more of these matters were not enacted into legislation is due to the fact that the Senate and House majorities were from opposing parties and because the House was operating under a set of rules that made legislation well-nigh impossible.

When the House convened it elected John G. Carlisle of Kentucky its Speaker, but it refused the customary procedure of adopting the rules of the preceding Congress. Instead, it authorized the Committee on Rules to draft and submit certain alterations which would give the House greater freedom in initiating and carrying through needed legislation. As the rules stood such freedom was impossible. Debate could be carried on almost interminably, and the minority could create unnecessary delay by dilatory motions and filibustering tactics. There was no machinery to give precedence to important measures. All bills reported from committees were placed on the calendar in hit-or-miss fashion, and the more important ones could be reached only by the suspension of the rules which required a two-thirds majority. A militant minority could and did block any measure it chose.[23] This situation the Democrats hoped to remedy through the recommendation of its Committee on Rules composed of Speaker Carlisle, Samuel J. Randall, William R. Morrison, Thomas B. Reed, and Frank Hiscock. But their hopes were not realized. On Decem-

[23] For a discussion of the House rules, see Paul DeWitt Hasbrouck, *Party Government in the House of Representatives* (New York, 1927); and DeAlva Stanwood, *History and Procedure of the House of Representatives* (New York, 1916).

ber 14 the committee made two reports—a majority report by Randall and a minority report by Morrison. Then while the House marked time and legislation waited, these two Democrats fought it out. The result was that no reform was accomplished and much legislation went by the board.[24]

Representative Wheeler took little part in the discussion of the changes in rules. He was a comparatively new member, for one thing, and he was also very busy with other matters. As a member of the Committee on Military Affairs it again became his duty to bring the troublesome Fitz-John Porter case to the attention of the House. This he did in a speech which was almost a repetition of his former one delivered two years earlier. This time the bill passed the House and went to the Senate. There a bitter battle ensued—a battle so acrimonious that it was termed "the Third Battle of Bull Run." [25] The Republicans were determined that the Democrats should not have the privilege of correcting the injustice and the Democrats were equally determined to do so. Finally, however, a sufficient majority was mustered to pass the House bill unamended, and thus it went to Cleveland for his signature. A Democratic President signed the bill which restored, in a measure, the honor and reputation of a Yankee general.

Having thus seen the Porter case disposed of, Wheeler turned his attention to nearly every matter before the House. His speechmaking became proverbial. He spoke often and on a wide range of topics—"Little flyaway speeches on every conceivable topic" one newspaper

24 Henry J. Ford, *The Cleveland Era* (New Haven, 1919), 92–107.
25 Ben: Perley Poore, *Reminiscences of Sixty Years in the National Metropolis* (Philadelphia, 1886), II, 487.

called them.[26] His wide reading and thorough preparation of even the simplest speeches often made him seem
pedantic, yet none can deny that they are convincing
when seen in print. His speech on the Sundry Appropriations Bill will illustrate this. The House was considering
the matter of a bill for constructing storm, cold-wave,
and other weather signals over the United States, more
particularly along the Gulf coast. Wheeler was highly
in favor of this and in indicating his approval he displayed a map "indicating the general track of the most
destructive cyclones for the last hundred years" which
he himself had prepared. Within the tropics, he said,
there was a belt of calms which extended from the West
Indies eastward nearly to the African coast. The width
of this belt varied from sixty to two hundred miles and
its confines varied according to the season: in midwinter
being only one hundred miles north of the equator, and
in midsummer seven hundred miles farther north. "This
brings the belt of calms to that part of the Atlantic
Ocean which lies between the group of islands, Trinidad, Martinique, and Guadaloupe, on the west, and the
African coast on the east." "This belt of calms," he went
on, "is due to the heat of the sun near the equator,
which expands the atmosphere near the surface of the
earth and causes it to rise . . . thus causing cyclones
and hurricanes." [27]

It would be interesting to know just how many of his
colleagues knew or cared where Trinidad, Martinique,
and Guadaloupe were, but they would find out many
new things if they listened to the speeches of the gentle-

[26] Chattanooga *Daily Times,* August 8, 1897, in Clipping Files,
Wheeler Papers.
[27] *Cong. Record,* 49 Cong., 1 Sess., 6359.

man from Alabama. Before long he was lecturing on the so-called "Oleomargarine bill" which would restrict and tax the sale of this butter substitute. Wheeler opposed the bill, but he found it necessary to go into the history of oleomargarine from its very discovery. It took him ten closely printed pages of history, statistical tables, Supreme Court decisions, platform declarations, and expert opinion to say that he considered the bill "inquisitorial, iniquitous, and unjust." [28] But this oleomargarine question was more important than might appear on the surface and Wheeler's remarks typify the position taken by most of the Southern Senators and Representatives on an issue of vital importance to the rapidly growing Farmers' Alliance movement. During the 1880's synthetic food products began to make their influence felt in certain economic and political circles. Chief among these new products were oleomargarine and lard compound. Both of these vegetable products came into direct competition with the dairying and hog-raising industries of the Middle West and caused the National Farmers' Alliance to advocate government control of them.[29] In 1886 the dairy interests appealed to Congress for relief, showing by their petitions that oleomargarine was about to capture their butter market.[30] But these Westerners received scant consideration from the representatives of Southern farming interests. So Wheeler was voicing the almost unanimous opinion of his Southern colleagues when he pointed out: "If this measure should increase the profits of the dairymen of

[28] Wheeler, *Selections*, 1886, p. 272.

[29] Herman C. Nixon, "The Cleavage Within the Farmers' Alliance Movement," in *Mississippi Valley Historical Review* (Cedar Rapids), XV (1929), 25–26. Professor Nixon was one of the first to point out the importance of the oleomargarine bill.

[30] *Cong. Record*, 49 Cong., 1 Sess., 4865.

the North and Northwest, just in the same proportion
will it decrease the profits of the producers of cotton
and the stock raisers of the South." The butter produced in his district, he pointed out, was insufficient to
supply the needs. Therefore, it was evident that raising
the price of oleomargarine would enhance the value of
each pound of butter consumed by the people of Alabama.[31] Thus was revealed a rift in the ranks of the
embattled farmers, a rift which goes far toward explaining the lack of success encountered by the agrarian Alliance movement in the South. Oleomargarine was not
the only difference; the Negro question, prices of cotton
bagging, barbed wire, lard compound—all these questions conspired to prevent a real union of Southern and
Western agrarians.

The disagreement between Southern and Western
farmers over oleomargarine was but one manifestation
of the fact that sectional and economic differences in
American life were growing more acute. The Civil War
had preserved the Union politically, but nothing could
save it from economic divergence. As the Cleveland administration got under way it became increasingly evident that there was no unanimity of opinion as to the
facts of economic life or of national policy. The fact
is that America was growing so rapidly the pace was becoming confusing. Between the years 1880 and 1890 the
population increased by twelve millions and national
wealth grew to the then staggering figure of sixty-five
billions of dollars. During the same period the number
of manufacturing plants increased by a hundred thousand, the value of domestic manufacturing leaped four
billions of dollars, the number of wage earners doubled,
and the exports from farm and factory began to reach

[31] *Ibid.*

the outer fringes of the globe.[32] America was growing—growing in the middle, as later events revealed, and becoming corpulent and unsteady. Economic classes presented programs which would favor their own groups and thought little of a consistent national plan. Captains of industry sent their representatives to the Congress to protect their interests; the West and South had their free silverites; labor began to clamor for a hearing in national affairs; the farmers were in veritable revolt. A legislative program was well-nigh impossible unless one group should dominate all the rest.

In spite of the vacillation and lack of consistency which was becoming more and more apparent, men "always came back . . . to three great subjects—currency, the tariff, and administrative reform." To use the words of a modern historian: "Politics was like a weary waltz in some huge triangular ballroom; the airs and the partners changed, but the circling dancers pivoted upon the three identical corners." [33] Lower the tariff! Repeal the Bland-Allison silver bill! Reform governmental administration! These became the familiar slogans.

The Democratic party in 1884 had pledged itself to "revise the tariff in a spirit of fairness to all interests." [34] President Cleveland in his first annual message to Congress pointed out that "a certain reduction should be made in the revenue derived from a tax upon the imported necessaries of life." [35] In his second annual message delivered December 6, 1886, the President became more definite and urgent in his tariff recommendations.

[32] Arthur M. Schlesinger, *New Viewpoints in American History* (New York, 1925), 249.

[33] Nevins, *Grover Cleveland,* 340.

[34] Kirk H. Porter, *National Party Platforms* (New York, 1924), 119.

[35] James D. Richardson (ed.), *A Compilation of the Messages and Papers of the Presidents, 1789–1897* (Washington, 1896–1901), VII, 341.

Income was far outrunning expenditures, he informed the legislative branch, and there soon would be a large surplus in the Treasury. Such a situation, Cleveland thought, boded no good for the country. If it should be allowed to continue "we should then be confronted with a vast quantity of money, the circulating medium of the people, hoarded in the Treasury when it should be in their hands, or we should be drawn into wasteful public extravagance with all the corruption and national demoralization which follows in its train." [36]

But despite platform pledges and Presidential admonition, nothing in the way of tariff reform was accomplished by the Forty-ninth Congress which adjourned on March 3, 1887. As a matter of fact, the Democratic party was almost hopelessly divided on the issue. During the first session of that Congress the so-called "Morrison bill" had been introduced providing that lumber, salt, wool, hemp, flax, and other miscellaneous articles be put on the free list, and that the duty on cotton and sugar be reduced. The bill was never discussed, for Morrison's motion to proceed to its consideration was defeated. During the rest of the session no attempt was made to revive it, but in July, 1886, a motion was again made to proceed to the consideration of revenue bills and was again defeated. [37] As a substitute for the Morrison bill, Samuel J. Randall of Pennsylvania introduced a resolution to remove taxes on tobacco, fruit, brandies, and spirits used in the arts; entire remission of duties on lumber, jute, and a slight reduction on miscellaneous articles. [38] The plan was thoroughly protectionist and

[36] Taussig, *Tariff History of the United States*, 252.

[37] House Resolution, No. 9702, in *Cong. Record*, 49 Cong., 1 Sess., 6756.

[38] Nevins, *Grover Cleveland*, 385.

was never reported from committee. These two plans then, Morrison's and Randall's, constituted the only efforts made by the Democrats to reform the tariff at the short session.

The Randall plan reveals the rapidly widening issue which was appearing within the Democratic ranks. There clearly was a protectionist group which proposed to fight the President's tariff reforms. This group had as its leader Randall, but its followers were not entirely eastern. There was a rapidly developing protectionist group in the South. In 1886 Randall paid a visit to Alabama and was welcomed in the heart of this state's budding industrial region at Birmingham. "Peace, Pig-iron, and Prosperity" were the banners which greeted him there. A year later in Atlanta he was given a tremendous ovation when he appeared in response to an invitation formally to open the Piedmont Exposition. In General Wheeler's home district in North Alabama one paper expressed the estimate that "half the newspapers of North Alabama were supporters of the protection policies of Samuel J. Randall." [39]

Wheeler did not join with the protectionists of his own district, but before he had an opportunity publicly to express his views there came Cleveland's tariff message of 1887. After mature deliberation the President decided to welcome the Fiftieth Congress with a message devoted entirely to one issue—the tariff. He vigorously urged a general reduction of duties, and more especially the removal of the tariff on raw material.[40] His position was decided and outspoken and had the effect of committing his party unreservedly to a policy of opposition to the existing protective system, and of making this

[39] Moulton (Alabama) *Advertiser*, July 30, 1896.
[40] Richardson (ed.), *Messages and Papers of the Presidents*, VII, 589.

question more distinctly a party matter than it had been at any time since the Civil War.[41] It would be interesting now to see what the protectionist wing of the President's own party would do.

Immediately after the President's message, both the Republican and Democratic forces cleared for action and began to maneuver for position. At one o'clock in the afternoon, April 17, 1888, Roger Q. Mills of Texas, Chairman of the Committee on Ways and Means, proposed that the House should resolve itself into a committee of the whole for the consideration of matters pertaining to the tariff and revenue. It was the opening gun. For two hours the irascible gentleman from Texas pointed out the glaring defects of the Republican scheme of protection and pleaded for reform—for the support of the bill ultimately to be known as the "Mills bill." [42]

On May 4 Wheeler gained the floor in support of Mills, Cleveland, and tariff reduction. The House being in Committee of the Whole he had but five minutes to speak, but he used those minutes well. It was not, he thought, a time for partisanship and oratory. "The reform attempted to be accomplished by the bill under consideration is so important, and the benefits it seeks to confer upon our people are so far-reaching, that it merits our earnest thought and careful investigation, and, notwithstanding the popular demand for prompt action, I think prudence dictates that a subject so momentous in its effects should be approached with deliberation and caution." He was the warrior counseling calmness in the heat of battle. "The discussion of a question involving the interests, and therefore the hap-

41 Taussig, *Tariff History of the United States*, 253.
42 *Cong. Record*, 50 Cong., 1 Sess., 3057.

piness and prosperity of the great mass of the citizens of a free government, should be characterized by calm and judicious impartiality and intelligent conscientious sincerity of purpose to secure the highest possible good to the whole country." [43]

He then proceeded to lay down seventeen conclusions which "the statistics and other evidence which I have before me tend strongly to establish." His conclusions in general were: That a prohibitory tariff created and fostered trusts and combinations of capital; that the Republican tariff policy favored privileged classes, benefited the rich, and victimized the poor; that a protective tariff sometimes injured the very industries it sought to benefit; that American labor had been misled in believing that a tariff helped them; that our greatest prosperity had always been achieved under a low tariff; that a downward revision of the tariff was necessary to secure a foreign market for our products.[44]

Wheeler barely had time in the five minutes allotted him to lay down these propositions, but he extended his remarks in the *Record* into one of the longest treatises on the tariff in that compilation. When reprinted it covered 137 closely printed pages and proved a veritable mine of information of the much discussed subject. "His speech upon the tariff," commented the Washington *National Free Press,* "was universally admitted to be an inexhaustible arsenal of facts and deductions from which advocates of tariff reform drew ammunition without stint." [45] Wheeler was not a florid orator, but his printed

---

[43] Wheeler, *Selections,* 1888–1889, p. 90.   [44] *Ibid.,* 91 ff.

[45] March 17, 1889. Wheeler's habit of reading material into the *Record* came in for considerable comment from his contemporaries. "He had a habit as to speechmaking," Champ Clark wrote, "which was valuable to searchers after information. He would get a few minutes in which to address the House, and also leave to extend and

speeches were not surpassed for facts and logical treatments of varying subjects. Although he was not a member of the Committee on Ways and Means until 1894, the tariff issue, nevertheless, constituted one of the major interests of his Congressional career.[46]

The hectic debates on the Mills bill came to a climax on May 19 after two days of oratory. Then followed thirty days of maneuvering with only desultory speechmaking. Finally, on July 21 the vote came. Just before roll call began Randall sent in a letter to be read: "I fear my strength, by reason of recent illness, will not permit my presence in the House on that day," he wrote, "and, if absent, I want you to secure me a pair with someone who favors the bill, as I would, if present, record my vote in opposition to it." There was much cheering from the Republican side of the House and the Clerk began the roll call.[47] The result was the adoption of the bill by strict party vote of 162 to 149. The Democratic party had again placed itself on record as favoring tariff reform.

Following the adoption of the Mills bill in the House, the Senate with its Republican majority prepared a counter bill to strengthen the protective system. As in the House, the measure was adopted by a party vote, thus drawing very clearly the party lines and preparing for the Presidential battle of 1888.[48] The result was an

---

revise his remarks—a few minutes answered his purpose as well as an hour. Then he would set his four clerks to work gathering data, and would print a speech of several pages in *The Congressional Record,* exhausting the subject from his point of view." Clark, *My Quarter Century,* II, 46.

[46] Wheeler's committee assignments were: Public Lands, Expenditures of the Interior Department, Board of Regents of Smithsonian Institute, and Board of Visitors of the Military Academy.

[47] *Cong. Record,* 50 Cong., 1 Sess., 3057.

[48] Taussig, *Tariff History of the United States,* 254.

impasse. The Senate had one plan and the House another. All through the summer of 1888 the two bodies continued their sessions, threshing over reform and accomplishing little, if anything. National conventions met and nominated Cleveland and Harrison, and still the Congress held on, its terminal facilities apparently wholly impaired.

Early in October Wheeler got the floor to express again his tariff views—this time the Senate bill being the object of his attack. The House was trying to resolve itself into committee of the whole for the consideration of a bill to establish "a public park near the headwaters of the Yellowstone River." Representative Thomas C. MacRae of Arkansas discovered, however, there yet remained twenty-eight minutes of the morning hour which rightfully belonged to him. Accordingly, he yielded his time to Wheeler for a set speech on the tariff.[49] It was a speech bristling with strong adjectives and almost devoid of the usual statistical tables and logical propositions. In short, it was a campaign document charging the Republicans with everything except mayhem. Most of all Wheeler saw in the bill the real purpose of the Republican party. Behind all their talk about protection, patriotism, and the welfare of labor under the proposed Senate bill could be seen, if one looked closely enough, the party's real desire "to perpetuate the privileges whereby a few favored monopolists and corporations have gained enormous individual fortunes at the expense of the comfort and happiness of those by whose toil the wealth of the country is created." There would come a day of reckoning, however, and when that time came "as our ancestors at Runnymede wrung from King John the Magna Carta . . . so we

[49] *Cong. Record,* 50 Cong., 1 Sess., 9306.

will wring from the Senate of the United States a concession as valuable to the people of this land of freedom as was the Magna Carta to the downtrodden subjects of the proud English monarch." [50]

It was excellent oratory and quite characteristic of its day, but if Wheeler and his colleagues expected to "wring" anything from the Republican party they had selected a mighty poor time to do so. Within little more than a month after he had delivered this speech the people had elected a Republican President, a Republican Senate, and a Republican House of Representatives. Nevertheless, it was speeches like this, shouted loud enough and long enough, that made it possible for a superb young orator, William Jennings Bryan, one summer day in 1896 to face a milling, sweating horde of Democracy in convention assembled and there win for himself the Presidential nomination.

As a matter of fact, events for fifteen years before 1896 foreshadowed a showdown sooner or later. Agrarian unrest, the tariff, and money—all unsolved problems—pointed toward a day when half-measures and compromises would not suffice. And of these, none threw a longer or more ominous shadow than the government's monetary policy, for during Cleveland's first term the "silver blizzard" broke in a fury of oratory. And it was a blizzard in which party affiliations were lost sight of on both sides of the House. Many Democrats, among them Wheeler, refused to follow Cleveland's gold policy; and many Republicans came over to the silverites.

Wheeler retired to his subterranean office and came up with a long and scholarly dissertation on silver to match his previous one on the tariff, but he had little opportunity to discuss it before adjournment. Men

[50] Wheeler, *Selections*, 1886, p. 96.

were too busy with political oratory to pay much attention to the operation of Gresham's law, the relation of
the deflated dollar to prices, or the ratio of gold to silver.
He had time only to remind the House that low prices
and depression were due to deflation and that the way
out was through purchase of silver and the reduction of
the amount of metal in the gold dollar—a policy inter-
estingly prophetic of certain phases of the New Deal.[51]

[51] *Ibid.*, 95. See also, *Cong. Record*, 49 Cong., 1 Sess., 3300. Alonzo
B. Hepburn, *A History of Currency in the United States* (New York,
1915), Chap. XII, is an adequate discussion of the silver issue. See
also, Nevins, *Grover Cleveland*, Chap. XVI; and John D. Hicks, *The
Populist Revolt* (Minneapolis, 1931), Chap. XI.

Chapter XII

THE NINETIES

IT was with Wheeler that the Bourbons had won the
Eighth District from the wool hat boys, but after it was
apparently safe in the Democratic fold there arose many
of Wheeler's own party who were quite willing to take
over his seat in Congress and keep the district saved.
Chief among these aspirants was William Richardson
of Huntsville, probate judge of Madison County. Judge
Richardson was either the candidate or the moving force
behind the Wheeler opposition in every campaign from
1886 until the General resigned his seat after the
Spanish-American War. Richardson was never successful
in defeating Wheeler, but his efforts kept the campaign
going constantly with only slight pauses that came just
after election day. Well might Wheeler have used the
Queen's words to Alice: "Now, here, you see, it takes all
the running you can do to keep in the same place."

Because of these constant attacks by Richardson,
Wheeler found it necessary to devote a great deal of his
time to keeping his political fences in order. When one
consults his voluminous correspondence to find his views
on leading questions of the day he is rewarded by a great
mass of letters which tell practically nothing about his
views on national problems. "Your pension claim is being given my personal attention." "I cannot, as yet, find
out why your appointment has not gone through." "I

shall personally investigate your claim." "Please determine, if possible what reports Richardson is circulating." These and hundreds of similar ones are typical quotations from the great bulk of his letters. It is small wonder that he had to be at his office in the morning while his colleagues were yet in bed, and to remain at work long after they had retired at night.[1]

There were few mails which did not bring some form of his remarks extended in the *Record* into his district. The volume grew steadily year by year until his friends began to joke about it. It is related that on one occasion when the General was campaigning in mountainous Jackson County he wished to travel from one village to another. The only means of conveyance was the mail wagon of the Negro star route carrier. He applied to the Negro for permission to ride with him, but when he saw what his mode of transportation was he was somewhat taken aback. He saw a wobbly one-horse wagon piled high with mail bags and pulled by a decrepit nag apparently about ready to collapse. Surveying it all with the critical eye of a cavalry commander the General inquired imperiously, "Nigger, why don't you feed that horse something? He's about dead."

The Negro, wholly unaware of the identity of his guest, answered: "Well, I tell you, boss, There's some Congressman up dere in Washington what keeps sendin' speeches down here and it keeps my hoss pore haulin' 'em around." [2]

This ceaseless political activity, however, did not be-

---

[1] Houston *Post*, August 26, 1896, in Clipping Files, Wheeler Papers. Quotations selected at random from Wheeler Correspondence, Wheeler Papers.

[2] Judge J. J. Mitchell of Florence, Alabama, to the author, October 2, 1927. Judge Mitchell and General Wheeler were close personal and political friends.

cloud his thinking to the point where he was not aware of the changing conditions in his state and district. Writing in 1895 to George W. Ochs of the Chattanooga *News* he pointed out that "the agricultural interests of our region must share with rising industry the credit for the great increase in our wealth"; and that "It is gratifying to learn that only last week Bessemer steel was made in Chattanooga of ores found within easy access of that city." [3]

Wheeler obviously was aware that industrialism was beginning to make inroads upon the agrarian character of Southern life. His own district, the Eighth, and that represented by Oscar W. Underwood, the Seventh, were learning by the late 1890's to walk on their new industrial legs. North Alabama was digging coal from her mountains and listening to the hum of textile spindles. Hundreds of poor whites moved into the steel and textile towns of Birmingham, Sheffield, Florence, and Huntsville and there took up their new and strange trades and an even newer and stranger way of living. [4] An abundance of cheap labor, an excellent climate, inexhaustible natural resources, and adequate transportation facilities afforded by the Memphis and Charleston Railway and the Tennessee River made the region more than attractive to the industrialist.

Not only was Wheeler aware of the changing nature of economic life in his district, but he warmly approved of it. As early as 1886, before the industrialization of the South had begun, he pointed out in a speech in Congress

[3] Wheeler to George W. Ochs, August 5, 1895, in Wheeler Papers.

[4] Production of coal increased from 323,972 tons in 1880 to 8,394,-275 tons in 1900. Pig iron increased from 68,919 tons in 1880 to 1,184,337 tons in 1900. In 1880 there were 49,423 spindles in the state. This number grew to 79,324 in 1890 and to 411,328 in 1900. Moore, *History of Alabama and Her People*, I, 770.

that the South's advance "in all that makes a people great, rich, and prosperous is evidenced by no faltering or uncertain signs. She is coming—not to injuriously compete with our sister states of the North, but by her growing prosperity to aid them in the great strides they are taking toward unquestionable supremacy in the commercial and industrial affairs of the world." The old order was passing, he thought, and "the young men of the South are pressing forward in the race for prosperity with energy, vigor, and determination." [5]

And the rising industrialists of the district applauded the work being done by Wheeler in Congress. "There are in Sheffield and Florence in operation, being put in operation, and being built, eight large blast furnaces," wrote the President of one iron and coal company to Wheeler. "If the obstructions in the Tennessee River . . . could be removed, a great many more furnaces and other important industries could be started at these places, as the country round is full of iron. We all appreciate the great work and energy you have displayed working for this improvement. If you need any help in the Senate, Senator William E. Chandler would be a good worker." [6] Another president reminded his superintendent that Wheeler was the man rising Southern industry needed in Congress. "I simply want to say, as President of the Sheffield Coal, Iron and Steel Company, that the best interests of everyone, not only connected with that furnace at Sheffield but in my judgment in all business matters pertaining to Sheffield, is depending upon the completion of the canal around Colbert Shoals. Taking that view of the matter, I cannot but think that Gen-

5 Wheeler, *Selections*, 1893, p. 151.

6 E. W. Cole, President of the Sheffield & Birmingham Coal, Iron, and Railway Co., to Wheeler, February 22, 1896, in Wheeler Papers.

eral Wheeler is the party we want to represent that interest in Congress." [7]

As the above indicates, one of the chief interests of industry in the Tennessee Valley portion of Alabama was in seeing that the obstructions to navigation existing at Muscle Shoals and Colbert Shoals were removed; and it was by no means a new interest. As early as 1824 steps had been taken to overcome the obstacles that Muscle Shoals presented to navigation of the Tennessee River. In that year, John C. Calhoun, then Secretary of War, referred to the proposed canal around the shoals as third in rank among the projected improvements of national importance; and in 1826 a survey was made by a group of army engineers. During Jackson's administration an imperfect and narrow canal was constructed around the main obstruction, Muscle Shoals; but before anything was done at other points along the river, some of the dams gave way and the canal fell into disuse.[8] General Wheeler estimated that from 1827 to 1880 Congress expended approximately $1,684,000 for improvement of the Tennessee River, of which almost 95 per cent went for work on Muscle Shoals. From 1880 to the end of his career in Congress in 1899, Wheeler stated, he had secured $3,250,000 for the work, two and a half times as much as had been appropriated in the fifty-three previous years of its existence as a national problem.[9]

Wheeler appears to have aimed at more than mere

[7] A. W. Willis, President of the Sheffield & Birmingham Coal, Iron & Steel Co., to J. J. Gray, Superintendent of the same company, September 2, 1896, *ibid.*

[8] Summary of Muscle Shoals legislation taken from undated report in General Wheeler's handwriting, in Wheeler Papers. See also, report of the Chief of Engineers, United States Army, 1894, in Adjutant General's Office, Washington, D.C.

[9] *Ibid.*

assistance to rising industry, however. While he did not, of course, foresee the potential hydroelectric possibilities of Muscle Shoals, he did envision a region in which the industry of the miner, the skill of the artisan, and the labor of the farmer would be correlated in such a manner that a well-balanced and sound economic system would be the result. "Minerals, rich in quality and well-nigh inexhaustible in quantity, invite the miner's industry and the artisan's formative skill," he wrote. "Farms so fertile and easy of cultivation that they yield generous returns to the toil of the husbandman skirt the banks of the beautiful Tennessee" and made it possible to supply food for the entire region.[10] In short, his was a vision not entirely different from that of the Tennessee Valley Authority planners today. Almost any week day while Congress was in recess General Wheeler could be seen alone or in the company of an army engineer in a small boat on the river taking measurements, making observations, planning locks.[11] The great Wheeler Dam, which stands today near the point where he and his cavalry crossed that night in the sixties just before he met his future wife, is a worthy monument to his efforts.

Wheeler might have reflected on his legislative career at the close of the Fiftieth Congress with some degree of pride. It had not been particularly brilliant, but he had pushed the Fitz-John Porter case to a successful conclusion, had secured Muscle Shoals legislation, and had brought himself to the attention of his party through his ably prepared treatises on the tariff and on silver. But more than anything else he could pride himself on the

10 Wheeler, *Selections*, 1893, p. 169.
11 The newspapers of the district commented frequently on these river trips. Miss Annie Wheeler relates how her father enjoyed these surveys.

condition of political affairs in his own district. The agrarian revolt that had once threatened his own district, and which in 1886 was flaming anew in near-by East Tennessee, had been brought under control.[12] No leader had arisen since Colonel Lowe's death to rally the Independents. Too, General Wheeler's personal work at home and his speeches in Congress which often reflected his interest in the small-farmer group had gradually weaned it away from its independent course and had brought it into a unified Democratic party. There was every indication, he wrote Cleveland, that this unity might be maintained almost indefinitely if things were managed right.[13] And things were managed "right," for even the full force of Populism did not seriously threaten Wheeler's seat in Congress.

When the Clerk called the roll of the House at the opening of the Fifty-first Congress on the first Monday in December, 1889, there was confirmed a fact which was already quite well known. The Democrats had lost control of the House at the fall elections of 1888 and now the Republicans had control of the legislative and executive branches of the government. At one end of Pennsylvania Avenue was President Benjamin Harrison and at the other a Republican House and Senate. If one had cared to listen to the roll call he doubtless would have recognized many whose names irrespective of party affiliation ultimately came to occupy positions of prominence in American political life. In the House were such men as Thomas B. Reed and Nelson Dingley of Maine, William McKinley of Ohio, Charles F. Crisp of Georgia, Henry

[12] For an account of the Agrarian uprising in Tennessee, see Daniel M. Robison, "Tennessee Politics and the Agrarian Revolt, 1886–1896," in *Mississippi Valley Historical Review*, XX (1934), 365–80.

[13] Wheeler to Grover Cleveland, November 29, 1889, in Cleveland Papers (Division of Manuscripts, Library of Congress).

Cabot Lodge of Massachusetts, Richard P. Bland of Missouri, Samuel J. Randall and William Kelly of Pennsylvania, Wheeler of Alabama, Alfred Taylor and Benton McMillan of Tennessee, Roger Q. Mills of Texas, Robert M. LaFollette of Wisconsin, "Private" John Allen of Mississippi, and John G. Carlisle of Kentucky. For once in American politics the membership of the House in this "billion dollar Congress" seemed almost to outshine that of the Senate.

Reed and Carlisle were nominated by their respective caucuses for the Speakership, and since the former was of the majority party no one was surprised at his election. There were, however, many who were enraged when he initiated his "Czarish" parliamentary reforms. Since the attempt of the Democrats to reform the House rules during Cleveland's administration had failed, the situation at the beginning of Harrison's term with respect to rules and procedure remained unchanged. Dilatory motions and the absence of a quorum still could effectually block any legislation advocated by the majority party. But Reed soon served notice that the rules were to be changed. While the Committee on Rules debated proposed changes the Speaker put an end to the "absence of a quorum" method of delaying legislation by counting those members present who because of their failure to answer roll call were technically absent. If a member was in his seat the Speaker ruled he was present despite his silence.

Immediately there was a storm of indignant protest from the Democratic side of the House. Crisp quoted Shakespeare; Carlisle protested vehemently.[14] Wheeler presumed that there were still some Republicans who

[14] James A. Barnes, *John G. Carlisle, Financial Statesman* (New York, 1931), 168.

revered Abraham Lincoln and remembered that he had
once said: "No man is good enough to govern another
without consent." If a man perfect in all respects and of
unquestioned and infallible wisdom could be found,
then he might be intrusted with the sole governing
power, but Wheeler could not believe Speaker Reed was
that perfect man. "One man power is destructive to
liberty, and how much more dangerous is an unre-
strained rule of a majority," he added.[15]

Virtually every other Democrat in the House added
his voice to the chorus of protests, but the urbane Reed
went calmly about the business of pushing through the
Republican program of raising the tariff and reducing
the surplus in the Treasury. On April 16, 1890, Chairman McKinley of the Committee on Ways and Means
set the program in motion by introducing into the House
the tariff proposal destined to bear his name. He and the
Speaker united their efforts to hasten its adoption. Only
four days were allowed for debate and, since the Democrats could no longer use the quorum and dilatory motions to delay a vote, the measure encountered little
real opposition until it reached the Senate. The House
Democrats, of course, fought it, but they had been deprived of their principal weapons.

Wheeler did not choose to deliver his usual long and
extensive treatment on the tariff, but his remarks are
clearer for the omission of many details. He revealed
himself as a doctrinaire low-tariff adherent. His views
were made known in 1884, he said, and he did not expect to change them as long as he lived. He was not opposed to industry because he came from a state which in
1890 "manufactured more iron than any other State of
our Union except Pennsylvania and Ohio"; rather, he

15 Wheeler, *Selections,* 1893, p. 27.

was denouncing an upward revision because he believed that a lowering of rates was "essential to the permanent success of manufacturers as much as it is to the farmers." [16] With him the tariff was not a local problem, but one involving world markets. To reduce trade barriers, he thought, would permit a free exchange of goods and relieve "our home markets glutted by over-production."

Wheeler's chief interest in the McKinley bill, however, was in its agricultural aspects rather than the industrial. The American farmer "with a leaky roof, a mortgaged farm," he thought, would be seriously injured by the new tariff rates. "What has the Republican party done for the farmer in this bill?" he inquired. Under previous Republican tariffs, he answered, the exports of corn had dropped from $54,000,000 in 1880 to $13,000,000 in 1890. Likewise, exports of bacon, ham, and pork had decreased 50 per cent in the same time, while that of wheat had slumped from $150,000,000 to $42,000,000. In the face of these astounding figures, he stated, the McKinley bill proposed to burden the farmer further by increasing the tariff on wire for his fences, trace-chains, iron ties, cottonseed oil, and oleomargarine.[17] There was, as he saw it, not one single feature of the bill which would aid the Southern farmer, and this fact was enough to condemn the bill in his sight, for he was adopting a portion of the rising agrarian cause as his own. In Nebraska Bryan was doing a similar thing—advocating a great many of the reforms being preached by the Alliance-Populist groups, but as earnestly endeavoring to see these brought about through the Democratic party rather than through a third party.

Perhaps no speech more clearly indicates Wheeler's

[16] *Ibid.*, 26.   [17] *Ibid.*, 117.

interest in the rising tide of agrarianism and at the same
time illustrates the middle course he was taking in politics than one delivered in defense of the Farmers' Alliance movement. The McKinley bill had passed and the
hectic session of the Fifty-first Congress was drawing to a
close in August of 1890 when he again publicly espoused
the cause of the farmers. Representative Samuel R.
Peters of Kansas had, it seems, in a passing remark characterized the leaders of the Alliance movement as having
many of the appearances of demagoguery, and Wheeler
rose to state that "this most positively is not true of the
South." Farmers, he thought, were as a class "the best
citizens of our land, the most industrious, the most law
abiding, the best debt-paying." Yet these same men are
branded as demagogues because they venture to "come
and ask Congress to do them justice." Every other trade
and occupation, he stated, had a lobbyist at the doors of
Congress except the farmer. Such a state of affairs was
dangerous, for he believed as did Jefferson that "if we
want the government to go on in its purity; if we want a
government based upon honor, virtue, intelligence, and
hard solid judgment," then leave power in the hands of
the farmers. If he had his way about it he would give
them relief by supplying an adequate money circulation
through free coinage of silver; by improving rivers and
regulating railroad monopolies; and "as far as practicable
bring our farmers face to face with the purchasers of
their products." [18]

This speech probably was the direct result of the farmers' movement which was making rapid strides in his
own district. In fact, the first Alliance movement in Alabama had been organized in 1887 only a few miles from
Wheeler's home. Others were soon thereafter established

[18] *Ibid.*, 157.

in surrounding counties, and, under the direction of Reuben F. Kolb, State Commissioner of Agriculture, the movement gained in power and importance.[19] Wheeler did not find it difficult to adhere to many of the principles enunciated by the Alliance. While he did not support Kolb's political ambitions he did believe with him that "the farmer should be our first concern in Alabama." [20]

If Wheeler thought the McKinley bill sectional he had even more reason to believe the same about the "Force bill" of the Fifty-first Congress. This measure, House Resolution 11045, introduced by Lodge from the Committee on Election of the President and Vice-President on June 25, 1890, provided for Federal supervision of Congressional elections in districts where a small percentage of the voters might request it. It was under consideration only seven days in the House, but six of those days were as charged with sectional and partisan bitterness as any similar period during the Reconstruction debates of 1865–1866.[21]

Although the bill theoretically would apply uniformly to all sections of the country, it was evident that its object was the supervision of elections in the South. In that, the Southern representatives saw a return of carpetbag days and Negro supremacy. Even Northern Democrats were quick to grasp the significance of the bill and to fly to the assistance of the South. From the remarks of Representative Roswell P. Flower of New York near the beginning of the debate, that "it is a bill to try to elect a Republican Congress this fall," to those of "Pri-

19 Thomas M. Owen, *History of Alabama and Dictionary of Alabama Biography* (Chicago, 1921), I, 564.
20 Wheeler to Reuben Kolb, September 3, 1889, in Wheeler Papers.
21 *Cong. Record,* 51 Cong., 1 Sess., 6505 ff.

vate" John Allen of Mississippi near the close, that "I know of no parliamentary language and no language consistent with my position in the church that would enable me to characterize it," the members of the House ran the gamut of invective. All the old skeletons of Reconstruction, alleged Southern disloyalty, and the Tilden-Hayes controversy were disinterred and paraded up and down the aisles of Congress. Those who had hoped with Wheeler that there might be sectional peace were doomed to disappointment by the conduct of the Republican leaders. The Democrats resorted to all the parliamentary tactics left them after the "Reed Reformation" to delay the matter, but they were not able to prevent a vote.

Wheeler's speech of June 30 is almost an epitome of the Southern position. The bill was, he said, "inexpedient, fearful, atrocious, diabolical." In addition to that it was unconstitutional. It was inexpedient, he thought, because Northern interference with the question of Negro suffrage in the South could bring only bitterness and strife. The thing for the North to do was to follow the advice given them by a former carpetbag governor of South Carolina who went back to Boston and told the people that the patriotic duty of all Northerners was "to let the negro alone." [22] If the bill should pass, Wheeler thought, and an attempt be made to enforce it in the South "it would do more toward turning back the wheels of civilization than can be corrected by years of effort on the part of those who devote their best endeavors to secure a free and pure ballot and an advanced and progressive civilization."

In defending his thesis that the bill was unconstitutional Wheeler quoted authorities from Glanville and

22 Wheeler, *Selections*, 1893, p. 93.

Bracton to the latest decisions of the United States Supreme Court "or any other judicial tribunal of last resort that ever existed." To Lodge he ascribed "incredible
errors" and to prove it quoted the same sources as the
gentleman from Massachusetts had used and pointed out
the errors made by him. To Wheeler it seemed "absolutely incredible that an educated gentleman sent to
represent a cultivated constituency" could be so "incor-
rect, illogical, and unlawyer-like." [23] If Lodge would only
read a little more carefully his constitutional law books
he would find that "no writer upon the Constitution ever
ventured to expound so fearful a heresy" as that proposed in the bill.

But Democratic efforts to kill the measure availed them
nothing. Republican leaders were able to bring it to a
vote on July 2, and it passed by a vote of 155 to 149.[24]
When the bill reached the Senate it was sidetracked in
favor of the pending Sherman Silver bill, and, despite
Republican attempts to revive it, was never enacted.

On the two other important measures of the Fifty-first
Congress, the antitrust and the silver purchase bills,
Wheeler voted, but did not participate in debate. His
views on silver were well known already. He favored free
and unlimited coinage when he came to Congress, he
favored it in 1890, and in 1896. He stood as firmly upon
his free-silver convictions as he did upon his low-tariff
views. He did not say why he voted against the Sherman
Silver Purchase Act, but it is not improbable that he did
so because he considered it as much a half-way measure
as the Bland-Allison bill was. Almost all the other ardent
free-silver men who opposed the bill did so for this
reason. Wheeler favored the Sherman Antitrust Act and
voted for its passage. Here, as in the case of silver, he did

23 *Cong. Record*, 51 Cong., 1 Sess., 6941.   24 *Ibid.*, 7226.

not explain his vote; but it is only necessary to know that the Alliance favored the regulation of monopolies to understand why he supported the measure.

The Fifty-first Congress passed tariff, silver, and anti-trust acts, and numerous pork-barrel measures designed to reduce the surplus; but the program did not receive the endorsement of the people at the polls in the election of 1890. The Fifty-second Congress consisted of 235 Democrats, 88 Republicans, and 9 Independents, a complete reversal of the results in 1888. In the Senate there was a Republican majority of only six.[25]

How much of the credit for the Republican defeat may be attributed to the Alliance movement is a matter for some conjecture, but it may be said that the "embattled farmers" did wield a powerful influence in determining the results.[26] In Alabama Wheeler had no Populist opposition, but the state-wide situation gave warning that a storm was gathering on the political horizon. There were five candidates for the gubernatorial nomination in Alabama in 1890, and on the first ballot in the convention Reuben F. Kolb, Alliance man, led all the rest. It soon became apparent that he could be defeated only by a union of the other candidates against him. This union was perfected, resulting in the nomination and election of Thomas G. Jones, Democrat. Kolb supported the nominee, but he also began to lay plans for 1892.[27]

Thus when Wheeler returned to Washington for the meeting of the Fifty-second Congress in December, 1891, he was more aware than previously of the power which the farmers' movement was wielding. The Democratic

[25] For an interesting map of the results, see Lester B. Shippee, *Recent American History* (New York, 1930), 184.

[26] Forty-four members of the House were known as Alliance men. See Hicks, *The Populist Revolt*, Chap. VI.

[27] William G. Brown, *A History of Alabama* (New York, 1900), 307.

party should, he thought, "adjust itself to new circumstances." [28] The obstacles were too great to allow him as a Democrat to form a real union with the Populists, for there were certain features of the movement which did not have his approval nor that of other leading Democrats who took a middle course between Bourbonism and outright Populism. Wheeler believed in government regulation but not in government ownership of railroads. He disagreed with the Populist advocacy of a subtreasury plan and, above all, he fought their attempts to launch a new third party because he believed such a party would threaten the unity of the South. In fact, when the matter is boiled down, there was little except free silver upon which Populists and Democrats could unite. The representatives of all three parties did a great deal of talking about the welfare of the farmer and laborer, but when they got together to discuss actual ways and means of promoting that welfare it was found that widely divergent economic and political interests prevented any concerted action.

The Democrats organized the House in the Fifty-second Congress, elected Charles F. Crisp of Georgia speaker, and then settled down to months of comparative legislative inaction preceding the Presidential election of 1892. An attempt was made to repeal the Sherman Silver Purchase Act and Wheeler made a long speech favoring the repeal, but the times were not propitious for legislative action. There was a Democratic House, a Republican Senate and President, and, clamoring for recognition, a third party—the Populist. All eyes were turned on the coming election and the time of the House was spent largely in jockeying for position and making speeches for campaign purposes.

[28] Quoted in Huntsville *Democrat,* August 16, 1892.

A violent quarrel between Wheeler and Thomas E.
Watson, Populist member from Georgia, illustrates what
was occurring in scores of instances on the floor of the
House. On Tuesday, July 26, Wheeler explained to the
House his opposition to the pending $5,000,000 appro-
priation for the Columbian Exposition to be held in
Chicago. The people of Alabama, he said, were opposed
to the appropriation and would be until all threat of the
Force bill was removed. But soon he wandered from his
subject and began an attack on the Populist movement
in the South. "Our third party friends of the South seem
to have allowed themselves to be deluded by the siren's
song," he said. "Do not our third party friends in the
South know that the unity of the South is the only possible means of our salvation, and yet these gentlemen
follow Senator [William A.] Peffer who says in effect that
his use of the subtreasury is to break the solid South, and
this would enable the Republican party to manacle and
trample our people under foot as they did when they had
the Southern States in their power."

At this point "Sockless" Jerry Simpson interrupted to
ask what "the gentleman means when he speaks of the
third party." "To what party does he refer?" he queried.

"Your leader in this House," Wheeler replied, apparently unwilling to name Watson personally, "opposed a
measure the purpose of which was to give the people information with regard to the character of the election bill
intended to be forced upon them."

"Does the gentleman refer to the Prohibition party?"
Simpson facetiously demanded.

"No," Wheeler replied, "he refers to the party to which
the gentleman from Georgia (Mr. Watson) is the leader.
When we met here last December it was my hope we
could all vote together. I have never voted for any meas-

ure which was not Democratic and which was not for the benefit of the people. When I read the *Congressional Directory* I saw that my friend from Georgia was a Democratic elector for the grand old State of Georgia in 1888, and that he was elected to Congress as a Democrat from the district in which I was born and around which the dearest recollections are associated. When I read this I could not believe he could lend his influence to strengthen a party whose leaders were seeking to divide the white people of the Southern states." [29]

The fighting Populist from Georgia jumped to his feet to reply immediately, but Wheeler refused to yield to him and the matter went over. The next day, however, Watson replied in a singularly dispassionate and moderate speech. He was a Democrat he said, except that he had not entered the Democratic caucus and had not voted for Crisp for speaker, but if things like that were to be taken as criteria for party loyalty then the "tail" of the Democratic ticket, "Mr. Adlaidaho Stevenson" likewise must be condemned, for he also had refrained from participating in the caucus and had "consorted with Greenbackers and other leprous persons." Therefore, he warned Wheeler, the gentleman had better shut up before he exposed just how disorganized the Democratic party really was. He had, he said, opposed the printing of the Force bill because it was "merely a campaign document which the millionaires who contributed to the Democratic campaign fund should have paid for themselves." [30]

But Wheeler was not content to let the matter drop with this mild exchange of blows. In Alabama the Populists and Democrats were fighting it out for control of the state elections and the Democrats very badly needed some campaign material. Wheeler, it was charged,

[29] *Cong. Record,* 52 Cong., 1 Sess., 6817 ff.   [30] *Ibid.,* 6875.

thought he could supply some of this needed ammunition if he could personally discredit Watson on the floor of the House. This he attempted to do on July 27, just a few days before the convention was to meet in Montgomery to select a nominee for governor. Arising to a point of personal privilege Wheeler sent to the Clerk's desk a marked copy of Watson's book, *Not a Revolt: It is a Revolution*. The sections marked charged that in Congress "drunken members have reeled about the aisles, a disgrace to the Republic." Furthermore, "drunken speakers have debated grave issues on the floor and in the midst of maudlin ramblings have been heard to ask: 'Mr. Speaker, where was I at.' " This Wheeler considered a grave insult to the whole House as well as to himself.[31]

There were cries from the House for "regular order," but, to quote a contemporary account: "Mr. Wheeler would not down and . . . insisted upon being heard. Mr. Wheeler then proceeded to answer the speech made by Mr. Watson on Wednesday, and he was frequently called to order by Mr. [Julius C.] Burrows of Michigan and repeatedly requested by the Speaker to confine himself to the question of privilege. But Mr. Wheeler declined to do so and was permitted to proceed for a quarter of an hour longer. When a remark about the organization of the Society of the Sons and Daughters of the Revolution called forth another point of order from Mr. Burrows, he requested information as to what the organization of that society had to do with the question of privilege."

The chair again appealed to Wheeler to confine his remarks to the question and Reed of Maine in his most appealing fashion plaintively inquired if the Speaker could not suggest "some remedy for this affliction." "The

[31] *Ibid.*, 6931–32.

Speaker's patience was now well-nigh exhausted, and with firmness he directed the gentleman from Alabama to confine himself to the question before the House, or take his seat. The Chair would not allow the gentleman willfully to violate the rules of the House. Mr. Wheeler said that he did not wish to embarrass the Chair in any manner; he would, therefore, resume his seat." [32]

Watson arose to reply and, like Wheeler, proceeded to wander from the question of privilege to the general plight of the Populists. William J. Coombs of New York called the irascible gentleman to order but was repulsed with the statement that no Representative from New York could bulldoze him; and he hoped he made himself clear. Then he launched into a defense of his book, assuring the House with laughter that he had not entered into a partnership with Wheeler to advertise the book. "I say," he roared, "that every word in that book is literally true, and all men that have been here keeping their eyes open and wanting to admit facts will admit that these facts are literally true."

Then ensued general confusion and sounds of hissing from all sides. Edward H. Funston of Kansas protested that the hissing was a disgrace to the House but Watson waved him aside, bawling that he was perfectly able to care for himself. More members were now on their feet and here and there were stray voices calling for the regular order; and in the midst of it all towered Watson shaking his fists and gesticulating. Only when the Sergeant at Arms intervened was order restored. [33] A committee was appointed to investigate, and for the next few days this "committee on jagology" conducted its hearings to the amusement and amazement of the country. Even-

[32] Savannah *Morning News*, July 30, 1892.
[33] *Ibid.* See also, Woodward, *Tom Watson*, 211 ff.

tually it reported Watson's charges untrue, and apparently everyone was relieved to have the matter hushed.

And there sat "Little Joe." Whereas he had meant only to make a campaign document for home consumption, he had created a major political issue.

There was a great need for campaign material in Alabama. When Wheeler reached his home in August of 1892 he found the state in the midst of one of the bitterest political fights in its history. The Populists were making a strong effort under the leadership of Kolb to carry the state elections and there was grave danger that Alabama might go Republican or Populist in the national race. Wheeler had a Republican, W. B. Austin, running against him for Congress. The whole state was seething.

The trouble began on June 9 when the state Democratic Convention met in Montgomery to nominate a state ticket. Kolb was a candidate for the Democratic nomination for governor, but when the convention refused to choose him instead of endorsing the incumbent, Governor Jones, Kolb bolted and held a separate convention which nominated him and selected a delegation to represent Alabama in the Democratic Convention scheduled to convene in Chicago. The delegation was not seated at the Democratic Convention, but this in no way indicated that it did not represent a powerful faction in Alabama.[34]

As the campaign got under way it became increasingly evident that it would be a close race. By the middle of July political street fights and shooting affrays were becoming common.[35] The Bourbon press was violent in its denunciations of the "Kolbites" as the Populists were called. They were, one paper thought: "Like the red re-

---

[34] Brown, *History of Alabama*, 312.
[35] Montgomery *Advertiser*, quoted in Florence *Herald*, July 14, 1892.

publicans of the great French Revolution. They come before the people with the cry of Liberty, Fraternity, and Equality upon their lips. Like them they have promised to their hearers and followers a season of confiscation. Like them, they have sought to inflame the passions of the masses. . . . They have promised a new order of things in which the poor shall be rich and the rich shall be made poor. They have appealed to the vices, passions, woes, and prejudices of humanity. They have poured out the dregs of slander upon fair reputation, have subsidized a press, and have appealed to ignorance instead of intelligence." [36] A Democratic leader wrote Cleveland that the "Kolbites are the greatest political menagerie that was ever seen in Alabama." [37] "Kolb and the Republican party are working hand in hand to carry Alabama over to the enemy," warned the Huntsville *Democrat,* "and yet some are blinded by their prejudices and so unscrupulous as to cling to their fallen leader." "Can you vote for a man," this paper continued, "who will inaugurate a policy worse than the carpetbag rule of the reconstructionists?" [38]

Wheeler described the situation in a letter to Cleveland on August 22:

On Wednesday last the disappointed Kolb element, and the Weaver faction fused, and agreed to support the Weaver electoral ticket, and efforts are being made to induce the Republicans to support the Weaver ticket in the hope that they can thus carry the State and take Alabama from the Democratic column. If that plan cannot be carried out they will join as many disaffected Democrats as possible to the

[36] Florence *Herald,* August 4, 1892.
[37] H. D. Clayton to Cleveland, August 22, 1892, in Cleveland Papers.
[38] July 21, 1892.

Peoples party in the hope of taking off sufficient Democrats to carry the State for the Republican ticket.[39]

But Wheeler thought he saw a way out of the difficulty. The chief issue, he informed Cleveland, was silver. The people of Alabama believed in free silver and were reluctant to support the Democratic ticket because of the former President's well-known gold standard position. "I tell the people," he wrote, "that Mr. Cleveland's opposition to free coinage of silver is based upon the fear that disaster would result from our adopting free coinage when Great Britain and Germany and some other countries still adhered to the gold standard and that I am confident you would warmly unite in the advocacy of free coinage if these nations would adopt free coinage also." He then appealed to Cleveland to make some such view as this public in order that it might be used to combat Populism in the South. "Moderate concessions and wise counsel" would be required if Alabama was to be held in the Democratic column; [40] but if Cleveland made any statements for Southern consumption they did not come out in the campaign.

In his own district Wheeler was waging his campaign against his Republican opponent, but he does not appear to have been as much concerned about his own election as he was about the state-wide situation. There was little actual danger that he would be defeated, but as the summer wore on the Populists appeared to be gaining in strength over the state. Wheeler found it embarrassing to urge his people to support a man for President whose views on money were directly contradictory to his and

[39] In Cleveland Papers.
[40] Wheeler to Cleveland, August 22, 1892, *ibid*.

that of the majority of his constituents. But his fealty to the Democratic party and his fear that the Populists would split the solid South led him to support Cleveland. In September he made another appeal to Cleveland asking him to say something which would pacify the Southern free-silverites, but again the Democratic nominee was silent.[41]

When the ballots were counted in November it was found that Alabama would cast its electoral vote for Cleveland, but the governor's race was undetermined. Both Kolb and Jones claimed the victory. Charges of fraud were hurled back and forth as an investigation became imminent. Jones was declared to be duly elected; but there are many men in Alabama today who will declare that Kolb's majority was near forty thousand votes.

The Fifty-third Congress assembled on August 7, 1893, in response to President Cleveland's call for a special session. The country as a whole was in a disturbed state of mind. Big business was uneasy, a financial depression threatened, labor was seething with unrest, the South and West were in open political revolt over Populism and free silver, the President and his cabinet were worried to distraction by office seekers, doubt and uncertainty were everywhere apparent.[42]

Amid more than the usual commotion incident upon an opening session of Congress came the President's message, "a notably tactful and moderate document," which reviewed the uncertain business situation and attributed most of the country's ills to the operation of the Sherman Silver Purchase Act.[43] He recommended its repeal and set Congress to work upon the task. On August 11 William

41 *Id.* to *id.*, September 18, 1892, *ibid.*
42 Nevins, *Grover Cleveland,* Chap. XXVIII.   43 *Ibid.,* 433.

L. Wilson of West Virginia opened the debate by pre-
senting the administration with an able argument. Following him other repeal advocates spoke before well-
filled galleries. Then the free silverites had their inning.
On the sixteenth William Jennings Bryan was recognized
and delivered a lengthy speech opposing repeal.[44] Then
came another young man of some forensic ability, Joe
Bailey of Texas, who ably seconded what Bryan had said.
Bland of Missouri, who had been fighting for free silver
while Bryan and Bailey were both still college youths,
joined his voice in the protest against repeal.

Wheeler, though long an earnest advocate of free and
unlimited coinage, took little part in the debates. He
read a free-silver speech into the *Record* for home consumption and voted against repeal; but he did not see
active service on the floor of the House. He was not a
powerful orator like Bryan and he did not possess Bailey's
dominant personality, and so he stepped aside while they
led the fight. But there is another probable reason why he
limited his activities: he was unwilling to widen the already dangerous breach in his party by actively opposing
the administration's monetary policy. His letters to Cleveland during the campaign of 1892 indicate that he was
unwilling to see the Democratic party wrecked on the
rock of free silver. Thus he took a middle course on repeal. Wheeler was a Democrat first, then a silver advocate. He firmly believed that "the success of Democracy
alone can insure us prosperity and happiness." [45] Here he
was displaying the same characteristics he had shown
during the 1860's when he had supported his general-in-
chief Bragg in the face of that leader's growing unpop-
ularity. Cleveland was the Democratic chief and although

44 *Cong. Record,* 53 Cong., 1 Sess., 400.
45 Wheeler, *Selections,* 1893, p. 495.

Wheeler could not support all of his policies he could and did refrain from openly fighting them.

While the House debated its repeal bill, a similar bill with a clause favoring bimetallism had been introduced in the Senate. There, as in the House, debate was prolonged and violent. It was not until October 30 that the bill was passed. Two days later the House concurred by a vote of 194 to 94, and Cleveland had weathered another free-silver storm.[46] By November 3, adjournment day, many Congressmen were already on their way home for a month's respite before the regular session began in December.

When they returned after their brief vacation they were set to work upon the tariff. The wheels of revision had been set turning as soon as the silver repeal bill had passed the House. Wilson, who had led the repeal fight, now undertook to pilot a tariff measure through the shoals of Democratic bickering and Republican opposition. The so-called "Wilson Bill" was introduced into the House on December 19, 1893, and pushed vigorously to a successful termination on February 1, 1894. But the comparative ease with which the bill passed was not an index to its popularity. Many Democrats were not satisfied with its provisions. Wheeler was very positive that the iron and coal industry did not need protection, while his colleague in the House, William C. Oates of Abbeville, Alabama, was equally insistent that these products should be protected.[47] Although all the Alabama representatives voted for the bill on its final passage, their remarks in debate show a wide divergence of opinion even within a single state.

Wheeler's opposition was due to the fact that he considered the bill too much of a compromise with the pro-

46 *Cong. Record,* 53 Cong., 1 Sess., 3067.   47 *Ibid.,* 2 Sess., 1250.

tectionists. He wanted a thorough-going tariff for revenue such as "the Democratic party has advocated for seventy-five years." In his investigations he found even higher duties than those imposed by the McKinley bill, and "one hundred and twenty classes of articles upon which the duty proposed by the Wilson bill are precisely the same as the duties imposed under the McKinley bill." This, he pointed out, was not to signify that he opposed the bill and would vote against its passage but that the House might correct "certain features . . . which are susceptible of improvement." [48]

There were other groups who opposed the bill. Louisiana sugar growers wanted their product protected; so did West Virginia coal interests. And there was a liberal sprinkling of the Randall followers who were chronically opposed to the lowering of a tariff. But on February 1 the malcontents buried their sectional interests and voted 204 to 140 for passage of the bill.[49]

The long struggle which the bill encountered in the Senate and its ultimate passage as the amended Wilson-Gorman Act need not be related here. President Cleveland allowed the bill to become a law without his signature as he turned his attention to the financial panic, labor troubles, and foreign affairs.

Party welfare might also have claimed a part of the President's interest had he been more of a politician, for the Democratic party was undergoing profound changes. The metamorphosis which had begun with the agrarian unrest of the 1880's was now perfectly evident and to loyal party men like Wheeler it was a trying time. Wheeler was unfailingly loyal to the name of Democracy, but that name was at times not very meaningful. To him in theory at least it meant the party of the masses, the

[48] *Ibid.*, 1271. [49] *Ibid.*, 1796.

South in particular. His Democratic party would stand for free silver, low tariff, and an income tax. To others the Democratic party should stand for sound money, tariff compromise, and a recognition of the importance of various big business interests. To this latter group, many thought, belonged Cleveland, the party chief. Rapidly these two groups were drawing away from each other and in the dilemma Wheeler chose the role of discretion. He quietly went about the routine duties of looking after the interests of his district in local matters and let other men split the party. His activities upon the floor of the House were slackened considerably. No longer were there the "little flyaway speeches on every conceivable topic" nor the long elaborate treatises upon silver and tariff. Younger men carried on the fight while he retired to his office in the capitol basement to conduct committee affairs and receive the scores of daily callers.[50] Always he was alert and sprightly, however, as he bounded from committee room to committee room and back to his office again. "He will run into a committee room," one paper observed, "and if he finds there a group of men talking on any subject in which he is interested will drop his hat and coat on the floor, and in two minutes he will be in the thick of a heated argument. Some ponderous member of the committee will get up and leave the room, inadvertently step on the hat, and in a twinkling the brave little man is up and smoothing out his battered headgear with the greatest surprise, wondering how on earth it came to be on the floor." [51] And there were those who were outspoken enough to say that the General probably was more picturesque than useful.[52]

[50] Philadelphia *Times,* July 6, 1894, in Clipping Files, Wheeler Papers.

[51] Houston *Post,* August 23, 1896, *ibid.*

[52] *Ibid.* A defense of Wheeler.

His committee duties took him away from many of the party fights on the House floor. During his entire tenure of office he had been a prominent member of the Military Affairs Committee and now was on the Ways and Means Committee. In addition, in 1894, he was a member of the Board of Visitors of the Military Academy, a Regent of Smithsonian Institute, and a member of the Committee on Dedication of Chickamauga and Chattanooga National Park. Part of the time he was out of the city on inspection trips either to West Point or to Chattanooga and a great deal of his time in Washington was consumed in helping frame and steer through Congress necessary legislation touching the army.[53]

His efforts to build up the Military Academy are noteworthy. He was an alumnus of the institution and that fact naturally would lead him to care particularly for its interests. But his solicitude for its welfare extended beyond a personal interest. He believed that the extension of our commerce would inevitably lead us into war and that if war came "the first important step in preparation . . . should be to prepare a corps of thoroughly educated and accomplished officers." The army as a whole, however, should not be a large one. "I think," he said, "we should have a very small army well drilled, and the perfection of discipline and administration, with officers so thoroughly educated as to be ready for any duty and equal to any emergency." [54] Economy, he thought, should be practiced in all branches of the military service; and, it might be added, Congress took his and others' advice to the extent of so crippling the army that when the war with Spain came the country found itself in a state of unpreparedness.

[53] Philadelphia *Times,* July 6, 1894, in Clipping Files, Wheeler Papers.

[54] *Cong. Record,* 53 Cong., 1 Sess., 4243.

Wheeler's kindly and obliging disposition and his willingness to help people who came to Washington on business of one kind or another also took a great deal of his time. He had been in Congress since the early 1880's and his familiarity with official Washington caused people to flock to him for assistance. "When he is on the floor of the House," a newspaper reported, "nearly everybody at the Capitol wants to talk to him about something, so that his time is continually occupied with miscellaneous matters." [55] In December of 1894 he was appointed a member of the Committee on Ways and Means and after that, except on important occasions, he was hardly seen on the floor of the House. But he could be found early and late in his subterranean office or "dashing in and out of the House, through the corridors, and into the office rooms with the speed of a record breaking sprinter." [56]

The political situation in his home state had greatly improved since the election of 1892. The elections of 1894 had been devoid of the bitterness of former years. Many who were Populists in 1892 were now coming back into the fold, Wheeler wrote the President.[57] But, though Wheeler did not add it, they were not coming back as Cleveland Democrats, and when Alabama had an opportunity she supported the Bryan element in the Chicago convention and in the election of 1896. But Wheeler was satisfied. He had seen the Democratic party "adjust itself to new circumstances"; he had seen it change leadership; he had seen the efforts of Populists to split the Solid South fail; and although Bryan had been defeated he believed the future of the party was assured.[58]

[55] Houston *Post*, August 23, 1896, in Clipping Files, Wheeler Papers.
[56] *Ibid.*
[57] Wheeler to Cleveland, August 24, 1894, in Cleveland Papers.
[58] *Id.* to William J. Bryan, December 16, 1896, in Wheeler Papers.

Chapter XIII

OFF TO WAR

" 'I AM deeply sorry, Mr. President,' " Cleveland is reported to have said to McKinley on returning from the inauguration exercises, " 'to pass on to you a war with Spain. It will come within two years. Nothing can stop it!' " [1]

No person was in a better position to predict such a thing than the outgoing President. During his second term of office he had been flooded with letters, petitions, memorials, all demanding that something be done about the Cuban situation. Letters came to him from people in all walks of life—letters from the poor and ignorant scrawled with a pencil on cheap paper, letters from the wealthy and learned on crested stationery. All demanded that the President intervene in Cuban affairs.[2] The same spirit had been more than apparent in Congress. The Committee on Foreign Relations during the sessions of the Fifty-third and Fifty-fourth Congresses was literally deluged with petitions and resolutions demanding Cuban recognition, Cuban independence, Cuban investigation.[3] Senators and Representatives talked openly of intervention, of war, of atrocities perpetrated on the Cu-

[1] Quoted in David S. Muzzey, *The United States of America* (New York, 1933), II, 294.

[2] In Cleveland Papers.

[3] The volumes of the *Cong. Record,* 53 and 54 Congresses, are replete with speeches on this subject.

bans, of the glorious part Americans should play in protecting weak and downtrodden peoples. Republicans and Democrats alike joined in the general bellicose uproar, but the noise was loudest on the Democratic side, particularly with the Southerners. Senator Wilkinson Call, Florida Democrat, introduced his eighteenth resolution for United States recognition of belligerency in Cuba.[4] Immediately he was joined by Senator John T. Morgan, Democrat of Alabama, who in turn was supported by Republican Henry Cabot Lodge of Massachusetts. Democrat George G. Vest of Missouri and Republican John Sherman of Ohio added their voices in approval of intervention. In the Lower House there was less discussion, but the attitude of that body is clearly revealed when it adopted without much of a fight the Senate resolution by a vote of 247 to 27. The first step toward actual war had been taken even though the resolution was little more than a gesture.

No small amount of credit for the inflamed state of the American mind thus revealed through direct appeals to the President and through representatives at Washington must be given to the newspapers of the period. They did not mirror public opinion; they molded it. For months prior to the inauguration of McKinley the Hearst and Pulitzer papers had been engaged in their well-known contest to determine which could tell the bloodiest and most gruesome tales of atrocities in Cuba.[5] Headlines screamed the awful "truths" about reconcentration camps. The insurgents were always good and noble, the Spanish always low and dastardly. Naïve and untruthful

---

[4] *Ibid.*, 53 Cong., 3 Sess., 152.

[5] The part played by the newspapers is well portrayed in Marcus M. Wilkerson, *Public Opinion and the Spanish-American War* (Baton Rouge, 1932). See also, Walter Millis, *The Martial Spirit: A Study of Our War with Spain* (New York, 1931).

as many of these dispatches were, however, the effect on the American mind cannot be overlooked. If the insurgent "patriots" had wished to subsidize outright American newspapers and many members of the Congress they could not have improved on the propaganda being daily served the American public. It is not strange that the war came; the wonder is that these papers did not bring it on earlier than 1898. Perhaps if Cleveland had not been in the White House they, with Congress, might have.

A less resolute man in many respects than Cleveland, McKinley was not able to ward off the impending struggle. The newspapers continued and even increased their daily servings of fresh incendiary material from Cuba. Hardly had the Fifty-fifth Congress convened before its members were threshing over again the old troublesome questions of recognition, intervention, status of belligerency, and allied problems. And events in Cuba played into their hands. A famine broke over the island in 1897 and immediately there was a reaction in the Congress. A bill was introduced to provide $50,000 for Americans on the island who might be hungry, and with it went a rider calling for genuine recognition of belligerency. Immediately the jingoes were on their feet, and chief among them was Wheeler. Republicans and weak-kneed patriots might talk of this being a mere rebellion in Cuba but to him it was war. Had not the Spanish Minister, Señor Práxedes Mateo Sagasta, informed the Cortes a few days earlier that Spain had sent two hundred thousand troops to Cuba and still had failed to reconquer the island? Of course, Señor Sagasta meant that in all the years of trouble Spain had sent two hundred thousand troops there, but "Fightin' Joe" didn't interpret it that way. Instead, he saw "two hundred thousand Spanish soldiers in line of battle in the Island of Cuba" and, what was worse, "eight hundred American citizens are driven from their property, despoiled of their estates, impounded and corralled and starving in the towns and villages of Cuba." That, he thought, called for action—and yet he beheld around him in Congress "men who have forgotten that honor and chivalry are the priceless heritage of the American people." To these sadly misinformed pacifists Cuba might seem "blessed with profound peace" but to the old warrior whose nostrils scented powder again it was suspiciously like war. For three years, he said, the Congress had been told "of the slaughter of the insurgents in battle and the sound of musketry shooting down helpless prisoners including . . . Cubans and Americans." This "reign of the Nero of the nineteenth century, King Weyler the First," must be terminated.

At this point his time expired, but he was given an additional two minutes to bring his speech to a torrential climax. "I do not know how others may vote or what others may say," he cried,

but I for one proclaim on this floor that war, cruel, brutal, murderous war, does exist in that gem of the ocean—that beautiful Queen of the Antilles—and I here assert that it is our duty as the Representatives of the greatest people upon earth to so declare in the highest councils that exist under the canopy of Heaven.

If this declaration [of belligerency] will aid our brethren struggling for liberty, we are only doing what we promised to do when God vouchsafed victory and liberty to us. If we fail to do this, we are recreant to our pledges to Christianity, to civilization, to humanity and to God. [Loud applause] [6]

[6] *Cong. Record,* 55 Cong., 1 Sess., 1198.

This was in May of 1897, and during the next few months before war actually began Wheeler became more and more bellicose. No longer was he the pedantic and gentle scholar who loved to deliver long treatises on the tariff and on money. No longer was he the sprightly and almost comic little figure who darted in and out of committee rooms. He was now a fiery crusader—a gentle, mild-mannered little fellow who could suddenly blaze with fury—and now he was blazing.

In January of 1898 he delivered another speech on Cuba and Spanish affairs. He was "amazed," "mortified," and "astounded" that his Republican friends on the other side of the House should openly admit that they were afraid of war if intervention should come. Suppose war did come. Was there anyone who would sacrifice honor for peace—that is, anyone except these pusillanimous Republicans who were afraid war would ruin their business? Was money more important than liberty and national honor? In some quarters, he was afraid, the answer seemed to be in the affirmative, and this was such pacifism as that which "dragged down the great Empire of Assyria and Rome and Greece and Carthage from the highest to the lowest grade of nations." He would like to reply to the tariff speech of Dingley, he said, but when it came to a question of "honor and glory of my country on the one side and dollars and cents on the other" his voice could always be found on the side of "honor, glory and chivalry." "God forbid," he concluded, "that the growing generation should prefer to be money changers rather than brave soldiers, fighting, and if need be dying, in the front rank of battle." [7]

[7] *Ibid.*

"Fightin' Joe" did not have to wait long to see the young generation fighting and dying. On February 15 the *Maine* was blown up in the harbor at Havana and Republicans were soon forced to choose war. Before they did, however, there elapsed a brief period of calm in which it seemed that hostilities might be averted; and this worried Wheeler no end. On March 30, just the day after the President transmitted the report of the *Maine* investigating committee to the Congress, a group of some fifty Republicans presided over by Representative Albert J. Hopkins of Illinois held a caucus and demanded that their party actively support intervention in the Cuban affair. The malcontents were forced into line again and nothing came of the caucus; but it did afford Wheeler another opportunity to make a speech on liberty, honor, and chivalry. The caucus, he said, had caused a "sound of triumphant joy throughout the length and breadth of this land of liberty. The feeling of humiliation which has weighted down American hearts was at last dispelled." With high hopes he had come to the session that morning expecting to see the Republican party "do its duty." But what did he encounter? Surrender—abject surrender of the fifty malcontents. "Early this morning," he chided, "the people hastened to this hall. They came to hear the rights of the people proclaimed in tones of thunder; they came to be told that the sufferings of the patriots of Cuba had at last reached the ears and hearts of the great Republican party; they came to see patriotism triumph." They had come to see a brave revolt, but the galleries looked down to see and hear every one of the revolters vote "no" on intervention. He was disgusted. "Mr. Speaker," he said, "I know of no more certain way to bring on war than the action of the Republican party this morning.

Already this surrender . . . has been cabled to Madrid and has no doubt encouraged the Spaniards to assume a more defiant attitude." [8]

On that same day of March 30 he introduced a resolution providing for intervention and it was sent on its way to join twenty-nine similar ones then reposing in the rooms of the Committee on Foreign Affairs. Then he took a train home in order to get his personal affairs in shape before war came. He was not only going to help bring on this war—he was also going to help fight it. He, along with the others, seemed to know that it was only a matter of days before the pressure on the Congress would make war inevitable.

When war came in April, 1898, one of the first to offer his services to the President was Wheeler. In fact, he had filed his application with the War Department before he presented his resolution for intervention. Now that the final blow had come he had merely to remind the President: "In case of trouble with Spain, remember that my tender of service is on file in the War Department." [9] His letter was given to the newspapers and the headlines began to shriek: "FIGHTIN' JOE TO FIGHT AGAIN." "BLUE AND GRAY UNITED." "GRIZZLED JOE WHEELER DRAWS HIS SWORD AGAIN." And the response from the country was instantaneous. From a nephew of Colonel John Bonham of Alamo fame came a request: "My father commanded the Third Alabama in some of the hardest fights during the late Civil War. I herewith make an application for a commission on your staff." [10] From Louisiana State

8 New York *Journal,* March 31, 1898, in Clipping Files, Wheeler Papers.

9 Wheeler to William McKinley, February 16, 1898, in Wheeler Papers.

10 E. F. Bonham to Wheeler, April 17, 1898, *ibid.*

University, Professor David F. Boyd, former rebel and erstwhile friend of General Sherman wrote: "Though I am now 63 years old I have not been sick a day in nearly 40 years. I feel as strong and active as ever I was and believe I could do good military duty." [11] From Chicago a traveling salesman wrote: "Yourself, General Forrest, and Morgan gave us cavalrymen lots of trouble years ago. I missed two shots which I meant for you. It would give me a great deal of pleasure to enlist under your leadership. I have been a commercial traveler for nearly 30 years. I am ready at any time to kick my sample case in the gutter and go shoulder to shoulder with the friends of the South to defend and honor the flag." [12]

Some gentle pressure was brought to bear on Wheeler by his family to keep him from going to war, however.

"Father," one daughter is quoted as saying, "you surely had fighting enough to do from sixty-one to sixty-five; let the young men go to war this time."

"Daughter," he replied, "if a fish had been out of water for thirty-three years, and suddenly came in sight of a great pond, he'd wiggle a little, at any rate." [13]

And wiggle Wheeler did, right into the army. He received a summons from the White House on April 26.[14] Arriving there about half-past eight in the evening he was ushered into the presence of the President, the Attorney General, the Secretary of War, and other public officials gathered to discuss the appointment of officers for the approaching conflict.

"General," the President is quoted as having said, "I have sent for you to ask you if you want to go, and if you feel able to go."

11 March 9, 1898, *ibid.*
12 G. F. Binder to Wheeler, April 17, 1898, *ibid.*
13 Clark, *My Quarter Century,* II, 45.
14 McKinley to Wheeler, April 26, 1898, in Wheeler Papers.

"Yes, Mr. President," was the reply. "Although I am sixty-one years old I feel as strong and capable as when I was forty, or even much younger, and I desire very much to have another opportunity to serve my country."

Thus the matter was settled. After a private conference with McKinley, Wheeler left the White House assured of a commission as Major General of Volunteers.[15] It created an excellent impression on the public mind. A rebel general was to don the blue uniform he had discarded in 1861. The war was getting away to a fine start.

Wheeler left Washington bustling with warlike preparations and reported for duty at Camp George H. Thomas, Chickamauga, Georgia, Major General John R. Brooke commanding. Hardly had Wheeler arrived, however, before he was ordered to Tampa "to command the cavalry in the expedition now leaving." General Nelson Miles, the order informed him, was leaving Washington immediately and would meet him there.[16]

When Wheeler and Miles arrived at Tampa on June 1 they encountered activities most warlike, but highly unmilitary. For several weeks the regular army had been assembling in the immediate neighborhood of the huge and resplendent Tampa Bay Hotel, attracting to the rendezvous a horde of newspaper men, sight-seers, politicians, foreign officials, and hangers-on. These, together with the army staff officers, settled themselves in the rocking chairs on the porch, drank huge quantities of iced tea and talked of the prospects of the war. In the camp sites near by the troops fought sand gnats and mosquitoes and wondered dimly what all the confusion was about and when and if there was to be a war. Quietly

15 Joseph Wheeler, *The Santiago Campaign* (New York, 1899), 54.
16 Orders quoted in *ibid.*, 5.

and almost unobserved, Wheeler slipped into the scene. He was assigned a small room on the sunny side of the hotel where the thermometer hovered around 110° and when "with some embarrassment" he edged into the dining room for luncheon he was placed at a table far removed from the flower-laden ones reserved for officers and journalists. When his luncheon was not forthcoming one war correspondent with a touch of pity "let the little man have a goblet of iced tea out of his own pitcher and the half of an omelette" with the understanding that it was to be repaid in kind when the waiter should finally serve the elderly man.[17]

During the afternoon the same observer saw "the little man dashing about as cheerful as a cricket, here and there and everywhere." Always he was accompanied by a young companion almost his exact physical duplicate. Together they seemed to be looking after some sort of official business, yet no one apparently knew just who they were. Evening came and taps. The two slept in a small tent and were stirring with reveille. An orderly approached the tent.

"I have—I bring despatches and a bundle for the commanding general," he stammered.

"All right," said the young companion; "the general is here."

The bundle contained a uniform—a blue uniform—and when he stepped from the tent he was Major General Joseph Wheeler, United States Volunteers, commanding the cavalry.

A troop of cavalry came riding by at a stiff trot. The guidon proclaimed it was Troop A, Third Cavalry. It is said that the little man's eyes flashed and his lips trem-

17 Stephen Bonsal, *The Fight for Santiago* (New York, 1899), 54.

GENERAL WHEELER AND STAFF AT TAMPA, 1898

Standing, left to right: CAPTAIN W. A. CHANLER; LIEUTENANT JOSEPH WHEELER, JR.; LIEUTENANT M. S. STEELE; CAPTAIN P. W. WEST; LIEUTENANT J. H. REEVES; MAJOR W. B. BEACH.
Seated, left to right: CAPTAIN J. T. DICKMAN; GENERAL WHEELER; GENERAL GUY V. HENRY.

bled. Forty years before he had ridden boot to boot and saber to saber across the plains of New Mexico and Texas as a lieutenant of Troop A, Third Cavalry.

"And how does it feel, General, to wear the blue again?" asked an officer respectfully.

"It's only when I look at Joe and see his shoulder straps, that I realize that thirty seven years and four months have passed since I followed that guidon," was the response. "I feel as though I had been away on a three weeks furlough, and had but just come back to my own colors." [18]

Perhaps the journalist colored the picture a bit by his own imagination, but there is little doubt that Fightin' Joe and the young companion, his son, were glad of the opportunity to serve as fellow officers in blue uniforms.

On all sides the scenes of confusion bordered on chaos. The United States was wholly unprepared for war and no one seemed to know just how to go about getting her ready. At the close of the Civil War the government had a million veterans in arms, all well equipped for war at that time. Gradually the war material was sold or used up by issue either to the militia of the states or to the regular forces engaged in military operations on the frontier between 1865 and 1895. The supplies and materials that were not sold, but stored, were gradually reduced to a minimum, and the War with Spain found this country with a very small army—twenty-five thousand men—with war material sufficient to equip that force and furnish it with a small part of ammunition; but the tentage, transportation, and

[18] *Ibid.*, 57.

camp equipage were insufficient for military operations.[19]

Regulars being insufficient in numbers for the proposed invasion of Cuba, volunteers had to be depended upon. Congregating tens of thousands of men, many of whom were not uniformed, and scarcely any properly equipped, in great camps far-removed from their states, rendered it extremely difficult for them to be properly supplied with food, medical supplies, and equipment in general.[20] The port of Tampa, "the jumping off place" for the proposed expedition, was poorly situated for the handling of large shipments of troops and supplies. A single track connected the port with the city of Tampa nine miles away. Along this track was indescribable confusion. At one time there were over three hundred cars loaded with war supplies along the roads about Tampa, but the invoices and bills of lading were misplaced and officers were obliged to break open seals and hunt from car to car to ascertain whether they contained clothing, food, ammunition, or balloon material.[21] At another time fifteen cars loaded with uniforms were sidetracked twenty-five miles from Tampa and remained there for weeks while the troops were suffering for clothing.[22] The single track to Port Tampa gave way under the pressure and became more of an impediment than an aid in moving troops and supplies. Along the track officers could be found scurrying about

19 Annual Report of the Major General Commanding the Army, 1898, in House Documents, No. 2, 55 Cong., 3 Sess., 4.

20 Ibid., 8.

21 Nelson Miles to Russell A. Alger, June 4, 1898, in Correspondence from the Adjutant General U.S.A., Relating to the Campaign in Cuba, in Senate Documents, No. 221, 56 Cong., 1 Sess., Vol. II, 888. Cited hereafter as Cuban Correspondence.

22 Ibid.

looking for food and clothing for their men. Other officers were looking vainly for their commands, while
groups of soldiers lolled about without officers. Teamsters with mules looked for harness. Other teamsters
with harness looked for mules. Wheeler found several
of his volunteer regiments arriving without uniforms;
others had no rifles, tents, or packs; and one of his regiments expected momentarily had not arrived at all.
He was to command the Volunteer Cavalry, yet no
budding cavalryman knew whether he had a mount or
not. Indeed, Wheeler embarked for Cuba without knowing for certain how many horses and saddles were being
taken along. There was no way outside the realm of
clairvoyance that he could know.

Back at the hotel there was enacted a scene bordering
on the comic. General James F. Wade was the officer
in command when Wheeler arrived. A few days later
General William R. Shafter, slated for the command,
arrived. But Wade was Shafter's superior by virtue of
the fact that his commission was issued three days earlier
than Shafter's. Both generals, a bit embarrassed at this
state of affairs, retired to their apartments and the
corps was left without an official head. To complicate
the situation Fitzhugh Lee arrived resplendent in the
uniform of a major general. Thus there were three
major generals each of whom, according to the statements of his personal friends and of his staff, was the
officer designated to lead the army to Cuba. Finally, the
War Department made up its mind who was to lead
the expedition. Wade was sent to Chickamauga and
Shafter was officially designated as commanding officer.[23]

Meantime, war had actually begun. On April 27 a

[23] Bonsal, *The Fight for Santiago*, 60–61.

dispatch arrived at the Navy Department in Washington announcing that Commodore George Dewey's squadron of vessels had quit Hong Kong and was on its way to the Philippine Islands, the most convenient point to strike Spain in the Pacific. There at Manila Bay was accomplished on May Day, 1898, the destruction of Spain's fleet. While Dewey was thus occupied in the Pacific, Admiral William T. Sampson with the remainder of the American fleet was in Caribbean waters looking for the Spanish fleet which had on April 29 left the Cape Verde Islands under command of Admiral Pascual Cervera y Topete. Americans, the newspapers warned, might expect this squadron to bombard New York and other coast cities within a short time. The fear thus created was increased by the fact that no word was had of Cervera's fleet after its departure. Through the month of May the American people were still rejoicing over Dewey's feat, but dwellers along the Atlantic coast were in a state of perpetual suspense. Finally Cervera appeared. After considerable cruising about in Caribbean waters he had, on May 19, led his fleet into the harbor at Santiago. Sampson and Admiral Winfield S. Schley finally learning of this disposition of the enemy fleet noisily set about making plans to destroy it.

On June 7 Sampson wired the Navy Department:

Bombarded forts at Santiago 7:30 A.M. to 10 A.M. today June 5th. Have silenced works quickly without injury of any kind, though stationary within 2,000 yards. If 10,000 men were here, city and fleet would be ours within forty-eight hours. Every consideration demands immediate army movement. If delayed, city will be defended more strongly by guns taken from fleet.[24]

[24] Wheeler, *The Santiago Campaign*, 7.

He had steamed up within range of Santiago, observed the enemy fleet riding at anchor, and had turned his guns on the city's fortifications immediately to the rear of the harbor. But the city, to be taken, would have to be invested from the landward side. The troops at Tampa, therefore, should be sent immediately.

The grand strategy of the war thus unfolded itself. With Dewey controlling the Pacific, with Sampson and Schley holding Cervera in Santiago harbor, with the small Spanish army stationed within the city of Santiago, the situation looked promising indeed for the success of American arms. It seemed a comparatively simple military maneuver for the United States troops to move in behind Santiago, thus catching the Spanish between the army and the navy. As it developed, however, the movement was not quite so simple as the War Department anticipated.

In response to Sampson's message Shafter was ordered to load his men on the transports riding at anchor in Tampa Bay and hurry to Cuba. Shafter's response was: "I will sail tomorrow morning. Steam can not be got up earlier." [25]

But the loading proceeded slowly. It was found that many of the steamers were not suitable for transport service. They had been built largely for freight steamers and were not equipped for properly conveying troops and munitions of war. The accumulation of the large amount of supplies and war material at Tampa had crowded the place and the single track to the port was inadequate to transport troops and supplies the nine miles.[26] Again confusion reigned. Men, mules, and bag-

[25] William R. Shafter to Henry C. Corbin, June 7, 1898, 9 P.M., in *Cuban Correspondence*, 894.

[26] *Annual Report of the Major General Commanding the Army, 1898*, p. 12.

gage were hopelessly entangled. Divisions and brigades
were separated. Again men looked for their commands
and commands looked for their officers. The Rough
Rider regiment arrived at Tampa from Texas. Seeing
the confusion and anticipating that the command might
be left behind, Lieutenant Colonel Theodore Roosevelt
and Colonel Leonard Wood commandeered a train and
loaded the regiment aboard. Arriving at the port they
seized a transport, the *Yucatan,* and sent their men
aboard in defiance of everything and everybody.[27] At
the last moment the regiment was ordered to leave all
its horses and half its men for future transportation to
the scene of the war. A few horses were sent aboard,
but neither Wheeler commanding the cavalry nor anyone else knew whether in sufficient numbers to supply
the mounted men or not. Closing in behind the Spanish at Santiago was proving a rather complicated matter
for army officials.

But at last it appeared that most of the men were
aboard. The supplies, it was hoped, were also aboard.
The expedition was ready to sail. At the moment of
hauling up anchors, however, there came a message
from the Secretary of War. "Wait until you get further
orders before you sail." [28] A report had come to Washington that a Spanish warship was cruising in the Ba-
hama straits. The expedition must not go until this
danger was ferreted out and disposed of. Then followed
five days of waiting while the Navy looked for the war
vessel. Men and animals were crowded like sardines in
stuffy, inadequate transports while the tropical sun beat

[27] Arthur F. Cosby, "The Rough Riders," in J. T. Dickman (ed.),
*The Santiago Campaign: Reminiscences of the Operations for the
Capture of Santiago de Cuba in the Spanish-American War, June
and July, 1898* (Richmond, 1927), 105.

[28] Alger to Shafter, June 8, 1898, in *Cuban Correspondence,* 895.

mercilessly down on the decks. The animals were unloaded, many of the men came ashore, farewells had to
be said all over again. Finally, on June 14 the expedition sailed—803 officers and 14,935 men loaded on
thirty-six transports.[29]

The cavalry embarked on the steamers *Allegheny, Rio
Grande, Miami,* and *Yucatan.* Wheeler, for the first and
only time during his entire career, decided to jot down
events as they happened. As the expedition swung out
to sea he recorded:

Wednesday, June 15. The sky in the evening is perfectly
beautiful, the stars very bright, and appear much more
numerous than in more northern latitudes. At dusk we see
Tortugas Light and pass, leaving it to our right.

Thursday, June 16. At daylight we find ourselves under
the escort of a number of warships. The entire fleet, including
the naval vessels, numbers some fifty-five ships. We sail in
three columns, the columns being about one thousand yards
apart. My ship, the *Allegheny,* leads the right column, the
one nearest Cuba. The war-ship *Indiana* sails some thousand
or more yards to our front and right. . . . During all of
Thursday we sailed in an easterly direction keeping nearly
parallel to the coast of Cuba. Of course it is very warm, but
not so intolerable as one would imagine. We occasionally see
a strange sail, which generally turns out to be a despatch boat
or a freight vessel. . . .

Friday, June 17. Soon after daylight the fleet turned Southward, and by 8 o'clock we were running parallel to and in
sight of the shore of Cuba. . . . We are compelled to regu-
late our speed by that of the slowest vessel, and hardly make
more than nine or ten knots an hour. At 10 o'clock we are
passing the Cuban lighthouse at Paradone Principe. We can

[29] *Annual Report of the Major General Commanding the Army,
1898,* p. 12.

plainly see the barracks that are occupied by Spanish soldiers, and some contend they can see the men standing in front of the buildings. . . . Five p.m. See very high ground in Cuba. The sea has been very blue, quite as blue as blue indigo. At night the signalling of the war-ships is very interesting. . . .

Saturday, June 18. Remained at a standstill several hours this morning, for slow ships to catch up. At 2 p.m. we are passing Cape Lucretia, about the middle (measured east and west) of the province of Santiago de Cuba. We see high hills on the Cuban coast, estimated at from twelve hundred to fifteen hundred feet high. . . .

Sunday, June 19. . . . The sea is getting quite rough. At 3 p.m. the sea has become more calm, and we are in sight of Cape Maisa. The shore seems to be lined with high hills or mountains. . . . We see clouds of smoke; very possibly Spaniards preparing to retreat to Santiago. We are now about one hundred and twenty miles from that place.

Sunday night at 9 p.m., we have rounded the eastern end of the Island of Cuba, and are now sailing west to Santiago.

Monday, June 20. At daylight, we are about thirty miles east of Santiago. We see high mountains on the shore, probably two thousand feet high. Will close this before reaching landing place, as we must pack up for disembarkation.[30]

As Wheeler surveyed the little town of Daiquirí through his glasses from the deck of the *Allegheny* he could readily see that disembarkation could be accomplished only with difficulty. There were three other possible landing places, but Shafter, after conferring with the Cuban General Calixto Garcia had selected Daiquirí as the most desirable. Yet it had little to recommend it outside of the fact that it had a broad firm beach and was somewhat sheltered. It had no harbor, no usable

[30] Wheeler, *The Santiago Campaign,* 8–12.

piers, no facilities to assist in moving heavy baggage.
The horses, it became evident, would have to be dumped
overboard to swim ashore; the men and baggage transported in whatever small boats the naval vessels could
furnish.

As a preliminary to disembarkation the warships
raked the shore with shell fire to drive out any Spaniards
who might be lurking about watching the proceedings.
Hardly had this firing ceased when Wheeler, taking
along Colonel Wood and a few men, lowered away from
his ship and pushed through the surf to the beach.[31] He
had been among the first to offer his services at Washington; now, with the exception of Shafter and Sampson, he was the first to set foot on Cuban soil. Looking
around him he discovered a small flagstaff extending
above an ancient and dilapidated blockhouse situated
upon a rounded eminence. Quickly a man was dispatched to raise the regimental flag over the blockhouse.
Hardly had it been flung to the breeze before "the air
was filled with cheers, and whoops, and yells, the shriek-
ing of whistles and crashing of brass bands" from the
men and officers still held aboard the transports.[32]

Having thus planted the colors of the cavalry in a conspicuous place Wheeler left for an exploring trip toward
the interior, leaving the unloading of his command in
the hands of others. When he returned it was night.[33]
All day the unloading had proceeded unevenly. It appeared to one reporter that there was "no order, or
formation, either of the transports or of the small
boats." [34] Another observed that it was like the begin-

[31] Ibid., 14.

[32] John Bigelow, Reminiscences of the Santiago Campaign (New York,
1899), 82.

[33] Wheeler, The Santiago Campaign, 14-15.

[34] Bigelow, Reminiscences of the Santiago Campaign, 82-83.

ning of a boat race with all the craft maneuvering for position.[35] Many boats were overturned in the surf; men and animals threshed about in the water; baggage and supplies were lost. But the unloading proceeded. By the twenty-fifth Shafter could report: "With assistance of navy disembarked 6,000 men yesterday and as many more today. Will get all troops off to-morrow. . . . The assistance of the navy has been of the greatest benefit, and enthusiastically given. Without them I could not have landed in ten days, and perhaps not at all." [36]

[35] Richard Harding Davis, *The Cuban and Porto Rican Campaigns* (New York, 1898), 116.

[36] Shafter to Corbin, June 25, 1898, in *Cuban Correspondence,* 917–18.

Chapter XIV

GUÁSIMAS AND SAN JUAN

GENERAL SHAFTER'S orders issued on the morning of June 23 for the next day placed General Henry W. Lawton's regular army division in a defensive position at Siboney, eleven miles from the point of debarkation at Daiquirí. In this position he commanded the gap through the hills to Santiago, and in case the Spanish attacked it would be his task to hold them off until all men and equipment had been landed. General J. Ford Kent's brigade was also to be held near Siboney, while General John C. Bates's independent brigade of volunteers was to take position in support of Lawton. Wheeler's dismounted volunteer cavalry, including the Rough Riders, was to occupy a position to the rear of Bates. It was *intended* that these positions should be maintained until all troops and baggage were unloaded and the army properly organized for the march on Santiago.[1]

In such a position the cavalry would probably be the last division to see action, and apparently this greatly displeased Wheeler and his officers. They had come to Cuba to fight and not to wait in the rear while Lawton

[1] Shafter's Report, September 13, 1898, in Adjutant General's Office, Washington, D.C.

or someone else of the regular army got the glory. Accordingly, on the morning of June 24, while Shafter was still aboard ship, Wheeler engineered a maneuver unique in military annals. He took 964 men, neatly outflanked Lawton and the other divisions of his own army, and provoked a fight with the Spanish troops at Guásimas on the road to Santiago.[2] It was a movement which came as a complete surprise to Shafter and to all the other officers save General S. B. M. Young, Colonel Leonard Wood, Lieutenant Colonel Theodore Roosevelt, and, of course, Fightin' Joe; but it was successful, and success may cover a great amount of indiscretion.

The idea of attacking, General Wheeler wrote later, came to him after he had made his tour of exploration while the troops were debarking. He had met a group of insurgent Cuban officers and together they had prepared a rough map of the territory immediately surrounding Siboney. During the night of the twenty-third Wheeler showed this map to Young, Roosevelt, and Wood, and the four went into conference.[3] It was decided, Major William D. Beach of Wheeler's staff relates, that the position of the Spanish troops (who thus far had proved themselves little more than interested spectators) was too close to Siboney to render Lawton's, Kent's, and Bates's positions secure. Therefore, "General Wheeler determined to attack early the next morning and clear the way for the debarkation and assembly of our corps at Siboney." Roosevelt and Wood, it was decided, would take the left-hand trail from Siboney and strike the enemy's right. Wheeler and Young would take the other trail, assail the enemy's left, form a junction with the Rough Riders and drive the Spanish toward

[2] Wheeler, *The Santiago Campaign*, 16–38.
[3] Davis, *The Cuban and Porto Rican Campaigns*, 136.

Santiago.[4] The only hitch was that these officers had failed to notify the commanding general that they were thus going to make debarkation and assembly quite safe.

On the afternoon of the twenty-third, while Wheeler and the Cuban officers were reconnoitering and preparing a map, the troops of the First, Tenth, and First U.S. Volunteer Cavalry (Rough Riders) were dumped on the beach at Daiquirí. The word having been passed out that no action was contemplated until all men should be disembarked, the men organized sight-seeing expeditions. They "visited the ruins of the burning round-house, looked around in the fever infested shacks, ate green fruit, drank unboiled water, and otherwise violated existing instructions." [5] But their festivities were interrupted by marching orders. Shouldering their haversacks, blankets, and rifles they took up the march to Siboney. Wearily they trudged along through the coconut groves in the intense heat, weighed down with blanket-rolls and personal equipment. Originally it had been anticipated that all this baggage would be transported on horseback, but since the horses had been left in Tampa that was impossible; and so these dismounted cavalrymen met the situation in characteristic fashion —they simply discarded their excess baggage. The trail over which they marched became well marked—marked with discarded blankets, blouses, cans of food, and other personal articles.[6]

It was after dark when they reached Siboney and bivouacked not far from Lawton's regulars. Reveille

[4] William D. Beach, "Some Recollections of Santiago," in Dickman (ed.), *The Santiago Campaign*, 408. The author was Major of Engineers, U.S.V., and Chief Engineer of the cavalry division at Santiago.

[5] C. McK. Saltzman, "Some Recollections of the Engagement at Guásimas," *ibid.*, 398.

[6] *Ibid.*, 399.

was at four o'clock, but that was hardly necessary, for the night had been spent fighting off mosquitoes and the teeming thousands of land crabs. At six they were again ready to march. There was "considerable comment and enthusiasm" in the column when it was discovered that they were actually marching right through the infantry camp, an enthusiasm they would need before the day was over. Clear of the town, Wood, Roosevelt, and the Rough Riders swung off on the left trail and Wheeler and Young kept straight ahead. For a time both commands attempted to follow regulations concerning advancing into enemy territory. Advance guards and flankers were thrown forward, but soon they got lost or became entangled in the jungle undergrowth. The attempt to make an orderly advance was abandoned and the columns crept raggedly forward. The morning was hot, the trails rough, the undergrowth heavy. Here and there a trooper dropped from exhaustion. Soon, all who had not done so the afternoon before began relieving themselves of packs, tents, and blankets. Only the possible nearness of the enemy kept them going forward.[7]

About half-past seven Wheeler's command was halted and Captain A. L. Mills was sent forward to reconnoiter. In a few minutes word came back that the enemy had been sighted a few hundred yards ahead intrenched behind stone breastworks. Wheeler and Young rode forward to confirm Mills's observations. Orders came back for the leading troop to move left forward into line, after which the others were to deploy right and left. Straw hats were plainly visible over the breastworks, but there was some doubt as to whether they belonged to Cubans or Spaniards. Wheeler solved the problem by directing the commander of his Hotchkiss gun to

[7] Bigelow, *Reminiscences of the Santiago Campaign*, 89.

open fire. The mystery was solved; there was an answering volley from the breastworks and everyone knew it was the enemy at last.[8] At Wheeler's side a man dropped, shot through the belly with a Mauser bullet. "He was near me," Wheeler said later, "and I went to him just as he had fallen and could see no mark where he had been struck, yet he was in the last agony of death. . . . We undid his belt and there was just the least hole where the ball had gone right through his body." [9] Perhaps it was only then that Wheeler realized that this was different from the Civil War. Here in Cuba the enemy used smokeless powder, and rifles which had a range of over a thousand yards. Soon other men right and left were dropping dead or wounded into the palmetto brush. The regular troops found it impossible to move forward in line because of the mass of Spanish bayonet and other jungle growth which lay before them. Before long, companies were losing contact with each other and it was every man for himself.

At about the same time that Wheeler's attack had taken place the Rough Riders had also encountered the enemy. The command had been halted upon sighting the Spanish, the troops deployed right and left, and the order was given to fire. Captain Allyn K. Capron, leading the advance, fell mortally wounded. Sergeant Hamilton Fish was shot through the heart. Firing became heavier as the lines crawled slowly forward. Edward Marshall, correspondent of the New York *Journal,* was shot through the spine and sent to the rear in the agonies of death. "Cease firing and advance" was ordered, and the Americans advanced to within three hun-

---

[8] Beach, "Some Recollections of Santiago," in Dickman (ed.), *The Santiago Campaign,* 410.

[9] New York *Times,* August 19, 1898, quoting Wheeler.

dred yards of the enemy entrenchments and again opened fire.[10]

Wheeler's regulars could hear the firing of the Rough Riders but could only wonder at what progress they were making. As for themselves they were not going forward very rapidly. All the talk they had heard about the Spanish not fighting was being proved false. The casualties on the American side were mounting. Wheeler, it is reported, announced to his staff that he remembered no heavier musketry fire in any action he was engaged in during the Civil War. Major Beach, becoming alarmed at the lack of progress, reports that he suggested to Wheeler: "We have nine big regiments of infantry only a few miles back on the road. Let me send to General Lawton for one of them and close this action up."

"All right," Wheeler reluctantly answered.

Beach began the preparation of the message. "Shall I say 'request' or 'direct,' " he inquired of Wheeler.

" 'Direct,' " replied Wheeler after a moment.[11]

An orderly was called and the message sent to Lawton.

"Time crawled . . . the sun seemed to stand still as in the days of Joshua of old, and it seemed too awfully hot for words." Orders were no longer necessary; the firing was general all along the line. Finally, the head of the relieving infantry column swung into view and the Spanish forces withdrew. As they went, Wheeler shouted something about the "Yankees" being on the run, and

---

[10] Leonard Wood's Report, June 25, 1898, in Adjutant General's Office. See also, Theodore Roosevelt, *The Rough Riders* (New York, 1900), Chap. III.

[11] Beach, "Some Recollections of Santiago," in Dickman (ed.), *The Santiago Campaign,* 410. Wheeler reported that Beach was with him during the entire fight.

the engagement was over.[12] It was concluded before Lawton's men became engaged. Wheeler reported: "The moment General Lawton and the commander of his leading brigade, General [Adna R.] Chaffe, heard the noise of my engagement they promptly struck camp and marched to the front; but as the enemy broke and was in full retreat in a little more than an hour, they did not reach me until after the action was over."[13] There is no mention, however, of the orderly and his message.

After the fight there was general rejoicing. From Washington the Secretary of War wired Shafter: "The President directs me to send his thanks to you and your army for the gallant action of yesterday, which I gladly do."[14] Compliments were handed all around. Wheeler, although he had not witnessed their fighting, officially complimented Wood and Roosevelt for bravery. Wood, not to be outdone, made mention of Roosevelt's valor. "Fightin' Joe" was on everyone's tongue as they laughed about the "Yankee" mistake. Even Shafter admitted: "The engagement had an inspiring effect upon our men and doubtless correspondingly depressed the enemy." However, it would be interesting to know just what his real views were concerning the activity of his cavalry commander. Those views are not known, however; but Wheeler was given immediate orders "very positively" not to do any more advancing.[15]

---

[12] No one, not even General Wheeler himself, seemed to know exactly what his words were upon this occasion. Miss Annie Wheeler, who was in Cuba as a nurse, relates that she asked her father immediately after the battle what his words were and that he replied, "It was something about the 'Yankees' instead of the Spanish being on the run." Major Beach reports that the words were: "We've got the Yankees on the run."

[13] Wheeler, *The Santiago Campaign*, 40.

[14] *Ibid.*, 41.   [15] *Ibid.*

The fight at Guásimas was the only one preliminary to the actual siege of Santiago. After it was over Shafter could proceed with his plans for the campaign; that is, he could proceed unless some other highly individualistic officer should suddenly take it into his head to start a little war of his own.

Despite the questionable wisdom of Wheeler's precipitate attack at Guásimas, however, it did accomplish one thing; it removed the first barrier on the trail to Santiago. When, after the fight, Lawton's troops moved up to join Wheeler at Guásimas they found themselves much closer to the city than they had imagined. They were on a low plateau looking away across five miles of palm-studded country which came to an abrupt conclusion at the foot of a higher piece of ground called San Juan Hill. On this hill were Spanish fortifications; behind it lay the city and harbor.

Although the distance was short, that fact was in no way indicative of ease and simplicity in negotiating it. One narrow trail led away through an almost impenetrable jungle. Even on the high ground where Wheeler and Lawton bivouacked their men there was hardly space enough for a camp. As detachments of men arrived from the coast the situation became even more cramped. Gradually conditions came more and more to resemble the confusion so apparent at the embarkation at Tampa. As divisions moved forward it became apparent that the supply wagons were entirely inadequate. Men were left without food or were supplied with inferior stuff which quickly spoiled in the tropical heat. Men were chilled by sudden gusts of rain and then left steaming as the sun penetrated their woolen uniforms. Shafter fell ill, a victim of the heat. Wheeler came down with a fever. Man after man began to grab his belly as the bad food churned inside him.[16] It became increasingly evident that if there was to be a campaign at all it must come quickly.

After a week of inaction the army moved. It was decided that Lawton's division should reduce El Caney while Wheeler's and Kent's should go straight at San Juan. Lawton, after he had taken El Caney, should then join the other forces before Santiago. Captain George S. Grimes's battery of artillery was to take position at El Pozo to shell San Juan, while Capron's battery was to plant itself on a slight eminence some two thousand yards from El Caney.

On the night of June 30 Lawton permitted his men only a few hours of sleep and before daybreak on July 1 set them in motion toward El Caney. By seven o'clock they were in sight of the Spanish fortifications. A few minutes later Captain Capron opened fire with his artillery as the infantry deployed in the grass and commenced firing with their Krags. An hour of this accomplished little. The artillery fire was ineffective and the advance of the riflemen was extremely slow in the face of the severe rifle fire from the Spanish entrenchments. Noon came and still the enemy had not capitulated; in fact, their fire had not noticeably diminished.[17]

In the meantime, the movement toward San Juan had got under way. Wheeler, for four days barely able to remain in the field because of a fever, had temporarily relinquished his command to General S. S. Sumner. General Young, also ill, was replaced by Wood. Kent was able to retain his command of the regulars. At daylight on July 1, while Lawton was hammering at El

[16] See Gregory Mason, *Remember the Maine* (New York, 1939), Chap. XII.

[17] Lawton's Report, September 15, 1898, in Adjutant General's Office.

Caney, Sumner, Wood, and Kent moved forward. The cavalry divisions were allowed to take the lead. Once across the river they were to deploy to the right, command the approaches to the river, and wait for word of Lawton's success in his undertaking. Kent with his infantry division was to cross the river, deploy to the left, and likewise wait.[18]

The dismounted cavalry moved forward en masse to the intersection of the Santiago road and the river. As more men moved forward the narrow road became choked. Happily, however, they were concealed from the enemy by the woods on either bank of the stream; that is, they were concealed for a few minutes until the signal corps decided to notify the enemy of the exact position. With the American troops a mass of helplessness, the signalmen sent up a balloon with observers aboard. Instantly there was a crash of artillery and small arms from the Spanish which wounded several American officers and men. Fortunately for the cavalry the balloon was soon shot down by the enemy and so the crossing continued.

Across the river and deployed to the right Sumner found his men in a precarious position under the galling rifle fire from the Spanish. They could not stay where they were and yet there were no orders to advance and take the hill. Nothing was heard from Lawton except the sound of heavy firing in that direction. Kent had crossed and deployed to the left and was likewise subjected to heavy fire. Shafter was at the rear too ill to come and personally direct things; so was Wheeler. There seemed to be only one course—to storm the Span-

---

[18] The positions and movements of the army before Santiago are derived from the reports of the various participating officers. Reports in Adjutant General's Office.

ish position, and that was an extremely hazardous undertaking since little was known of the enemy's strength. Straight ahead before Sumner's position was fortified Kettle Hill, beyond that a marsh, and beyond that the right of San Juan Hill crowned with a house. In front of Kent was an open field and beyond that the left of San Juan Hill with a blockhouse on the summit.

The attack was begun by Kent on the left somewhere near nine in the morning. Sumner, apparently still without orders, delayed his attack an hour and then got under way. While Wheeler chafed in his tent and fought his fever, Sumner, Wood, and Roosevelt led 2,522 men up and over Kettle Hill, across the intervening marsh, and up the slopes of San Juan.[19] There was a great deal of confusion among commands. Regiments became mixed, but the fighting went on.[20] Across the marsh between Kettle and San Juan hills Roosevelt splashed

[19] According to Wheeler's Report, the following was the strength of the cavalry participating in the fight: First Brigade consisting of Third, Sixth, and Ninth Cavalry, 50 officers and 1,054 men; Second Brigade consisting of First, Tenth, and First Volunteers, 77 officers and 1,468 men.

General Wheeler came to the battlefield sometime during the day of July 1. In his *Santiago Campaign*, 118, Wheeler states: "I was up and ready for duty on the morning of July 1st." General E. J. McClernand, in "The Santiago Campaign," in Dickman (ed.), *The Santiago Campaign*, 22, says: "General Wheeler looked ill and it was thought he could do little more than observe. He, however, returned to duty from the sick list and rendered gallant and efficient service." Millis, in *The Martial Spirit*, 289, writes: "Somewhere in the confusion [morning of July 1] there was a wild message from Fighting Joe (who had arisen from his sick bed and was wandering more or less at large over the scene)." Davis, in *The Cuban and Porto Rican Campaigns*, 229, states that Wheeler did not assume active command of the cavalry until about four o'clock on the afternoon of July 1. Theodore Roosevelt, in *The Rough Riders*, 149, states: "Soon after dark [July 1] General Wheeler, who in the afternoon had resumed command of the cavalry division, came to the front."

[20] Roosevelt to E. D. Dimmick, July 31, 1898, quoted in Dickman (ed.), *The Santiago Campaign*, 421.

with his Rough Riders and some colored troops from
the Ninth and Tenth Cavalry. They reached the foot
of San Juan and began the ascent. Following them came
other lines of blue-coated figures. Roosevelt reached the
top only to find that some of the Tenth Cavalry had
gone to his left and reached the summit before him.
But the hill was won, at least temporarily, and the Spanish had retreated. Farther over to the left Kent's men
had likewise gained the top of the hill.

During the afternoon after the severest of the fighting was over General Wheeler took the field in spite of
his illness.[21] There was yet much work to be done. The
winning of the hill did not by any means insure that it
could be held. The enemy had merely fallen back to a
secondary position and had not ceased firing. Upon
reaching the crest of the hill late in the afternoon
Wheeler ordered breastworks to be constructed, and
preparations made to meet any possible counterattacks.
The men, he found, were so exhausted that they could
hardly swing the picks and shovels used in throwing up
breastworks. Their shoes were soaked with water from
wading the marshy ground, they had been drenched
with rain, they were hungry, and, what was worse, they
sorely needed reinforcements from Lawton, who was
still hammering away at El Caney. Notwithstanding
these circumstances, however, the men labored through
the night erecting breastworks, burying the dead, and
carrying the wounded back in litters. At midnight Bates
reported and was placed in a supporting position on
Wheeler's left, but Lawton did not make his expected
appearance to reinforce the right.[22]

So exhausted were the men, so poor the facilities for

[21] Shafter's Report, September 13, 1898, in Adjutant General's Office.
[22] Wheeler's Report, July 7, 1898, *ibid.*

treating the wounded, and so tardy was Lawton with the expected reinforcements, that many of the officers believed the hill should be abandoned and a position taken up somewhat to the rear. Wheeler, however, was of a different opinion. At 8:20 P.M. while the men and officers around him were busy with preparations for holding the place he wrote Shafter who was still in the rear:

The positions which our men have carried were very strong, and the intrenchments were also very strong. A number of officers have appealed to me to have our line withdrawn, and to take up a strong position farther back, and I expect they will appeal to you. I have positively discountenanced this, as it would cost us much prestige. The lines are now very thin, as so many men have gone to the rear with the wounded and so many are exhausted. We ought to hold on to-morrow, but I fear it will be a severe day. If we can get through to-morrow all right, we can make our breastworks very strong the next night.[23]

The morning of July 2 dawned clear and hot. Before sunrise the Spanish had begun a heavy fire destined to last throughout the day. About ten o'clock Lawton's division arrived from El Caney with the sorely needed reinforcements and went into position on the American right. Throughout the miserably hot day the American troops held their position. Toward sundown the Spanish fire let up and the American general officers retired to the rear for a conference with Shafter who still could not get out in the heat. This was to determine whether the army should fall back or remain where it was. Every officer apparently was allowed free expression of his opinion. A vote was taken which showed Bates, Wheeler,

[23] Quoted in Bonsal, *The Fight for Santiago*, 249.

and Lawton against retreat and Kent favoring it.[24] The
meeting adjourned and the officers went back to their
commands leaving Shafter to ponder the next step. It
is not difficult to imagine that he was a very perplexed
officer that night as he turned various alternatives in
his mind. The next morning he sent two astoundingly
different dispatches. At eight-thirty he sent one of these
to General Wheeler who, under a flag of truce, was to
transmit it to the Spanish General José Toral. It read:

I shall be obliged, unless you surrender, to shell Santiago
de Cuba. Please inform the citizens of foreign countries and
all women and children that they should leave the city before
10 o'clock to-morrow morning.[25]

But it was a different story he had to tell the Secretary
of War. Three hours after he had demanded the surrender of Santiago he wired Secretary Russell A. Alger
that Wheeler, Young, and General Hamilton S. Haw-
kins were ill and that he himself was still unable to be
about. Santiago was invested on the north and east, but
with a very thin line. Under the circumstances he was
"seriously considering withdrawing about 5 miles and
taking up a new position on the high ground between
the San Juan River and Siboney." [26]

That afternoon General Toral politely replied that
he would not surrender. Immediately Wheeler's headquarters was paid a visit by the British, Portuguese,
Chinese, and Norwegian consuls, who bore requests that
noncombatants be allowed to leave the town. If the city
were not fired upon before ten o'clock on the fifth, they
thought that all refugees might be properly cared for.
Wheeler on transmitting the information to Shafter received a reply. "Notify the consuls," Shafter instructed

24 *Ibid.*, 256.   25 In *Cuban Correspondence*, 946.   26 *Ibid.*, 941.

Wheeler, "that their request for delay until 10 a.m. on the 5th is acceded to, provided that Spanish forces inside of the city remain quiet." [27] To further his bluffing game he notified Toral that "in the interest of the poor women and children" he would withhold his fire until noon of the fifth.[28]

In the meantime, while all this land campaigning had been going on, the fleet under Sampson had been lying at the entrance to Santiago Harbor effectively bottling up the Spanish fleet. A month before, the young officer Richmond Pearson Hobson had sunk the collier *Merrimac* in the bottle-neck entrance and very nearly closed it. During the month of June the fleet had been comparatively inactive, but now with the army occupying the San Juan heights the time had come for a combined land and naval attack. On July 3, while Shafter was writing his dispatches to Alger and Toral, Admiral Sampson steamed away from the rest of his fleet on his flagship bound for Siboney. On the beach three horses waited to carry him and his party into the hills for a conference with Shafter. While the Admiral was away on this visit Cervera decided to send his flotilla from the harbor, a decision which meant destruction for his ships.[29] With Shafter besieging one side of Santiago and the American fleet now free to steam into the harbor and bombard the other side, there appeared to be little left for General Toral except surrender.

Shafter, apparently concluding that hostilities were about to cease, issued a general order commending the officers and men of his army for their gallantry in the actions at El Caney and San Juan Hill. General Wheeler

[27] *Ibid.,* 946.   [28] *Ibid.*
[29] A breezy account of the naval battle is found in Millis, *The Martial Spirit,* 293–315.

was singled out for special commendation. The order read:

To Major-General Joseph Wheeler, of the Cavalry Division, was probably given the most difficult task, that of crossing a stream under fire and deploying in front of the enemy's rifle pits. These he almost immediately charged and carried in the most gallant manner, driving the enemy from his strong positions to the shelter of the stronger works in the rear.[30]

Wood, Roosevelt, Sumner, Kent, Lawton, all were thanked by their commander.

But the surrender did not come as soon as anticipated. It was not until July 17, two weeks after the fight at San Juan and the destruction of the Spanish fleet that actual negotiations were concluded.

On the fifth, hundreds of refugees had begun pouring out of Santiago, most of them headed for El Caney. On the seventh the formal exchange of Spanish prisoners for Lieutenant Hobson and his companions was concluded. On the ninth another formal demand was made for surrender and was refused. On the eleventh the bombardment was resumed with the navy joining in but doing little damage. By July 13 General Miles had arrived at army headquarters in Cuba and he, together with Shafter and Wheeler, had an interview with the Spanish commander. After it was over Miles notified the Secretary of War that General Toral felt that he could not conclude definite terms of surrender without instructions from his government.[31] The next day, July 14, Miles, Shafter, and Wheeler again were in conference with Toral. Because of a misunderstanding brought about by the fact that interpreters confused the

[30] General Orders, No. 21, July 4, 1898, in Adjutant General's Office.
[31] Miles to Alger, July 13, 1898, quoted in Wheeler, *The Santiago Campaign*, 122.

conversations this interview was unsuccessful, but it resulted in Wheeler, Lawton, and Lieutenant J. D. Miley being appointed commissioners to negotiate the terms of surrender.[32]

Wheeler, being senior member of the commission, prepared the necessary papers and went to the meeting place between the lines at two o'clock on the afternoon of July 15. After two hours' discussion, the Spanish commissioners returned to Santiago for further instructions, returning to the conference at six with the information that it would be necessary to postpone further negotiations until the next morning. Upon objection to this procedure from Wheeler the Spaniards agreed to return with their General that same evening at half-past nine. The negotiations were concluded by midnight and officially confirmed on the morning of the sixteenth.[33]

Early on the morning of July 17 mounted orderlies rode along the lines at Santiago carrying a message: "The commanding general's compliments and the division and brigade commanders accompanied by their staffs are to assemble at corps headquarters to witness the surrender of the Spanish forces." [34]

There was no cheering, for the order had closed by prohibiting any demonstration on the part of the American troops. Truces like this had been common every few days, and the Spanish troops might not understand that this one was final. Cheering on the part of the *Americanos* might be the signal for a fresh attack.

By the time all the generals, staff officers, and orderlies had assembled in response to the order there were some two hundred in the procession. Slowly it moved out from headquarters, Shafter and Wheeler leading

32 Wheeler's account, *ibid.*, 124.   33 *Ibid.*

34 General Orders, No. 37, July 17, 1898, in Adjutant General's Office.

the way. Under an old tree midway between the lines it paused and there General Toral, resplendent in a blue linen uniform decorated with medals and gold braid, was presented. In striking contrast Shafter and Wheeler wore plain blue campaign uniforms. "One might have thought it was a meeting of old friends and not the acknowledgement of defeat," wrote a journalist who was present. "Smiles everywhere and bright looks from the defeated Spaniards more marked than from our own officers. Intense interest and curiosity was shown on both sides, for this was the first time the opposing forces had been afforded a good look at each other." [35]

"General Toral rode forward," the report continues, "and smilingly saluted General Shafter, who stretched forth his hand and heartily shook that of the Spanish general. He congratulated General Toral upon the bravery of his men and of their gallant defense of Santiago, and both expressed satisfaction that the campaign had closed. . . . There was no giving up of General Toral's sword, as it had been previously arranged that the Spanish officers should retain their side arms." A young naval officer stepped up and surrendered the lone Spanish vessel remaining in the harbor. Shafter, on horseback, received it with all solemnity explaining that he did not dismount because remounting would be a very laborious undertaking. Then followed a presentation of all the generals on both sides. The trumpets of a battalion of Spanish infantry struck up a quick march, the defeated soldiers marched by, depositing their arms, and the formal surrender was complete.[36]

[35] James F. J. Archibald, "The Day of the Surrender at Santiago," in *Scribner's Magazine* (New York), XXIV (1898), 413–16.
[36] *Ibid.*

But there were exercises yet remaining. The formal surrender had taken place about half-past nine in the morning. Immediately after, Shafter and Wheeler turned and rode toward Santiago followed by the staff officers, orderlies, two troops of the Second United States Cavalry, and the Ninth United States Infantry. Their destination was the Governor's palace at Santiago. There the American flag was to be raised and the city formally occupied.

As the cavalcade moved into the plaza in front of the palace, General Leonardo Ross y Roderigues, military governor, gave the officers an effusive Latin welcome and all the dignitaries moved inside to the audience hall. At one end of the room sat Shafter, Wheeler, and the Governor. Suddenly into the room swept His Eminence, Archbishop Saenz de Uturi, accompanied by several priests. His robes were of a rich purple and many decorations adorned his breast. He had come merely to pay his respects and his visit was of short duration. Previously he had boasted, it was rumored, that he could take ten thousand men and raise the Spanish standard over Washington. Now he chatted briefly with the victors and passed out in the direction of the cathedral, on the opposite side of the plaza.[37]

The assembly moved out into the plaza for the flag-raising ceremony, which was to take place at the stroke of twelve noon. The lines were drawn up, musical instruments were poised, two officers were on the roof with the flag. Suddenly a third figure appeared on the roof. He was clad in civilian clothes and carried a camera.

"Who is that man up there?" boomed Shafter from below.

[37] *Ibid.*

"A newspaper photographer, sir," answered Captain William H. McKittrick.

"Order him down."

"I have, sir, but he won't go."

"Then throw him down." [38]

The newspaperman beat a precipitate retreat and the ceremonies went on.

Promptly at the stroke of twelve by the cathedral clock, Captain McKittrick hauled the flag to the top of the mast, the band below played "The Star Spangled Banner," the officers uncovered, the troops presented, and Santiago passed into American hands. The war was over and it was farewell to Cuba's sickly dews and heat.

[38] Related to the author by the late Colonel Joseph Wheeler, Jr., U.S.A., who was the second officer on the roof.

Chapter XV

HOME TO WIKOFF

For nearly a month after the surrender there was little spectacular news from Cuba. The war was over, the troops were soon to be sent home, and the government was hastily erecting Camp Wikoff at Montauk Point, Long Island, to receive them.

Then suddenly the newspaper headlines began to shriek. "GENERAL WHEELER AND THE ROUGH RIDERS ASHORE AT MONTAUK" ran one. "CAMP WIKOFF HAILS HEROES OF SANTIAGO," went another. Roosevelt and Wheeler had arrived to receive the first welcome home just as they had been the first to fight in Cuba. Ragged, bearded, lean, and brown, 680 men of the Rough Riders landed at camp on August 15.[1] At the foot of the gangplank Wheeler and Roosevelt were met by delegations of newspapermen and dignitaries. There was a general shaking of hands and the crowd pressed forward to the very bayonets of the sentries along the pier. Women spectators carried small American flags and cheered lustily. "General Joe Wheeler, the veteran of two wars, showed hardly any traces of the hard campaign in which he played so prominent a part," reported one newspaper. "He walked down the gang plank with the agility of a boy. Beneath his white helmet his face looked perhaps thinner and more drawn

[1] New York *Journal*, August 15, 1898, in Clipping Files, Wheeler Papers.

than usual, but his eyes sparkled with joy at the home-coming, and as cheer after cheer went up for him he ran to the end of the pier and raised his helmet in acknowledgment." [2]

Roosevelt also came in for his share of the honors. "I have nothing to say for myself," he is quoted as saying, "but I have a lot of things to say about the regiment. They are a crowd of cracka-jacks, by George! I feel as strong as a bull moose and I have had a bully time. Was I wounded? Yes, I got a little scratch here on my right wrist. But I've got nothing to say for myself." [3]

All in all, with the bands playing "Home Sweet Home," the crowds cheering, the women weeping and waving tiny flags, it was a great day for "Fightin' Joe" and "Teddy." But the scene had its serious aspect. The troops were kept waiting in the broiling sun until nearly two in the afternoon. When they finally received marching orders many of them were exhausted. As they plodded through the ankle-deep sand their weakened condition became even more apparent. The first flush of excitement caused by touching home soil was spent and the reaction had set in. Women standing along the line of march were heard to sob as they saw the miserable plight of the troopers. Men unable to walk farther tumbled to one side, the papers reported, and lay there until rescued.[4] It was the first definite and concrete illustration afforded the country of what Cuba and inefficient army methods could do to strong men. Soon there would be long files of gaunt figures silently shuffling along the sandy road to Wikoff. These were the men who had left home a few months previously with a

2 New York *Times*, August 16, 1898, *ibid.*
3 New York *Journal*, August 15, 1898, *ibid.*
4 New York *Times*, August 16, 1898, *ibid.*

smile and a song. Now they were broken by the ravages of fever and flux.

On the sixteenth, the day after his arrival, Wheeler was summoned to Washington. Along the way he gave out interviews. At New York he praised Roosevelt and the Rough Riders and told the newspapermen stories of Guásimas and San Juan. Curious crowds gathered at railway stations along the way to catch a glimpse of the old warrior. At Washington the news gatherers surrounded him. No, he didn't know what the President wanted with him. No, he didn't know whether he would be a peace commissioner or not. Yes, he expected to take his seat in Congress in December. These and countless other questions were answered.[5]

After the conference with President McKinley he was able to give out more information. The President, he stated, had made him commander at Camp Wikoff pending the arrival of General Shafter. That was all, and he was on his way back to New York.

Upon his return the Rough Riders at Wikoff staged a celebration for their commander who had just been made commander of the whole camp. "Captain Woodbury Kane got lots of champagne for the feast. There were lots of eggs, too, rice, chocolate and delicacies of many kinds sent by Colonel Roosevelt, and there was much liquor for the boys sent by friends," the papers reported.[6] But in the midst of their feasting there arose the specter of disease.

Soon the newspapers changed their headlines from sentimental adulation to hysteria of another sort. "SOME OF OUR HEROES FORCED TO DRINK FROM A POLLUTED POND," one said. "NOT TENTS

[5] Washington *Times*, August 16, 1898, *ibid.*
[6] New York *World*, August 20, 1898, *ibid.*

ENOUGH AT MONTAUK," thought a second. "SICK SOLDIERS SLEEPING ON GROUND," noted a third.

Troops were arriving by the hundreds daily from Cuba. Camp Wikoff had been erected hastily after the surrender and was inadequate to care for the increasing stream of troops. Sanitation was poor, the supply of drinking water was inadequate, the hospitals were crowded, and governmental red tape complicated the whole situation. "The water supply went back on the camp last night," reported the New York *Times,*

and today was terrible. It was noon before some of the more distant troops received even one drink of water and then it was carted in barrels clear across the Point, and was hot and not refreshing. Hundreds of men under force of necessity drank the water out of Fresh Pond, and if this should have to be continued there may be serious results, for it was the drinking of this water by the men that is most dreaded by those who are warding off typhoid.[7]

But this was not all. Ill fortune seems to have overtaken the camp generally. General Young tripped over a wire and broke his arm in the fall. A few days before, his horse had run sideways into a telephone pole, injuring the general's foot. Many of the nurses were complaining of their treatment. They were overworked, they said, and hadn't enough food or decent sleeping quarters. General Wheeler and the medical chief were quarreling because the hospital staff did not like to take orders from regular army officers. More ships were arriving daily with their cargoes of sick soldiers. On September 3 the *Berkshire* arrived with 348 invalids. That same day the *City of Washington* brought only a colonel, his secretary, and two Negro servants. This large clean

[7] New York *Times,* September 3, 1898, *ibid.*

boat had brought only four passengers from Cuba, while the *Neuces,* a cattle boat, cleared the same day with 685 men aboard. The *Orizaba* also arrived on the third with 24 paymasters and a million dollars in gold. The gold had been sent to Cuba to pay the soldiers, but since it found no soldiers there it had followed them back to New York.[8]

Other pictures were given of bad conditions. One newspaper account tells of two trainloads of soldiers arriving in New York City from Camp Wikoff. "There was not a face that was not pinched and worn, not a leg that did not tremble and halt," the account runs. And as the stretcher bearers came from the trains in long files "men and women who had never seen these men before, and never would see them again, gave way to tears." [9]

As the newspapers broadcast the worst of conditions at Wikoff, hundreds of letters and telegrams poured in on the little commanding officer. The files of his correspondence today bear mute evidence of the fact that the position of commanding officer at Camp Wikoff was no easy one. Every mother in the land, it seems, wanted her son back. "In regard to my son," one mother wrote,

we feel very uneasy about him on account of the newspaper reports of the privation and suffering inflicted on the private soldiers. Although he has never uttered a complaint since he has been in the army, we hear from other sources of the cruel and horrible treatment inflicted on our soldiers under the pretense of humanity for our neighbors, and the whole country is in a state of excitement. I should not be surprised if the feeling should lead to a revolution of some kind.[10]

[8] *Ibid.*   [9] New York *Press,* September 3, 1898, *ibid.*
[10] Mrs. William Wade to Wheeler, September 1, 1898, in Wheeler Papers.

Some of the protesters dispensed with long distance methods and resorted to direct action. Every day, a newspaper reported, trains arrived at Montauk Point bringing "hordes of mothers, wives, sisters, and sweethearts, in search of warriors bold, crippled, scarred, or worn." Sunday and Labor Day, the same paper added, "witnessed at the camp many an irate woman on the warpath in behalf of some loved one." [11] It was difficult enough for Wheeler to supervise those in charge of sick soldiers, but when scores of hysterical women invaded the camp it was too much.

He attempted to allay the country's fears by defending the administration against charges of gross neglect and by pointing out that conditions were greatly exaggerated by the newspapers. On September 11 he gave out an interview to the press the substance of which was that the men knew they were going to meet hardships, disease, and death. They did not complain, he said, but seemed grateful to McKinley and Alger for the opportunity to fight. He admitted that "there is no doubt that there have been individual cases of suffering and possibly of neglect not only in Cuba, but since their arrival at this place"; but he insisted that the suffering was not of a serious nature.[12] Likewise, in his private correspondence, he denied that conditions were as bad as pictured. Most of the rumpus, he wrote Mark Hanna, was due to the fact that the newspapers were "addicted to misrepresentation." [13]

But he did not stop with a mere denial. He appointed General Adelbert Ames of the Volunteer army as his own private investigator. The General went to work

11 New York *Tribune*, September 11, 1898, in Clipping Files, Wheeler Papers.

12 New York *World*, September 2, 1898, *ibid.*

13 Wheeler to Mark Hanna, September 5, 1898, in Wheeler Papers.

and soon he was talking for publication. "I think the first thing to do with these troops is to send them home," he was quoted as saying. "The war is over and they are not needed now. This camp is in a disgraceful condition as it is now arranged." [14] What his final verdict was is not known, for even General Wheeler's private papers fail to reveal an official report, if one was made. The General's statements in the newspapers, however, did not make Wheeler's task any lighter.

Finally, Wheeler fixed the blame. It was, he said, the fault of Commissary General Charles P. Egan that the troops were suffering. Food which had been ordered from Washington stood in the cars for days while Egan pondered what official order was necessary to release it.

"It is not my fault," replied Egan. "General Wheeler should pay more attention to the routine of his duties. He called for supplies that were not allowed by law and was notified that my department would be forced to cancel the order for such goods." [15]

On September 3 the President himself visited camp for an inspection. With him were Vice-President Garret A. Hobart, Secretary of War Alger, Senator Fletcher D. Proctor of Vermont, Commissary General Egan, Quartermaster General Marshall I. Ludington, and the President's secretaries, John A. Porter and George B. Cortelyou. Accompanied by Wheeler as guide the entire party made an inspection of the camp. The first call was made at Shafter's tent. He had lately arrived from Cuba, and, although they found him in full dress uniform sitting in the door of his tent, he was too ill to rise.[16] Then the party passed up and down the rows of hospital cots.

[14] Binghamton *Republican*, September 1, 1898, in Clipping Files, Wheeler Papers.

[15] New York *Journal*, August 27, 1898, *ibid*.

[16] New York *World*, September 4, 1898, *ibid*.

Some of the patients were strong enough to rise and salute the President, but many lay listlessly on their cots and stared into space, too sick and wasted to know or care that their Commander-in-Chief was with them.[17] General Wheeler acted as interlocutor. As the party entered a ward he would announce in all dignity: "The President of the United States!" and as they proceeded down the aisles questions would be asked of the sick soldiers.

"Are you receiving good treatment? Is everything being done for your comfort?" were the usual questions.

And the usual answer was: "Yes, sir, we are treated all right, but we want to go home." [18]

When the party returned to General Wheeler's headquarters the President washed his face and hands in an old wooden basin and, according to newspaper reports, wept as he washed.[19] But he strengthened himself enough to make an evasive statement to the reporters. "I was very much pleased to meet the heroes of Santiago, and to observe their splendid spirits. What I saw of the care of the sick men in the hospitals by those in charge and by the noble women engaged in that work was especially gratifying to me." [20] Secretary Alger added: "I find things are in better condition than they were when I was here a week ago. I am well satisfied with the camp." [21]

Then the Presidential party prepared to return. As it was ready to reseat itself in the carriage there was a tumult and a thundering of hoofs. When the dust cleared away, there on his horse sat the effervescent Teddy with his broad smile. He had arrived just in

17 New York *Times*, September 4, 1898, *ibid.*
18 New York *World*, September 4, 1898, *ibid.*
19 Brooklyn *Eagle*, September 4, 1898, *ibid.*
20 New York *Times*, September 4, 1898, *ibid.*   21 *Ibid.*

MAJOR GENERAL JOSEPH WHEELER, U.S.V.,
1898

time to share in the ceremonies. His reward was a cordial handshake from the President and a hearty slap on the back from the Secretary of War. Then the Colonel with a group of his troopers acted as an escort for the cavalcade as it wound up the hill and out of sight.[22]

In the midst of his perplexities at Wikoff, General Wheeler suffered an almost crushing blow in the death of his youngest son. When the Wheelers had fared forth to war they made it almost a family affair. With the General had gone his son, Joseph, as a member of his father's staff; the daughter, Annie, as a nurse; and the youngest member of the family, Naval Cadet Thomas Harrison Wheeler, detailed to the cruiser *Columbia*. All had come through the war unharmed; but now, safely back at Wikoff, accident reduced the famous quartette to a trio. While surf-bathing, the youngest Wheeler and a companion were drowned. Sorrowfully the remaining members of the family bore the body back to Wheeler, Alabama, and there laid it to rest beside that of his mother.[23]

While in Alabama General Wheeler received confirmation of news which under different circumstances might have cheered him. The Democrats of the Eighth Congressional District had met in convention and chosen him as their candidate for Congress again. All other political opposition in the district had melted away.

The furor created by the press and by the relatives and friends of soldiers at Camp Wikoff made an investigation of army conditions well-nigh inevitable. There were two types of procedure which the administration might take—one a court-martial investigation, or the

[22] New York *World*, September 4, 1898, *ibid.*
[23] New York *Sun*, September 8, 1898, *ibid.*

second, a Congressional committee. President McKinley chose neither way, but appointed rather an unofficial committee of investigation consisting of a majority of staunch defenders of the administration. The personnel of the committee included: Major General Grenville M. Dodge; Major General Alexander McD. McCook; Colonel Charles Denby, former Minister to China; Brigadier General John M. Wilson, Chief of Army Engineers; former Governor James A. Beaver of Pennsylvania; Colonel James A. Sexton, commander-in-chief of the G.A.R.; former Governor Urban A. Woodbury of Vermont; Dr. Phineas S. Connor of Cincinnati; and Captain Evan P. Howell of Atlanta. Most of these gentlemen could be counted upon to let neither the reputation of the army nor the welfare of the administration suffer.

Deliberations were begun in the last days of September. General Shafter was not summoned. General Miles asked not to be called. Fitzhugh Lee found it inconvenient to be present. Wheeler was the sole officer of major importance who testified before the committee, and his testimony was little more than a repetition of his newspaper defense of conditions at Wikoff. As one newspaper expressed it "General Wheeler saw nothing and heard nothing wrong" during the whole war.[24]

Regarding conditions at Tampa prior to sailing he testified:

We were well located while we were there, but from inquiries I learned that there were fears of suffering when the weather should change. . . . I think there were about 18,000 or 19,000 troops there. I think they were well supplied with commissary stores. We were all under tents. I consider the men in the hospitals very well taken care of. The percentage

24 New York *Telegram*, October 6, 1898, *ibid.*

of sick was very small. There were few sick, of regulars or volunteers under my command. I went into the hospitals and saw all the men doing well.[25]

Continuing his testimony, General Wheeler admitted that when the troops sailed for Cuba there was, so far as he knew, no plan of campaign when they should land, but suggested that this didn't make so much difference because the men fought so bravely once they were in Cuba. There was, he said, an unusual amount of sickness during the stay in the trenches because of "the wet nights and hot days." He thought from 12 to 15 per cent of the men got sick; one of the troubles was that the men would not report their illness. Then, too, "it happened that the men would throw their rations and other things away. Our men carried their rations with them —three days rations—and when they were fighting they threw them away."

As to the promptness with which the wounded were attended, General Wheeler said he saw many attended to quickly, and though he also saw men crawling to the hospitals in the evening he supposed they had been overlooked. The hardtack and bacon were good. The field rations were not always supplied, but the men did not complain—they seemed proud to be at the front.

At Montauk blankets were well supplied. So were medicines, tents, delicacies, and everything else which was needed. Conditions there were far above the average army camp. In fact, one gathers from the testimony, Camp Wikoff was little different from a pleasant seaside resort.

[25] Washington *Times,* October 4, 1898, *ibid.* Wheeler's testimony is found in *Report of the Commission Appointed by the President to Investigate The Conduct of the War Department in the War with Spain,* in *Senate Documents,* No. 221, 56 Cong., 1 Sess., III, 3–56.

If the newspapers may be taken as a criterion, public opinion was somewhat divided on Wheeler's testimony. Many of the papers praised Wheeler and displayed his testimony as being a complete refutation of stories carried by the "yellow journals." "Probably no testimony that may be given before the committee investigating the charges of mismanagement of the recent war will go further to put an extinguisher upon the sensational clamor of yellow journalism than that of General Joseph Wheeler given yesterday," thought the Chicago *Post*. "His rank in the army of invasion and his previous service in the army of the Confederacy, to say nothing of his long and honorable career in Congress, give a weight and authority to his observations on the management and conditions of the campaign that will be sought in vain elsewhere." [26] The Richmond *Times* reserved the right to change its mind but thought "the testimony of General Wheeler is a strong point gained in advance for the persons under investigation." [27] Another Southern paper thought that "Joe Wheeler's word will go farther than that of any sensational newspaper or perpetual candidate for office." [28] "Whatever the other testimony may be, the fact is likely to stand that the most conspicuous complaints yet made have been entirely unfounded, since this appears on the evidence of one better qualified to know and to judge than any political critic, and in such high standing with Democrats that his evidence cannot be questioned," thought the New York *Tribune*.[29]

On the other hand, there were those who disagreed and thought that the value of the General's testimony

26 October 7, 1898, in Clipping Files, Wheeler Papers.
27 October 8, 1898, *ibid*.
28 Memphis *Scimitar*, October 7, 1898, *ibid*.
29 October 8, 1898, *ibid*.

should be discounted. "General Wheeler's testimony is singularly at variance with the statements of pretty nearly everybody that took part in the Santiago campaign," stated the Detroit *News*.

Even General Shafter himself has not expressed the supreme satisfaction with conditions which General Wheeler shows. Even the War Department has conceded that many things might have been done differently and better. . . . We are forced to believe that General Wheeler is a much better fighter than a military critic, and that even the present unsatisfactory system could never be improved if the change depended upon suggestions from General Wheeler.[30]

The New Orleans *States* thought that the General's "heroism is immeasurably greater than his head" and that a "dab of whitewash was being applied to the administration's conduct of the war." [31] The Washington *Times* stated that if the commission had been a legally constituted one, or a court-martial, General Wheeler would have told more, but since it was "a commission created and operated solely for political advertising purposes" the country should not be surprised that more was not revealed.[32] The New York *Times* in a conservative and apparently unprejudiced editorial thought:

General Wheeler is a man whose honesty is as undoubted as his courage, and it would be almost as difficult to imagine as to suspect any motive he could have for whitewashing the administration or its Secretary of War. There is, however, widespread surprise at the sort of testimony which the veteran has given before that absurd committee in Washington, and people are pondering deeply on the mystery of how a soldier so well informed and well intentioned can deduce from un-

[30] October 5, 1898, *ibid.*   [31] *Ibid.*
[32] October 6, 1898, *ibid.*

questionable facts conclusions so utterly at variance with those he was expected to reach.[33]

It would, of course, be easy to speculate on General Wheeler's testimony and to offer theoretical explanations as to why his conclusions were "so utterly at variance with those he was expected to reach," but the simple truth appears to be that, in spite of a rather uncritical attitude, Wheeler's testimony was, on the whole, reliable. It is quite likely that he was inclined to minimize the bad aspects of the situation and to see more of the good, but a careful study of his testimony and of the newspapers' reaction to it indicates that the real trouble lay in the fact that the Democratic press had counted on Wheeler, a life-long Democrat, to come to the aid of his party by testifying that the Republican administration had grossly mismanaged affairs at Camp Wikoff.[34] When Wheeler failed them in this they gave vent to their wrath in calling him names and accusing him of "whitewashing" the administration. But in the final analysis it appears that after the first few days of chaos at Wikoff the camp was conducted rather creditably and that Wheeler's testimony was not as far afield as might seem if one reads only the Democratic newspapers.[35]

Nothing of importance ever came from the commission. In its official report, it condemned not, neither did it exonerate. Very soon a series of peace jubilees began to take the mind of the people away from the horrors of the late campaign. At Philadelphia on October 27 there was a grand review of the veterans of the Santiago

[33] *Ibid.*

[34] These are the author's tentative conclusions. No study has been made of the situation at Camp Wikoff.

[35] *Ibid.* See Millis, *The Martial Spirit,* 365.

campaign. The President's carriage headed the parade
to the reviewing stand. There he and members of the
cabinet watched the procession go by. There was General Miles resplendent in full dress uniform with gold
braid. Then came governors of the various states. Then
came General Joe Wheeler, "short, gray-haired, gray-
bearded and affable, the picture of wiry activity and
cool courage," bowing to the right and the left.[36] The
night before, he had been a prominent speaker at the
Union League banquet and now here he was "being
made the recipient of the love of the most thoroughly
Northern city in the North." [37] It took the parade more
than three hours to pass a given point and as the crowd
showered the troops with sandwiches and confections
the evil days of Cuba and Wikoff were forgotten.

Almost immediately after this celebration Wheeler
left for the South on an inspection trip which would
occupy his time until the next jubilee, which would be
held in Atlanta in December. At Birmingham there was
a short ovation as the train paused. There was an official
reception and a banquet at Mobile. At Nashville he was
the honored guest at a number of brilliant luncheons
and receptions, and the local chapter of the Daughters
of the American Revolution presented him with a handsome sword.[38] From Nashville he journeyed to Chattanooga to address the Tennessee River Improvement Association in session there. Instead of talking about the
improvement of the Tennessee River, however, his remarks were devoted to the advocacy of a policy of national expansion. Annexation, he thought, was "a matter
that has passed beyond the point of discussion. The logic
of events has visited upon us these colonies, and it is

[36] Philadelphia *Inquirer*, October 28, 1898, in Clipping Files, Wheeler
Papers.
[37] *Ibid.*   [38] Nashville *American*, November 10, 1898, *ibid.*

our duty now to legislate and to do the most possible for the benefit of the inhabitants of these islands and the United States." [39] It was the beginning of a series of speeches which ultimately were to bring him into conflict with the leaders of his own party.

Congress convened on December 5, 1898, and General Wheeler was present to answer to his name, but he was present under rather peculiar circumstances. He was a Major General in the Volunteer army of the United States and also a member of Congress. In addition, he had, it appeared, lined up almost solidly with the Republican administration in as much as his testimony had helped save the day for the War Department and Secretary Alger. His public and private statements since the close of the war had all been highly imperialistic—all of which caused consternation within the Democratic ranks, consternation and irritation. Very wisely Wheeler refrained from participating in debates and from voting until his case had been decided.

Joseph W. Bailey of Texas, Democratic leader in the House, chose to make the issue a constitutional one. Article I, Section 6, was very clear on the point. "No person holding an Office under the United States, shall be a Member of either House during his Continuance in Office." Wheeler was holding two offices and this was clearly unconstitutional. The first step toward ousting the General was taken on December 19 when Bailey introduced a resolution directing the judiciary committee to report on the eligibility of Wheeler and two other similar cases.[40] The case was before the committee until February 4 when a report was made to the House. It

[39] Chattanooga *News*, November 29, 1898, *ibid.*
[40] New York *Herald*, December 20, 1898, *ibid.; Cong. Record*, 55 Cong., 3 Sess., 310.

was the opinion of the committee that Wheeler and the other officers involved held their seats unconstitutionally and that they should, therefore, be declared vacant.[41] The resolution, however, did not come to a vote until nearly a month later.

On February 28 a caucus was called by the Democrats to determine the party's stand on the general question of imperialism and expansion. Apparently sentiment was strongly anti-expansionist. It is difficult to know exactly what transpired in the caucus, but from newspaper reports it seems that sentiment was almost unanimous in condemning the Republican policy of expansion. Almost all the opposition to the party's stand came from Wheeler. "It was practically a unanimous affair," observed one paper. "The most notable feature of the caucus was the reception awarded to General Joe Wheeler of Alabama. He sounded an opposition note and was treated so coldly that he withdrew from the caucus shortly afterward before any vote was taken." [42] Another paper elaborated somewhat upon the unwelcome speech and declared: "The speech of General Wheeler was noteworthy in differing from the prevailing view. He urged that nothing should be done which could be construed as a lack of support of our soldiers. The hands of the President should be upheld, he said, when fighting was going on. As a matter of expediency also, he urged that the party should not oppose the war. Wars were popular, he declared, and at the present time the spirit of the people was shown by the fact that every boy had his drum and sword, while the mothers were proud of this patriotic spirit." [43]

41 New York *Times*, February 4, 1899, in Clipping Files, Wheeler Papers.
42 Washington *Post*, February 23, 1899, *ibid.*
43 New York *Press*, February 28, 1899, *ibid.*

This action of the caucus coming as it did just before the vote on the resolution to unseat was not in any way of assistance to Wheeler. When the vote came on March 3, it found the Democrats almost evenly divided on the issue. There were 43 Democrats, 21 Republicans, and 13 Populists, a total of 77, who favored unseating Wheeler. Those who wished to see him remain in Congress were 44 Democrats, 101 Republicans, and 1 Populist, a total of 146.[44] Joe Bailey had failed in his efforts to oust the General and as a result resigned his leadership of the minority.[45]

Wheeler, at this time, was in great favor with McKinley, but it appears his popularity was not so pronounced in the House of Representatives. Half of his own party had voted to unseat him. Now Speaker Reed took it upon himself to humiliate Wheeler publicly. The occasion was the appearance of General Shafter at the doors of the House chamber where, at the invitation of Wheeler, he was expecting to give the body some information on things military. While Shafter waited, Wheeler went inside to notify the House of his presence. On being informed by Speaker Reed that such a procedure was not allowed under the House rules Wheeler requested that the House take a recess while members met General Shafter.

The Speaker assumed a new dignity. "General Wheeler," he is quoted as saying, "the House of Representatives of the United States is bigger than any Major-General." [46] Humiliated, Wheeler was forced to

---

[44] New York *Times,* March, 4, 1899, *ibid.; Cong. Record,* 55 Cong., 3 Sess., 2751.

[45] Sam H. Acheson, *Joe Bailey: The Last Democrat* (New York, 1932), 130.

[46] New York *World,* January 10, 1899, in Clipping Files, Wheeler Papers.

meet Shafter outside and convey the information to him
that his views were not desired.

Then, too, the House refused to make a place for
Wheeler in the regular army. Army regulations provided for three major generals and all three places were
filled. In the appropriation bill pending before the
House there was an amendment which provided that
the number should be increased to four, it being generally understood that the fourth place was for Wheeler.
But when the bill was under consideration before the
Committee of the Whole House the Chairman ruled the
amendment not germane and it was lost.[47] The House
of Representatives seemed to be recovering from its war-
time hysteria and Wheeler was the unfortunate object
of its reforming spirit. But the President was not checked
in his attempts to keep Wheeler in the army. There was
a brigadier general's commission open in the Volunteer
army and Wheeler was appointed to this. His command
was the Fourth Army Corps with headquarters at Huntsville, Alabama. This location of headquarters only a
few miles from Wheeler's home enabled him to look
after both his political and military interests.

In December, 1898, however, the army post at Huntsville was abandoned. Early the next year Wheeler was
on a speaking tour of the East. At Bangor, Maine, he
was received with open arms by the Grand Army of the
Republic. At Boston the same organization presented
him with a sword at a great public dinner. At Trenton,
New Jersey, he was enthusiastically received.[48] Although
it was frequently mentioned he had once been a Confederate general, that was forgiven him now that he had
permanently donned the blue. The Grand Army of the

[47] Albany *Times-Union*, March 4, 1899, *ibid.*
[48] Boston *Journal*, May 31, 1899, *ibid.*

Republic, President Charles W. Eliot, Governor Roger
Wolcott of Massachusetts, Francis Lowell, and Josiah
Quincy vied with each other in paying him tribute.
The general sentiment was that Wheeler was a living
illustration of the fact that the South was loyal again
after her great mistake in 1861. But Wheeler was looking for more fighting instead of so much speech-making.
Although now within a year of the army retirement age,
his persistent entreaties that he be allowed to go to the
Philippines and help subdue Emilio Aguinaldo were
rewarded when the President on June 20, 1899, ordered
him to report to General Arthur McArthur at Manila.
Once again, father, son, and daughter were going to
war.

They reached Manila on August 21, and Wheeler
reported for what he expected to be active duty. Mc-
Arthur sent him to General E. S. Otis and Otis found
no duties for him.[49] Finally, he was given command of
the First brigade of the Second division but was not
ordered to active duty with it. August gave way to September and still Fightin' Joe was performing only routine inspection duties and writing long letters to the
newspapers back in the States. On September 3 he wrote
McArthur: "I would like very much to be with the
troops of the brigade which are nearest the enemy, and
also to be near the troops of my command." [50] But this
request brought no action. October came and with it
what Wheeler thought was the promise of a fight. From
his headquarters he could hear the roll of musketry in
the distance. The alarm was spread, the troops were

[49] Pittsburgh *Dispatch*, April 29, 1900, *ibid.*

[50] Wheeler to Arthur McArthur, September 3, 1899, in *Annual Report of the Lieutenant General Commanding the Army, 1900,* in *House
Documents,* No. 2, Pt. VI, 56 Cong., 2 Sess., 205. Cited hereafter as *Report, Lieutenant General, 1900.*

assembled, and then it was discovered that the noise came from a near-by basement where Filipino women were crushing grain with huge wooden pestles.[51] October passed, the rainy season came with November, and still Wheeler had not seen the action which he desired. On the seventeenth, almost four months after his arrival, he made another request. "I beg you will pardon me for again asking for active service against the enemy when I have completed this work," he wrote.[52]

Doubtless General Wheeler's age made McArthur hesitate to send him into the swamps during the hot season. The heat of Cuba had been a bit too much for Wheeler and conditions in the Philippines were certainly no better. Too, Wheeler's prominence and the fact that he was accustomed to commanding might complicate the situation on the firing line if he were sent there. Already Wheeler had given reporters permission to go into forbidden territory against McArthur's orders; and, although it made Wheeler popular with the reporters, it was not conducive to the maintenance of discipline.[53] But in the face of Wheeler's importunity McArthur finally sent him to his command.

He joined his brigade just in time to participate in the last fight with Aguinaldo's troops. On November 12 General McArthur's headquarters were at San Fernando on the railroad some forty miles north of Manila, while Aguinaldo and the insurgent congress were at Tarlac, thirty-five miles farther north. In between Tarlac and San Fernando the American and insurgent troops con-

[51] Related in Atlanta *Journal,* November 7, 1899, in Clipping Files, Wheeler Papers.

[52] Wheeler to McArthur, November 17, 1899, in *Report, Lieutenant General, 1900,* Pt. VI, 229.

[53] Brooklyn *Standard-Union,* November 8, 1899, in Clipping Files, Wheeler Papers.

fronted each other. The center of the insurgent line was on the railroad a short distance north of Angeles, the flanks extending two or three miles to the right and left.[54] There had been what the newspapers termed "battles" at Santa Rita, Porac, and Angeles during September and October, which had resulted in the insurgents being driven back to their capitol at Tarlac. Fighting had been sporadic, almost of a guerrilla nature. Nearly always the attacks of the insurgents took place near nightfall when the confusion would be greatest among the United States troops fighting on unknown territory.

But the opposition offered by these insurgents was more annoying than effective, and when Tarlac fell the opposition was crushed.

Wheeler was in active command of his brigade during the campaign, but there was little of a dramatic nature for the newspapermen to report. Those incidents, however, which made interesting copy were seized upon. At Tarlac after the battle, for example, Wheeler went on an inspection tour. The railroad connecting the town with Manila had been cut by the insurgents. Upon examination Wheeler found that the most serious break in the road was where it crossed a small stream now swollen by fall rains. In order to determine the condition of the girders lying on the bottom of the stream he undressed and dived into the muddy water where he conducted a submarine examination.[55] On another occasion a private was wounded in the knee and was about to drop unnoticed by the trail when Wheeler came riding along with his aides. Seeing the man's plight Wheeler

---

[54] Wheeler's Report, September 10, 1900, in *Report, Lieutenant General, 1900*, Pt. VI, 255.

[55] *Ibid.*

dismounted and ordered the wounded man to ride his horse for the rest of the day.[56] While such events did not add a great deal to the success of the campaign, yet they did increase Wheeler's popularity and offer proof that he was not too old to fight.

Wheeler remained in the Philippines until January 15, 1900, when he returned to Washington apparently expecting to resume his duties in Congress. But McKinley had a place much more to the General's liking. The President commissioned him a brigadier general in the Regular Army and on June 16, 1900, sent him to Chicago to assume command of the Department of the Lakes, a position he was to hold until his retirement in the fall of the same year.[57]

This retirement gave him leisure for travel and social activities. There was another Eastern speaking tour. During the summer of 1901 he was reported as being "the social lion of Newport." [58] He traveled to Mexico as a representative of a gun and ammunition company; he traveled in Europe where he witnessed the maneuvers of the French and German armies and where he and Lord Roberts began the organization of the Pilgrims Society. Although he maintained his legal residence in Alabama, his activities were confined largely to the East during the last five years of his life. He was prominently mentioned for various official positions: Police Commissioner of New York, Secretary of War, and Vice-Presidential nominee. None of these, however, were actually tendered him.

[56] Philadelphia *North American*, May 11, 1900, in Clipping Files, Wheeler Papers.

[57] Wheeler's Report, September 10, 1900, in *Report, Lieutenant General, 1900*, Pt. VI, 256–57. Wheeler retired September 10, 1900.

[58] Washington *Times*, August 31, 1901, in Clipping Files, Wheeler Papers.

Across Brooklyn Bridge toward Manhattan slowly moved a caisson draped with intermingled Confederate and United States flags. Following the caisson walked a riderless horse, and behind the horse was a long procession of troops, carriages, and people walking. Slowly the cavalcade made its way through lanes of bared heads along Broadway to Fifth Avenue and thence to St. Thomas's Church on Fifty-third Street. As the long line passed in solemn review the word spread among the onlookers that General Wheeler was dead. There was a hush and a silent tribute. On Thursday, January 25, 1906, while visiting in the home of his sister in Brooklyn, the same home whence he had gone as a cadet to West Point, the old fighter had passed away. After brief services at New York the flag-draped casket was transferred by rail to Washington where it lay in state at St. John's Episcopal Church. There the great and the near great filed past the bier. Confederate veterans and members of the Grand Army of the Republic mingled with Spanish war veterans and formed the procession which followed the body to the national cemetery. There a withered Confederate who had been Wheeler's bugler during the 1860's sent across the silent slopes of Arlington the clear notes of "taps, lights out." [59]

[59] New York *Herald,* January 29, 1906; Washington *Post,* January 29, 1906, *ibid.*

CRITICAL ESSAY ON AUTHORITIES

Manuscript Material

General Wheeler's life falls naturally into three main divisions: The Civil War period, the political period from 1880 to 1898, and the Spanish-American War period from 1898 until his death in 1906. For each of these there exists some manuscript material, but the greater bulk of it deals with the last two phases of his life. By far the most important collection is that made by Miss Annie Wheeler of her father's correspondence and private papers. This collection at the Wheeler home, Wheeler, Alabama, consists of several hundred pieces, mostly letters, but also includes manuscript speeches, bills, ledgers and account books, photographs, newspaper clippings, and other similar material. Although a disappointingly large number of the letters are from constituents on inconsequential topics, occasionally the researcher encountered one which shed considerable light on the General's personality or on his position regarding a local or national problem. There seems to have been a growing tendency on General Wheeler's part after 1890 to keep copies of important letters which he wrote, and this fact proved a boon to the researcher.

The Cleveland Correspondence in the Division of Manuscripts, Library of Congress, was unindexed when the author had access to it, and his task was much like looking for the proverbial needle in a haystack; but he was rewarded by several letters from Wheeler which illuminated certain of the General's political views during the Populist period in Alabama.

Also in the Division of Manuscripts is the Beauregard Correspondence in which the author located the report of Assistant Inspector General Alfred B. Roman of the Confederate army on Wheeler's alleged depredations in Georgia and

South Carolina during the war. This report goes far toward clearing up a situation that other writers on Wheeler have avoided or have failed to treat with any degree of objectivity.

Miscellaneous manuscript material includes: two letters from William H. Wheeler concerning his brother, in the Miscellaneous File of the State Archives, Atlanta, Georgia; records of St. Paul's Episcopal Church, Augusta, Georgia; five letters written by Mollie Weakely to her mother in Florence, Alabama, describing conditions at Mobile and Pensacola during the spring of 1861; and the political memoirs of Judge Thomas J. Taylor of Huntsville, Alabama. This last manuscript, now in possession of Judge Taylor's son of Huntsville, was especially valuable in clearing up certain points in the Lowe-Wheeler controversy.

The chief sources of information concerning the early history of the Wheeler family in Augusta, Georgia, are the records of the Tax Collector's Office of Richmond County from 1826 to 1845, and the deeds, contracts, wills, and mortgages recorded in the office of the Judge of Ordinary of Richmond County, Books S, V, and XX. The Circuit Court Criminal Docket of Lawrence County, Alabama, 1872–1890 (Moulton), bears evidence of General Wheeler's prominence as a lawyer.

Printed Correspondence

An absolute essential for the writer on the Civil War is, of course, *War of the Rebellion: A Compilation of the Official Records of the Union and Confederate Armies*, 130 vols. (Washington, 1880–1901). Although parts are scantily edited and contain a great mass of indigestible material, the series is indispensable as a source on events as they happened day by day in the field. It is also valuable as a check against statements made in after years in the memoirs and reminiscences of leading participants in the war.

For the Spanish-American War a much less complete work is *Correspondence from the Adjutant General U.S.A., Relating to the Campaign in Cuba* (*Senate Documents*, No. 221, 56 Cong., 1 Sess., II). This was supplemented by manuscript material in the Adjutant General's Office in Washington.

Other printed material in the nature of correspondence

and reports includes: Ulrich B. Phillips (ed.), *The Correspondence of Robert Toombs, Alexander H. Stephens, and Howell Cobb,* in the American Historical Association, *Annual Report,* 1911, Vol. II (Washington, 1913); and James D. Richardson (ed.), *A Compilation of the Messages and Papers of the Presidents, 1789–1897,* 11 vols. (Washington, 1896–1901).

Government Documents: State and National

In addition to the local court records listed under manuscript material, the report of the banking committee of the Georgia legislature, recorded in *Acts of the General Assembly of the State of Georgia,* 1833 (Milledgeville, 1833), is a valuable source of information on the elder Joseph Wheeler's career as a banker.

The *Report of the Adjutant General of the State of Tennessee of the Military Forces of the State from 1861 to 1866* (Nashville, 1866), the author found valuable in tracing the military records of Union soldiers from Tennessee. Also of great value in studying the political phases of the Civil War is the *Journal of the Confederate States of America,* 7 vols. (*Senate Documents,* No. 234, 58 Cong., 2 Sess.).

For the Congressional career of General Wheeler the volumes of the *Congressional Record* (1882–1898) are essential. Also used was *Selections from the Speeches of Hon. Joseph Wheeler,* 7 vols. (Washington, 1883–1896). These selections are taken largely from the *Congressional Record* and obviously constitute what Wheeler considered his most important pronouncements.

For information concerning certain phases of the Spanish-American War and the occupation of the Philippines, the *Annual Report of the Major General Commanding the Army, 1898* (*House Documents,* No. 2, 55 Cong., 3 Sess.), and the *Annual Report of the Lieutenant General Commanding the Army, 1900,* 7 vols. (*House Documents,* No. 2, 56 Cong., 2 Sess.), are valuable. Of particular worth concerning operations of the army in Cuba is the *Report of the Commission Appointed by the President to Investigate the Conduct of the War Department in the War with Spain,* 8 vols. (*Senate Documents,* No. 221, 56 Cong., 1 Sess.).

Contemporary Newspapers and Periodicals

General Wheeler subscribed to several clipping bureaus, with the result that over a period of years a great mass of newspaper clippings accumulated in his home. After her father's death, Miss Annie Wheeler sorted and arranged these clippings in several large scrapbooks, being careful to mark each clipping with the date and the name of the newspaper. These range all the way from lengthy feature stories to short news notices, and, since Miss Wheeler did not delete those unfavorable to her father, these clipping files serve as an excellent collection of source material. Clippings from the following newspapers were used: Memphis *Scimitar,* 1898; Nashville *American,* 1898; Boston *Journal,* 1899; Albany *Times-Union,* 1899; Pittsburgh *Dispatch,* 1900; Atlanta *Journal,* 1899; Binghamton *Republican,* 1898; New York *Herald,* 1898, 1906; New York *Tribune,* 1898; New York *World,* 1898, 1899; New York *Journal,* 1898; New York *Times,* 1898; New York *Press,* 1898, 1899; New York *Sun,* 1898, 1900; New York *Telegram,* 1898; New York *Evening Post,* 1906; Washington *Times,* 1898, 1899, 1901; Washington *Post,* 1899, 1906; Philadelphia *Inquirer,* 1898; Philadelphia *North American,* 1900; Philadelphia *Times,* 1894; Brooklyn *Standard-Union,* 1899; Brooklyn *Eagle,* 1898; Chattanooga *Daily Times,* 1897; Chattanooga *News,* 1898; Houston *Post,* 1896.

In addition, files of the following newspapers were examined: Augusta (Georgia) *Chronicle,* 1862; Augusta *Constitutionalist,* 1863; Memphis *Appeal,* 1863; Nashville *Dispatch,* 1865; Nashville *Daily Press and Times,* 1865; Savannah *Morning News,* 1892.

The weekly newspapers of Wheeler's Congressional District furnish a great deal of material on his various political campaigns. The files of the Florence (Alabama) *Gazette,* 1880–1885, were utilized, as were those of the Huntsville (Alabama) *Democrat,* 1880–1896, the Huntsville *Independent,* 1880–1896, and the Huntsville *Gazette,* 1880–1896. The Florence *Gazette* and the Huntsville *Democrat* were old-line Democratic papers; the Huntsville *Independent* reflected the views of the Independent-Greenback party, while the Huntsville

Gazette proclaimed itself the leading Negro newspaper of the state. The Tuscumbia *North Alabamian,* 1880; Florence *News,* 1882; Florence *Herald,* 1892; and Moulton (Alabama) *Advertiser,* 1896, were also examined.

Among the contemporary periodicals, articles pertinent to the study were found in the following: *Southern Literary Messenger* (Richmond), XXXVIII (1864), 231–38; *Harper's Weekly* (New York), XLII (1898), 601–602; *Scribner's Magazine* (New York), XXIV (1898), 412–18.

Autobiographies, Memoirs, and Reminiscences

The memoir published long after the event has happened is, of course, often unreliable as historical evidence. Particularly is this true of many of the memoirs of Federal and Confederate officers who sought to justify a certain course of conduct; but when checked against other sources much may be gleaned from them.

In studying Wheeler's career in the Civil War the following memoirs were consulted: Myrta Lockwood Avery (ed.), *Recollections of Alexander H. Stephens: His Diary* (New York, 1905); Virginia Clay-Clopton, *A Belle of the Fifties* (New York, 1910); Basil W. Duke, *Morgan's Cavalry* (New York, 1906); *id., Reminiscences of General Basil W. Duke, C.S.A.* (New York, 1911); Ulysses S. Grant, *Personal Memoirs of U. S. Grant,* 2 vols. (New York, 1885); John B. Hood, *Advance and Retreat* (New Orleans, 1880); Joseph E. Johnston, *Narrative of Military Operations, Directed, During the Late War Between the States, by Joseph E. Johnston* (New York, 1874); James Longstreet, *From Manassas to Appomattox* (Philadelphia, 1896); William H. Russell, *My Diary North and South* (New York, 1863); William T. Sherman, *Memoirs of General W. T. Sherman Written By Himself,* 2 vols. (New York, 1891); G. Moxley Sorrel, *Recollections of a Confederate Staff Officer* (New York, 1905); Edward L. Wells, "A Morning Call on General Kilpatrick," in *Southern Historical Society Papers* (Richmond), XII (1884), 123–30; Joseph Wheeler, "An Effort to Rescue Jefferson Davis," in *Century Magazine* (New York), LVI (1898), 85–91.

Reminiscences touching the latter phases of Wheeler's life

include: James F. J. Archibald, "The Day of the Surrender at Santiago," in *Scribner's Magazine* (New York), XXIV (1898), 413–16; John Bigelow, *Reminiscences of the Santiago Campaign* (New York, 1899); Stephen Bonsal, *The Fight for Santiago* (New York, 1899); Champ Clark, *My Quarter Century of American Politics,* 2 vols. (New York, 1920); Richard Harding Davis, *The Cuban and Porto Rican Campaigns* (New York, 1898); J. T. Dickman (ed.), *The Santiago Campaign: Reminiscences of the Operations for the Capture of Santiago de Cuba in the Spanish-American War, June and July, 1898* (Richmond, 1927); Ben: Perley Poore, *Reminiscences of Sixty Years in the National Metropolis,* 2 vols. (Philadelphia, 1886); Theodore Roosevelt, *The Rough Riders* (New York, 1900); Joseph Wheeler, *The Santiago Campaign* (New York, 1899).

By far the most valuable work in the nature of a collection of memoirs touching the Civil War is Robert U. Johnson and Clarence C. Buel (eds.), *Battles and Leaders of the Civil War,* 4 vols. (New York, 1887–1888). This set, written by surviving officers of both the Federal and Confederate armies, is perhaps the best single secondary source on the Civil War. Although many of the statements made should be checked against the *Official Records,* the set remains a monumental work.

Biographies

Two books have been written on the Civil War career of General Wheeler. These are W. C. Dodson, *Campaigns of Wheeler and His Cavalry* (Atlanta, 1899), and John W. Dubose, *General Joseph Wheeler and the Army of Tennessee* (New York, 1912). Both books are lacking in objectivity and often gloss over controversial events in Wheeler's life. The former is rich in anecdotal material of doubtful origin, although some of the stories were related by Wheeler himself. No full length biography of Wheeler has been published. In fact, the only published work on the latter phases of Wheeler's career is a small volume in the nature of a eulogy written by T. C. DeLeon and entitled *Joseph Wheeler: The Man, The Statesman, The Soldier* (Atlanta, 1899).

It is an interesting commentary that adequate biographies

of many of Wheeler's fellow officers in the Confederate army have not been written. There is no life of General William J. Hardee, and no definitive ones of Generals Joseph E. Johnston, Braxton Bragg, John B. Hood, and Wade Hampton. Perhaps Forrest's life has been more adequately treated than that of any major Confederate officer in the West, there being three biographies of him extant: Thomas Jordan and J. P. Pryor, *The Campaigns of Lieut. Gen. N. B. Forrest and of Forrest's Cavalry* (New York, 1868); John A. Wyeth, *Life of General Nathan Bedford Forrest* (New York, 1901); and Andrew Nelson Lytle, *Bedford Forrest and His Critter Company* (New York, 1931). The last is by far the most dramatic, although Mr. Lytle has drawn heavily upon Wyeth's book.

Biographies of Confederate officers in addition to those of Forrest which have been used in this study are: Elizabeth Cutting, *Jefferson Davis, Political Soldier* (New York, 1930); William E. Dodd, *Jefferson Davis* (Philadelphia, 1907); H. J. Eckenrode, *Jefferson Davis, President of the South* (New York, 1923); H. J. Eckenrode and Bryan Conrad, *James Longstreet: Lee's War Horse* (Chapel Hill, 1936); Douglas Southall Freeman, *R. E. Lee: A Biography*, 4 vols. (New York, 1934–1935); A. J. Hanna, *Flight into Oblivion* (New York, 1938); Robert M. Hughes, *General Johnston* (New York, 1893); Robert McElroy, *Jefferson Davis: The Unreal and the Real*, 2 vols. (New York, 1937); Don C. Seitz, *Braxton Bragg* (Columbia, S.C., 1924); Edward L. Wells, *Hampton and His Cavalry in '64* (Richmond, 1899); Howard Swiggett, *The Rebel Raider: a Life of John Hunt Morgan* (Indianapolis, 1934).

For the Atlanta campaign B. H. Liddell Hart, *Sherman: Soldier, Realist, Statesman* (New York, 1929), is particularly valuable, as is the work of another English military critic, Alfred H. Burne, *Lee, Grant and Sherman* (New York, 1939). Although the latter work cannot be strictly classified as a biography, it is, with the exception of a few errors in dates, one of the best treatments of the generalship of Lee, Grant, and Sherman the author has encountered. His discussion of the Atlanta campaign is particularly good. J. T. C. Fuller, *The Generalship of Ulysses S. Grant* (New York, 1929), is also worth study.

Of great value in studying Wheeler's political career were: Daniel M. Robison, *Bob Taylor and the Agrarian Revolt in Tennessee* (Chapel Hill, 1935); C. Vann Woodward, *Tom Watson, Agrarian Rebel* (New York, 1938); Edwin A. Alderman and Armistead C. Gordon, *J. L. M. Curry* (New York, 1911); Allan Nevins, *Grover Cleveland, A Study in Courage* (New York, 1932); James A. Barnes, *John G. Carlisle, Financial Statesman* (New York, 1931); Sam H. Acheson, *Joe Bailey: The Last Democrat* (New York, 1932). The two compilations, *Biographical Directory of the American Congress, 1774–1927* (Washington, 1928), and *Dictionary of American Biography,* 20 vols. and index (New York, 1928–1937), were, of course, indispensable. Thomas M. Owen, *History of Alabama and Dictionary of Alabama Biography,* 4 vols. (Chicago, 1921), and Ben LaBree (ed.) *The Confederate Soldier in the Civil War* (Louisville, 1895), were consulted for miscellaneous biographical material. *The Historical Register and Dictionary of the U.S. Army,* 2 vols. (Washington, 1903), is valuable in tracing the enlistment and subsequent careers of minor army officials.

Histories and Monographs

Good general works on the Civil War are rather numerous. The author has found that, next to *Battles and Leaders,* Walter G. Shotwell, *The Civil War in America,* 2 vols. (New York, 1923), is one of the best balanced accounts. J. G. Randall, *The Civil War and Reconstruction* (New York, 1937), is excellent, but the nature of the work prohibits more than a bare outline of military campaigns. Louis Philippe Albert d'Orleans, Comte de Paris, *History of the Civil War in America,* 4 vols. (Philadelphia, 1875–1888), is strongly pro-Union in sentiment. George J. Fiebeger, *Campaigns of the American Civil War* (West Point, N.Y., 1914), is an excellent summary. From this work and Thomas L. Livermore, *Numbers and Losses in the Civil War* (New York, 1901), the author obtained considerable information on the organization of the armies in the West. Livermore, however, is of little value with respect to the cavalry arm of the service. James K. Hosmer,

The Appeal to Arms, 1861–1863 (New York, 1907), is still valuable for the period covered.

More recent popular accounts of the Civil War are Robert S. Henry, *The Story of the Confederacy* (New York, 1931), and Fletcher Pratt, *Ordeal by Fire* (New York, 1935). The former is more accurate and more valuable than the latter.

For illustrative material Francis T. Miller (ed.), *The Photographic History of the Civil War,* 10 vols. (New York, 1911), is unexcelled. Many of the articles accompanying the photographs are highly inaccurate, however.

In studying strategy and tactics the author found G. F. R. Henderson, *The Science of War* (New York, 1905), of great value. Alonzo Gray's *Cavalry Tactics as Illustrated by the War of the Rebellion* (Fort Leavenworth, 1910), is excellent. Useful also are: George T. Denison, *History of Cavalry from the Earliest Times with Lessons for the Future* (London, 1877); J. Roomer, *Cavalry: Its History, Management, and Uses in War* (New York, 1863); L. E. Nolan, *Cavalry: Its History and Tactics* (London, 1860); Joseph Wheeler, *A Revised System of Cavalry Tactics for the Use of the Cavalry and Mounted Infantry, C.S.A.* (Mobile, 1863); *Regulations for the Army of the Confederate States* (New Orleans, 1861).

For Wheeler's brief period in the Southwest immediately before the war, Henry Inman, *The Old Santa Fe Trail* (New York, 1898), and Hubert H. Bancroft, *A History of Arizona and New Mexico* (San Francisco, 1899), proved valuable. Helpful in studying his student days at West Point was Morris Schaff, *The Spirit of Old West Point* (Boston, 1907).

General works covering the period of Wheeler's life after the Civil War are legion. For information on the Wheelers in Georgia, Charles C. Jones and Salem Dutcher, *Memorial History of Augusta, Georgia* (Syracuse, 1890), is useful. Works on Alabama history which treat the period of Wheeler's Congressional career are: William G. Brown, *A History of Alabama* (New York, 1900); Walter L. Fleming, *The Civil War and Reconstruction in Alabama* (New York, 1905); Albert B. Moore, *History of Alabama and Her People,* 2 vols. (New York, 1927); John B. Clark, *Populism in Alabama* (Auburn, 1927); James E. Saunders, *Early Settlers of Alabama*

(New Orleans, 1899); W. Brewer, *Alabama: Her History, Resources, War Record, and Public Men* (Montgomery, 1872).

General works treating the broader national problems of Wheeler's day include: Arthur M. Schlesinger, *New Viewpoints in American History* (New York, 1925); David S. Muzzey, *The United States of America*, 2 vols. (New York, 1933); Lester B. Shippee, *Recent American History* (New York, 1930); John D. Hicks, *The Populist Revolt* (Minneapolis, 1931); Alonzo B. Hepburn, *A History of Currency in the United States* (New York, 1915); Kirk H. Porter, *National Party Platforms* (New York, 1924); Henry J. Ford, *The Cleveland Era* (New Haven, 1919); Frank W. Taussig, *The Tariff History of the United States* (New York, 1914); Holland Thompson, *The New South* (New Haven, 1919); Alex M. Arnett, *The Populist Movement in Georgia*, in Columbia University *Studies in History, Economics and Public Law*, CIV (New York, 1922).

Paul DeWitt Hasbrouck, *Party Government in the House of Representatives* (New York, 1927), and DeAlva Stanwood, *History and Procedure in the House of Representatives* (New York, 1916), were consulted concerning House rules. Donald Davidson, *The Attack on Leviathan* (Chapel Hill, 1938), contains an excellent philosophical discussion of agrarianism.

Two general and one specialized work on the Spanish-American War deserve mention. Walter Millis, *The Martial Spirit: A Study of Our War with Spain* (New York, 1931), is racy, but, on the whole, an accurate book. Gregory Mason, *Remember the Maine* (New York, 1939), is of less value. Marcus M. Wilkerson, *Public Opinion and the Spanish-American War* (Baton Rouge, 1932), is an excellent treatment of newspaper propaganda in its relation to the war with Spain.

Three articles by Thomas R. Hay shed considerable light on certain phases of Wheeler's Civil War career by treating movements with which Wheeler was connected. These are: "The Battle of Chattanooga," in *Georgia Historical Quarterly* (Savannah), VIII (1924), 121–41; "The Atlanta Campaign," *ibid.*, VII (1923), 19–43, 99–118; "Braxton Bragg and the Southern Confederacy," *ibid.*, IX (1925), 289–99. Also useful on the Civil War period were: John A. Wyeth, "General Wheeler's Leap," in *Harper's Weekly* (New York), XLII (1898), 601–602, and [J. William Jones (comp.)], "Treatment of Prisoners During the War Between the States," in *Southern Historical Society Papers* (Richmond), I (1876), 113–327. Useful for the Kentucky phases of the war is E. Merton Coulter, *The Civil War and Readjustment in Kentucky* (Chapel Hill, 1926).

Touching certain phases of Wheeler's political career are: Daniel M. Robison, "Tennessee Politics and the Agrarian Revolt, 1886–1896," in *Mississippi Valley Historical Review* (Cedar Rapids), XX (1934), 365–80; Herman C. Nixon, "The Cleavage Within the Farmers' Alliance Movement," *ibid.*, XV (1929), 22–33; J. P. Dyer, "The Final Struggle for Democratic Control in North Alabama," in *Alabama Historical Quarterly* (Montgomery), VI (1930), 370–81; Daniel M. Robison, "From Tillman to Long: Some Striking Leaders of the Rural South," in *Journal of Southern History* (Baton Rouge), III (1937), 289–310; Benjamin B. Kendrick, "Agrarian Discontent in the South," in American Historical Association, *Annual Report,* 1920 (Washington, 1923), 265–72.

INDEX

403